JOHN DEWEY

THE MIDDLE WORKS, 1899–1924

Volume 7: 1912–1914

Edited by Jo Ann Boydston
With an Introduction by Ralph Ross

Carbondale and Edwardsville
SOUTHERN ILLINOIS UNIVERSITY PRESS
London and Amsterdam
FEFFER & SIMONS, INC.

Manufactured in the United States of America
Designed by George Lenox

Editorial expenses for this edition have been met in part by grants from the National Endowment for the Humanities. Publishing expenses have been met in part by grants from the John Dewey Foundation and from Mr. Corliss Lamont.

Library of Congress Cataloging in Publication Data (revised)

Dewey, John, 1859–1952.
The middle works, 1899–1924.

Vol. 7 has introd. by Ralph Ross.
Includes bibliographies and indexes.
CONTENTS: v. 1. 1899–1901.—v. 2 1902–1903.—v. 3. 1903–1906.—v. 4. 1907–1909.—v. 5. 1908.—v. 6. 1910–1911.—v. 7. 1912–1914.
1. Dewey, John, 1859–1952. 2. Education—Philosophy. I. Boydston, Jo Ann, 1924– II. Title.
LB875.D34 1976 370.1′092′4 76–7231
ISBN 0–8093–0881–9 (v. 7)

The Middle Works, 1899–1924

CONTENTS

INTRODUCTION

By Ralph Ross

In Dewey's review of William James's *Essays in Radical Empiricism,*[1] he remarked "much of his influence is due to the remarkable vitality and picturesqueness of his style." He went on at once to say that literary style alone did not account for the influence, but one wonders if there was a rueful note in the comment on style by a man who confesses in these pages to an awkward prose. James was indeed a superb writer and one can be sure his quality was not just a result of care, rewriting, and polishing because nowhere is the bite, compression, and vigor of his style more evident than in his personal letters.

Dewey was a truly poor writer only on occasion, when what he said did not reveal what he meant. Usually his prose is adequate to his meaning; he gives the impression of knowing exactly what he is about, thrusting rapidly to the focal point of an argument and whisking peripheral matters away. When he takes the time he needs to be clear, he manages it, and can even create startling and apt imagery, although it is often graceless. Thus he expresses the idea that traditional epistemology presupposes a static universe by saying that in such a theory "knowledge is a kodak fixation."

The enormously personal quality of James is matched by Dewey's impersonality, which tells you the way of the world, not how John Dewey feels about it. Yet he is not aloof, like Santayana, as though looking down from Olympus; he is in the thick of things, even passionate about them, but his passion is in his advocacy, not in private response. He can even make it seem there is no private world in him to which he can retreat and in which he can live for a time. Perhaps he sometimes regrets his impersonality. Such regret may be implicit in picking particular sentences from James, and

1. This volume, p. 142.

calling them, admiringly, "precious." Dewey writes of James's characteristic "belief that the world itself has an element of unfinishedness in it and that one of the standing errors of philosophers has been to attribute to reality a completeness which as matter of fact it does not possess" (p. 143). James says this in the passage Dewey chooses with just that personal response Dewey rarely shows:

> The "through-and-through" universe seems to suffocate me with its infallible impeccable all-pervasiveness. Its necessity, with no possibilities; its relation, with no subjects, makes me feel as if I had entered into a contract with no reserved rights, or rather as if I had to live in a large seaside boarding house with no private bedroom in which I might take refuge from the society of the place. . . . The "through-and-through" philosophy seems too buttoned-up and white-chokered and clean-shaven a thing to speak for the vast, slow-breathing, unconscious Kosmos, with its dread abysses and its unknown tides (p. 143).

The philosophical pieces in volume seven of *The Middle Works of John Dewey,* as distinct from the educational essays, deal to a great extent with other philosophers. Dewey writes about Bergson, Royce, and McGilvary at some length and, in book reviews, about Schiller and James. Some hesitation might have existed, for he suggests that it may be better to develop his own ideas than to respond to criticism (which he was not doing in the case of Bergson, but was with Royce and McGilvary), yet he clarified his thought by answering critics, and with clarification came development.

What emerges is implicit in the review of James. There Dewey said that radical empiricism would be more influential than pragmatism on professional philosophers, and he quotes Ralph Barton Perry to the effect that James himself toward the end of his life thought it more important. Already, in 1905, Dewey had committed himself to a version of radical empiricism in an article called "The Postulate of Immediate Empiricism" (*Middle Works* 3:158–67). He had also committed himself more and more to the doctrine of realism, calling himself a pragmatic realist to mark a distinction from other kinds of realists, especially perhaps critical realists like Santayana and Roy Wood Sellars, and his immediate empiricism and realism came together in the naturalism he talked so much about later.

Despite Santayana's description of Dewey's naturalism

as "half-hearted," it was much more thoroughgoing than most and caused as many problems for his critics as his pragmatism, especially because Dewey saw pragmatism and naturalism as making a single philosophy. By his fifties, when he wrote the papers in this volume, his philosophy was almost thoroughly formed, and his major works, which came afterwards, restated and expanded his ideas, facing the challenges of new shifts and quakes in philosophical grounds. Perhaps the most novel development of his thought was in aesthetics, culminating in *Art as Experience* in 1934, in which all the chief strands of his philosophy came happily together.

In this period of 1912 to 1915, when Dewey was pitting himself against important adversaries, his talents as a critic were fully evident. All criticism is from a position which is often implicit and so somewhat unclear and perhaps inconsistent. The minimal position of the critic is a belief in consistency and clarity, and it is with those in mind that he criticizes. But Dewey criticizes from an explicit philosophy, which he does not hide but tries to establish against the philosophy he examines, testing the power of his own theories to cope with the problems treated so differently by others. This explains his special critical mastery, especially since the ordinary tools of the critic are a second nature: analysis of meaning, concern for consistency, prediction of consequences, and so on.

The pragmatic naturalism from which Dewey criticized was far more developed by 1912 than naturalism would be by most others as late as the 1930s. Then there was a tendency to define naturalism as a single intellectual method for use in all areas of inquiry, thus ruling out of philosophy faith, the supernatural, the mystical, and the intuitive. Dewey had held a similar position for a long time and, in believing that man was as natural as stones, trees, and stars, had pressed on to reveal the characteristically human as natural, and thus included mind, consciousness, values, and ends in nature. That meant that it was as natural for a thing to be known as it was for it to grow, and as natural for it to be changed purposely as a result of its being known as it was for it to decay or erode. It also meant that mind and consciousness lost any non-natural spiritual quality and became organic functions or relations of knowing and awareness, rather than private entities.

In consequence, Dewey opposed philosophies in which mind and consciousness were entities which existed apart from their contents or in which it was the function of mind (and perhaps of human life at its best) only to know. What of making, using, directing, foreseeing, and so much else? His opponents, Dewey thought, were still in bondage to the old separation of mind and matter. It seemed obvious to him that the evolutionary function of mind had been to guide behavior so that people could adapt themselves to their environment and adjust that environment to themselves in the interest of surviving and living better. That the mind should now be a knower for the sake of knowing, with no trace of its original function, struck him as untrue. Civilization had, of course, liberated the minds of some, especially in a leisure class, from a host of immediate perils, and that liberation had perhaps brought an exuberance which made pure knowledge, thinking for its own sake, seem an ideal fulfillment. The spectator of affairs, not the participant, the understander of action, not the actor, not even the intelligent actor who understood in order to act more effectively, were celebrated as ideal types. Against this type of philosophizing, Dewey pitted an acute awareness of the continuing perils and problems of men, which reflection might resolve, and accused the "knowers" of being innocent of the values of knowing.

It is from this standpoint that Dewey confronts Bergson and Royce. Bergson deals with ordinary experience as a sieve which strains the useful and desirable but allows all else to pass through its holes. Our concern with need and action dictates what we experience; the vital, acting animal perceives what accords with his life, perceives under the category of usefulness, and perceives thus in both daily life and science. Philosophy, however, is concerned with reality, unstrained and undistorted, as it is for itself. From this standpoint, Bergson can come to an aesthetic, in which Dewey has little interest at this time but which became important to people like T. E. Hulme,[2] authorized translator of

2. T. E. Hulme, "Bergson's Theory of Art," *Speculations* (London: Routledge & Kegan Paul, 1949 [first edition, 1924]), pp. 141–67.

Bergson's *An Introduction to Metaphysics*, whose considerable influence brought many men of letters and the arts to make a sharp distinction between the perceptions of daily life and the perceptions of art.

As Hulme described Bergson's view of ordinary perception it was far from the disinterested perception of reality that characterizes art.

> Life is action, it represents the acceptance of the utilitarian side of things in order to respond to them by appropriate actions. I look, I listen, I hear, I think I am seeing, I think I am hearing everything, and when I examine myself I think I am examining my own mind.
>
> But I am not.
>
> What I see and hear is simply a selection made by my senses to serve as a light for my conduct. My senses and my consciousness give me no more than a practical simplification of reality. In the usual perception I have of reality all the differences useless to man have been suppressed. . . . Things have been classified with a view to the use I can make of them.[3]

Science, too, has its purposes, and scientific perception is thus partial and limited. But art penetrates to undistorted reality, as does philosophy, or metaphysics, aided by an intuition which replaces the needs of action with the inner movement of reality. This duality in Bergson, one important theme among many others in his philosophy, offended Dewey as all dualisms did, but particularly offended him because some ultimate reality was removed from the world in which the questing, adapting human organism acted, and because mind, memory, and life were separated from that organic action that Dewey conceived as the process of life itself. Life and mind became entities in Bergson, however much he tried to avoid it, and in the end he held a panpsychic belief that the material universe is a kind of consciousness. A good part of the argument hinged on perception, and Dewey was happy to agree with Bergson that perception was colored by organic needs and intentions, but he insisted that just that account of perception revealed the interplay of organism and environment and was the clue to follow in trying to understand nature, rather than a deviation to avoid.

3. Hulme, "Bergson's Theory of Art," p. 158.

Dewey's response to Josiah Royce's paper brought a different emphasis, ultimately a social one. Royce had combined his own version of Absolute Idealism, although using many of its stock ploys, with a great concern for instrumentalism which he doubtless acquired from his friend and colleague William James. Royce did not argue for three levels of truth, as F. H. Bradley did, but he found three "motivations," of which instrumentalism was one, which should be combined in a higher synthesis. That there was no intelligent way to refuse to follow him to these heights was obvious to Royce, and his ploys were used to make that clear. They were of the same kind Bradley thought would discomfit his critics when he published *Appearance and Reality* in 1893. There, on the first page of the Introduction, he writes:

> The man who is ready to prove that metaphysical knowledge is wholly impossible has no right here to any answer. . . . He is a brother metaphysician with a rival theory of first principles. . . . To say the reality is such that our knowledge cannot reach it, is a claim to know reality; to urge that our knowledge is of a kind which must fail to transcend appearance, itself implies that transcendence. For, if we had no idea of a beyond, we should assuredly not know how to talk about failure or success.

Royce had been working on symbolic logic and mathematics when he wrote his article on the problem of truth and, although he added the voluntarist twist that thought is basically will, he believed he had found absolute truth in logical relations, defining the granite basis of that truth as propositions whose denial implied their affirmation, although perhaps in a different form. As C. I. Lewis put it elegantly in telling what it meant for p to be necessarily true: "The truth of p can be deduced from its own denial." Royce thought that symbolic logic and mathematical progress had brought a new situation for the philosopher, and he was not alone in that belief. Bertrand Russell was saying that philosophy no longer had to go to science, hat in hand, to ask for truth. Royce, however, still insisted on absolutes. Yet this "new" attempt to find absolute truth in formal necessity is just the old ploy dressed in new and elaborate trappings. What Bradley was implying was that the absolute truth that there was a reality transcending appearance was a proposition that was necessary because its truth could be deduced from its denial.

In arguing the old case in the same way, Royce was trying to rest his argument on a new logic, not the Idealist logic of Bosanquet and Bradley. "That there are absolutely true propositions," he wrote, "the existence of the science of pure mathematics proves" (p. 437). Even if logic and mathematics are hypothetical in character, their assertions are absolutely true, presumably because in all cases when "if p, then q" is true, p and q being propositions, that q follows from p is absolutely true. For all this new interest of his, it is most instructive that Royce's examples are of the same kind as Bradley's and need no new logic at all. Royce thinks we cannot get rid of the postulate of an absolute truth and illustrates that by saying: "We can define the truth even of relativism only by asserting that relativism is after all absolutely true" (p. 436). And in an instance suspiciously like Bradley's, he argues: "If I say: 'There never was a past,' I contradict myself, since I assume the past even in asserting that a past never was" (p. 436). Perhaps every word (the old Idealistic logic) is thought to have a referent in "Reality" and by using the word "past" I assume its referent. It seems unpleasant to suggest that if I say "There never was a mermaid," I would contradict myself in the same way, but I think it is fair enough. That I should know what a word means if I am to use it is a sensible admonition but it does not imply that the meaning is an existent.

Dewey did not respond to any of this Idealist argument; there was by then a tradition of avoiding it as though it were a morass. But he attacked the reason for it, in Royce's article, as he understood that reason. Royce had understood the instrumentalist theory of truth as based on verification of consequences, and he thought of verification as an individual act, and so private. Also, truth is valuable, but value is a personal matter, perhaps even internal to "states of consciousness." Hence the need for the Absolute and absolute truth, which transcend the private and the personal and are objectively valuable. At bottom, perhaps, is the instrumentalist's reliance on experience. For Royce, experience is always some one person's experience, cut off from other people's experiences, hence private and incapable of vouching for public and objective facts. What we must do, then, is accept on credit what other people say about their experiences ("credit" being a vivid metaphor from James) and that is a dubious base for truth.

Dewey was stung and reacted sharply. This was the same sort of "reasonable" statement that had been made again and again in criticism of James, leading him to publish *The Meaning of Truth* in 1909, but no response seemed to be understood. Thus Dewey wrote of Royce's treatment: "Speaking for myself, I may say that if I had any such nihilistic, anarchistically egoistic notion of the individual man, of his doings, states, tools and results, I should probably be willing to resort to an absolute to escape my 'own' awful isolation and selfishness" (p. 68). Criticisms like Royce's probably assumed that the sensationalistic empiricism of the seventeenth and eighteenth centuries underlay the "experience" of the instrumentalists, whereas it was one of their chief critical targets. For Dewey there was no gulf between private and objective experience because, as he put it tersely in *Experience and Nature*, what we experience is nature. Where there is a difference between what two people perceive, tests and further perception can bring agreement.

The "live creature" Dewey talks about constantly is continuous with a racial organic life and it is as fully social as it is organic. Verification is not private at all; it is social. And we cannot function with any sanity unless we are willing to credit the experience other people have. But we do not take anybody's word, without question, about experiences we have not had. We accept it tentatively, "on probation," until there is corroboration and verification. Unless we learned from the experience of others, sometimes duplicating it ourselves, we would learn precious little. It is the social nature of life and experience that gives us the transpersonal quality of knowledge that an absolute is supposed to yield. Indeed, Dewey guesses that the Absolute is only a reification of the social quality of experience.

There is in this volume a paper of Dewey's called "What Are States of Mind?" that was read to the Philosophical Club and, so far as we know, never before published, which expands the argument in the article on Royce. A "state of mind" is not an internal psychic entity, a mind, consciousness or soul, but a frame of mind, an emotional disposition which is exhibited in a particular kind of behavior. The chief reason for distinguishing the emotional attitude as personal from the situation in which behavior operates is social, that is, political, legal, and moral, so that responsibility for results can be allocated. But that distinction is made retrospectively in analysis. In the original experience the state of mind has no independent existence, but is a quality of the experienced situation. Dewey recalls James's theory of emotion (which became famous as the James-Lange theory because of James's generosity), in which an emotion is the feeling of the sum total of organic changes that result from a stimulus, rather than a psychic state resulting from those changes. On a broader view, Dewey thinks this is not so much a theory of emotion, of which he would have to be somewhat critical, as it is an indication of how states or frames of mind would have to be described if they became the subject matter of psychology. For "psychical states" as private entities, he believes, never arose from empirical psychology but entered psychology illegitimately from traditional epistemology.

So far this analysis develops the position from which Dewey criticized Bergson and Royce. But "What Are States of Mind?" also contains an important move toward Dewey's later and more fully elaborated philosophy, a hitherto lost link in the chain of his intellectual biography. Continuing his interpretation of James, or rather his insight into what James missed when framing his theory, Dewey says that what are called psychical states are not separable from organic reactions, nor are they antecedents or concomitants of them, but are the *qualities* of the reactions. The "psychical state," however, which is no more than the state or frame of mind is, once again, the result of retrospective analysis. Actually, it has no independent existence in experience, as pointed out before, but now Dewey goes on to say that in experience it is a *quality* of the situation, of the experienced subject matter. This is a start, not the only one perhaps, in a growth that led to the idea that there was a pervasive quality in a situation, and that it colors and pervades the entire situation. The word "situation" was used later to describe a complex existent characterized by a single quality which controlled the terms of thought. Thus anger, a frame of mind, may be the pervasive quality of a situation and color all its elements. The same set of elements with a different quality—elation, love, or hope, for example—are differently colored and have a different character.[4]

The idea of underlying pervasive quality, broached in this article, was of great importance to Dewey's mature philosophy, but it is tenuous, difficult to grasp. The pervasive quality is unifying and is felt, rather than thought. That statement must be supplemented by the further statement that the unifying quality in any subject matter defines the meaning of feeling. When angry, we do not at once perceive the anger itself; we see the objects of our anger differently. Later, when we think about our anger, we may be calm; in any event we have thus made it an object in another situation. Metaphorically, a pervasive quality is the personality of a situation, and the elements of the situation are for the moment pervaded by that personality. And feeling is the way we experience a situation, rather than a subjective response to it.

The earlier empiricists notwithstanding, association is not by contiguity or similarity but by unifying quality, and may be based on habit. A work of art is an especially good example of a situation. We see a painting and know at once that it is by Goya or is Goyaesque. We know this, if we have adequate training, as we know a sonata is by Mozart, quickly, before we have analyzed the detail, and when we do examine the detail it is Goyaesque or Mozartian. In all of this there is clearly some relation to gestalt psychology, and Dewey's philosophy of immediate experience now hinges on the only "given" he finds in experience, which is the immediate existence of a total pervasive quality. Thought finds its background, point of departure and regulative principle in that quality.

4. Although Dewey refers to this general idea in a number of places, the *locus classicus* is "Qualitative Thought," *Symposium* 1 (1930): 5–32. Reprinted in *Philosophy and Civilization* (New York: Minton, Balch and Co., 1931), pp. 93–116.

In this same fascinating paper to the Philosophical Club, Dewey tries to make his thought compatible with the inner life so regularly neglected (even seemingly denied) in most of his writing. After all, if mind and consciousness are not internal entities and if feeling and emotion are qualities of situations, it is hard to know what "inner life" means. Dewey makes his move, as he often does, by appeal to ordinary language. "The accident was depressing," he says, "and I was depressed; these are but two names, given from the spectator's point of view, to that which in its own occurrence and of its own right is one and the same situation" (p. 38). How is it that we discriminate two aspects of the situation and think of one as objective and the other as subjective? Because we have discovered that when we want to predict and to bring about change we do not get very far dealing with a depressing accident but we may with a depressed man.

When, in earlier history, the human race punished inanimate objects (retributive justice rather than deterrence) and understood human immorality as the result of pollution, which was contagious and might affect a whole population (as in the *Oedipus Tyrannos*), it was difficult to change things or influence behavior. Thus we have developed different techniques for dealing with physical things and with human conduct. As we act upon organic attitudes and reactions in order to modify or direct them, we tend to speak or think of them as motives, the springs of action, and to attach them to individuals as unique persons. In a sense, Dewey does not really believe there is this inner realm (for it is only our emotional attitudes detached from their full context of occasions, causes, and functions), to which we are somehow confined and in which we discover our very being, but thinks that religions and the arts have convinced men of its existence. It is one thing to search our souls and hearts, metaphorically, to discover our relations to persons and things, but it is quite different to think we search our souls and hearts, literally, in order to discover ourselves, apart from things and all other persons. The former is a vivid and dramatic way of speaking; the latter is superstition.

In the dramatic arts characters of all sorts are portrayed

in a great variety of situations; through empathy with these characters we have vicarious experiences. It is easy enough to feel that we have entered the internal life of someone else and perceive a world refracted through his personality. But in the last few centuries, as Dewey sees it, the arts have become subtler and often treat the "inner life" as their direct subject matter, thus more fully disconnecting emotional attitudes from the world in which they originally function, and cultivating them in some isolation and for their own sake.

Having identified that "inner life" which is missing in most of his work, Dewey is ambivalent about it. I think it is hardly overstating Dewey's case to see the "inner life" as a kind of intellectual construct created by dissociating or fragmenting the living reality of experience. But it is not, even in Dewey's view, a fiction. It is a genuine fragment of experience to which a growing subjectivity brings attention, and, although it is too often treated as though it had no context but is the fundamental repository of meaning and value, it can be isolated, found, and used. Dewey's ambivalence consists, first, in fearing that morality thus becomes subjective and private; and he was justified in his fears not so many years later when it became the fashion for philosophers to translate "This is good" as "I prefer this," sometimes adding "and I would like you to prefer it, too." Yet Dewey knew, also, that the "inner life" pursued vigorously brought increased sensitivity to the meanings of life and a perception of nuances in the quality of living. And such a life is quite accessible; as he put it eloquently: "No man is so poor in this world's goods or in fame or friends that he cannot afford an inner world of this kind as a buffer, a refuge and a private theatre" (pp. 41–42).

The relations between Dewey's general philosophy and his theory of education are many, as are the relations between his theory of education and his political theory; his thought was too seamless for any intellectual undertaking to be a separate statement. He was still in this period deeply concerned with education and was on the way to his most comprehensive account of the subject, *Democracy and Education*, published just three years after his long monograph, or short book, *Interest and Effort in Education*, 1913, in this volume. Of his influential earlier work, *The School and Society* was published in 1899 (*Middle Works* 1:1–109) and *The Child and the Curriculum* (*Middle Works* 2:271–91) appeared in 1902.

Like so many others, Dewey wrote far more clearly when he was not writing technically. Part of the reason, of course, is a difference in difficulty in the subjects themselves, but another part is the assumption that the philosophical reader is trained to understand difficult and technical matter, but the educator and the layman are not. To insure that the latter understand, the writer must be more lucid; he must also give more examples and refer regularly to the ordinary activities of life. Dewey managed that very well, and still his enormous influence on educational thought was often misdirected, because it was easier to read the oversimplified commentaries of followers and critics, who might or might not get Dewey's ideas straight.

Interest and Effort in Education is a good example of the quality of Dewey's mind and thus is a reason for his host of followers. The book is a direct statement and elaboration of Dewey's belief, page after page, with no deviations, excursions, or hesitations. It is like a ball of twine, unstrung in a perfectly straight line until the ball is completely unpacked; the reader has the rare satisfaction of following a fully understood argument as it is thoroughly articulated. And the position is held strongly; there is nothing tentative about it. The pages are full of confident phrases like "it is absurd that," "as a matter of fact," "it is a mistake to."

Although Dewey did not write about human nature as such in this book, as he did later in *Democracy and Education*, he assumed a set of beliefs which had germinated early in his thinking. He was thus quite prepared, when it came, for the dominance of the idea of culture as the chief category in anthropology, and he showed a sophistication about it that none of the cultural anthropologists could match. When he published *Freedom and Culture* in 1939 he brought his whole philosophy and his vast knowledge of the history of philosophy into play. Even though it was written as a popular book and attempted no solutions, *Freedom and Culture* put the problem of nature and nurture in quite a new way. "There is here," Dewey wrote, "a field which has hardly been entered by intellectual explorers:—the story of the way in which ideas put forth about the makeup of human nature, ideas supposed to be the results of psychological inquiry, have been in fact only reflections of practical measures that different groups, classes, factions wished to see continued in existence or newly adopted, so that what passed as psychology was a branch of political doctrine."[5]

Following this clue, Dewey was able to show that a presumably fixed human nature could not explain cultural variety and that social "forces" could not account for what men do, for a social "force" was a predetermined (and often political) interpretation of all observed behavior, whether that behavior accorded with the interpretation or did not. There was a constant interplay between person and culture, each altering the other. The great error in understanding that interplay was to treat each cultural configuration as if it were based on an original human nature.

Part of what made the concept of culture congenial to Dewey was his early treatment of the person, motivation, and the inner life in their relation to environing conditions, in which he did not distinguish the former sharply from the latter. Another part was his treatment of knowledge as a process of inquiry, not passive, but active, not usually sudden and spontaneous, but serial. Education was the principal area in which he tested his theories and gave them practical warrant. In *Interest and Effort in Education* he defined "motive" as "the name for the end or aim in respect to its hold on *action*, its power to *move*" (p. 181). (There is more than a touch of Aristotle's "final cause" here, which is also a first cause.) In consequence, he could warn against attaching motive too strongly to the person because that would detach it from the end in view. It is wrong in educating the child to seek for a motive in him to learn some subject instead of seeking the motive in the subject, that which can and does bring the child to want to learn it. Of course there must be a reason in the child's powers, interests, and stage of growth

5. John Dewey, *Freedom and Culture* (New York: G. P. Putnam's Sons, 1939), p. 29.

that connects him with an end or aim related to the subject, and that connection is what motivates.

As for the active process of inquiry, Dewey finds it obvious that the infant as well as the adult does things in the course of knowing and in order to know. The infant seizes, grasps, and moves objects which confront him; he does not get to know them passively, and the knowing includes learned behavior. Interest is close to motive: it is engagement with some activity because of its recognized value or inherent fascination. It is the heart of learning. Had there existed in 1913 a doctrine of positive reinforcement in the fashion of B. F. Skinner, Dewey might have attacked it directly and at length. As it was, he thought of such "motivating" behavior as a sort of bribe, only externally related to the real question of interest in the subject. External satisfactions that induce performance are quite different from what Dewey wants of the student: a concern with the work to be done as a means to an end that attracts him. The end, however, must not be an external reward, like a wage, but an aim intrinsically connected to the means in such a way that it grows out of it, and so permeates the means that it can interpret it and give it a new significance.

Dewey has been misunderstood by those who think his famous "learning by doing" means the substitution of action for thought. On the contrary, he was concerned with the intimate relation of theory and practice, and knew that even practice might be intellectual, since learning is a process of coming to know; though an experiment to test a hypothesis is practice that brings knowledge, so is an imaginary experiment. To an equal extent, Dewey has been misunderstood by those who think he minimizes the importance of meaning and of the power of abstract thought. To the contrary, meaning is basic to his concept of experience and his theory of learning; it is the meaning of what we experience that stirs us, stimulates action, and allows us to evaluate intelligently. The aesthetic experience, for example, is suffused with meaning and could not exist otherwise. As for abstraction: the measure of a mind is its power of abstraction. The learning process culminates in the ability to grasp meanings and think abstractly.

What does bother Dewey about conventional education is what he calls "the false sense of abstraction." This false sense is based on the belief that the mind can function apart from objects, that it can be occupied with symbols that are not signs of anything, and so are abstract in that they are abstracted from subject matter and, in having no referents, contain no real meaning. Sometimes, however, subject matter is introduced, but as mere exercise, to strengthen the mind as lifting barbells strengthens the body. That is the sheerly academic, in the pejorative sense of the word, for it bears no fruit in the world in which we live and find our joys and sorrows. This false sense of abstraction may be based on the fictions of an internally isolated mind and an external subject matter.

I have been emphasizing aspects of Dewey's general philosophy as they enter his theory of education and are developed in concrete application because even people who read Dewey seriously today are likely to read either his general philosophical writings or his education texts, but not both. The kind of confusion this generates is evident in the republication in a single paperback volume, by the University of Chicago Press in 1956, of *The Child and the Curriculum* and *The School and Society*, with an Introduction by Leonard Carmichael. Carmichael tries to place Dewey's thinking about education in its time, a time before two world wars, a time when, he thinks, a naïve optimism was still possible, when one did not have to worry about establishing fixed values which alone can withstand the barbaric inroads of such horrors as Nazism.

"Dewey was a consistent relativist," Carmichael comments, and he writes of Dewey's "simple naturalistic psychology of more than a half-century ago."[6] But Dewey finished *Democracy and Education* in 1915, when World War I was already under way, and in it there was far more continuity with his earlier writings than discontinuity. That was not because Dewey could not face that war's great shattering of public myth and unreflective values but because he had

6. John Dewey, *The Child and the Curriculum* and *The School and Society* (Chicago: University of Chicago Press, Phoenix Books, 1956), Introduction by Leonard Carmichael, p. vii.

already faced it, at least in great part. The "simple naturalistic psychology" was less psychology at all than it was a complex epistemology. And the "consistent relativist" did not suddenly seek absolute values because he was not, as say Clyde Kluckhohn was, a cultural relativist in the sense in which every culture had its own warrant and, in some way, was therefore as good as any other culture. One of the marks of Dewey's sophistication about culture was that he knew that some cultures were good and some bad and that there were ways to discover which was which. His constant concern with value was a concern to discover by a process of inquiry which values to hold. In a simple relativism it is assumed that because each culture has its own dominant values, which are woven into the very fabric of that culture, we can take for granted that each culture has the values it needs, those that are proper to it. But if we can criticize dominant values in our own culture, as we do, why cannot we criticize dominant values in any other culture?

Dewey never believed that when one is in Rome he should do as the Romans do, for that might mean throwing Christians to the lions, an act no more justified because Romans did it than if cannibals had. Carmichael ends by saying that Dewey "wrote from a heart that was full of faith and energy when the pages of our violent and bloody century were still uncut."[7] The two books in the volume Carmichael introduced were first published in 1900 and 1902, so perhaps his words may address just those books. But the revised edition of the earlier book, *The School and Society*, appeared in 1915. And Carmichael shows no sign of knowing that Dewey did not die until 1952 and was a "premature" anti-Communist and anti-Fascist. All this is to the point that perhaps Dewey's work in education should be enough to show his general point of view, but when questions arise about his educational theory they cannot be answered readily without reference to other books of his on other subjects. The same point can be made about reading all of Dewey except for his work on education, especially because the latter includes example and evidence to a much greater extent than the former.

7. Carmichael, Introduction, p. xii.

A matter of great importance to Dewey in much of his philosophy, educational, social, political, aesthetic, is the relation of industry to civilization. Logically, it is rooted in his instrumentalism and his refusal to keep mental and physical activities in separate compartments or to value the one and deprecate the other. The recurrence of the theme in his educational writings is the counterpart of its recurrence in different terms in his other writings. Dewey stresses "labor" as the beginning of the word "laboratory," which is a scientist's *work*room, and he emphasizes the experimental in science, which involves not only thought but physical operations. Verification brings knowledge, and verification takes place through experiment or observation in the laboratory. Science itself is one of man's greatest achievements, not just because it is delightful to know (although it should be), but because its uses may free man from mechanical, routine, arduous labor and allow both the creation of what we hold dear and the elimination of what we oppose, by creating the conditions for the existence of the one and destroying the conditions for the existence of the other. In short, science can contribute to a better life and that includes work that has become meaningful and leisure that is fruitful.

In the educational pieces in this volume, Dewey's chief concern with vocational training is that it not be separated from general, or liberal, education. Thus the vocational student should take his place in society as a full-fledged member rather than merely as one of the working class and he can learn to grasp the significance of the work he performs by understanding its relations to history, science, art, society, and culture in general. Dewey's interest in a progression of studies for the child, moving from play to work to theory is not only that it is the best sequence for growth in intellectual skills and the ability to cooperate, but that it also teaches the relation of work to play and thought. This may be even more important for the child who will go on to the liberal arts than to the child who will become a vocational student.

Of all the agencies that foster the democratic spirit, the public school is, for Dewey, foremost. Where else can children from all walks of life spend years in an atmosphere of relative equality, both of opportunity and of treatment? How else would the children of the rich and the poor meet and play with each other? In what better way could the same ideals of citizenship and civic responsibility be taught and shared? As the problem of democracy enters the argument, it becomes clear that Dewey's great commitment to the democratic idea bears on vocational education, too, for an illiberal vocational training breeds and perpetuates a class structure whose rigidities are alien to democracy. A working class devoid of general education and untouched by a spirit of public responsibility is ready for autocratic rule or for thoughtless rebellion stirred by the voice of the demagogue.

Just as Dewey demands that work move on, in education, to theory, from cooking to chemistry, and that practical skills like telling time lead up to the stars, so in his writing a consideration of work brings him to politics, morals, society, and art. As one goes on, from work to thought, and from work to art, so one returns from them to work. Liberal education, too, leads to careers, usually careers in the professions, the arts, and the sciences, and includes politics and diplomacy. The politician and the lawyer were, in the best circumstances, trained for their work by their education. But that work includes regular dealings with those who do other work, the working class. And so the circles of ideas widen, like those in a pool into which a stone has fallen.

Among the many dualisms Dewey rejects is that of labor and leisure. Nor is he patient with the idea that more leisure and higher wages have any real bearing on the problem, which is that of the mechanical, routine character of drudgery, for the time being intensified, not minimized, by technology. The solution is meaningful work and the satisfactions of the worker. By no means is this restricted to a working class, for it is true of any kind of work. Leisure should not only bring rest and refreshment, but time for civic and cultural activities in their full range.

In understanding the relation of one's work to the rest of one's life, and the relation of both to the work and lives of others, one may grasp the moral import of one's behavior. For that begins with knowledge of the conditions and consequences of choice and action. One chooses at first out of appetite and desire. But it is only when the initial choice is judged by the conditions and consequences that determine it and result from it that one is on the way to moral decision. Morality thus, for Dewey, has its root in knowledge and prediction and its flower in choice based on them. Here again, some form of science is an indispensable condition, for the choice of means that will yield our ends requires a knowledge of the causes that will bring about desired effects. And then, in the choice of ends, we must bring into play as best we can their relation to the whole of our lives.

In his treatment of art, Dewey rejects another form of the same dualism of vocational and liberal, labor and leisure, that muddy the intellectual waters of education, politics, and society. That duality appears in aesthetics as a separation of the useful and the fine arts. To keep the distinction rigid in our time is to make the useful arts mean and the fine arts superfluous, like an extra layer of frosting on a rich cake. Yet the dualism is age-old and has been defined differently in other and older cultures. Ancient Greece enshrined it by a separation between those who worked with hands and tools and those whose medium was words. The former were mere artisans; the latter might be artists. The distinction is obvious enough when it is applied to a cobbler and a poet. But among artisans, by definition, were numbered the sculptors, architects, and painters. In consequence, Phidias was an artisan but Euripides an artist.

Today the machine has intervened and useful articles are stamped out on an assembly line. But if one sees a continuity rather than an absolute disjunction between the useful and the fine arts, it is easier for him to understand that a growth in civilization would occur if the ideas of art and its satisfactions permeated the making of all kinds of things. As it is, other interests dominate so much of what men make that American cities, and recent cities almost everywhere, are depressingly ugly in many of their sections, and some altogether ugly. Civic architecture can ennoble or blight. The surroundings of millions of men, in which most of them have their entire daily lives, are a weight crushing the very idea of beauty, and in the teeming slums crushing other ideals by which civilization is built. The two are not unconnected. In Dewey's terms there are modes of expression not usually thought of as art which have the same qualities that a fine work of art has. The eighteenth century was much taken with the idea of the sublime; like beauty, it was a great quality of great art. But conduct, too, can be sublime and it, too, has its beauties. The penetration of the aesthetic into the marrow of life is desirable, and if works of art could enter the consciousness of all society they would help effect that penetration.

Above all, what I have tried to do in the small compass of this Introduction is to indicate how the pages in this volume illuminate, and are part of, a large and growing philosophical attitude toward the world. Dewey was less concerned with exact solutions to problems than he was with what he believed to be the fruitful way to state and to view them. His polemic was not a direct onslaught on the solutions offered by others so much as an attempt to uncover their assumptions, which were historically and culturally grounded and so, unwittingly, supported a society that is not ours and a knowledge that is less complete or misleading. Every philosophy expresses the ethos and world view of a civilization, and Dewey would gladly accept the charge that he spoke for ours. But he has been criticized, with gross unfairness, as accepting the technical, manipulative, prosperity-oriented aspects of America. In fact, he rejected them soundly. In speaking for a civilization, one should not forget, as Dewey never did, to be its critic, and criticism rests on a choice of its better qualities against its worse. This choice assumes standards of choice; as Dewey put it once, philosophy is a criticism of criticisms. Its high office is to seek for basic grounds. Insofar as Dewey did that deliberately, and in full awareness of the implications of his quest, he tried to express more than the world view, at its best, of our brave and dangerous new world. To that he added what he thought was the continuing truth behind all life and all civilization. In truth, his life's work is a massive achievement.

Essays

PERCEPTION AND ORGANIC ACTION

Every reader of Bergson—and who to-day is not reading Bergson—is aware of a twofold strain in his doctrine. On the one hand, the defining traits of perception, of common-sense knowledge and science are explained on the ground of their intimate connection with action. On the other hand, the standing unresolved conflicts of philosophic systems, the chief fallacies that are found in them, and the failure to make definite progress in the solution of specific philosophic problems, are attributed to carrying over into metaphysics the results and methods of the knowledge that has been formed with the exigencies of action in view. Legitimate and necessary for useful action, they are mere prejudices as respects metaphysical knowledge. Prejudices, indeed, is too mild a name. Imported into philosophy, they are completely misleading; they distort hopelessly the reality they are supposed to know. Philosophy must, accordingly, turn its back, resolutely and finally, upon all methods and conceptions which are infected by implication in action in order to strike out upon a different path. It must have recourse to intuition which installs us within the very movement of reality itself, unrefracted by the considerations that adapt it to bodily needs, that is to useful action. As a result, Bergson has the unique distinction of being attacked as a pragmatist on one side, and as a mystic on the other.

There are at least a few readers in sympathy with the first of these strains who find themselves perplexed by the second. They are perplexed, indeed, just in the degree in which the first strain has left them convinced. Surely, they say to themselves, if the irresolvable conflicts and the obscurities of philosophy have arisen because of failure to note the connection of every-day and of scientific knowledge with the

[First published in *Journal of Philosophy, Psychology and Scientific Methods* 9 (1912): 645–68.]

purposes of action, public and private, the clarification of philosophic issues will arise by correcting this failure, that is to say, by the thorough development of the implications of the genuine import of knowledge. What an emancipation, they say to themselves, is to come to philosophy when it actively adopts this discovery and applies it to its own undertakings!

Perhaps it is because of unredeemed pragmatic prejudice that I find myself among those who have this feeling of a baffled expectation and a frustrate logic. Nevertheless, the feeling indicates a genuine intellectual possibility, a legitimate intellectual adventure. The hypothesis that the same discovery that has illuminated perception and science will also illuminate philosophic topics is an hypothesis which has not been logically excluded; it has not even been discussed. It may, then, be worth trying. Any notion that this road has been closed in advance arises from confusion in reasoning. It rests upon supposing that the unresolved antitheses of philosophic systems and the barriers that arrest its progress have been shown to be due to importing into philosophy, from common life and from science, methods and results that are relevant to action alone. If it had been shown that the evils of philosophy have resulted from *knowingly* carrying over into it considerations whose practical character had all along been *knowingly* acknowledged, then the conclusion would follow that philosophy must throw overboard these considerations, and find a radically different method of procedure. But this is a supposition contrary both to fact and to Bergson's premises. Why not, then, try the other hypothesis: that philosophic evils result from a survival in philosophy of an error which has now been detected in respect to every-day knowledge and science? Why not try avowedly and constructively to carry into philosophy itself the consequences of the recognition that the problems of perception and science are straightened out when looked at from the standpoint of action, while they remain obscure and obscuring when we regard them from the standpoint of a knowledge defined in antithesis to action?

We are thus carried a step beyond the mere suggestion of a possibly valid adventure in philosophy. If a conception of the nature and office of knowledge that has been discarded for common sense and for science is retained in philosophy, we are forced into a dualism that involves serious consequences. Common-sense knowledge and science are set in invidious contrast not merely with philosophy—a contrast that they might easily endure more successfully than philosophy—but with "reality." As long as the notion survives that true knowledge has nothing to do with action, being a purely theoretical vision of the real as it is for itself, insistence upon the operation within perceptual and conceptual "knowledge" of practical factors *ipso facto* deprives such "knowledge" of any genuine knowledge status. It gives us not reality as it is, but reality as it is distorted and refracted from the standpoint of bodily needs. To condemn all other "knowledge" (as *knowledge*) to the realm of fiction and illusion seems a high price to pay for the rescue of philosophy from the ills that it may be suffering from.

Thus we are compelled to go still further. A philosophy which holds that the facts of perception and science are to be explained from the standpoint of their connection with organically useful action, while it also holds that philosophy rests upon a radically different basis, is perforce a philosophy of reality that is already afflicted with a dualism so deep as seemingly to be ineradicable. It imports a split into the reality with which philosophy is supposed to deal exclusively and at first hand. We account for perception and science by reference to action, use, and need. Very well; but what about action, use, and need? Are they useful fictions? If not, they must be functions of "reality," in which case knowledge that is relevant to action, useful in the play of need, must penetrate into "reality" instead of giving it a twist. With respect to *such* characters of the real, a purely theoretical vision of intuition would be refracting. Suppose that conceptions mark fabrications made in the interest of the organic body. Are the organic needs also fabrications and is their satisfaction fabrication? Either that, or else the conceptual intelligence which effects the development and satisfaction of the needs plays a part in the evolution of reality, and a part that can not be apprehended by a mode of knowing that is antithetical, in its merely theoretic character, to them. From the standpoint of philosophy, accordingly, the analytic intellect, space, and matter—everything related to useful action—must be irreducible surds, for reality as apprehended in philosophic cognition by definition omits and excludes all such affairs.

Precisely the same order of considerations applies to the theory of knowledge. Were it not for the survival in the court of last resort and of highest jurisdiction of the old idea of the separation of knowledge and action, Bergson's special analyses would point to very different conclusions from those that constitute his official epistemology. The connection with action of the characteristic methods and results of knowledge in daily affairs and in science would give us a theory of the *nature* of reflective intelligence, not a theory of its *limitations*. When theoretic and disinterested knowledge cease to occupy a uniquely privileged position with respect to reality, there also cease to be any motive and ground for denying the existence of theoretic and disinterested knowledge. Such knowledge is a fact exhibited *in* sympathetic and liberal action. Its contrast is not with the limitations of practical knowledge, but with the limitations of the knowledge found in routine and partisan action! Genuine theoretic knowledge penetrates reality more deeply, not because it is opposed to practise, but because a practise that is genuinely free, social, and intelligent touches things at a deeper level than a practise that is capricious, egoistically centered, sectarian, and bound down to routine. To say the same thing the other way around, if it were not for the assumed monopolistic relation to reality of a knowledge disconnected from organic life, reference to action would cease to be a distorting, or even a limiting, term with respect to knowledge. The reference would be wholly explanatory and clarifying. Just as complications attaching to the questions of the relation of mind and body, or the self and its stream of mental states, are disentangled, and the elements in question fall into ordered perspective when viewed from the standpoint of the growth of an intelligently effective action, so with the other questions of philosophy.

It is high time, however, to make a transition from these general considerations to the special problems to which they are relevant. In this paper, I propose to deal with their bearing upon the topic of perception. Before directly attacking it, I must, however, introduce some further general considerations in order to make clear the bearing of what has been said upon what is to follow. Take the matter purely hypothetically. Imagine a philosophy which is convinced that the peculiarities of perception remain opaque, defying genuine analysis, as long as perception is regarded as a mode of theoretical cognition, while they become luminous with significance when it is treated as a factor in organic action. Imagine also that this conviction is conjoined with a belief that there is something in the nature of organic action marking it off so definitely from the truly real, that the latter must be known by a radically heterogeneous operation. Imagine that in the further course of the discussion the dualism in reality presupposed in this mode of treatment threatens to break out, and to break down the account. What is likely to happen? Are we not likely to find, at first, a sharpening of the antithesis between the special topic under consideration (whether it be perception, space, quantity, matter) and pure knowledge and genuine reality; and then, as the metaphysical consequences of this dualism come to view, a toning down of the antithesis between the two, by means of the introduction into each of reconciling traits that approximate each to the other? And surely this is one of the marked traits of the Bergsonian procedure. Suppose, however, we had commenced, not with the view that is afterwards corrected, but with the corrected view. Would not then the special analysis of the specific topic (perception or whatever) have assumed a very different form from that in which it is actually found? And is it not *a priori* likely that the original account will not be found quite consistent even in its own nominal sense? Is it not likely that there will be already present in it elements that, inconsistent with the notion of the sheer opposition of useful action and reality, point to the correction to be later made?

I have asked the above questions not because I expect the reader to answer them, much less because I expect in advance an affirmative answer, but to put the reader in possession at the outset of the point of view from which the following criticism of Bergson's account of perception is written, and, in outline, of the technic of its method. As has been sufficiently intimated, I shall not question his main thesis: the description of perception as a factor in organic action. Neither shall I be called upon to question the specific terms in and by which he carries on this description: the central nature of indeterminate possibilities and the preoccupation of perception with the physical environment, not with mental states. My point is rather that so far as these traits receive due development we are carried to a conclusion where reference to useful action ceases to mark an invidious contrast with reality, and, accordingly, indicates a standpoint from which the need of any rival mode of knowledge, called philosophical, becomes doubtful.

It is not enough to say that perception is relative to action: one needs to know *how* it is relative, and one needs to know the distinguishing traits of action. And so far as Bergson's account makes perception relative to action, that is, makes knowledge qualified by possibilities (by freedom), and *useful* in affording an efficient development of free action, we are taken where the antithetical dualisms of space and time, matter and spirit, action and intuition have no belonging. Let the reader recall the honorific use of "life" in Bergson and his depreciatory use of "action," and decide whether the following sentence (the most emphatic one that I have found in his writings in the sense just indicated) does not break down the barriers supposed to exist between action and life, and connect perception with an action which is naught but the process of life itself. "Restore, on the contrary, the true character of perception; recognize in pure perception a system of nascent acts which plunges roots deep into the real; and at once perception is seen to be radically distinct from recollection; the reality of things is no more constructed or reconstructed, but touched, penetrated, lived."[1]

Place in contrast with this sentence such statements as the following: "My conscious perception has an entirely practical destination, it simply indicates, in the aggregate of things, that which interests my possible action upon them" (p. 306);

1. *Matter and Memory*, English translation, pages 74–75. The significance of the passage stands out the more if one calls to mind that, from the other standpoint, recollection is the index of the real, of time and spirit, while perception, since connected with action, is tied down to space and matter.

and this: "When we pass from pure perception to memory, we definitely abandon matter for spirit" (p. 313). Must not such a view of perception flow from quite another analysis, or at least from another emphasis, from that which yields the conception that in perception we *live* reality itself? I have finally reached a point where I can state what seems to me to be a specific oscillation between inconsistent views in Bergson's account of perception, while it will also be evident, I hope, that the discussion of this oscillation is not a picayune attempt to convict a great writer of a mere technical inconsistency, but involves the whole question of the validity of the knowledge that is connected with action, and of the need in metaphysics of another kind of knowledge. One view of perception implicates indeterminate possibilities (and hence time, freedom, life) in the quality of its operation, subject-matter, and organ; the other regards indeterminate possibilities as conditions *sine qua non* of the act, but not as qualifying either its nature as an act or that of its subject-matter. Our long introduction is now at an end. We come to the details of Bergson's account of perception.

I

Perception, according to Bergson, must be approached as a problem of selection and elimination, not as one of enhancement and addition. If there were more in the conscious perception of the object than in its presence, the problem of the passage from the latter to the former would be wrapped in impenetrable mystery. Not so, if its perception means less than its presence, since all that is then required is to discover the condition that might lead to the abandoning by the unperceived object of some of its entire being (p. 27). In the search for this condition, we begin by noting the trait characteristic of the existence of the subject in its entirety. Since the physical world is always a scene of complete transmitting, by equal and opposite reactions, of energy, it follows that "in one sense we might say that the perception of any unconscious material point whatever, in all its instantaneousness, is infinitely greater and more complete than ours, since this point gathers and transmits the influences of all the points of the material universe" (p. 30). Anything, accordingly, that would eliminate some of the transmitting power of some part of the total physical system would throw the phases of this blocked part into contrast with the rest of the system, and thereby into a kind of relief equivalent to its perception. Introduce a living body, with its special interests, and this is just what happens. The activity of the organism allows all influences, all movements, that have no interest for it, to pass immediately through it. With respect to them it is a neutral transmitter like any other part of the total system. But those movements that are of concern to it are singled out, disengaged (pp. 28–29). They are held up, as it were, as a highwayman holds up his intended victim preparatory to exercising upon him the function of robbery that defines a highwayman. This arrest and detachment throws the traits of the things with which it is concerned into relief: they are perceived. From this interpretation of perception are derived its main traits. It is concerned directly with physical things, no mental states intervening; the perceived objects are arranged about our body as their centre; they vary with changes of the body; the extent of the field perceived increases with growth in the variety and scope of our organic interests. Above all, perception is primarily a fact of action, not of cognition.

In making this summary I have tried to leave out of account considerations which would tell one way or another as respects the double analysis of perception to which I referred above, making my account as neutral as may be. The account must now be complicated by referring to the considerations slurred over. In the first place, the fact must be emphasized that in Bergson's professed view (that which leads in the end to invidious contrast with true knowledge of reality) the change from the total world to the perceived part is merely quantitative; it is *merely* a diminution, a subtraction. The relation is just and only that of part and whole. "There is nothing positive here, nothing added to the image [object], nothing new. The objects merely abandon something of their real action."[2] Perception "creates nothing; its office, on the contrary, is to eliminate from the totality of images [objects]

2. *Ibid.*, page 30. The omitted half of the last sentence will be noted later.

all those on which I can have no hold, and then, from each of those which I can retain, all that does not concern the needs of the image [object] which I call my body" (p. 304). This notion of sheer diminution and elimination of most of the parts and aspects of a whole supplies the official definition of pure perception: "a vision of matter both immediate and instantaneous" (p. 26); "an uninterrupted series of instantaneous visions, which would be a part of things rather than of ourselves."[3]

The position that seems inconsistent with this one might be arrived at deductively from the stress laid, in the definition of perception, upon indeterminateness of action: upon the operative presence of genuine possibilities. Consider such a statement as the following:

> Is not the growing richness of this perception likely to symbolize the wider range of indetermination left to the choice of the living being in its conduct with things? Let us start, then, from this indetermination as from the true principle, and try whether we can not deduce from it the possibility and even the necessity, of conscious perception. . . . The more immediate the reaction is compelled to be, the more must perception resemble a mere contact; and the complete process of perception and of reaction can then hardly be distinguished from a mechanical impulsion followed by a necessary movement. But in the measure that the reaction becomes more uncertain, and allows more room for suspense, does the distance increase at which the animal is sensible of the action of that which interests it. . . . The degree of independence of which a living being is master, or, as we shall say, the zone of indetermination which surrounds its activity, allows, then, of an *a priori* estimate of the number and distance of the things with which it is in relation. . . . So that we can formulate this law: *perception is master of space in the exact measure in which action is master of time.*[4]

The passage is quoted because of its statement of the central position of indeterminate action. The explicit reference (in the last sentence) to time *suggests* what I regard as the true doctrine, but a careful reading shows that this ref-

3. *Ibid.*, page 69. The reader familiar with the doctrine of space and time in Bergson does not need to be reminded that perception as an *instantaneous* section (non-temporal, non-durational) in an instantaneously complete field inevitably aligns perception with matter to the exclusion of time, mind, and reality as it would be envisaged from within.
4. *Matter and Memory*, pages 21, 22, 23. It is perhaps superfluous to multiply references, but see also pages 28, 29, 35, 37, 67, 68.

erence can not be taken as an assertion of that conclusion. On the contrary, Bergson evidently means that the indeterminateness only acts as a sort of negative condition, a condition *sine qua non,* to throw into relief those objects which have a possible concern for the indeterminate action. As he says elsewhere, it operates "to filter through us that action of external things which is real, in order to arrest and retain that which is virtual" (p. 309). Again the effect is spoken of as one of disassociation, of disengaging (p. 41). The objects "detach from themselves that which we have arrested on the way, that which we are capable of influencing" (p. 29). He speaks of indetermination acting as a sort of mirror which brings about an apparent reflection of surrounding objects upon themselves (pp. 29, 46). Again, the body "indicates the parts and aspects of matter on which we can lay hold: our perception which exactly measures our virtual action on things thus limits itself to the objects which actually influence our organs and prepare our movements."[5]

All such statements but emphasize the doctrine of mere subtraction, of diminution, as the essence of the act of perception. And if I now quote some passages which seem to have a contrary sense, it is not because I attach any great importance to what may be casual verbal inconsistencies, but because the passages bring to the front a contrasting notion of the facts themselves. The part of the sentence that was omitted in our earlier quotation after saying that objects merely abandon something of their real action "in order to manifest their virtual action" reads: "that is, in the main *the eventual action of the living being upon them.*" (Italics mine.) To the same effect he says (p. 59) around my body "is grouped the representation, *i.e.*, its [the body's] *eventual* influence upon the others [objects]." So (p. 68) perception is said to "express and measure the power of action in the living being, the indetermination of the movement or of the action *which will follow upon the receipt of the stimulus.*" (Italics mine.) Again, "perception consists in detaching, from the totality of objects, the possible action of my body upon them." Most significant of all, perhaps, is the following: "Perception, understood, as we understand it, measures

5. *Ibid.*, page 233. Compare "It eliminates from the totality of images all those on which I can have no hold." *Ibid.*, page 304.

our possible action upon things, and thereby, inversely, the possible action of things upon us" (p. 57; italics mine).

As I have just said, I shall try not to attach undue importance to the mere wording of these passages. It is easy to substitute for the phrase, "bodies upon which we may act," the other phrase, "our possible action upon bodies," and yet *mean* the same thing, verbally opposed as are the two phrases, especially as the idea that perception "measures" our possible action upon things seems to afford a connecting link. But the verbal opposition may be used to suggest that there follows from Bergson's theory of the dependence of perception upon indeterminateness quite another view of the perceived subject-matter than that of quantitative elimination. If we allow our mind to play freely with the conception that perceived objects present our *eventual* action upon the world, or designate our possible actions upon the environment, we are brought to a notion of complication, of qualitative alteration. For the only way in which objects could conceivably designate our future actions would be by holding up to view the objective effects of those actions; that is to say, presenting the prior environment as it will be when modified by our reactions upon it. Perception would then be anticipatory, prognostic; it would exhibit to us in advance the consequences of our possible actions. It would thereby facilitate a choice as respects them, since the act of appreciating in advance the consequences that are to accrue from incipient activities would surely affect our final action.

So far as the *subject-matter* of perception is concerned, we are led to substitute for a material cut out from an instantaneous field, a material that designates the effects of our possible actions. *What* we perceive, in other words, is not just the material upon which we *may* act, but material which reflects back to us the consequences of our acting upon it this way or that. So far as the *act* of perception is concerned, we are led to substitute an act of choosing for an act of accomplished choice. Perception is not an instantaneous act of carving out a field through suppressing its real influences and permitting its virtual ones to show, but is a process of determining the indeterminate.

So far we have, however, simply two contrasting positions placed side by side. What are the grounds for preferring one view to the other? I shall first take up the formal or dialectic analysis of the elements of the situation as Bergson describes them, and then consider his account of perception as choice, closing with his account of the place of the brain in the act of perception.

II

I think it can be shown that the idea of perception as bare instantaneous outstanding of part of an instantaneous larger world is supported only by a rapid alternation between the two conceptions of real and of possible action; and that the moment we hold these two conceptions together in a way that will meet the requirements of the situation we are bound to pass over to the other idea of perception, the one involving a qualitative change of antecedents in the direction of their possible consequences.

The difficulty in Bergson's professed account may perhaps be suggested by the following passage: "If living beings are just centers of indetermination . . . we can conceive that their *mere presence* is equivalent to the suppression of all those parts of objects in which their functions find no interest" (p. 28; italics mine). But can we conceive anything of the kind, even if we allow our imagination the most generous leeway? We seem to be caught in a dilemma. Either the living bodies are engaged in *no* action, are *merely* present; or else they are really acting. If the former is the case, then no influence is exercised upon the environment, not even a suppressive or relinquishing one. If the latter, the action must modify the bodies upon which it is exercised. We get either less or more than abandonment. Does it not seem *a priori* probable that the idea of perception as the outcome of a sort of purely negative action is but a half-way station between the notion of no perception at all and of perception as an environment modified through a characteristic response of the living body? For we *can* conceive that some act of the organism in accord with its peculiar interests, some gesture, or active attitude, might *accentuate* the parts of the world upon which the organism is interested to act, and that this stress might be equivalent to their perception.

Perhaps, however, our hard and fast dilemma is due to our ignoring just the points upon which Bergson insists: indeterminateness and possibilities. But the dilemma appears to repeat itself. Are the possible actions of the organism *merely* possible? Even if we admit (what seems to me inadmissible) that *mere* potentiality is an intelligible conception, we are still far from seeing how it could exercise even a suppressive influence. But if possible activities mean (as it seems to me they must mean to have a meaning) a peculiar quality of real actions, then we get real influence indeed, but something more and other than sheer elimination and suppression. If we look at it from the side of indetermination, the logic is not changed. Either indetermination and uncertainty mean a qualitatively new type of action, or they mean the total absence of action.

Perhaps I can now make clearer what I meant by Bergson's alternation between real and possible action. The act of carving out a portion of the entire field must be a real act. It is complete at one stroke, all at once. This by itself gives a sheer quantitative limitation. But this act of eliminative selection is still to be accounted for. So we have recourse to the presence of possible actions. What is let go is that upon which the organism can not possibly act; what is held to is that upon which it can act. Bergson thus strings the two conceptions one after the other in this way: *Logically,* possibility antecedes (that is, implies and requires) an act of selection; *really,* the act of selection precedes the actualization of possible actions, furnishing the field upon which they are to operate. Bergson seems to vibrate between the real action of possibilities, and the possible action of real (but future) actualities. The former designates an act that is, however, more than instantaneous, that is a process; and that does more than cut out, that qualifies the material upon which it operates, so as to prepare the way for a subsequent action. The latter expresses something that will be instantaneous when it comes and that may be conceived (perhaps) as having only an effect of diminution, but that, unfortunately, is not present to have any effect at all, save as, to meet the requirements of the situation, it suddenly changes to a present real action of possibilities, that is, to a distinctive *quality* of selective action. The same dialectic operates (as we shall shortly see) upon the side of the environment. On the one hand, the perceived subject-matter indicates *possible* action upon the organism, something which has been acquired in the act of perception. But on the other hand, as the perceived subject-matter is an instantaneous section out of a homogeneous totality, any possibilities which the subject-matter can present must have been already in its possession. But as this contradicts the notion of complete presence, we are again forced to the conception of possibility as something conferred by the organism.

Bergson seems to recognize that the bare inoperative presence of potentialities (the conception which seems to provide a middle term between possible future real actions and present real action of possibilities) will not, after all, suffice to account even for a diminution of the physical environment. We somehow *arrest* the influences proceeding from those bodies that we are capable of acting upon. This act of arrest receives some positive characterization in the following passage. After stating that physical bodies act and react mutually by all their elements, he goes on to say: "Suppose, on the contrary, that they encounter somewhere a certain spontaneity of reaction: their action is in so far diminished, and this diminution of their action is just the representation which we have of them" (p. 29). Here we have the most explicit statement that I have been able to find of the *modus operandi* of the act of suppression. It is treated as a real act, and in so far meets the necessities of the case, while at the same time spontaneity is suggestive of possibilities. We will admit, without caviling, that spontaneity of action describes a peculiar type of action, one which, instead of following the physical principle of equal and opposite reaction, merely diminishes the real efficacy of the influences that it encounters. But even so, we have only a *real* action of a peculiar unusual sort in this reduction of the efficacy of the objects. If, however, spontaneity means that the organic act is already charged with potentiality, its manifestation might *convert* the energy of the environment into a form that would involve the inhibition, for the time being, of its usual physical mode of efficacy. But suppression *through conversion into a different form* is a radically different thing from suppression by mere diminution. This latter might, by lowering the resistance that it would otherwise encounter, give a better chance for some subsequent organic activity to express itself, but this would be the limit of its significance. Such a state of affairs would involve no indetermination, and there is no sense in calling the subsequent action a possible action. It is simply a postponed action, bound to occur if the spontaneous action intervenes. It is simply the real future action of which we have spoken. In short, it does not fulfill the conditions for the emergence of the unperceived into the perceived.

Upon occasion, however, Bergson states the situation differently. As stated in a passage already quoted, we allow "to filter through us that action of external things which is real, in order to arrest and retain that which is virtual: this virtual action of things upon our body and of our body upon things is our perception itself" (p. 309). I pass over the question of how this view is to be reconciled with the statements to the effect that perception "limits itself to the objects which *actually influence our organs* and prepare our movements." The point to notice is that virtual or potential action is transferred from our body and made a property of the objects, the peculiarity of our action now being that it isolates this property of the objects. This point of view is even more explicit in such a statement as the following:

> Representation is there (that is, in the universe), but always virtual—being neutralized at the very moment when it might become actual, by the obligation to continue itself and to lose itself in something else. To obtain the conversion from the virtual to the actual it would be necessary, not to throw more light upon the object, but on the contrary to obscure some of its aspects, to diminish it by the greater part of itself, so that the remainder, instead of being encased in its surroundings as a *thing*, should detach itself from them as a *picture* (p. 28).

The extraordinary nature of this passage stands out if we recall that the express definition of the physical is complete actuality, total lack of virtuality. Even more significant, however, than this contradiction is, for our present problem, the complete shift of the point of view. Potentiality to begin with was wholly on the side of the living being, just as actuality was the essence of the world. But since any act of elimination, of diminution, affected by the living being would obviously be a real act of a certain kind, the exigencies of the logic require that potentiality be attributed to the object, the real action of the organic being now treated merely as an occasion for the display of this potentiality. But whenever the exigencies of the argument require reference to the indeterminateness of the action of *living* beings, to mark them off from non-living things, potentiality retires from the object to take up again its exclusive residence in the living being.[6]

Quite likely the reader has been brought to a feeling that we are not any longer considering perception at all, but are engaged simply in performing dialectic variations on the themes of actuality and possibility, indeterminateness and determinateness. Let us then attempt to translate the conceptions over into their factual equivalents. I think that the es-

6. It is worth considering whether this dialectic does not throw light upon Bergson's panpsychic idealism. It seems as if his final attribution of panpsychic quality to matter were simply a generalization, once for all, of the circular logic we have just noticed. If (*a*) we define perception as a conscious representation on the basis of potentiality, and then (*b*) fall back on the inherent potentiality of the universe to account for the diminution of the field characteristic of the conscious representation, it follows as matter of course that the universe itself is already consciousness of some sort (*cf.* page 313). "No doubt also the material universe itself, defined as the totality of images, is a kind of consciousness, a consciousness in which everything compensates and neutralizes everything else, a consciousness of which all the potential parts, balancing each other by a reaction which is always equal to the action, reciprocally hinder each other from standing out." Here we have, I think, the key to his entire treatment. Let anything throw the whole out of balance, and a piece of this total consciousness stands out. The cut-out portion is a *conscious* representation just because the whole from which it is cut is conscious. But why is the whole called consciousness? Simply because perception is conscious and perception is a part cut out from a homogeneous whole. But there must be something to effect the cutting out; the whole does not cut itself up. Hence the need of referring to the differential presence of the organism as a centre of indeterminate possibilities. But to stay by this standpoint would connect all the eulogistic traits that are employed in designating philosophic intuition with crises of organic activity. Hence potentiality and freedom are transferred back to the whole, which accordingly makes matter into consciousness once more.

sential of Bergson's view may be correctly stated about as follows: The indeterminateness of the action of a living being serves to delay its motor responses. This delay gives room for deliberation and choice. It supplies the opportunity for the conscious selection of a determinate choice—for freedom of action. But the delay of motor response also signifies something from the standpoint of the world: namely, a division within it. Certain of its movements are still continued through and beyond the organism; with respect to them, there is no delaying response. Consequently those other movements of the world to which response is postponed are sundered; they are thrown into relief, cut out. Moreover, it will be noted that the material that thus stands out presents just those movements upon which the possible, or postponed, responses of the organism may take effect. Material thus cut out and having such reference to subsequent organic actions constitutes pure perception.

The ingenuity of this account is indubitable. For my own part, I think it gives the elements of a true account. But it is possible to arrange these elements quite differently and thereby reach quite a different result. The revised account reads somewhat like this. External movements are involved in the activities of an organism. If and in so far as these activities are indeterminate, there is neither a total, or adequate stimulus in the movements, nor an adequate total response by the organism. Adequate stimulation and adequate response are both delayed (the delay is an effect, not a cause or condition, as it seems to be in Bergson's account). The partial responses, however, are neither merely dispersed miscellaneously upon the environment, nor are they merely possible. They are directed upon the partial stimuli so as to *convert* them into a single coordinated stimulus. Then a total response of the organism follows. This functional transformation of the environment under conditions of uncertain action into conditions for determining an appropriate organic response constitutes perception.

What is the difference between the two views? According to the first, perception *is* a stimulus, ready-made and complete. According to the second, it is the operation of *constituting* a stimulus. According to the first, the object or given stimulus merely sets a problem, a question, and the process of finding its appropriate answer or response resides wholly with the organism. According to the second, the stimulus or perceived object is a part of the process of determining the response; nay, in its growing completeness, it is the determining of the response. As soon as an integral and clear-cut object stands out, then the response is decided, and the only intelligent way of choosing the response is by forming its stimulus. Meantime organic responses have not been postponed; a variety of them are going on, by means of which the environing conditions are given the status of a stimulus. The change effected in the environment by the final total organic act is just a consummation of the partial changes effected all through the process of perception by the partial reactions that finally determine a clear-cut object of perception. This means that the perceived subject-matter at every point indicates a response that *has* taken effect with reference to its character in determining *further* response. It exhibits what the organism *has* done, but exhibits it with the qualities that attach to it as part of the process of determining what the organism is *to do*. If at any point we let go of the thread of the process of the organism's determining its own eventual total response through determining the stimulus to that response by a series of partial responses, we are lost.

III

We have now to consider the same situation, but this time from the standpoint of the act of choice concerned in it. Our previous discussion prepares us for the points at issue. We may anticipate an alternation between two conceptions, introducing into a choice alleged to be complete in an instantaneous act, traits which belong to a choice among future possible acts. The circular reasoning will disappear, we may also anticipate, as soon as substituted for the alternation between a present choice and a future choice, each of which owes its character to the other, a temporal act of choice, that is, a *choosing*.

Bergson's nominal theory is that the selective elimination

is itself a choice. "Our consciousness only attains to certain parts and certain aspects of those parts. Consciousness—in regard to external perception—consists in just this choice."[7] Such a choice seems, however, exactly like a "choice" exhibited in the selective or differential reaction of a metal to an acid. The metal also "picks out" the form of energy upon which it can act and which can act upon it.[8] Permit, however, the phrase to pass as a metaphor; or permit, if you will, the metaphor to pass as a fact. There is here no indetermination of any kind; nothing undecided and no need of any subsequent choosing. The choice being complete, the reaction of the organism follows at once, or as soon as its time comes. But now there enters upon the scene a present effect attributed to future possible actions. There are many possible acts lying in wait. Otherwise the choice, the relinquishing and the standing out, would not have occurred. Somehow, therefore, the perceived object sketches and measures the many possible acts among which a choice has to be made before a

7. *Ibid.*, page 31; *cf.* page 304: "Perception appears as only a choice."
8. Considerations of space compel me to omit many matters of interest which are relevant to the topic. But I can not forbear here a word of reference to Bergson's earlier mode of statement of the point at issue between idealism and realism. The reader will recall that he sets out from a statement of the two ways in which objects—called, for convenience, "images"—may vary. In one system each varies according to all the influences brought to bear upon it; in the other, all vary according to the action of *one privileged* object, the organic body. The former system describes the physical world; the latter, the perceived world. But *some* of his descriptions of the peculiarities of the latter surely refer as well to the traits of the former. Thus "I note that the size, shape, even the color of external objects is modified according as my body approaches or recedes from them; that the strength of an odor, the intensity of a sound, increases or decreases with distance" (page 6). Surely, however, the intensity of an influence exercised by any physical body upon another physical body varies with distance. Shape and size, regarded as the angular portion of the total field subtended, vary with distance in the same physical way; so does color with the change in intensity of light effected by distance. Thus choice, as here defined, is only a name for the *specific* action one body exercises upon others. But in his final formula is stated the *peculiar* kind of a change in the physical system effected by the organic body in perception: things not merely change with its changes, but change so as to reflect its "*eventual* action" (p. 13). Here, indeed, is a genuine criterion of distinction; and our further discussion of choice is simply a development of the consequences of introducing reference to *eventual* action into its nature.

determinate response can occur. The circle is before us. The present complete choice makes possible a presentation of future possibilities; the future possible acts operate to define the peculiar nature of the present act.

The two sides are brought together in the consideration that the perceived object reflects or mirrors our state of suspense, of hesitation, the conditions with respect to which we have to choose. It is unnecessary to go over the ground already traversed; if I have not succeeded in laying bare the circular reason nothing I can add now will be of any avail. But we may note two consequences applicable to the situation as it takes form with respect to choice. Since the unperceived world is, by definition, one that is completely actual in itself—since, in other words, the world as physical already has its mind all made up—this view implies the introduction into the perceived world of a quality contradictory to the conception of a mere quantitative selection. Choice, even though instantaneously complete choice, has done something positive after all. But of greater moment is the fact that a subject-matter of perception that merely mirrors our own hesitation is of no use in resolving that hesitation. If we insist upon looking at it as marking a choice, the choice is simply to be undecided as to a choice. The perceived object just gives back to us, indifferently, sullenly, uninstructively, our own need of a choice. Such a perception could never participate in the "office of *ensuring our effective action* on the object present."[9] Our later choice among possible actions will then be as blind and random as if perception had never intervened. What is the likelihood of an act so chosen being effective, appropriate? Better had it been to have remained in the frying-pan of complete mechanism than to have jumped into the fire of purely random action.[10]

9. *Ibid.*, page 84. Italics mine. In its context the quotation refers to the role of the cerebral mechanism in perception, but, by hypothesis, it must be capable of transfer, without injustice to the logic, to the perception as the chosen object.

10. It may be objected that we have here ignored the distinction between pure and concrete perception and the need of memory to effect the change of the former into the latter, and thereby have treated the essence of the account of pure perception as if it were a difficulty in the account. Pure perception, we may be told, does present us with exactly the indeterminateness which reflects our own hesitation. It gives the field with respect to which choice has to be made. It sets a question to which the

Note how the difficulties disappear if we regard the act of perceiving as a temporal act, as *choosing*. Follow out literally the idea that our reactions *are uncertain*, not merely "allowing room for suspense," but *involving* suspense (p. 22).

Since any reactions that we actually make must, no matter how charged they are with uncertainty, modify the environment upon which they exercised,[11] we shall have as the counterpart of the act a field undergoing determination. So far as reactions are dominantly uncertain we shall expect, indeed, to find the subject-matter vague and confused—and we do so find it. But an indefinite reaction may have a certain

---

motor response has to find a reply (see, for example, page 41). What guides the motor response in finding the reply is not perception but memory. "Though the function of living bodies is to receive stimulations in order to elaborate them into unforeseen reactions, still the choice of the reaction cannot be the work of chance. This choice is likely to be inspired by *past experience*, and the reaction does not take place without an appeal to the *memories* which analogous situations may have left behind them. The indetermination of acts to be accomplished requires, then, if it is not to be confounded with pure caprice, the *preservation* of the images perceived" (page 69, italics mine; see also pages 103 and 114). I have no doubt that this quotation represents Bergson's view; perception puts the question, and only puts the question; memory helps the motor response to find the effective and appropriate answer. Even though my whole argument seems left hanging in the air with its underpinning knocked out, I must postpone consideration of this point of view till an explicit discussion of memory is undertaken. But certain indications may be suggested at this point. The assumption leaves totally unexplained the sudden transformation of a physical world totally devoid of virtuality (see pages 80 and 81 for the statement that if the physical world had virtuality it might be the cause of consciousness) into a world that is as perceived nothing but potentialities. Matter as perceived is now pure freedom: mind as memory is pure determination. But more significant to the present problem is the recognition that action based on pure perception is a matter of "chance," of "pure caprice." If such be the case, how can the object of pure perception provide any clue to the recall of the proper memory? Why is not that a work of chance, of caprice? But most significant of all is the preestablished harmony set up between perception and memory, space and time, matter and mind, by this view that perception sets the problem to which an alleged radically different power uniquely supplies the answer. For like all preestablished harmonies it testifies to the probability of a prior artificial separation.

11. It will be interesting to watch the logic of those neo-realists who connect the act of perception with the organism instead of with "consciousness" when they develop their views in detail. Professor Montague's theory of potential energy as the physical side of consciousness seems to avoid the snares, but if I mistake not, potential energy which is all located at one spot instead of marking a stress in a larger field alleges an unprecedented physical fact.

focusing that will further define its subject-matter so that it will afford the stimulus to a more effective subsequent response, and so on till the perceived matter gets outline and clearness. If, however, the reactions continue wholly and only indeterminate, the confusion of the subject-matter will remain, and, correspondingly, the indeterminateness of response will persist. The only perception that can be a useful part of the act of choosing a useful response will be one that exhibits the effects of responses already performed in such a way as to provide continuously improving stimuli for subsequent responses. The only way in which a living being with indeterminate possibilities of action can be intelligently helped to their determination by perceived objects is by having perceived objects serve as anticipations of the consequences of the realization of this or that possibility. And only through a presentation in anticipation of the objective consequences of a possible action could an organism be guided to a choice of actions that would be anything except either mechanical or purely arbitrary. Perception can prepare our further movements effectively and appropriately in the degree in which it continuously provides the stimuli for them. In words of Bergson's own which can not be bettered: "That which constitutes our pure perception is our dawning action, in so far as it is prefigured in those images [namely, objects]. The *actuality* of our perception thus lies in its *activity*, in the movements which prolong it."[12] Take this passage seriously and literally, and you have the precise view of perception here contended for. It is not a choice accomplished all at once, but is a process of choosing. The possible responses involved are not merely postponed, but are operative in the quality of present sensori-motor responses. The perceived subject-matter is not simply a manifestation of conditions antecedent to the organic responses, but is their transformation in the direction of further action.

IV

In the references which we have made in this discussion to sensori-motor responses we have already implicitly

12. *Ibid.*, page 74. Italics in the original.

trenched upon our last topic: the body, as implicated in perception. Just what part does the brain have, in the act of perception? The reader need not be reminded how central is this aspect of the matter for Bergson. From one standpoint, his entire discussion of perception is intended as a demonstration that the brain is not the cause of conscious representations, but is, and is solely, the organ of a certain kind of action. The undoubted correspondence between the *facts* of the subject-matter of perception (the conscious representations) and brain events is to be explained, not by invoking materialism or psycho-physical parallelism (both of which depend upon regarding perception as a case of knowledge instead of action), but by showing that both the conscious representations and the brain states are functions of nascent or potential action. The "representations" designate action on the side of its material, the environing conditions; the brain movements designate it on the side of the organs intimately involved in it (pp. 35, 309). The correspondence is that of material and tool of action, like that of soil and plow with reference to the act of sowing seed.

The reader is invited to traverse the field for a third and last time. We have, once more, to see how Bergson provides all the factors of an adequate statement; how he places them in temporal alternation to each other and thereby renders them incapable of performing the office attributed to them; and how the account stands when it is corrected by making the factors of actuality and indeterminateness contemporaneous instead of successive.

The nervous system, being a physical structure, is a medium of the transmission of movements, and is only that. Consequently any correspondence or correlation that can be made out between the brain processes and the object of conscious perception (the so-called conscious content or representation) must be in terms of correspondence of modes of movement. The nervous process concerned in the act of perception must be describable, in other words, in a way analogous to the peculiar type of action that is exhibited in the perceived object. The marks that distinguish cortical action from the so-called reflex action of the lower structures furnish the clue. In the latter, the incoming movement is shunted at once into a return movement. In the former the paths of communication are immensely multiplied and the nature of transmission correspondingly complicated. The same incoming stimulus has many outgoing paths open to it. Thus the brain has a double office. On the one hand, it provides a mechanism by which peripheral disturbance, upon reaching the spinal cord instead of being deflected into its immediate reflex track, may be put in flexible connection with other motor mechanisms of the cord. The cortical cells termed sensory "allow the stimulation received to reach *at will* this or that motor mechanism of the spinal cord, and *so to choose* its effect."

On the other hand, as a great multitude of motor tracks can open simultaneously in this substance to one and the same excitation from the periphery, this disturbance may subdivide to any extent, and consequently dissipate itself in innumerable motor reactions which are merely nascent. Hence the office of the brain is sometimes to conduct the movement received to a *chosen* organ of reaction, and sometimes to open to this movement the totality of the motor tracks, so that it may manifest there all the potential reactions with which it is charged, and may divide and so disperse. . . . The nervous elements . . . do but indicate a number of possible actions at once, or organize one of them (p. 20).

With respect to the matter under discussion, the significant element is the statement that *sometimes* the brain has one office—allowing a *chosen* reaction to proceed; and *sometimes* another office—to permit its dispersal into a number of channels. The same duality is repeated in the statement that the brain indicates a number of possible reactions *or* organizes one of them. The alternation already considered here presents itself overtly and externally. And the dilemma is presented in an equally definite way. So far as there is choice, organization of a fixed path, there is just a single actual response. So far as there is dispersal in many paths, there are many actual responses. In neither case does possibility, or choice among possibilities, show its face. At the same time, there is indicated the true state of affairs: the brain expresses the operation of organizing one mode of total response *out of* a number of conflicting and partial responses.

We can of course imagine that the dispersal of energy

among many paths is so extensive as to be equivalent to a practical inhibition, for the time being, of any definite action upon the environment. For the time being, the expenditure of energy (barring what leaks through) is intraorganic, or even, anticipating the dispersion into sensori-motor tracks to be mentioned shortly, intracerebral. We might identify this temporary inhibition of overt response with the gap in the instantaneously completed transmission which throws part of the material world into relief. But this identification proves too much. If the dispersal is into *motor* tracks, these discharges are just so *many* overt and disconnected acts in an incipient or nascent condition.[13] They are not the incipiency of one *appropriate* act. No provision is made, none is suggested, for recalling them so that in place of the multitude of dispersive tendencies there may be one concentrated act. With reference to the performance of this one act—that alone could meet any need of life—these dispersive activities are just so much waste energy. They sketch, not what we are going to do, but what we *are* doing futilely.

The single path opened may, however, be said to represent a choice of the effect to be attained if it is regarded as a process of coordinating, for greater efficiency, a number of competing partial tendencies. Similarly, these tendencies may be said to represent possible incipient acts (possible paths of choice) if they are brought into contemporary, not alternating, connection with seeking and finding the single most effective line of discharge. Completely real and really complete just as they are when their dispersive character is isolated, they are incipient acts with reference to a unity of organic attitude which they take part in establishing.

The method of realization of the contemporary relation of discovering a unified response to a multitude of dispersive tendencies is incidentally mentioned in Bergson's allusion to the intervention of the "cortical cells termed sensory." All direct motor shunting, whether unified or dispersive, is of the reflex type. Only because of the complication of a situation by the continuation of an incoming stimulus to *sensori*-motor areas in intricate interconnection with one another, can there

13. Compare what was said earlier about the reality of future acts, page 15, above.

be that suspension and choosing which constitute the act of perception. This act is as genuinely motor as eating, walking, driving a nail, or firing combustibles, and involves a like change in the environment upon which it takes effect.[14] But its motor peculiarity is that it takes effect not in such acts as eating, walking, driving, firing, but in such acts as tasting, seeing, touching. The motor response, as long as the act of perception is continued, is directed to *moving* the sense-organs so as to secure and perfect a stimulus for a complete organic readjustment—an attitude of the organism as a whole. This is made possible precisely in so far as the incoming disturbance is "dispersed" not into motor tracks, but into *sensori*-motor areas.[15] In the reciprocal interactions of these sensori-motor areas (their reciprocal stimulation of one another) is found the mechanism of coordinating a number of present but ineffectual motor tendencies into an effective but future response.

Let us suppose the disturbance reaches the brain by way of the visual organ. If directly discharged back to the motor apparatus of the eyes this results not in a perception, but in an eye-movement. But simultaneously with this reaction there is also a dispersal into the areas connected with tasting, handling, and touching. Each of these structures also initiates an incidental reflex discharge. But this is not all; there is also a cross-discharge between these cortical centres. No one of these partial motor discharges can become complete, and so dictate, as it were, the total direction of organic activity until it has been coordinated with the others. The fulfillment of, say, eating, depends upon a prior act of handling, this upon one of reaching, and this upon one of seeing; while the act

14. Not, of course, that the act is, as such, a change of the *perception* (that would involve us in the *regressus ad infinitum* of which the neo-realists have rightly made so much), but that perception *is* the change of the environment effected by the motor phase.

15. It is doubly significant that Bergson alludes to the sensory elements involved without in any way amplifying the allusion. The allusion is necessary in order to supply the basis for the uncertain character of the situation in which perception occurs, and for explanation of its inherent future reference. It is not amplified because the whole explanation of sensory features in Bergson's scheme is found in memory. "Memory" is thus again found implicated in the very heart of pure perception.

of seeing necessary to stimulate the others to appropriate execution can not occur save as it, in turn, is duly stimulated by the other tendencies to action. Here is a state of inhibition. The various tendencies wait upon one another and they also get in one another's way. The sensori-motor apparatus provides not only the conditions of this circle, but also the way out of it.

How can this be? It is clear that if, under the condition supposed, the act of seeing were overtly complete it would *then* furnish the needed stimulus of reaching, this to handling and so on. The *sensory* aspect of the apparatus is, in its nature, a supplying of this condition. The excitation of the optical area introduces the *quality* of seeing connected (through the simultaneous excitation of the areas of reaching, tasting, and handling) with the specific *qualities* of the other acts. The *quality* of movement, or action, supplied by the sensory aspect, is, in effect, an anticipation of the result of the act when overtly performed. With respect to determining the needed stimulus, it is *as if* the overt responses in question had been actually executed.[16]

The reader may regard this account as speculative to any degree which he pleases. Personally I think it outlines the main features of the act of perceiving. But that is neither here nor there. The question is whether or no it furnishes the terms of an account which shall avoid the dilemma in which Bergson's account is held captive, while remaining true to the three requirements of his method of definition: namely, that the brain be treated as an organ for receiving and communicating motion; that indeterminateness be introduced as a specifying feature; that brain processes correspond to subject-matter perceived, as an organ of action corresponds to the material of its action.

Our analysis of Bergson's account is now completed. The reader will decide for himself how far we have been successful in showing that his professed account of perception depends upon alternation between two factors which, if they are

16. Here we find the *modus operandi* presupposed in our account of perception as a process of obtaining, by partial reactions to partial stimuli, the determinate stimulus which will evoke a determinate response. See *ante*, p. 19.

involved at all, must operate contemporaneously, not alternately. He will judge for himself of the value of the account of perception obtained when these factors are treated as contemporaneously operative. I may however be pardoned for reminding him that if the argument has been successful in its two purposes, the traits that are alleged to demarcate perception and the objective material with which it deals from a reality marked by genuine presence of temporal considerations have disappeared. Perception is a temporal process: not merely in the sense that an act of perception takes time, but in the profounder sense that temporal considerations are implicated in it whether it be taken as an act or as subject-matter. If such be the case, Bergson's whole theory of time, of memory, of mind and of life as things inherently sundered from organic action needs revision.

WHAT ARE STATES OF MIND?

"For we move in a world known to us only in symbols. The colors are not in the flowers, but only in our minds." I hasten to reassure the members of the Club by saying that this quotation—borrowed for the occasion from a non-philosophical writing—is not preliminary to a discussion of idealism and realism—though I cannot guarantee that the outcome, if sound, will be without bearing upon that disputatious topic. But the purpose of my paper is to raise a question of descriptive fact. What specific facts does the phrase "in our minds" *denote*? Or what facts capable of specific detection and description does the term "states of mind" denote?

As the rules of the Club call, I believe, for a summary of the paper, it may prove helpful if I give one at the beginning instead of at the close.

1. A state of mind means (and means only) a *frame* of mind: that is an emotional disposition as exhibited in a certain mode of behavior.

2. The preposition "*of*" in the phrase "state of mind" denotes an objective, not a possessive, genitive. That is, it denotes that behavior is qualified with a distinctive quale which may be called "psychical" or "mental"; not that there is a mind or consciousness or soul as its subject, substance, agent, sex stuff, place of residence or association.

3. The subject of possession and reference is a living organism-as-actually-implicated-in-a-mal-adjusted-situation. This hyphenated phrase is meant to indicate that the distinction of an emotional attitude of an agent—a person—and of a thing is derived, not original, in experience. What exists in its own right is a situation possessed of "tertiary qualities" as well as primary and secondary; or a situation in which a dis-

[Delivered by Dewey at the New York Philosophical Club on 21 November 1912. Previously unpublished typescript from the Philosophical Club Papers, Special Collections, Columbia University.]

tinctive qualitative reaction towards a distinctively qualitatively toned environment occurs; these two descriptions being but different ways of analytically naming one and the same fact.

4. The derived distinction of personal or emotional attitude and impersonal thing or object comes from a sharpening of interest in the connexion of agencies and consequences, due to the fact that consequences are better and worse in various degrees. In some cases "tertiary quales" cannot be used either (1) as means of producing certain results, or (2) as reliable indices of probable consequences. In other cases, the opposite occurs. Tertiary qualities are deliberately eliminated in the first case, leaving physical objects; and are specifically located and cultivated in the other, yielding conscious personalities.

5. The chief agency in effecting the distinction is social (political-legal-moral). The distinction is primarily made to locate responsibility for results, and to secure results socially esteemed. That is, a living human organism becomes a psychical or conscious being for himself in the degree in which he is socially treated as the author, through means of his emotional dispositions, of certain consequences. In ultimate analysis, a state of mind is a moral fact; that is, a spring of action valued in terms of its consequences.

6. This primary influence is reinforced and often overlaid by others; among which the following are prominent:

(i) The dramatic arts.

(ii) Individualistic morals—individualistic in the sense of employing standards and exacting attitudes that have no well-defined contemporary social embodiments or sanctions. This influence is especially strong when associated—as it generally is—with ideas about divine beings.

(iii) The discovery and exploitation of the value of emotional attitudes for sentimental and literary purposes. So far as the modern "inner world" or "realm" is not a political-moral fact, it is mainly the expression of this motive, which may take the form either of a refined egotism or of literary art, or both.

(iv) In certain circles, the scientific reflex of the foregoing factors (in psychology) is important.

As I have outlined much more than I shall attempt to develop adequately, the above summary is to be regarded as a synopsis of what net result I should try to make out if I had time; and I shall make no pretense of sticking to it literally in the pages that follow.

I

In colloquial English, no one is in doubt about the meaning when it is said that so and so is in a "state of mind." The impression conveyed is that he is in a "state of nerves"—that is in a disposition of behavior towards things and persons which evinces an emotional attitude of irritation and impatience, that will make things disagreeable for his associates. Leave out the special connotation of *irritable* behavior and of disagreeableness as a companion, and we have in this ordinary phrase a better indication of the nature of mental states than is conveyed in some of the tomes on epistemology. A state of mind is an essentially emotional attitude or disposition, this attitude or disposition being characteristic of certain conditions of organic agents. And in order that there may be no doubt of the scope of my meaning—or the extent of my error—I will say that I intend this statement to apply to any and every fact that has a qualification for the title of psychical or mental state: sensations, ideas, images and volitions, as so-called states of consciousness as such.[1] When a psychologist writes: "If I look at grass I have a sensation of green" he means one of two things. He means either that when he looks at grass he sees that the grass is green; or that he is thrown into a peculiar personal state. In the former case, the statement has no psychical context or subject-matter; it pertains to a quality of the object, grass, not to a quality or state of mind. It is probably true that the grass is green, but it is certainly false that the mind is, or that the

1. There is of course another meaning of all these phrases with respect to which they denote certain *functions* of knowledge and action. In this sense they are not *emotional* attitudes, but then neither are they "states of consciousness."

greenness of grass is attached to or resident "in" the mind.[2] And to go on and say that the grass is also in the mind, because it is made up of sensations like green, even if it were true, would so obviously break down the entire distinction between a state of mind and anything else, that it would make meaningless the use of the phrase "state of mind" as a differential or distinguishing phrase. Or if it still had any specific sense, it would have to be sought, and the hypothesis of its being an emotional condition of an organic agent would be as good as any other. But on the other hand, if the term "sensation" has reference to mental state, it refers to an excitation or thrill of the organism on seeing red—a stirring of life like the material of which poetry is woven or upon which the "sensational" newspaper thrives.

There is a general implication—a principle of a fundamental nature—involved in James's theory of emotion which he does not seem to have suspected himself. This principle emancipated from its local setting furnishes not so much a theory of emotion as an indication of the true nature of states of mind as the subject-matter of psychology. The organic resonances and reverberations which in James's theory constitute what he calls "the mind stuff" (the quotation marks are his) of an emotion are in truth the stuff out of which every "state of mind" is constituted. We have to recall that the concept of "psychical states" dominating orthodox psychology is not of psychological origin; its birth-mark and heredity are not scientific but epistemological. Its origin is in the philosophical situation that generated the traditional "metaphysical" problem of the relations of mind and matter. This situation is historically natural and explicable, conditioned on the one hand by religious ideas of the soul and on the other by the practical non-existence of physiological and biological science. But in so far as we cut loose from a speculative assumption which, finding its way into introspective psychology, was uncritically taken to be a self-evident datum, and try to start instead from ideas and facts that are congenial to the science of our own day, the natural point of departure is quite other.

2. To say that because certain molecules or certain vibrations are not green that the *grass* isn't green is one of those astonishing equivokes so current in epistemology.

The primary datum to any mind approaching the subject freed from merely historical prepossessions would be, I am confident, a centre of life, a struggling living being whose efforts to live depend for their success and failure upon the kind of reactions made to the world in which it lives. This unprejudiced observer (a rhetorical figure, as your acute minds have detected, for the present writer) would also find it natural that certain new qualities should attend the activities characteristic of a living being. For its reactions are always biased; they have a tendency to continue or maintain themselves, which contrasts strikingly with the indifference of activities of non-living beings to their outcome. Living beings alone have a destiny, a fate and, consequently, a career or history.[3] That this defining trait should exist in specifically differential qualities of behavior is inevitable—otherwise it would not be at all.

Like all other existences a living being vibrates with and to changes in its surroundings, though with extraordinary delicacy and intensity of susceptibility. In addition these responsive changes have a tendency to modify the surroundings in a direction favoring their own continuation. We talk of a certain self-conserving tendency that marks the phenomena of life; and perhaps there is in some of our talk a concealed suggestion that the living being exercises the tendency directly upon and within itself. But a moment's reflection makes us aware that upon the whole the influence of organic acts is exerted upon the environment; and that in the long run self-conservation is absolutely dependent upon the nature of the changes thus produced in the surroundings. Only indirectly, by a utilization of its environment, does an organism manage to go on being an organism. Every reaction of a living being to stimuli of its environment is fraught, accordingly, with a bearing upon its future success, its own continued being.

It is not claimed that this peculiar quality of organic, as distinct from inorganic, behavior, namely its interested or

3. This statement is not meant to deny that non-living things as implicated or culminating in the specific actions of living beings may have a genuine history.

concerned character (I use those words in a purely objective sense) is identical with what are termed psychical existences and states. It is claimed, however, that it furnished the natural point of departure in any search to identify and describe such states. At this point the reference to James's theory becomes pertinent. The quales out of which *he holds the emotion as a conscious fact to be*[4] *built are precisely the* qualities that mark the deeper-seated adaptive reactions to the organism of its own environment. James's own statement is exclusively interested in the establishing of the fact as a fact of observation. He is curiously indifferent to its meaning or interpretation. Hence while he dwells upon the role of quickened or retarded heart-beats, of changes of breathing, circulation and locomotor apparatus, disturbances of digestion, secretion and excretion, in supplying the material of our consciousness of an emotion, he does not dwell upon the role of those organic changes in the life-struggle of man. His failure to bring this matter into the foreground is responsible, I think, for most of the objections brought against his theory considered as a description of fact. But this significant organic connection is there implicit, and needs only to be brought to express recognition. When it is thus brought forward, his denial of an antecedent (or parallel) separate psychical state which is "expressed" in peculiar bodily postures, flushes, tremblings, etc. etc., suggests the generalization to which I referred earlier: All so-called psychical states are neither antecedents nor concomitants, in a separate realm of existence, of organic reactions, but are the very qualities *of* these reactions. Making a separation which is non-existent (and hence misleading if taken to be more than an emphatic mode of speech) they are consequences, outcomes, products, records, or organic reactive changes involved in the effort of an organism to adapt its actions to changes in its surroundings. Fear, anger, curiosity, hope, love, elation, abasement are characteristic episodes in the vibrating career of success and failure of a living thing; as consciously psychical, they are the

4. The italicized words are introduced as a reminder that in its popular usage an emotion is much more than a fact of consciousness—namely, an active disposition to behave towards things and persons in a specific way.

material of an individual organism's apprehension of its own characteristic attitudes.

No wonder then that "consciousness" in the sense of psychic existence[5] is private, inner, fleeting, individualized, and at the same time characterized by a double-facedness which has been the source of all kinds of extraordinary theories of "transcendence," "transsubjective reference," ejection and projection. For the organic reaction is always (i) to an immediately urgent change and is always of (and so "within") just this or that particular organism whose own especial fortune is at stake; while (ii) it is always *at* or *from* or *with* some change of the environment.

In the latter portion of the foregoing paragraph I have gone, however, beyond what the prior discussion justifies. The discrimination of certain qualities of the situation and their reference to the organism's status and career (the identification of them, in short, as conditions of the organism or subject instead of as conditions of the environment) is a derived fact, an intellectual acquisition. It is equally fallacious to suppose that the primary fact of experience is a psychical state which then has to get extradited into an objective world or is a physical object of strictly physical qualities, exhibiting, however, a perplexing tendency to be clothed upon with animistic and other illusory properties. The primary and the persistent occurrence in the way of experience is a Res, an affair, a concern, a moving complex situation in which so-called, primary, secondary and tertiary qualities are indissolubly blended or fused,—or from which, speaking more correctly, they have not yet been analyzed. We are constantly subject to a retrospective fallacy. Looking back there is the sad event *and* the saddened me; the fearsome bear *and* my fright; the encouraging symptoms *and* my elated hopefulness. But the original situation came with no such duplicity. The

5. I use the quotation marks and the qualifying phrase to mark off the topic of discussion from consciousness in the sense of awareness. It seems to me useless to try to legislate for language, and insist that one or other of these senses is alone proper. They both exist in common speech as well as in technical literature. The real question is as to just what facts are meant by each sense, and how these facts are linked up with each other—if at all. While I have pretty firm opinions on the latter point, they do not enter into the scope of this paper.

accident was depressing and I was depressed; these are but two names, given from the spectator's point of view, to that which in its own occurrence and of its own right is one and the same situation. The "state or frame of mind" has no independent existence, not even as consciously referred to the adaptive struggles of a human organism, to say nothing of being in the orthodox, psychical realm of traditional epistemology and psychology. It was a quality of the situation of experience; of the experienced subject-matter, and it requires as distinctive an act of intellectual analysis to abstract it and refer it to the life-process of an organism as its source and home as it does to attribute the color of something implicated in the situation to vibrations of ether.[6]

II

If then the empirical situation in itself is neither psychical nor physical, "subjective" nor "objective," biological nor cosmical, how does it get discriminated into these two classes of existence? The clue to the answer is found, I think, in the continuity of empirical situations. They are found to be connected with one another. One is used as prognostic or indicative of another and is treated as productive of another. And, to condense a history that has required thousands of years to accomplish itself even partially, it has been found that to regard the angriness of the sun or the dismalness of the weather as efficient causes of subsequent events or as reliable signs of what is likely to occur is to frustrate power of expectation and stultify power of direction. Hence from the standpoints of efficiency in the production of consequences and dependability in forecasting them, the tertiary qualities have been extruded from one whole class of objects, the secondary qualities following suit in due time. The physical object—the object of physical science—is an object constituted wholly in terms of these two functions of relationship to consequences. On the other hand, the angriness of a *man* has turned out to be both a good basis for prediction of what he is

6. This section corresponds roughly to the first three points in the prefixed summary.

likely to do and an important factor in effecting certain kinds of results. Naturally then personal behavior has been set off as a type of behavior contrasting with physical behavior; or the distinction of persons and things has grown in sharpness and precision.

The making of the distinction owes much, if not everything, to social influences. The human race began with whipping, beating, burning and otherwise punishing inanimate objects, as it began with cajoling, bribing and soliciting them precisely as if they were actuated by moral tendencies. And conversely the race treated human beings as if their moral qualities were a matter of physical pollution, contagion and transmission. Out of this experiment conducted for a long time in the interest of influencing behavior certain results have been won. We now have one technique for modifying the behavior of physical things and we have another for affecting the behavior of persons. Certain organic attitudes and responses have been lifted into positions of great conspicuousness and centrality because it is found that through them and through them alone are the social processes of education, control, punishment and award effective. It is mere superstition, however, to suppose that we operate upon certain inner states which are purely psychical—a meaningless concept, since no one has ever suggested even in outline what might be the *modus operandi* of such a procedure. But we do operate upon certain individualized organic attitudes and inchoate reactions so as to give them this turn or that and to secure this result or that. These attitudes are by these processes of education and esteem and condemnation isolated for purposes of cultivation and elimination. They are recognized as the controllable springs to action—as motives in short. As motives capable of social modification and having consequences of general social import they gain a vivid coloring and value of their own; they become distinctively personal states, dispositions of mind, frames of mind, emotions attached to an individual recognized in his particular individuality.

The whole theory of "objective personalities" built up by reasoning from analogy to own exclusively private states of consciousness (supposed to be experienced from the start in their privacy) is in curious contradiction with a whole body of facts which in another context we unhesitatingly accept. We attribute "states of mind" much more readily to other people than to ourselves; we are quite certain that another person is angry when, in exactly the same situation, we are sure that we are but executive instruments for carrying the objective conclusions of an impartial reason. We are quite sure that another man has insulted us because of his purely private spitefulness, and that we in response are actuated by no merely personal wish to get even, but by an impersonal interest in seeing the eternal laws of universal justice vindicated. Roundly speaking, it is only because of social pressure and education that we ever recognize that *we* have any "states of mind" at all. Others insist in pointing out that we are angry and in reprobating us therefore and in treating us as beings who are composed out of anger, as if it were for the time being the very stuff out of which our innermost souls are made. Thus in time (though always in a more or less half-hearted and reluctant way) we learn to regard ourselves as beings possessed of peculiarly private states.

It would be impossible to overstate, I think, the extent to which this social-moral influence had been at times accentuated by the substitution of relations to God or to some metaphysical or cosmic principle (as the Stoic Nature) for the ordinary social interactions. When attention is fixed upon our own attitudes, our own motives, not because our legal liabilities and the daily social exactions and expectations of others require it, but because some invisible being demands a searching of hearts and because the personal and private attitude in respect to this ultimate principle is a condition of virtue or salvation (or some other highly generalized conception of destiny), subjectivity gets a boost from which it never wholly recovers. The heaven above and the hell below this "middle earth" of ours are then none too large a screen upon which to project the drama of our inner emotional life.

III

I add other influences which intensify the sense of an inner separate realm of psychical existences, and which, joined with other factors, have finally led many people to believe that what in reality is but the complex of our emotive attitudes towards the world of persons and things is a wholly detached and incommunicating world to which we are native born and within which we are always confined. Every form of dramatic art depends upon the fact that it is possible to secure a play of emotional reactions by mimic situations. The peculiar qualities that mark our organic behavior form our sense of life—our sense of struggle, of achievement and defeat and of the infinite series of shades of suspense and escape that lie between success and failure. The dramatic arts, from the dance and pantomime out of which the drama proper grew to the dramatic poem and novel and argument, involve a technique for purposely invoking this sense of life in its varied forms by presenting artificial stimuli—artificial from the standpoint of the actual life-struggle—which call out inchoate organic reactions. We vicariously enjoy the experiences of hero and criminal; of saint and general, of clown and sage. The artificiality of the situation emphasizes the unreality of the emotions (the states of mind) from the objective point of view, and it also stimulates (as of course it springs from) a tendency to enjoy and live in these states, simply as states, apart from their normal functions in behavior. The whole tendency is to draw a line about them as a separate region. The extent to which this dramatic motivation has coincided with certain phases of both Roman and evangelical Christianity need only be mentioned.

The dramatic tendency, as just conceived, has not been adequate to the ends of art in the last few centuries however. It is too coarse in its movements and in its results. Modern music, poetry, fiction, confessional and autobiographical literature, even painting, exhibit the possibilities of exploiting the "inner life" as a source not merely of artistic enjoyment but as specific subject-matter of art. The reflex effect of this attitude, falling in as it has done, with the moral and religious influences before mentioned, has been incalculable. All "cultivated" people are more or less Sentimental Tommies, constantly aware of the possibility of detaching their own emotional attitudes from the "real objects" that call them out and with reference to which they originally function in behavior, and of cultivating them for their own sake. No man is so poor in this world's goods or in fame or friends that he cannot afford an inner world of this kind as a buffer, a refuge and a private theatre. My language suggests, probably, the undesirable features accompanying this development of subjectivity. Undesirable features there are, and they complicate all our moral questions—if only because they have tended to make moral problems themselves matters of this inward landscape. But I need hardly point out that, on the other hand, a large part of our increased susceptibility to the meaning of life, the multiplication of subtle and delicate shades in the quality of life, as actually lived out in overt behavior and social intercourse, is due to precisely this same source.

I conclude by saying that the introspective psychologist as concerned (in the traditional formulation of his task) with states of consciousness as such is entangled in three distinct streams: One, mentioned earlier, is the historic heritage from the epistemology of Descartes, Locke and Hume. Another is the interest in motives and in emotional states of mind represented by education, law and other agencies of social direction, and by the inner realm of literary and personal exploitation. The third is his own distinctive contribution as a psychological observer. He has an interest, namely, in detecting the vast range of organic attitudes and reactions that are involved in our intercourse, as living beings, with things. In this interest he isolates them and identifies them by becoming aware of the "states" that appear when these attitudes are artificially reproduced and analyzed into their minor constitutive factors. In this sense, the psychologist himself secretes the states of consciousness which he observes. He secretes them as signs of different characteristic modes of response which in the hurlyburly of life escape our attention. Troubles begin only when, under the influence of the aforementioned tradition borrowed without scientific warrant from metaphysics, the psychologist tells you that the sensations by which he locates the bodily reactions which mediate the perception of distance and direction *are* the stuff out of which space has been built up—or at least out of which its perception, as a complex of these sensations, is built.

In conclusion I should like to say that I am quite aware that this paper is almost as much of a mere summary of possible positions as is the summary officially designated as such; and also that it is in no sense an argument, but only an exposition, or, if you please, only an assertion. But my experience in conversations upon the topic of "mental states" as traits of behavior has been that the difficulty in advancing the conception lies not so much in finding or following arguments, as it does in getting the point of view from which it appears to some persons intelligible and intelligent to hold that so-called states of mind are in truth qualities of a certain type of behavior. And in what I have read as well as in what I have heard in more casual conversations, I have formed the opinion that contrary definitions, descriptions and analyses of "consciousness" are not so much demonstrative appeals to reason as also developments of a chosen point of view.

THE PROBLEM OF VALUES[1]

All members of the Philosophical Association owe a debt of gratitude to the executive committee for formulating the question to be discussed at the next meeting. I am aware of no better way of expressing my own gratitude than to comply promptly with the request of the committee for submission of additional formulations of the question.

I shall first make a few remarks upon the formulation by four members of the committee.[2] I assume that in the question, "Is value something which is ultimate and which attaches itself to 'things' independently of consciousness, or of an organic being with desires and aversions?" the "or" is to be understood as marking a genuine alternative between "consciousness" and an "organic being with desires and aversions," not as indicating that the latter clause is in apposition with consciousness or explanatory of it. The alternative is genuine and important: for some may be inclined to connect the existence of values with organic behavior and yet not be willing to equate desires and aversions with "consciousness" —in fact, they may go so far as to hold that "consciousness" (in whatever sense the term is here used) is itself dependent upon matters connected with the desires and aversions of an organic being. Since, however, unconscious desires and aversions may appear to some to involve a contradiction in language, it would seem better to substitute a more objective term, such as selections and rejections; or better yet, to generalize the matter and make the alternative in question to be

1. This paper is presented in response to the request of the committee that further formulations of this problem be submitted for publication.
2. E. B. McGilvary et al., *Journal of Philosophy, Psychology and Scientific Methods* 10 (1913): 168.

[First published in *Journal of Philosophy, Psychology and Scientific Methods* 10 (1913): 268–69.]

simply that of connection with the *behavior* of organic beings.

When the question is thus understood, some doubt arises as to the force of the term "ultimate" in the first alternative. Are values if regarded as variables of organic behavior less ultimate than if regarded as things irrespective of connection with organic behavior? And if the answer should be in the affirmative, what is the ground upon which this answer rests?

I have no doubt a successful discussion may be had on the basis of the formulation already presented. In some respects, however, the formulation seems unnecessarily tied up with the idealistic-realistic controversy. I recognize that this complication has the advantage of preserving continuity in the discussions from year to year; yet it is possible that the questions at issue might, in the present juncture, be dealt with in the end more effectively if approached by a flank movement. At all events, I venture to submit the following list of questions:

1. Can the question of the status of values in philosophic discussion be approached apart from the question of the status of qualities?

2. Can values be separated from traits of organic behavior? If organic behavior has its own distinguishing traits, does the affirmation that values are traits of organic behavior imply their "subjectivity"? If so, in what sense? Does connection with organic behavior imply their dependence upon awareness?

3. Do values antecede, or do they depend upon valuation —understanding by valuation a process of reflective estimation or judgment?

4. If they antecede, does valuation merely bring them to light without change, or does it modify antecedent values? Does it produce new values? If the latter occur, are the modification and production merely incidental or are they essential?

5. Can the place of intelligence in behavior in general (and in moral conduct in particular) be understood without implying that reflection reorganizes antecedent natural values?

6. What is the meaning of appreciation? Is it a particu-

lar mode of apprehending (knowing) values, or is it a name for the direct presence of values in experience? How is it related to valuation and criticism?

7. Does the presence of values in experience in general (or say religious values in particular) have an evidential import? That is to say, does the existence of religious values, for example, prove the existence of any class of objects beyond the values themselves? Or, again, does the presence in experience of any type of values purport to make the mind aware of something in the environment, taking that word in its widest possible sense? [This question may profitably be considered in connection with the first question, regarding qualities.]

8. If the answers to these questions should be in the negative, is the significance of such values for experience and for philosophy thereby determined to be null or illusory? Can an affirmative answer to this question be maintained except on the assumption that all experience is, *ipso facto*, intended to be an awareness of objects?

PSYCHOLOGICAL DOCTRINE AND PHILOSOPHICAL TEACHING[1]

Abstract methodology has long seemed to me the dreariest field among all the territories, waste and fertile, occupied by philosophy. That philosophy—which, in the last analysis, means some philosopher—should, by means of a general philosophical position, attempt to catalogue the various provinces in the domain of learning, to set forth their respective boundaries, to locate their capital cities and fix their proper jurisdictions, appears to me an undertaking more likely to reveal the limitations of the philosopher's experience, interests, and intelligence than to throw light upon the subject. In discussing the relations of philosophy and psychology, I therefore disavow any attempt to pass upon what psychology must be or ought to be; I am content that psychology should be whatever competent investigators in that field *make* it to be in the successful pursuit of their inquiries. But a teacher and student of philosophy is within his scope when he reflects upon what philosophy in its own past has done in fixing the standpoints, ruling conceptions, and procedures of present psychology, and in raising questions as to the after-effects of this influence—its bearing, namely, upon present philosophical study and teaching.

From this point of view, I say without more ado that, so far as I can observe, the larger part of the time and energy of teachers of philosophy is taken up in the discussion of problems which owe their existence—at least in the way in which they are currently formulated—to the influence of psychology. In its dominant conceptions and professed methods,

1. A paper prepared for the joint discussion of the American Philosophical and Psychological Associations, on the Standpoint and Method of Psychology, New Haven, December 30, 1913.

[Read at the joint discussion of the American Philosophical and American Psychological Associations on "The Standpoint and Method of Psychology," 30 December 1913. First published in *Journal of Philosophy, Psychology and Scientific Methods* 11 (1914): 505–11.]

this psychology is a survival of a philosophy which is daily becoming more incredible and more irrelevant to our present intellectual and social situation. Grant that philosophy has no more to do, intrinsically, with psychology than it has with any other positive science, the fact remains that philosophy is neither taught nor studied, neither written nor read, by discarnate logical essences, but by human beings whose intellectual interests, problems, and attitudes, to say nothing of their vocabulary, are determined by what they already know or think they know in cognate fields. Let a man be as persuaded as you please that the relation between psychology and philosophy is lacking in any peculiar intimacy, and yet let him believe that psychology has for its subject-matter a field antithetical to that of the physical sciences, and his problems are henceforth the problems of adjusting the two opposed subject-matters: the problems of how one such field can know or be truly known by another; of the bearing of the principles of substantiality and causality within and between the two fields. Or let him be persuaded that the antithesis is an unreal one, and yet let his students come to him with beliefs about consciousness and internal observation, the existence of sensations, images, and emotions as states of pure consciousness, the independence of the organs of action in both observation and movement from "consciousness" (since the organs are physical), and he will still be obliged to discuss the type of epistemological and metaphysical problems that inevitably follow from such beliefs. The beliefs do not cease to operate as intellectual habits because one gravely hangs the sign "philosophy" over the shop whence one dispenses one's philosophical wares.

More specifically: The student of philosophy comes to his philosophical work with a firmly established belief in the existence of two distinct realms of existence, one purely physical and the other purely psychical. The belief is established not as speculative, not as a part of or incident to the philosophy he is about to study, but because he has already studied two *sciences*. For every science at once assumes and guarantees the genuineness of its own appropriate subject-matter. *That* much of naïve realism even the later study of epistemology hardly succeeds in displacing.

Given this established "scientific" background, it does not require much reflection to effect a recognition of problems of peculiar difficulty. To formulate and deal with these difficulties, then, becomes the chief work of philosophical teaching and writing. If it is asked what are the nature and scope of these difficulties, the simplest way of answering is to point to the whole industry of "epistemology." There are many ways of formulating them with technical specificality, no one of which, however, is likely, within the limits of space I can afford, to receive general assent, even as a bare statement of difficulties. But I venture upon the following: The physical world is, by received conception, something with which we become acquainted by external observation and active experiment. But the true nature of perception and action, as means of knowing, is to be got at only by introspection, for they are, by received theory, purely mental or psychical. The organ, the instrument, and the method of knowing the external world thus fall within the internal world; it is psychology that tells us about them in telling us about sensations, images, and the various associated complexes that form the psychical apparatus of knowing. But now how can these psychical states, these phenomena of consciousness, get outside of themselves and even know that there is a "real" or "external" world at all, much less whether what is known in any particular case is the "real" object, or is a real object modified by a mental contribution or a mental translation, or whether the sensation or image, as the only object immediately "known," is not itself the real object? And yet since sense-perception, observation of things, and reflective inquiry about these things, are among the data that psychological introspection studies, how can it study them unless there are such things to study? In this simple dialectic situation one may find implicit the endless circle of *epistemological* realism and idealism in their many varieties. And, one may also search not in vain for traces of attempts to solve these same problems in philosophies that professedly are purely empirical and pragmatic.

Let me attempt, in the interests of clearness, another statement that is not quite so formal. The student of philosophy comes to his work having already learned that there is a separate psychic realm; that it is composed of its unique entities; that these are connected and compounded by their own unique principles, thereby building up their own characteristic systematizations; that the psychic entities are by nature in constant flux, transient and transitory, antithetical to abiding spatial things; that they are purely private; that they are open to internal inspection and to that only; that they constitute the whole scope of the "immediately" given and hence the things that are directly—non-inferentially—"known," and thus supply the sole certainties and the grounds of all other beliefs and knowings; that in spite of their transient and surface character, these psychic entities somehow form the self or ego, which, in turn, is identical with the mind or knower. The summary of the whole matter is that with states of consciousness and with them alone to be and to appear, to appear and to be certain, to be truly known, are equivalents.

Can any one, I ask, ponder these conceptions and not admit that they contain in germ (and in actively flourishing germ) the substance of the questions most acutely discussed in contemporary philosophy? If such be the case, then the statement that philosophy has no more connection with psychology than with any other science expresses not a fact, but a revolution to be accomplished, a task to be undertaken. One has, I think, either to admit that his philosophizing is infected with psychology beyond all cure, or else challenge the prevailing conceptions about the province, scope, and procedure of psychology itself.

One who has already denied to himself the right to undertake in the name of philosophy the revision and reinterpretation of the work of a special science may well seem to be precluded from making any such challenge. In setting forth such a self-denying ordinance, I also made, however, the statement that a philosopher is within his scope when he looks in a science for survivals of past philosophies and reflects upon their worth in the light of subsequent advance in science and art. The right to undertake *such* a critical revision can be queried only by those who measure the worth of a philosophical problem by the number of centuries in which it has been unsuccessfully discussed.

There is, then, at least *prima-facie* ground for holding that the orthodox psychological tradition has not arisen within the actual pursuit of specific inquiries into matters of fact, but within the philosophies of Locke and Descartes, modified perhaps in some regards by the philosophy of Kant. With all due respect to the scientific findings of any group of inquiries, I can not find it in my heart to extend this disposition of acquiescence to the first tentative escapes from medieval science. I have not the time or the disposition herewith to prove that the notion of psychic states immediately given, forming the sole incontrovertible basis of "knowledge," —*i.e.*, certainty—and having their own laws and systematizations, was bequeathed by seventeenth-century philosophy to psychology, instead of originating independently within psychology. That is another story, and yet a story whose materials are easily accessible to all. My present purpose is the more restricted one of pointing out that in so far as there are grounds for thinking that the traditional presuppositions of psychology were wished upon it by philosophy when it was as yet too immature to defend itself, a philosopher is within his own jurisdiction in submitting them to critical examination.

The prospects for success in such a critical undertaking are increased, if I mistake not, by the present situation within the science of psychology as that is actually carried on. On the one hand, there are many developments (as in clinical psychology, in animal, educational, and social psychology) that decline to lend themselves to the traditional rubrics; on the other hand, a certain discrepancy between the researches actually carried on by experimentalists and the language in which alone it is supposed to be proper to formulate them is worrying an increasing number of psychologists, and is increasingly seeming to impose upon them the restrictions of an irritating and cumbersome artificiality. If one went over the full output of the laboratories of the last five years, how much of that output would seem to call, on its own behalf and in its own specific terms, for formulation in the Cartesian-Lockean terms? Supposing the slate were cleared of historic traditions, what would be the natural way of stating the object, method, and results of the inquiries?

When psychologists themselves are breaking away, in at least a considerable portion of their undertakings, from *exclusive* preoccupation with their inherited apparatus, the philosopher is not called upon to assume the whole burden of piety.

As a specific illustration, one may point to the change that will come over the spirit and tenor of philosophic discussion if the activities and methods of behaviorist psychologists grow at the expense of the introspectionist school. The change could hardly fail to be radical, as soon as there was a generation of teachers and students trained in the behaviorist point of view. It would be radical because the change effected would not be an affair of different ways of dealing with old problems, but of relegation of the problems to the attic in which are kept the relics of former intellectual bad taste.

Even a well-wisher (from the philosophic side) to the behaviorist movement must, however, express a certain fear and a certain hope. To sum them up in a single statement, it is possible to interpret the notion of "behavior" in a way that reflects interests and ideas that are appropriate only to the context of the type of psychology against which the behaviorist movement is professedly a protest. The limitation of behavior, for example, to the activities of the nervous system seems to me to express a by-product of the older problem of the relations of mind and body which, in turn, was an outcome of the notion of the mental (or psychical) as constituting a distinct realm of existence. Behavior, taken in its own terms and not as translated into the terms of some theoretical preconception, would seem to be as wide as the doings and sufferings of a human being. The distinction between routine and whimsical and intelligent—or aimful—behavior would seem to describe a genuine distinction in ways of behaving. To throw overboard "consciousness" as a realm of existences immediately given as private and open only to private inspection (or introspection) is one thing; to deny, on the basis of a behavior of the nervous system, the genuineness of the difference between conscious (or deliberate) behavior and impulsive and routine behavior is another thing. The obliteration of the conscious in its adjectival sense (as a quality of some types of response) because it is not discoverable by inspection of the operation of neurones or muscles seems to be the product of ways of thinking congenial only to a separation of physical and purposive action. And this separation would surely not arise if one *began* with behavior, for the separation implies an ascription of independent existence to the mental, on the basis of which alone some acts may be termed purely physical.

There is certainly every reason to think that the behavior of the nervous system is an important element in human behavior; there is reason to think that it is the crucial element in the mechanism of human behavior. But unless we start with behavior as more than physical, as meaning the sum total of life-attitudes and responses of a living being, and take these attitudes and responses at their face value, we shall never be able to discover the existence and importance of the nervous system as the mechanism of behavior. There must be genuine functions of which it is the operative mechanism, if it is to be identified as a mechanism.

Perhaps one example will make clearer what I am driving at. The psychology of immediately given conscious existence was compelled to treat meanings as simply aggregates of elementary states of consciousness, whose existence and aggregation as conscious things are open to immediate introspection. The behaviorist, in reaction from the artificiality and inadequacy of such a view, looks for some fact of ostensible, overt movement that may be identified with thought, *i.e.*, meaning-functions. Quite naturally he fastens upon physical changes in the vocal apparatus. These movements open to objective detection and registration *are* what the other school had termed thought—consciousness as meanings, concepts, judgments, reasonings, or whatever. For my own part, I do not doubt that vocalization, including overt laryngeal changes, furnishes the mechanism of the greater part (possibly the whole) of thought-behavior. But to say that we can tell what speech or meaningful behavior *is* by examining this mechanism is putting the cart before the horse; the fact of speech behavior must be given as a primary fact before we can identify any particular set of structures as concerned in its exercise. The behavior standpoint means, unless it is sheared down in behalf of some unexpressed preconception, that speech is just what men *do* when they communicate with others or with themselves. Knowing the apparatus through which this doing is carried on, we doubtless know more about it than we should otherwise know; by this discovery we bring the doing under better control. But to say that physical movements, when the concrete empirical qualities of language are eliminated, *are* language is to begin by mutilating the facts. Exactly the same considerations apply to purposive behavior—that is, conscious behavior, the event from which "consciousness" is derived by making an adjective into a noun. Purposive behavior exists and is given as a fact of behavior; not as a psychical thing to be got at by introspection, nor as physical movement to be got at by physical instruments. It *is* and it *exists* as movements having specific qualities characteristic of them. We may distinguish between the movement and the quality, and thereby make a distinction between the physical and the mental. The distinction may serve to bring the performance of the function under greater control. But to ascribe independent complete existence to the movement, to say that *is* deliberate behavior, behavior having meaningful or conscious quality, is a fallacy of precisely the same kind as ascribing complete and independent existence to purpose as a merely psychical state. And it is a fallacy that flourishes only in an atmosphere already created by the belief in "consciousness"—just as the latter belief could hardly have arisen save in an atmosphere where all concrete behavior, all achievable action, was regarded as degraded and insignificant in comparison with religious contemplation that related men to a truly spiritual world, which was wholly extra-worldly, supernatural, and hence wholly non-physical.

I am only suggesting a continuation of the same line of thought when I say that in so far as behaviorists tend to ignore the social qualities of behavior, they are perpetuating exactly the tradition against which they are nominally protesting. To conceive behavior exclusively in terms of the changes going on within an organism physically separate in space from other organisms is to continue that conception of mind which Professor Perry has well termed "subcutaneous." This conception is appropriate to the theory of the existence of a field or stream of consciousness that is private by its very nature; it is the essence of such a theory. But when one breaks loose from such a theory he is authorized to take behavior as he finds it; if he finds attitudes and responses toward others which can not be located under the skin, they still have the full claim to recognition.

The teacher of philosophy has, therefore, at the present time a deep concern with the way in which psychology is developing. In the degree in which he feels that current philosophy is entangled in epistemological questions that are artificial and that divert energy away from the logical and social fields in which the really vital opportunities for philosophy now lie, he will welcome every sign of the turning away by psychologists from subjective immediatism; every sign of a disposition to take a more objective, public, and outdoor attitude. The future of the teaching of philosophy for the next generation seems to be intimately bound up with the crisis psychology is passing through. Anything that tends to make psychology a theory of human nature as it concretely exists and of human life as it is actually lived can be only an instrument of emancipation of philosophy.

NATURE AND REASON IN LAW

In Pollock's *Expansion of the Common Law*, there is found the following interesting passage from St. German, written early in the sixteenth century:

> It is not used among them that be learned in the laws of England, to reason what thing is commanded or prohibited by the Law of Nature and what not, but all the reasoning in that behalf is under this manner. As when anything is grounded upon the Law of Nature, they say that Reason will that such a thing be done; and if it be prohibited by the Law of Nature they say it is against Reason, or that Reason will not suffer that to be done.[1]

It is a commonplace to the student of the history of law that this identification of natural and rational, and the equating of both with the morally right, has been at various times a source of great improvements in law. Professor Pound has recently designated the stage in the development of law that follows upon and corrects many of the abuses of the stage of strict law as that of equity or natural law. He says:

> The capital ideas of the stage of equity or natural law are the identification of law with morals; the conception of duty and the attempt to make moral duties into legal duties, and reliance upon reason rather than upon arbitrary rule to keep down caprice and eliminate the personal element in the administration of justice.[2]

Aside from the introduction of equity, the abolition of technicalities which obstructed rather than furthered justice, the adoption by the courts of usages that were more reasonable than those perpetuated in older law, the idea of the subordination of government to social ends, and the furtherance

1. Pollock, *The Expansion of the Common Law*, p. 109.
2. 27 *Harvard Law Review*, p. 213.

[First published in *International Journal of Ethics* 25 (1914): 25–32. Reprinted in *Characters and Events*, ed. Joseph Ratner (New York: Henry Holt and Co., 1929), 2: 790–97.]

of humane international relations are a few of the many services rendered by the identification of the natural with the reasonable. Looking back and taking the intellectual temper and equipment of the times into account, it is hard to see what other intellectual instrumentality could have done the work effected by the concept of natural reason in the seventeenth and eighteenth centuries. In view of such facts the title given by Pollock to the Law of Nature, "a living embodiment of the collective reason of civilized mankind,"[3] is not so much out of the way as it seems to the philosopher who has been trained to look with suspicion upon any reference to Nature as a norm; and who is conscious of the seemingly individualistic, if not anti-social connotation of the term in political philosophy. But even in Locke, careful analysis shows that the limitation of governmental action to the protection of pre-existent natural rights is much more an assertion of the subordination of governmental action to ends that are reasonable, or moral, than appears from a hasty reading. Restricting the action of government by moral considerations, that is to say considerations of reason, is what Locke is chiefly concerned with.

But, unfortunately, nature and reason are ambiguous terms; hence their use as equivalents of what is morally desirable is subject to diverse interpretations. Nature also means the existent, the given, the antecedent state of things; or the present state of things so far as that is connected with the antecedent condition by causal laws. Appeal to nature may, therefore, signify the reverse of an appeal to what is desirable in the way of consequences; it may denote an attempt to settle what is desirable among consequences by reference to an antecedent and hence fixed and immutable rule.

Accordingly, while at one time or with some people, or with some persons part of the time, natural justice meant that which commends itself to the best judgment of the most experienced or to the collective common sense of the race, as over against the conventional and technical justice of inherited legal rules; at other times it meant acceptance of the given state of distribution of advantages and disadvantages.

3. *Expansion of Common Law*, p. 128.

Such a view of natural justice finds, for example, a typical representative in Herbert Spencer. It is, so to speak, purely accidental that such philosophies have been what we lately call individualistic as against collectivistic or socialistic. The essential thing in them is the subordination of the human, whether several or conjoint, to the given, to the physical. The central feature of the *laissez-faire* doctrine is that human reason is confined to discovering what antecedently exists, the pre-existent system of advantages and disadvantages, resources and obstacles, and then to conforming action strictly to the given scheme. It is the abnegation of human intelligence save as a bare reporter of things as they are and as a power conforming to them. It is a kind of epistemological realism in politics. That such a doctrine should work out, no matter how personally benevolent its holders, in the direction of *Beati possidentes*, is inevitable.

This mode of interpretation affected the idea of Reason as well as of Nature, not merely because of the historic equating of Reason and Nature in judicial philosophy, but for special reasons. To the century that felt the influence of Newtonian science, Nature was more Reason than human reason itself. Human reason was reason only as a faculty of retracing the wisdom, harmony, the uniform and comprehensive laws, embodied in Nature—that is, in the physically given world. The Lockean and Deistic identification of Reason with God, the benevolent ordainer and arranger of things, flavored even the most free-thinking speculation of the times. Those who prided themselves that they had no fear of God attributed to Nature the same optimistic benevolence that had characterized the God of natural religion. In order to be really reasonable and moral in action, that is, to act in behalf of good consequences, one had but to get his own interfering intelligence out of the way, and permit Nature, true Reason, to execute her own harmonious and benevolent designs. With respect to Reason as to Nature, the emphasis upon individualism was extraneous and secondary; the intrinsic and primary thing was the denial of a characteristic, a unique function, to human intelligence. Nature, not human thought, determined the formation of true purposes.

If I trace an analogous movement in the decisions of the courts relative to due diligence and undue negligence, it is not for the sake of demonstrating the influence of this type of philosophy upon the minds of judges; that would be somewhat absurd. But there *is* demonstrable, in my opinion, a parity of logic; and in addition there was probably some indirect influence in so far as this mode of thought was in the air. Reason is appealed to as a standard of action. A man's liability depends upon whether he uses the proper degree of reasonable care and prudence. But what measures this? Obviously ordinary prudence is a vague and relative matter—relative in the sense of varying with the circumstances of the situations, as the courts have pointed out. But this very vagueness and variability make the more necessary some principle for detecting the meaning of reasonable in special cases. It is obvious at a glance that the reference to what reasonable and prudent men do or would do in similar cases has exactly the ambiguity we have been dealing with. It may mean reasonable in the sense of involving the kind of foresight that *would*, in similar situations, conduce to desirable consequences; or it may mean the amount and kind of foresight that, as a matter of fact, are customary among men in like pursuits, even though it be demonstrable that, upon the whole, the customs involve deplorable consequences.

That this ambiguity is not merely a theoretical possibility is evidenced by the course of court decisions in the matter of the due diligence of employers in the last half-century. While, in some cases, the courts have taken the position which identifies reason with foresight of specific consequences, the general tendency for a long time was to identify reasonable prudence with the ruling customs of the trade, no matter how unreasonable those customs themselves were when looked at from the standpoint of the sort of consequences they tend to produce. For a long time the Supreme Court was almost alone in saying:

Ordinary care on the part of a railway company implies, as between it and its employees, not simply that degree of diligence which is *customary* among those intrusted with the management of railroad property, but such as having respect to the exigencies of the particular service, *ought* reasonably to be observed . . . such watchfulness, caution, and foresight as, under all the circumstances of the particular service, a corporation controlled by careful, prudent men *ought* to exercise.

The court cannot give their assent to the doctrine that ordinary care in such cases "means only the degree of diligence which is customary, or is sanctioned by the general practice and usage which obtains."[4] Such a quotation, on the contrary side, as the following, from a federal court, shows well the different interpretations of reasonable care put upon the obligations of the corporation to the general public it served and to those for whose services it paid:

As respects travel on steam railways many of the courts of this country hold the carrier bound to keep pace with new inventions in the direction of safety. But this rule is an exceptional one, established upon grounds of public policy, and for the safety of human life. It has never been applied to the relation of master and servant.[5]

When we consider the implications of the contract from the side of the employee, as these have been developed through court decisions with respect to the assumption of risks, we find yet another aspect of the same matter. No Kantian philosopher ever went further in ascribing a ready-made antecedent faculty of reason to man than the courts, in endowing the laborers of this country with unbounded foresight of the consequences implied in taking a job; and no transcendentalist ever went further in assuming that this antecedently possessed reason was in a position to make itself effective in action. As far as the workmen were concerned the courts were committed to the idealistic assumption: *Mens agitat molem.* In its application, this meant that risks which the laborer ran as matter of fact in the performance of his habitual duties were assumed to have been deliberately or intentionally undertaken by him. The whole doctrine of the assumption of risk was, in pragmatic effect, a rendering of brute physical situations in terms of purpose or reason.

In short, in substance although not in form, the reasonable or "natural" was identified with the antecedently given,

4. Wabash Ry. Co. v. McDaniels, 107 U.S. 454, 460; italics are mine.
5. Ennis v. The Maharajah, 40 Fed. 785.

with the state of affairs that customarily obtained, not with the exercise of intelligence to correct defects and to bring about better consequences. From the side of the employer, it meant *Beati possidentes*, To him that hath shall be given; from the side of the employee, *Vœ victis*, From him that hath not shall be taken away even that which he seemeth to have.

It would not be difficult to trace the same logic in the denial of the principle of liability without fault. Under certain conditions, the doctrine is doubtless reasonable, in the sense in which reasonable means due foresight of consequences. Under other conditions, where industrial pursuits bring about different consequences, the doctrine that in pure accident of misadventure it is reasonable for the loss to lie where it falls, is, when laid down as a dogma, the deliberate identification of the reasonable with the physically existent, and wilful refusal to use intelligence in such a way as to ameliorate the impact of disadvantages.

Fortunately, many of the specific things dealt with in this paper are now by way of becoming historic reminiscences. But for this very reason they may the better illustrate the main thesis of this paper. The principle of natural law and justice in the sense that technical and official legal rules need to be adapted to secure desirable results in practice may well be accepted. But we also find that one of the chief offices of the idea of nature in political and judicial practice has been to consecrate the existent state of affairs, whatever its distribution of advantages and disadvantages, of benefits and losses; and to idealize, rationalize, moralize, the physically given—for customs from a philosophical point of view are part of the physical state of affairs. By reading between the lines, moreover, we find that the chief working difference between moral philosophies in their application to law is that some of them seek for an antecedent principle by which to decide; while others recommend the consideration of the specific consequences that flow from treating a specific situation this way or that, using the antecedent material and rules as guides of intellectual analysis but not as norms of decision.

My point is practically made. But, in concluding, I will

say that I see nothing new in principle in the recent attempt to rehabilitate the principle of natural rights by connecting it with the nature of consciousness.[6] The problem is the same whether we use the older word "reason" or the newer word "consciousness." Is consciousness taken as a possessed fact, something given in some men, and relatively lacking in others? Then we have still a physical morals—a worship of consciousness or intelligence in name; a denial, an abdication of it in fact, since what already exists is taken as the norm of action, in spite of the fact that intelligence is concerned with what the given may lead to. But if by "consciousness" we mean interest in desirable consequences and if we include in its attribution to a person the perception that similar intelligence is desirable in others (a man being stupid or unconscious so far as he does not effectively recognize this fact), then we have a situation where reference to individualism is irrelevant and misleading,[7] and where the significant thing is the need of the exercise of intelligence to bring about conditions that will develop more intelligence—a version of natural law to which I heartily subscribe.

I would suggest that the question of the moral right of the employer to exploit (as by means of the doctrine of the assumption of risk) the inferior intelligence of the employee affords an admirable opportunity for removing the ambiguity that still, to my own mind, affects the doctrine of natural rights as developed in chapter four of Fite's *Individualism.* The author seems, especially in his criticism of other views, to be falling back upon intelligence as a physical fact, that is, as a given thing. But when he is as anxious to show that

6. Warner Fite, *Individualism*, Longmans, 1911.
7. What would one think of a physiologist who today in describing the digestion of food lugged in the "individual," or the fact that all circulation is "individual" as an enlightening and explanatory fact? To dwell upon a conception of consciousness that identifies it with impartial and comprehensive foresight, and then to insist that "consciousness is individual" in a way that qualifies or denies the natural implications of the prior conceptions, seems to be on a par with the procedure of the physiologist, who, after telling us that circulation is a matter of specific fact, thinks to add or change something by hitching the facts on to an "individual." Either Professor Fite's individual *is* the intelligence over again, or it is something assumed ready-made, never analyzed or described, and yet used to negate the essential traits of intelligence.

his theory is "generous" as another school is to show that its views are "social," he appears to shift to the view that identifies intelligence with effective foresight of impartially and comprehensively distributed consequences. If he means the latter, the difference between it and what other people call a social view of intelligence is verbal; if he means the former, the difference is, pragmatically, fundamental and insurmountable. And, I repeat, while we hear much about intelligence, the effect of any theory that identifies intelligence with the given, instead of with the foresight of better and worse, is denial of the function of intelligence.

A REPLY TO PROFESSOR ROYCE'S CRITIQUE OF INSTRUMENTALISM

The republication by Professor Royce of his important address at the International Congress of Philosophy at Heidelberg, upon the Problem of Truth,[1] will set many persons to reviewing the problem, and some, perhaps, to considering it for the first time. Its criticisms of the instrumentalist position are so searching and its statements of that position so eminently fair—that is to say, intelligent—that, as one of those expounded and criticized, I should feel at once professionally stupid and personally unappreciative if I made no effort at response. I shall not attempt, however, to traverse the entire field but shall, in the main, confine myself to one point which Professor Royce has made peculiarly his own: The indispensableness to the instrumentalist theories of truth, even as working empirical theories, of a recognition of the social implications of ideas and beliefs. This indispensableness appears, to Professor Royce, fatal to the instrumental conception; to me it seems its essence.

In gist, Mr. Royce contends that if one admits the instrumental conception to be sound "as far as it goes," one is thereby bound to go a good deal farther—all the way to absolutism. Or, in his own words:

> Instrumentalism, consequently, expresses no motive which by itself alone is adequate to constitute any theory of truth. And yet, as I have pointed out, I doubt not that instrumentalism gives such a substantially true account of man's natural functions as a truth seeker. Only the sense in which instrumentalism is a true account of human life is opposed to the adequacy of its own definition of truth.[2]

There is a sense in which—so Professor Royce repeatedly states—instrumentalism is (or better, "contains") a correct

1. *William James, and Other Essays*, Essay IV. New York, 1911.
2. P. 429, this volume.

[First published in *Philosophical Review* 21 (1912): 69–81. For article to which this is a reply, see this volume, Appendix 1.]

"report of the truth about our actual human life, and about the sense in which we all seek and test and strive for truth, precisely in so far as truth-seeking is indeed a part of our present organic activities."[3]

It is obvious (is it not?) that when a criticism is made from the standpoint of the acceptance of a certain conception, and when the critical procedure tries to show that acceptance in logical good faith is quite incompatible with the version of the conception bruited abroad by those most actively engaged in circulating it, it is then obvious, I say, that everything depends upon *what* meaning is attributed to the conception that one accepts, upon *how* one conceives the conception that he announces himself as accepting. *If* the conception of instrumentalism that is "accepted" is after all one's own conception rather than that of those who hold the definition of truth in question, what one has demonstrated at the end is that one's *own* conception of instrumentalism is logically compatible only with absolutism—a conclusion not entirely surprising at the hands of such an accomplished dialectician as Professor Royce.

My first task, accordingly, is a churlish one. I have to show that the logical success of Professor Royce consists in attributing to the instrumentalist certain ideas which are indeed Mr. Royce's own presuppositions, but which are quite foreign—in fact and in logic—to the instrumentalist's position. In short, Professor Royce has not, after all, adequately "accepted" the instrumentalist account even as an empirical account of truth-seeking and truth-testing, for in accepting it he has read into it things so obvious, so self-evident to him that it has not occurred to him that the instrumentalist makes his way, for better or worse, precisely and only because he has rejected and eliminated them. I call this task churlish. And so it is. When one considers how often the pragmatist and instrumentalist have been refuted by denying to them any vestige of sense, to say nothing of truth, how often they have been refuted by attributing to them wilful perversity of facts evident to any sane apprehension, it would be a grateful task to acknowledge the sympathetic and just

3. P. 427, this volume.

version—*in every point save one only*—of instrumentalism rendered by Professor Royce. But alas for one's natural piety; for present purposes it is just this one point that enters into the reckoning.

I

Let me quote at length a statement which an instrumentalist at once recognizes to be a sympathetic and just (if not complete) version of his own intention.

> Human opinions, judgments, ideas, are part of the effort of a live creature to adapt himself to his natural world. Ideas and beliefs are, in a word, organic functions. And truth . . . is a certain value belonging to such ideas.[4] But this value itself is simply like the value which any natural organic function possesses. Ideas and opinions are instruments whose use lies in the fact that, if they are the right ones, they preserve life and render life stable. Their existence is due to the same natural causes that are represented in our whole organic evolution. Accordingly, assertions or ideas are true in proportion as they accomplish this biological and psychological function. This value of truth is itself a biological and psychological value. The true ideas are the ones which adapt us for life as human beings.[5]

Alas, for that little—or big—word "psychological." How great, indeed, are the oaks that little acorns start; what a cataract the little crack in the dam finally lets through—and like samples of proverbial philosophy! Surely the unprejudiced reader would infer from the above statement that, though the term psychological is undefined, the criterion for its definition lies in the conceptions of "life," of "organic functions," of "adaptation to [better *in*] a natural world." And the inference would correctly represent the point of view of

4. The omitted words are, "in so far as we men can recognize truth at all." The phrase thrown into an exposition made professedly from the standpoint of the instrumentalist is significant. Even Mr. Royce cannot wholly free himself from the notion that instrumentalism's account of truth is a statement of what truth is "for us" as distinct from some absolute truth or truth for itself. Of course, from its own standpoint, it is a statement about truth, about the sole intelligible meaning of the term truth.
5. P. 416.

the instrumentalist. But, as Professor Royce proceeds, "psychological" is employed to designate the merely private, the merely personal, and, at times, even the internal, transient "states of consciousness." Then the "psychological" swells and swells, till it swallows up the "live creature," the "natural world" and "biological functions." And if the instrumentalist wants them back (and he must get them back if he is to carry on his business) he must go to the Absolute to take out a license.

The instrumentalist

account of human organic and psychological functions may be—yes, is—as far as it goes true. But if it is true at all, then it is true as an account of the characters actually common to the experience of a vast number of men. It is true, if at all, as a report of the objective totality of facts which we call human experience. It is true, then, in a sense which no man can ever test by the empirical success of his own ideas as his means of controlling his own experiences. . . . If instrumentalism is true, it is true as a report of facts about the general course of history, of evolution, and of human experience—facts which transcend every individual man's experience, verifications and successes.[6]

The logic of this passage gives a narrow and exclusive sense to "individual man's experience," "his own ideas, his own experiences," a sense so narrow and exclusive as to throw between personal experience and "objective human experience" or the historic experience of the race, a gulf so deep and wide that only the Absolute *ex machina* will bridge it and bring the objective human experience and the individual's experience together.

The contrast is explicit in such a passage as the following:

For no man experiences the success of any man but himself, or of any instruments but his own; and the truth, say, of Newton's theory consists, by hypothesis, in the perfectly objective fact that generations of men have really succeeded in guiding their experience by this theory. But that this is a fact no man, as an individual man, ever has experienced or will experience under human conditions.[7]

6. Pp. 428–29.
7. P. 428. Yet Professor Royce, an individual man, knows this objective fact!

Here we have the logic exposed. Men are individuals; therefore whatever is experienced is one's own individual experience; or, individuals experience only themselves, and their exclusive possessions, which are, in fact, parts of themselves. The ground I plow is my own ground; I plow it with my own instrument, my own plow; the harvest—the success—is my own. Therefore the ground was never anybody else's; it is impossible for me even to see from it any other person's land (unless I secure a transcendental telescope); it is impossible for my plow to plow other persons' land; and the harvest, being mine, must be mine only, and therefore unsharable by others.

To my mind there is just one interesting question about such a view as this of the "individual" and of "his own"—the historic question. What ever led intelligent human beings to such a conception of human individuality and of its acts and states? What led to the identification of the individual with the private, and of the private with the merely private, with the absolutely exclusive and isolated? We are not now concerned however with a question of fact, but with a question of logic. Only as he assumes that the instrumentalist does and must presuppose this monopolistic, all-swallowing octopus of an individual and "his own," does Professor Royce "accept" the instrumentalist account, and argue to its necessary implication of the Absolute. Speaking for myself, I may say that if I had any such nihilistic, anarchistically egoistic notion of the individual man, of his doings, states, tools and results, I should probably be willing to resort to an absolute to escape my "own" awful isolation and selfishness. For selfishness is agreeable only when it involves others. But even so, such atrophied logical sense as may be supposed to survive even in an instrumentalist would haunt me with a suspicion that this Absolute was but another of my purely personal belongings, the most precious of my private possessions in appearance, and, in fact, a huge joke that some peculiarly private part of my private being was working off on my more accessible private properties. For, to consider the matter logically, it is passing strange that the private nature of my experience makes it impossible for me to be aware of such a prosaically limited matter as the existence of Sir Isaac

Newton while it absolutely warrants the absolute truth of my belief in something which includes Sir Isaac Newton along with everything else past, present and future. Surely the proverb concerning straining at a gnat and swallowing a camel should be brought down to date.

But we are getting too far away from the instrumentalist's position as he himself "accepts" or conceives it. Let us try, with a more unbiased sympathy, to take that point of view from which "human opinions, judgments, ideas, *are part of the effort of a live creature to adapt himself to his natural world,*" where beliefs are organic functions, and experiences are organic adaptations involving such functions; and where the issue—the success or failure—of these adaptations constitutes the *value* of the beliefs in question. Is there any conceivable way in which a person who had adopted (with however moderate an understanding of what he was about) such a position could still hold that the natural world was merely his own idea; that a live creature was just one of his own private entertainments or conceits, and that organic functions in their tools and results were confined to his own insides?

It is not necessary to enter into a definition of "psychological" upon the basis of the instrumental conception. But it must be conceived in accordance with the fundamental position of the live creature adapting itself to a natural world. And one of the most rudimentary traits of a live creature is its continuity with a racial organic life, just as that of an environment is its spatial diversity and its temporal perdurance. Without these features, adaptation and organic function are the most empty sort of term. Follow out the implications of *such* conceptions instead of the conception which Mr. Royce holds (and with great and fatal generosity lends to the instrumentalist) and the gulf between the objective human experience and the supposedly purely subjective individual experience disappears. Life individuates itself, and particular individuations appear and disappear. But the individuation is a trait of life; it is not the mystery of a private, isolated somewhat which destroys all the natural traits of life to replace them with its own quite opposite traits. We are not to interpret "life" in accord with some psychological preconception of the merely personal; we are to interpret the personal in accord with the functions of life.

A particular passage may serve to bring out the difference of conception. After stating what the truth of the Newtonian conception would consist in from the instrumental point of view, Professor Royce goes on to ask about the sense in which the statement of the historic episode of the formation and success of Newton's theory is itself true. Unless the instrumentalist is quite stupid, he will, I take it, apply his own criterion. It is true by the same token; it enables predictions, it gives control, it facilitates intercourse, it clears the path of obscurities, it guides (instead of obstructing) new observations and reflections, it brings men together instead of dividing them—so far as it is acted upon and thus genuinely asserted. But this path seems to Professor Royce to be quite closed to the instrumentalist.

> Newton is dead. As mortal man he succeeds no longer. His ideas, as psychological functions, died with him. His earthly experiences ceased when death shut his eyes. Wherein consists to-day, then, the historical truth that Newton ever existed at all, or that the countless other men whom his theories are said to have guided ever lived, or experienced, or succeeded?

Such statements followed by such a question are well calculated to inspire one with a feeling of despair regarding the possibility of arriving at any philosophic understanding. Newton is dead; therefore how can I assert as truth that he ever lived? The obvious answer is so obvious and so easy that it cannot be relevant to what Mr. Royce has in mind: the answer, namely, that Newton cannot be dead unless he once lived, and that, organic life being what it is, if he lived in the seventeenth century, he is surely dead by this time. I cannot imagine any beliefs operating and succeeding as organic functions in the development of life unless such simple and ordinary beliefs as these are capable of working, and working with a reasonable degree of success. If the propositions were that Newton is dead, though he never lived; or that because he was living in the seventeenth century, he must be living now, I can see how the propositions would offer difficulties to a pragmatic theory; I confess I do not see how they could "work." Seriously, and not in levity, this seems to me the inevitable answer and the only answer that instrumental theory can make to the question just cited.

But equally I have no doubt this reply is quite irrelevant to what Professor Royce had in mind. And, accordingly, I shall have to make a guess as to what presuppositions underlie the question and address a reply also to them. There are a number of phrases in the discussion which lead me to infer that Professor Royce identifies truth with existence. Now if the truth about Sir Isaac Newton's existence is the same thing as that existence itself, it is quite sure that no possible present experience will yield truth. For the working in experience of a belief or conception for its control, guidance, clarification, for social intimacy and emancipation, will not operate to raise Sir Isaac Newton *in propria persona* from the grave; it will not in short constitute (or reconstitute) his *existence*. But instrumentalism never pretended to encroach on the idealistic privilege of creating natural existences by formulating truths about them. It is content with the humbler task of describing how men do as matter of fact recreate, transform, *some* natural existence by intellectual formulations about *some other* existence. (The successful transformation of some things by use of intellectual formulations about other things being what instrumentalism calls the truth of these formulations.)

I know of no *a priori* compulsion to formulate conceptions or beliefs regarding Sir Isaac Newton; it is a safe guess for instance, that many an Oriental potentate has gone to his grave about whom no belief will ever be entertained, just as the vast majority of natural happenings go by without being reflected upon. But when there is a specific need for thinking, and a specific hypothesis emerges in response to the need, it is needful that we should have some way of testing its value, of developing it to the point of being true or false. And acting upon the hypothesis to select and collate data, to predict, to guide new observations and reflections, to organize the seemingly discrepant and to illuminate the hitherto obscure is the way. The success of the hypothesis upon and along this way is its truth.

If, however, the death of Sir Isaac Newton, and the cessation of his experiences, carried with them the absolute interruption of organic life, of all experience, if his experience, in other words, operated in absolute discontinuity in matter and method from mine and mine from yours, I can well see that the instrumentalist would be put to it to frame any idea about Newton, to say nothing of verifying it. But the difficulty would not be confined to the instrumentalist. Even the absolutist would, in such a situation, be unhelped by the Absolute. And if instrumentalist and absolutist alike do make judgments about Newton and, within certain degrees of approximation, arrive at successful outcomes, it is because life, experience, has its own continuities and sociable relationships.

And this brings me to my second guess about the difficulty which Professor Royce feels his question to involve. He presupposes, again, the completely egoistic, exclusive nature of Newton's experience—his life, his acts—on one side, and of mine on the other. "His ideas, as psychological functions, died with him." But did they? And if they did, what are we going to do about it, even with the help of the conception of the Absolute? For so far as they "died with him," the problem is not that of some eventual verification of our ideas about his ideas, but of our having any idea about his ideas.

In short, we come again to our basic statements: one about the instrumentalist, the other about Professor Royce's position. (*a*) By calling Newton's idea, his theory, a *function*, instrumentalism means to emphasize precisely that it *was* a function—to insist upon the need of reinterpreting the adjective "psychological" from the standpoint of function—an organizing and organized act, public, objective, impersonal just as surely as private, individual, personal. Certain images, a certain emotional tone of inward landscape, may be said to have "died" when Newton died. But to say that his idea of gravitation, as a vital *function*, died with him is to traverse the facts. Newton acted through it, lived it out, so adequately, that it became an integral part of the activities of educated men and scientific inquirers throughout the civilized world. Since this transmissive operation is just one of the things that is included in the conception of "success" of a vital function, one is not accepting the standpoint of instrumentalism when one conceives the vital function as something which renders impossible this transmissive operation. That the idea was made true means precisely that as a *function* it did not die.

(*b*) As to the logic of Professor Royce's own conception. Professor Royce says of certain statements about Newton: "No doubt all these historical and socially significant statements of mine are indeed substantially true" (p. 428). Professor Royce would doubtless also hold that there is a countless multitude of doings and sufferings of Newton about which we cannot now make any intelligible statements. So far as the "substantially true statements" are concerned, does not Professor Royce (and everybody else) fall back upon the procedure of which instrumentalism is simply a generalized description? And as far as the other to us non-existent "truths"[8] are concerned, does the conception (or the Being) of the Absolute help us one bit? Upon the Absolutist theory, what explanation can account for this partiality on the part of the Absolute? Why has it rendered certain events so opaque and silent and others so transparent and communicative? Is there any explanation that does not take us back to the instrumentalist terms—terms of vital doing under conditions of natural and social need, adaptation and success? And so far as our belief in the existence of the Absolute is concerned, why should we adopt a different logical procedure from that which has brought us to believe certain things about Newton? If the continuities, the transmissive bearings of life, of experience, suffice in the case of Newton to enable certain intellectual formulations—reflections—to prosper while dooming others to defeat, why, if the Absolute exists, should we not, *a fortiori*, wait till conditions have made the conception of its existence one that works out under tests? And, lacking these instrumental tests, what right have we to assert the truth of what, by Mr. Royce's own hypothesis, is a purely private, personal idea?[9]

8. Not "truths," but events, on any except a preordained idealistic basis.
9. "Instrumentalism in so far correctly defines the nature which truth possesses *in so far as we ever actually verify truth*," p. 430 (italics mine).

II

As respects certain truths, some instrumentalists—Professor James particularly—have made much of the significance of vicarious social verification. In Mr. Royce's words:

> Since we are social beings, and beings with countless and varied needs, we constantly define and accept as valid very numerous ideas and opinions whose truth we do not hope personally to verify. . . . If we personally do not verify a given idea, we can still accept it then upon its credit value. We can accept it precisely as paper, which cannot now be cashed, is accepted by one who regards that paper as, for a given purpose, or to a given extent equivalent to cash.[10]

This procedure Professor Royce accepts as an actual procedure, while he holds that reliance upon it is inconsistent with the instrumental conception of truth,—that, consistently, instrumentalism must identify the act of giving credit with truth itself, that is to say, anything is true to which we find it expedient to give credence at a given moment. Mr. Royce disclaims being an intellectualist of the rationalistic type, but he employs the good old rationalistic device of rigid alternatives. Either the assertion which I accept on credit *is* already true (truth belongs to the assertion anyway) or else by its truth I mean simply that I give credit to it. The former alternative surrenders instrumentalism; the latter puts it in the position of making truths offhand, while you wait—the sanctioning of caprice, whim, etc.

For reasons which I hope will appear presently, I am particularly interested in the implications of the "credit" notion with respect to its content. Before dealing with this phase of the matter, it seems necessary, however, to devote space to the formal dilemma. Upon close inspection it will be found, I think, to resemble most cases of formal alternatives in philosophic discussion. Two extremes are set up as exhaustive, while as matter of fact multitudes of other alternatives glide freely through wide-open intervening meshes. What *should* it mean upon the instrumental theory to ac-

10. P. 430.

cept some view or idea as true upon social credit? Clearly that such an acceptance itself works. And if the environment, the medium of action, be social could any other method save that of accrediting the results of experience in others be expected to work? There is nothing so licentious about the matter as Professor Royce's abstract logic would make out; the acceptance upon credit is subject to precisely the same sort of tests—of working under conditions—as acceptance on the basis of more direct personal verifications. What is indicated is that the social medium of life is as continuous as we have seen life itself to be. One has verified in innumerable cases that under certain conditions one can trust to the experience and the reports of others; one has found out that the limits between one's own experience and that of another are quite arbitrary and elusive. Besides this general verificational background, there is the specific verification, through working, of *acceptance* of this particular belief upon the credit and authority of some particular group of persons. And besides, there is frequent verification through the experiences of others who have given credit to these assertions—a method which could be made to appear vicious by the logic of abstractionism, but which, in inductive logic, is independently cumulative and hence confirming. In short, one doesn't, as an instrumentalist, accept arbitrarily on credit; he accepts on probation, hypothetically, just as one accepts his own hypotheses when they first occur to him. As this acceptance is confirmed by his works, the acceptance becomes a genuine accrediting; it has received the kind of trying by experimental tests in life that the conditions permit. That this is the way in which sensible men proceed can be shown by an argument *ad hominem*, indicating that even an absolutist must *actually* so proceed. Let us admit with Professor Royce that to the assertion in question truth or falsity already inherently belongs. Now, being unable to verify the matter directly, what shall be my attitude? I cannot, by hypothesis (Professor Royce's own hypothesis), be sure whether it is true or false, although I am sure it is already either one or the other. According to Professor Royce the only recourse possible is to accept or reject, just arbitrarily, by whim, by what seems agreeable at the moment. In short, the dilemma is one which applies only to those who hold Mr. Royce's view, and for them it takes the form of a choice of the two alternatives: Complete scepticism as to what is the truth or falsity of most things in history and nature, or else the loosest go-as-you-please most wayward opinionatedness. Other people employ the cautious testing of the kind and amount of credit to be given to others' ideas and reports that is described in the instrumentalist account.

As I have already stated, I find my significant interest attaching to the conception of social credit, and to the implied analogy of belief with credit in business, for this suggests that my *personal* experience is itself social in origin, matter and outlook. In good business, it is intimated, there is some value behind the *credit*; namely, in the philosophic analogy, truth. In purely speculative business, on the contrary, there is nothing but credit behind the credit: the instrumental theory of truth in the philosophic analogy. Now that business, modern business, is done so largely on credit seems to me a significant fact, and one which is peculiarly important for the instrumental theory. For so far as modern business proceeds upon a credit basis, it does *not* rely upon equating credits to values preexisting; modern manufacturing and commerce would go into wholesale bankruptcy were such its basis. It proceeds upon the basis of the *potentialities* of what already exists, upon the *future* operation of industry, good faith and consumption to realize these potentialities. Only in times of panic is there a falling back upon the past, upon the already existent store. And the immediate effect of the insistence upon backing *from behind* of already extant values is to restrict business. There must, indeed, be something behind—fields, woods, mines, human labor, human intercourse, mutual trust, desires, etc. But the credit is not measured by them—not by them just as back there, behind. It is measured by an anticipated future use of them. It is not a matter of their being there in a finished state; it is a matter of their expected consequences, when something is done to them and with them. Credit operates for the more effective and varied use of what is there; not to reduplicate it in some parallel series. And it is the outcome, the actual consequence, that confirms or condemns any particular giving of credit.

I have no wish to base conclusions or theories on a possible analogy. I do wish, however, to secure its full suggestive force. Credit exhibits a possible future outcome operating as present factor to guide and enrich the conditions whose possibilities it relies upon. So does intelligence. Both involve a risk, an uncertain speculative element; both involve, therefore, the need of check and test, of responsibility to the achievement of ends, the production of consequences. Both involve something "behind" them, prior existences; but neither of them is a reiteration or reinstatement of the prior; both are concerned with the potentialities of things, and take effect in endeavor to make potentialities real. And as credit is distinctly a social phenomenon, so is the accrediting which marks the life of thought. Social verification is not, taken by and large, a *pis aller*, in default of "personal" verification. It, and it alone, *is* verification; personal verification is but a step on this social road—an encouragement, an authorization to go ahead. Experience, life—just as is that phase of experience called business—*is* social, and it exhibits this sociability nowhere more than in the continuity, the interpenetration, the reciprocal reinforcement of meanings and beliefs. Instead of an Absolute being required to substantiate this social phase of the life of intelligence it is much more probable that the Absolute is a somewhat barren and dry isolation and hypostatizing of the everyday sociality of experience. The accrediting of others' experience is the fact that our personal experience is so much other and more than the narrow personal private matter upon whose "acceptance" Mr. Royce founds his dilemma.

If then, I were to try to gather together the significant strands of instrumentalism in opposition to Professor Royce's welcome of it as a convenient road to absolutism, I should say that as method for philosophy it indicated a more severe intellectual conscience; less free and easy use of the concept of Truth in general and more careful use of truths in particular to designate such conceptions and propositions as have emerged successfully from the test conditions that are practically appropriate. In substance, as distinct from form or method, I should say it meant recognition of intelligence as the way in which future possible consequences became effective in the present—the recognition of real time and real potentiality—and a recognition of the utterly false character of the prevailing notion of the sheer privacy, the egotistic isolation, of experience, of conscious life. The case is immensely understated when we restrict ourselves to the possibility of pragmatic verification of acceptance of beliefs on credit from others—adequate as is the noting of this possibility for the purpose of securing exemption from Professor Royce's dilemma. The fact is that the life, the experience (including the organic acts of ideas, opinions, judgments, etc.) of "individual man" is already saturated, thoroughly interpenetrated, with social inheritances and references. Education, language and other means of communication are infinitely more important categories of knowledge than any of those exploited by absolutists. And as soon as the methodological battle of instrumentalism is won—as it will be, not by instrumentalists, but by the constantly increasing influence of scientific method upon the imagination of the philosopher—the two services that will stand to the credit of instrumentalism will be calling attention first, to the connection of intelligence with a genuine future, and, second, to the social constitution of personal, even of private, experience, above all of any experience that has assumed the knowledge-form.

IN RESPONSE TO PROFESSOR McGILVARY

With the editors' kind permission, I shall group together my responses to the three articles which Professor McGilvary has been kind enough to devote of late to my writings.[1] I shall take them in the order of their publication.

1. Regarding my article in which I argued that if the ego-centric predicament marked a ubiquitous fact and so was a true predicament it left the controversy between the idealist and the realist insoluble and, in fact, meaningless, I should like to say that so far as I know there is nothing in that article which attributes to Professor Perry the belief that it is a true predicament. I had no such intention; it was the situation, not Professor Perry's views, that I was dealing with; and besides I was not sure what his attitude was, as there are things in his writings that could be interpreted both ways. I certainly never thought of arguing that a realist *must* accept the predicament as real; although I was convinced (and still am) that any realism which regards the self, ego, mind, or subject as necessarily one of two terms of the knowledge relation can not escape the predicament. So far as Professor McGilvary's argument is concerned, *if* the predicament is a predicament, he has fallen into a fallacy which, upon retrospection, I think he will find as amusing as he finds, upon occasion, my logic. He quotes the following from Professor Perry: "The same entity possesses both immanence by virtue of its membership in one class, and also transcendence, by virtue of the fact that it

1. "Realism and the Ego-Centric Predicament," *Philosophical Review*, May, 1912; "Professor Dewey's Awareness," *Journal of Philosophy, Psychology and Scientific Methods*, Vol. IX, p. 301; and "Professor Dewey's Brief Studies in Realism," *Journal of Philosophy, Psychology and Scientific Methods*, Vol. IX, p. 344.

[First published in *Journal of Philosophy, Psychology and Scientific Methods* 9 (1912): 544–48. For articles to which this is a reply, see this volume, Appendixes 2, 3, and 4.]

may belong also to indefinitely many classes." In comment, Professor McGilvary adds: "This means that when T stands in the complex $TR^c(E)$ it has 'immanence': but when this same T stands in some other complex TR^nT', it has 'transcendence' with respect to the former complex." *If* the predicament is genuine, a moment's reflection will make it obvious that the last formula is not complete. It should read $TR^nT'R^c(E)$. Any known relation among things, *if* knowledge involves a relation to an ego, is itself in relation to the ego.[2] That with respect to the subject-matter of knowledge, realism has the advantage over idealism of recognizing the importance of the relations that things sustain to one another was explicitly recognized in my article.[3]

2. In the second article, Professor McGilvary asks me two questions. In reply to his first, I would say that he is right in suggesting that I included "organic inhibitions" within the generic term "organic releases"—a careless way of writing. His second question is not so easily disposed of: namely, "Why are these 'organic releases' called 'the conditions of awareness' rather than awareness itself?" The passage of my own upon which Professor McGilvary bases his question reads as follows: "Of course on the theory I am interested in expounding the so-called action of 'consciousness' means simply the organic releases in the way of behavior which are the conditions of awareness, and also modify its content." Professor McGilvary's difficulty is a natural one: the passage should either have expanded or not appeared at all. I was alluding to the views of those

2. Since the text was written, Professor McGilvary's review of Perry's "Recent Philosophical Tendencies" has appeared (*Philosophical Review*, July, 1912). In this review Professor McGilvary states the point succinctly and vividly in this way: "How can we discount what is *ipso facto* counted in the very act of discounting?" (p. 466). This relieves Professor McGilvary from any imputation of incurring the fallacy mentioned above. But it makes me even more uncertain than before as to just why and how my article fell under his criticism.

3. "Nevertheless, I do not conceive that the realistic assertion and the idealistic assertion in this dilemma stand on the same level, or have the same value. The fact that objects vary in relation to one another independently of their relation to a 'knower' *is* a fact, and a fact recognized by all schools." *Journal of Philosophy, Psychology and Scientific Methods*, Vol. VIII., page 551—the article with which Mr. McGilvary is here dealing. [*Middle Works* 6:111–22.]

who hold that "consciousness" acts directly upon objects. Since my own view appears similar to this doctrine and has, as matter of fact, been identified with it, I threw in the above-quoted passage. My intention was to state that the difference made in objects was made not by a distinct or separate entity or power called consciousness, but by the distinctive type of behavior that involves awareness. The passage as I wrote it is worded with an unfortunate accommodation to the view I was criticizing. What I should have brought out was, first, that "consciousness" is short for conscious or intelligent behavior; and, secondly, that this kind of behavior makes its own distinctive difference in the things involved in its exercise. The unfortunate accommodation to which I refer (and which gives point to Professor McGilvary's query) is the seeming acceptance on my part of a dualism between organic action and awareness of an object. Cancelling this concession and remaining true to my own point of view, the distinction between organic action and the object known is replaced by the distinction of unconscious and purposive behavior with respect to objects. Strictly speaking, accordingly, upon my view the "organic releases" are neither conditions of awareness nor the awareness itself. They are a distinguishable element in intelligent behavior, "awareness" being another distinguishable element. I hope this makes my real meaning clear.

3. I have to confess that I am surprised by Professor McGilvary's last article. It starts by quoting from me (p. 345) a passage in which I state that until the epistemological realists have

> considered the main proposition of the pragmatic realists, viz., that knowing is something that happens to things in the natural course of their career, not the sudden introduction of a "unique" and non-natural type of relation—that to a mind or consciousness—they are hardly in a position to discuss the second and derived pragmatic proposition that, in this natural continuity, things in becoming known undergo a specific and detectable qualitative change.

So far the quotation from my article. Then follows immediately this amazing statement of Professor McGilvary. "The realists criticized are guilty, then, of believing that knowing is a sudden introduction of a 'unique' and non-natural relation." I call it amazing because I know of no principles of conversion, obversion, contraposition or any other mode of interpreting a proposition by which the passage quoted is transformable into what Professor McGilvary makes out of it. *Idealists* hold that knowledge is a unique and non-natural relation of things to mind or consciousness, and they make this belief the basis of the doctrine that things thereby have their seemingly physical qualities changed into psychical ones. This idealistic doctrine has been attributed to pragmatists; at least it has been attributed to me, as possibly Professor McGilvary may recall. That realists are not in a position to consider the actual nature of the pragmatic doctrine that knowing makes a difference in things till they have dissociated the premisses upon which it rests from the premisses upon which the idealistic conclusion rests, may, I think, be stated without being turned into a statement that realists are "guilty" of holding the obnoxious doctrine.

So far as this portion of his article is concerned, it seems to rest upon the supposition that I was hitting at some person or persons, instead of examining a position. In talking about presentative realism, I thought I made it clear that by presentative realism I meant the doctrine that knowledge is presentation of objects, relations, and propositions to a knower, such presentation occurring (according to this kind of realism) both by perception and by thought. I can assure Professor McGilvary (and others, if there be others that need the assurance) that I never supposed that my criticism applied to any except to those to whom, by its terms, it does apply. Mr. McGilvary says: "Mr. Dewey has, in the commendable way so characteristic of him, made his criticisms as impersonal as possible." I could gladly have foregone the compliment if this impersonal examination of a problem had been taken as, in good faith, of the essence of the article. The identification of mind, soul, with the self, the ego, and the conception that knowledge is a relation between the object as one term and the self as the other, are perhaps the most characteristic and permeating traits of the doctrines of modern philosophy. As yet the realists, with two partial exceptions, have not explicitly developed a theory regarding the self—or subject—and its place or lack of place in knowledge. The problem seems to me important enough to repay attention.

In the latter part of Mr. McGilvary's article, there is a point presented which does not depend upon dubious mind-reading of my intentions. In my earlier article I had stated "the very things that, from the standpoint of perception as a natural event, are conditions that account for its happening are, from the standpoint of perception as a case of knowledge, part of the object that ought to be known, but is not." Mr. McGilvary questions the "ought"—questions, in fact, is a mild term. It denotes, according to him, "*a priori* legislation," "sheer dogmatism," "licentious intellectualism." Before doing penance in sackcloth and ashes, I will remark that *ought* sometimes means "ought as a matter of logical conclusion from the premisses." It was in that sense the ought is used in this passage, so that if I am in error my sins are not of the kind mentioned, but consist of inability to connect premiss and conclusion properly. To go into that matter would involve pretty much a recapitulation of my entire article. I content myself here with pointing out that I was dealing with the doctrine that a seen light is, *ipso facto*, a knowledge (good or bad) of its cause, say an astronomical star, and with the bearing of this doctrine upon the idealistic contention concerning the numerical duplicity of the star and the star as "known" in perception—that is, the immediately visible light. And my point was that if the seen light is *per se* knowledge of the star as a real object, the physical conditions referred to can not be appealed to (this "can not" is intended in a purely logical sense) in explanation of the deficiencies and mistakes of the perceptual knowing, since they are, according to the doctrine, part of the object known by the perception. Mr. McGilvary's illustration regarding a wedding and the events that lead up to it is interesting, but not relevant, as there is no contention, so far as I am aware, that the event called a wedding is, *ipso facto*, a knowledge of that which caused it. It is somewhat "amusing" that the illustration fits perfectly what I said about the adequacy of the naturalistic explanation when applied to the happening of the perception as an event, but has no visible tie of connection with the doctrine that the perception is, *ex officio*, a knowledge of the "real" object that produced it.

SHOULD MICHIGAN HAVE VOCATIONAL EDUCATION UNDER "UNIT" OR "DUAL" CONTROL?

I am glad to say that without departing in any way from the notes I had prepared for this discussion, I can endorse heartily the general trend of the remarks of the last speaker and find myself in harmony with them.

The question *is* a question of method of procedure; of means, not of the end. It would be very unfortunate if any one here got the impression that because there are two sides as to the best method of procedure, there is a similar diversity of opinion about the end in view. The question we discuss assumes that it is desirable for the State of Michigan to have a system of industrial education which will pay more attention than does the present system to the education of wage-earners, of those who are going into gainful occupations in manufactures and in agriculture. The difference of opinion is as to the best method of getting at the matter.

I quite agree also with the previous speaker in holding that it is necessary to secure the close cooperation of existing educational agencies and of those agencies which are concerned with the new and supplementary measures to be put into operation in behalf of industrial education.

I wish to say also that I think we are both somewhat embarrassed by a lack of any clear definition of the terms "unit" and "dual" control. I certainly am not here to criticise the Wisconsin system. It would not be any of my business, and it would be in bad taste; but more especially I am not here to criticise it because it is not an example of what I should call dual control. On the contrary, it has certain of the fundamental features of unit control in it. It is a mixed scheme, I should say, not out and out one or the other. The hearty cooperation which, according to Dean Reber's ac-

[Delivered at the Seventh Annual Meeting of the National Society for the Promotion of Industrial Education, 23 October 1913. First published in the Society's *Bulletin* 18 (1913): 27–34.]

count, has frequently been secured in Wisconsin between the two sides indicates that they do not have there a thoroughgoing dual system. The local school board appoints the local industrial board, and the superintendent of schools is an ex-officio member of that board. It is not at all surprising then that these superintendents of schools being on that local industrial board, and being in the general organization or conference, of which he spoke, should have had a thoroughgoing opportunity fully to represent the general educational interests of the community.

I am given to understand, although Mr. Reber knows more about the facts than I do, that it is quite customary for the general school board, in appointing the industrial board, to appoint some of its own members. He referred to the fact that they often appoint those who had been on the regular school board; and sometimes those who are on the board. I am informed that in one case, (one of the most important industrial centres of Wisconsin and one which was reported as finding that the existing scheme works well), the existing school board appointed themselves as the sole members of the industrial vocational education board. I suppose there is no reason why, under the law in the case, every school board in Wisconsin should not do precisely that same thing. I do not know whether in that case they would have dual control in Wisconsin or unit control; but if you please to call it dual it is certain that the evils that are likely to attend the dual system are minimized.

What Does Unit Control Mean?

To guard against further misapprehension I wish to make it clear also that unit control does not mean that there will simply be what you might call unit *schools*. There is nothing in the principle of unit control that in any way prevents specialized industrial schools being established and administered as experience shows to be desirable.

The main and practically the only argument I shall advance for the unit control is then what Dean Reber has already emphasized: the importance of hearty cooperation. As a practical question, the question is, I should say, for the State of Michigan, one of expediency, one of policy. Everybody knows that it is very much easier to talk about industrial education or any kind of educational change than it is to carry it into effect. The pedagogues in America, of whom I am one, are only too willing to talk and write and argue about things. It is said that the "hot-air engine" is more fully developed in America than in any other country in the world, and that applies to the pedagogical aspects of our nation as well as to others.

At best there are plenty of practical difficulties in the way of the development of industrial education. What is the best thing we can do in the way of getting an adequate establishment of this new movement?—for in this country it is new. Under the circumstances it is certainly bad policy to do anything which will leave the existing school authorities and the existing school agencies indifferent to this new movement; and very bad policy to do anything which will make them antagonistic. Absolutely to divorce the movement from existing educational instrumentalities and put it under separate control is a measure of absolutely last resort, a measure of desperation. I think that educators ought to consider carefully their own attitude in the matter, and realize that it is possible for them to take an attitude toward this new movement that will furnish a stronger argument for separation than those who are now in favor of separation can possibly offer. If it should be found that the extending of unified control should smother the beefsteak of industrial education with so much of the onion sauce of academic studies that the substantial nutriment was no longer recognizable by anybody, then I for one should be in favor of separate control as a measure of desperation, of last resort. But this method of desperation we need not contemplate at present.

I cannot put my views better than they have been put by Mr. Kreuzpointer, a representative of the Committee on Industrial Education of the American Foundrymen's Association, who speaks therefore, from the industrial standpoint:

> Just as no judicious manufacturer would discard valuable machinery when the readjustment and strengthening of some

parts would save the installing of new machinery, so your committee thought it for the best to devote its energies to helping in the readjustment of the already existing highly organized system of public schools in order not to lose its valuable help in preparing, thru differentiated courses in the elementary schools, those who will enter the industrial schools when leaving school.

Making due allowance for over-conservatism and of the absurd claim of many, especially high school teachers, that industrial education has no cultural value, your committee believes that much of the unsympathetic attitude of the school people towards industrial education has been fostered by the manner with which the subject of industrial education has been forced upon them, and the blaming of the teachers for conditions which were caused by too much politics, social and business influences entering the school, for the presence of which the teachers were the least responsible.

Your committee, weighing these circumstances and believing that the unsympathetic attitude referred to is steadily diminishing as the teachers become better acquainted with industrial education, therefore thought it best not to deprive industrial education of the valuable cooperation of the existing organization. This mutual misunderstanding between the school people and the industrial people is largely due to the haste and necessity of late years to give to the industries the badly needed skilled help, and under the spell of the prevailing optimism it was believed we could make out of our schools a "Jack-of-all-education" the same as until quite recently it was thought every boy was fit for a "Jack-of-all-trades." We are finding out the need of separate industrial schools, but this should not lead us to the wasteful method of creating an independent system of industrial education with a distinct organization.

It seems to me that is the voice of reason, of common sense, of good judgment. It is the part of efficiency, it is the part of economy, it is the part that makes for permanent and lasting success, to utilize to the full the existing agencies supplementing them and extending them in such ways as are found necessary to give industrial interests a larger influence in the existing scheme than they have at present.

I have quoted one thing from Mr. Kreuzpointer. I am perfectly willing to quote and endorse something else that he says:

The universities and colleges are united in prescribing to the high school what kind of preparation they are to give to the students entering college and the colleges are very energetic in seeing to it that they get from the high schools what they want. There is no reason why the industries and the workingmen should not likewise get together and, instead of denouncing the schools and school people as backward and incompetent (which is not always true and only creates a feeling of distrust and resentment) prescribe to the schools what preparation they want for the young people going into the industries; and insist upon getting it just as the colleges do.

I would not, however, absolutely endorse the words of this statement, though I would its sense. I do not think the effect upon the high schools of so much dictation and prescription from the colleges has been wholesome; and I do not think that employers and workingmen should absolutely dictate or prescribe to the schools what should be done as preparation for social life. But I do say that we need more cooperation between teachers, the existing school authorities, and the business man and the laboring man. Certain traditions have been in too exclusive control of our schools; and we need the advice and assistance of those community interests represented by employers and wage-earners. But we need them in the interest of the community welfare, not in behalf of their own special class interests.

Schools Are What the People Demand

It is absurd to say, although it is said sometimes (not, I think, by people of experience or judgment) that the teachers are responsible for the evils, the backwardness, the overscholasticism of the present system; that they are exclusively responsible. Of course, we teachers must bear our share of the blame; we are partly to blame, but we are far from being exclusively or mainly to blame. The teachers are not in control of the schools. The schools are in the control of the community, and if they have carried out an overacademic and an overscholastic policy, it is because that is as far as the average public sentiment of the average community has advanced up to this time.

One of the good things about such an association as this is that it moves the public opinion of the community—upon which any system of public schools depends—forward to recognize the need of new and supplemental agencies within the school system. The alternatives are not that the schools shall stay just where they are, or that we shall have a new and totally different school system under the independent control of employers and laboring men. These are *not* the alternatives. As Mr. Kreuzpointer indicates it is up to the business men and the laboring men to make their influence felt more than they have made it felt upon the educational system of the community. There is no reason why the business men of the community should confine their attention to school affairs to keeping down taxes. It is possible for them also to see to it that the community is getting its money's worth out of existing school taxes; and even to see to it that they pay more taxes in order that the community may furnish its children in the future the kind of education that is really needed for our public welfare.

There is one other feature of the Wisconsin movement which illustrates the whole situation and the need for unit control. Dean Reber brought out the fact that their work there has reference to continuation work; to continuation schools for children who have left school between the ages of fourteen and sixteen (if fourteen *is* the age for getting working papers as it is in so many of our northern states). The movement there is to provide that these children shall at least have part-time schooling along with their wage-earning vocation. That is a very important part of vocational and industrial education. In many places it is the line of least resistance, I think, for immediate action; but it is *only* one part of the problem; and it will be very unfortunate if many states, especially states that are more distinctly industrial and manufacturing states than is Wisconsin,—states like Illinois, Ohio, New York, Pennsylvania, Massachusetts, and Connecticut—(I will leave it to the audience to judge whether Michigan or Wisconsin is further advanced in distinctly manufacturing lines), it will be very unfortunate for such states to segregate the continuation school movement from other phases of the industrial education movement.

Prevocational Education

The continuation school assumes that many children have left school at fourteen and simply asks: "What can be done for them now that they have left?" If that were the whole of the problem it is quite open to argument whether the Wisconsin system (a half-dual one) or some more unified system, would be the better, especially for a state like Wisconsin. But, it is not the whole of the problem. Bound up with this matter is the question of prevocational education. What preparation are the children below fourteen years of age, who in such large numbers leave school in the fifth and sixth grades, getting that bears upon their future callings in life? There is also the question of more distinctly specialized industrial school and trades school for those who do not leave, and of keeping many of those who now leave in schools that make them more skilled.

Now, to isolate one of the three phases of the problem and leave the other two untouched is very unfortunate; it is unfortunate from both sides. All of the continuation education, prevocational education and skilled industrial education need to be dealt with in relation to each other and in their entirety. This can be done only when the people considering those problems are also responsible for the entire educational system of the state and of the community.

Shall we assume that children *must* leave school at fourteen? This assumption is the chief fallacy in the argument which separates the control of the continuation school from the control of other forms of public education. Continuation education is at best simply a remedial measure, a measure of doctoring up and patching up a situation that is wrong. Let us first attack this assumption that children have got to leave school and go into the trades at fourteen. When they do, of course, we want to do something for them, and something more adequate and systematic than anything we are now doing in the way of part-time schooling. But the fundamental necessity is to change the educational system so these children shall not leave in such large numbers at the age of fourteen, and so that when they do leave they will have an industrial intelligence and efficiency that are totally beyond the capacity of fourteen-year-old children.

Now, will an agency primarily interested in caring for children *after* they have got into industry at the age of fourteen or fifteen by the nature of the case either be familiar with, or interested in, this great question of the modification of the existing school system? As one school man has recently put it, the thing we ought to be interested in is in stopping the waste and the slaughter that is going on with the children, and not simply in utilizing their carcasses better after the slaughter has occurred.

I do not say that the degree of separate control, found in the Wisconsin plan, is absolutely fatal to taking this larger and more complete view of the plan; but I do say it is not favorable to it; and I add that thoroughgoing dual control would be fatal. The problem here is a large problem. It cannot be solved hastily. It has to be solved step by step; and while we shall have to use the experience of Germany, England, and of Scotland, (and be willing to utilize it more than we have done in the past), it is, after all, our own problem which has got to be worked out, and worked out in our own way. Let us not compromise the working out of it by introducing divisions and antagonisms at the start. We need the cooperation of the manufacturer, we need the cooperation of the labor union; we need the cooperation of the teacher and of the existing school authorities; we need the cooperation of the social settlements, the social workers, the philanthropists, the legislators, and the statesmen who are interested in preventing the human waste that is now going on. It may take a little longer to secure definite results if we take the larger human position, and go at industrial education as a matter of importance to the whole community and one requiring cooperation of all its factors than it would to start a separate plant in behalf of employers and of the children who now leave school at fourteen. But, this isolation method will certainly lead to reactions which will, in the end, bring even these small remedial matters into disrepute. The safest course is the one predicated upon the interests of the community as a whole and worked out in a complete and rounded out scheme representing all factors in a unified school system.

A POLICY OF INDUSTRIAL EDUCATION

The habitual American attitude towards public education is, to say the least, paradoxical. Belief in publicly supported education is the most vital article of the average citizen's creed. Money devoted to educational purposes makes the largest item in the budget, and payment of taxes for school purposes is accompanied with the least amount of grumbling. The man who ridicules his legislature, who is suspicious of his judiciary and openly flouts his police system, is enthusiastic about public education. But the connection of the public with its schools ends for the most part with their support. There is next to no provision for public control, and that little is generally felt to be a nuisance when it extends its activities beyond the financial support of the schools under its nominal charge. The direction of educational policy is no part of statesmanship; the divorce of school from politics—which presumably means matters of public policy—is thought to represent the ideal state of things. Educators have reciprocated by taking an astonishingly slight interest in the public functions attached to their own work. Social settlements, amateur philanthropists and voluntary associations, rather than professional educators, have agitated the questions of child labor and juvenile crime, of adequate recreative facilities and the wider use of the school plant, and even of preparation for making a livelihood.

That our *laissez passer* methods have worked as well as they have indicates a certain soundness in our social life, as well as at least a temporary adaptation to our needs. That these methods will work as well in the future may be doubted. The formation by Congress of a Commission on National Aid to Vocational Education, composed of two

[First published in *New Republic* 1 (1914): 11–12.]

Senators, two Representatives and five laymen, reflects both the traditional system and the feeling of need for its change. Not one of the five lay members is a professional educator. While the Commission recommends the giving of aid, and drafts a bill which would involve an initial annual grant to the states of a million and a half dollars, rising to the sum of seven millions through a period of years, there is no thought of provision for a minister of education. The Federal Board in control is to consist of the Postmaster-General, with the Secretaries of the Interior, of Agriculture, of Commerce and Labor. The Commissioner of Education is to remain an executive clerk, although with somewhat enlarged clerical duties. The proposal is characteristic of our tradition. We are far from the day when direction and supervision of publicly supported education will be a public function.

Meantime the existence of an official Federal Commission is evidence of the changing situation. Congress is hardly likely to pass the bill which is recommended. Legislative action is of doubtful value till the subject of industrial education has been more thoroughly discussed. It is more important that it be treated as part of a general statesmanlike policy toward education than that immediate isolated steps be taken for furthering the agricultural and trade instruction of youth over fourteen. There is as yet no public opinion as to the standpoint from which education for industry should be approached, or the aims which should control the undertaking. The reasons thus far advanced for making industrial training an organic part of public school education are an undigested medley. The need of a substitute for the disappearing apprenticeship system, the demand of employers for more skilled workers, the importance of special training if the United States is to hold its own in international competitive commerce, figure side by side with the educational need of making instruction more "vital" to pupils.

The oft-cited experience of Germany as to the importance of industrial education must be weighed in connection with the purpose which has dominated her efforts. This has been frankly nationalistic. The available statistics indicate that the effect of industrial education upon wages has been almost negligible, skilled workers receiving but little more than unskilled. But the effect of industrial education upon the worker's individual wage or happiness was not the animating motive. Germans claim with justice that their systematized and persistent applications of intelligence to military affairs, public education, civil administration, and trade and commerce, have a common root and a converging aim. The well-being of the state as a moral entity is supreme. The promotion of commerce against international competitors is one of the chief means of fostering the state. Industrial training is a means to this means, and one made peculiarly necessary by Germany's natural disadvantages.

One does not need to grudge admiration for the skill and success with which this policy has been pursued. But as a policy it is extraordinarily irrelevant to American conditions. We have neither the historic background nor the practical outlook which make it significant. There is grave danger that holding up as a model the educational methods by which Germany has made its policy effective will serve as a cloak, conscious or unconscious, for measures calculated to promote the interests of the employing class. It is the privilege of large employers of labor to supplement public schooling by classes which they themselves support in order to give the special knowledge and skill required in their operations. There are many interesting and successful attempts of this kind. It is natural that employers should be desirous of shifting the burden of this preparation to the public tax-levy. There is every reason why the community should not permit them to do so. Class against class, there is no reason why the community should be more interested in the laboring class than in the employing class, save the important reason that the former constitutes a larger part of itself. But every ground of public policy protests against any use of the public school system which takes for granted the perpetuity of the existing industrial régime, and whose inevitable effect is to perpetuate it, with all its antagonisms of employer and employed, producer and consumer.

In the lack of enlightened public opinion as to the place of industrial training in the public schools in a would-be democracy, even the enumeration of commonplaces may be of some help; unfortunately they are not as yet current commonplaces. In the first place, its aim must be first of all to keep youth under educative influences for a longer time. Were it not for historic causes which explain the fact, it would be a disgrace that the larger portion of the school population leaves school at the end of the fifth or sixth grade. Irrespective of its causes, the continuance of this situation is a menace. Meagre as are the efforts already put forth in adapting industry to educational ends, it is demonstrated in Chicago, Gary and Cincinnati, that such adaptation is the first need for holding pupils in school and making their instruction significant to them. In these places the aim has not been to turn schools into preliminary factories supported at public expense, but to borrow from shops the resources and motives which make teaching more effective and wider in reach.

In the second place, the aim must be efficiency of industrial intelligence, rather than technical trade efficiency. Schemes for industrial education thus far propounded ignore with astonishing unanimity many of the chief features of the present situation. The main problem is not that of providing skilled workers in the superior crafts. Taken by itself, this is a comparatively simple problem. But it cannot be taken by itself, for the reason that these crafts are the ones already best organized and most jealous of efforts to recruit their numbers beyond the market demand, and for the reason also that automatic machinery is constantly invading the province of specially trained skill of hand and eye. Wherever automatic machines develop, high specialization of work follows. In the larger cities even the building trades now represent a grouping of a very large number of separate occupations, demanding for the most part simply skill in managing machines. The automobile is a complicated machine, nevertheless ninety-five per cent of the labor of manufacture in the cheaper cars is unskilled. Such facts are typical. The rapid change by means of new inventions of the forms of machine industry is another controlling consideration. The mobility of the laboring population in passing from one mode of machine work to another is important. Such facts cry aloud against any trade-training which is more than an incidental part of a more general plan of industrial education. They speak for the necessity of an education whose chief purpose is to develop initiative and personal resources of intelligence. The same forces which have broken down the apprenticeship system render futile a scholastic imitation of it.

In a word, the problem in this country is primarily an educational one and not a business and technical one as in Germany. It is nothing less than the problem of the reorganization of the public school to meet the changed conditions due to the industrial revolution. In view of this consideration, the absence of all educators from the Commission on National Aid to Vocational Education has a peculiar significance. Professional educators are not free from blame, because of their indisposition to face the question of educational reorganization. But to leave educators out of the discussion of an educational problem is a curious proceeding. They will have to take a large share in the execution of any plan which may be adopted. If they cannot be trusted to have a responsible share in the making of the plan, the chances of their successful execution of it are indeed slight. The situation also adds peculiar significance to the fact that the Commissioner of Education is made by the bill an executive clerk of various departments of the Government which have direct concern with certain forms of industry but none with education. It is not an immediately important question whether there be a minister of education in the Cabinet. It is a fundamentally important question whether or no a Federal policy with respect to industrial education be initiated which relegates the educational interest to the background.

SOME DANGERS IN THE PRESENT MOVEMENT FOR INDUSTRIAL EDUCATION

There is no greater need at the present time than a closer understanding and working agreement between those interested on general philanthropic and social grounds in the prevention of child labor and those interested in educational reform. It is not enough to keep children out of the factory and the shop till they have reached a certain age. Every success in raising the age level for labor of children should be accompanied by steps in a constructive educational policy so that youth, when they finally leave school, shall have a general education which fits them not only to find a better paying job, but a line of occupation suited to their own capacities and one in which there is a future for growth. Professional educators, on the other hand, need to awaken from the lethargy through which they have permitted non-educational associations to take the lead in measures for the amelioration of the condition of children. They should recognize their opportunities and their responsibilities and take an aggressive part in the formation and execution of all legislative and administrative measures concerned with the welfare of children.

The problems of vocational guidance and industrial education are by no means solved, and without intelligent cooperation of educators and reformers the newly awakened enthusiasm on these matters will result in hasty and superficial action. Thus it is absurd to talk about "vocations" in connection with the labor of children under sixteen at least, but the phrase is likely to have, with some people, an influence which it would not have were the ordinary words "finding jobs" substituted for the high sounding "vocational guidance." To encourage children under sixteen to leave

[First published as "An Undemocratic Proposal" in *American Teacher* 2 (1913): 2–4. Revised and reprinted in *Child Labor Bulletin* 1 (1913): 69–74.]

school by assisting them to find jobs is a mischievous enterprise. There are nineteen chances out of twenty that any work they can get into will prove a blind alley both industrially and economically. Enthusiasm for vocational guidance should exhibit itself first in encouraging children to stay in school till they have an education which will fit them for work where there are genuine openings ahead; secondly, in guiding public opinion and activity to modify the regular school work so that it shall have a more genuine connection with social opportunities; thirdly, to provide supplementary agencies so that children when they do leave to go to work shall continue under some educational supervision that will counteract the tendency of almost any trade at the present time to arrest their further growth. Only as a last resort in desperate individual cases should agencies for vocational guidance act as labor placing bureaus.

Industrial Education Dangers

The kindred question of industrial education is fraught with consequences for the future of democracy. Its right development will do more to make public education truly democratic than any other one agency now under consideration. Its wrong treatment will as surely accentuate all undemocratic tendencies in our present situation, by fostering and strengthening class divisions in school and out. It is better to suffer a while longer from the ills of our present lack of system till the truly democratic lines of advance become apparent, rather than separate industrial education sharply from general education, and thereby use it to mark off to the interests of employers a separate class of laborers.

These general considerations have a particular application to the scheme of industrial education which has been proposed for adoption by the next legislature of the State of Illinois—one of the leading industrial states of the Union, and containing its second largest city. This scheme proposes a separate State Commission of Vocational Education, wherever the community may wish to develop any form of industrial education. In other words, the entire school system of the state as a whole and of such communities of the state as may desire to do something definite in the direction of industrial education is split into two for the education of all above fourteen years of age. Since whatever a state like Illinois may do in such a matter is sure to have influence in other states in this formative period, educators all over the country should be aroused to help ward off what, without exaggeration, may be termed the greatest evil now threatening the interests of democracy in education.

The statement of the scheme ought to be enough to condemn it. The least reflection shows fundamentally bad features associated with it. First, it divides and duplicates the administrative educational machinery. How many communities have such an excess of public interest in education that they can afford to cut it into two parts? How many have such a surplusage of money and other resources that they can afford to maintain a double system of schools, with the waste of funds and the friction therein involved? Second, the scheme tends to paralyze one of the most vital movements now operating for the improvement of existing general education. The old-time general, academic education is beginning to be vitalized by the introduction of manual, industrial and social activities; it is beginning to recognize its responsibility to train all the youth for useful citizenship, including a calling in which each may render useful service to society and make an honest and decent living. Everywhere the existing school system is beginning to be alive to the need of supplementary agencies to help it fulfill this purpose, and is taking tentative but positive and continuous steps toward it. The City of Chicago in this same State of Illinois probably ranks behind no other city of the country in the extent and wisdom of the steps already taken, steps which will of necessity be followed by others just as fast as those already taken demonstrate their efficiency.

These two movements within the established American public school system, the proposed scheme, if adopted, will surely arrest. General education will be left with all its academic vices and its remoteness from the urgent realities of contemporary life untouched, and with the chief forces working for reform removed. Increasing recognition of its public and social responsibilities will be blasted. It is inconceivable that those who have loved and served our American common school system will, whatever the defects of this system, stand idly by and see such a blow aimed at it. Were anything needed to increase the force of the blow, it is the fact that the bill provides that all funds for industrial education raised by the local community be duplicated by the state, although the funds contributed by the state for general school purposes are hardly more than five per cent of the amount raised by local taxation.

Thirdly, the segregation will work disastrously for the true interests of the pupils who attend the so-called vocational schools. Ex-Superintendent Cooley of Chicago, who is understood to be responsible for the proposed bill in its present form, has written a valuable report on "Vocational Education in Europe." He quite rightly holds in high esteem the work and opinions of Superintendent Kerschensteiner of Munich. It is noteworthy that this leading European authority insists upon all technical and trade work being taught in its general scientific and social bearings. Although working in a country definitely based on class distinctions (and where naturally the schools are based on class lines), the one thing Superintendent Kerschensteiner has stood for has been that industrial training shall be primarily not for the sake of industries, but for the sake of citizenship, and that it be conducted therefore on a purely educational basis and not in behalf of interested manufacturers. Mr. Cooley's own report summarizes Mr. Kerschensteiner's views as follows:

> If the boy is to become an efficient workman he must comprehend his *work in all of its relations to science, to art, and to society in general*. . . . The young workman who understands his trade in *its scientific relations, its historical, economic and social bearings*, will take a higher view of his trade, of his powers and duties as a citizen, and as a member of society.

Whatever may be the views of manufacturers anxious to secure the aid of the state in providing them with a somewhat better grade of laborers to exploit, the quotations state the point of view which is self-evident to those who approach the matter of industrial education from the side of education, and of a progressive society. It is truly extraordinary that just at a time when even partisan politics are taking a definitely progressive turn, such a reactionary measure as the institution of trade and commercial schools under separate auspices should be proposed. It is not necessary to argue concerning the personal motives of the bankers and manufacturers who have been drawn into the support of the measure. Doubtless many of them have the most public spirited of intentions. But no one experienced in education can doubt what would be the actual effect of a system of schools conducted wholly separate from the regular public schools, with a totally different curriculum, and with teachers and pupils responsible to a totally independent and separate school administration. Whatever were the original motives and intentions, such schools would not and could not give their pupils a knowledge of industry or any particular occupation in relation to "science, art and society in general." To attempt this would involve duplicating existing schools, in addition to providing proper industrial training. And it is self-evident that the economical and effective way to accomplish this move is to expand and supplement the present school system. Not being able to effect this complete duplication, these new schools would simply aim at increased efficiency in certain narrow lines. Those who believe in the continued separate existence of what they are pleased to call the "lower classes" or the "laboring classes" would naturally rejoice to have schools in which these "classes" would be segregated. And some employers of labor would doubtless rejoice to have schools supported by public taxation supply them with additional food for their mills. All others should be united against every proposition, in whatever form advanced, to separate training of employees from training for citizenship, training of intelligence and character from training for narrow industrial efficiency. That the evil forces at work are not local is seen in the attempt to get the recent national convention on industrial education in Philadelphia to commit itself in favor of the Illinois scheme.

The only serious danger is that a number of sympathetic and otherwise intelligent persons should be misled, and on the basis of a justified enthusiastic support of the principle of industrial education (with whatever supplementary agencies that may be found necessary) jump to the support of this scheme, not realizing what is really involved in it. Such persons should first inform themselves as to what is actually being done already in this direction in the more progressive public schools, and should then devote their spare energies to backing up and furthering these undertakings, and to creating a public opinion that will affect the more backward and conservative public school systems. The problem is a difficult one, but many intelligent, though unadvertised, attempts are already making for its solution; and its difficulty is no reason for permanently handicapping the interests of both common school education and a democratic society by abruptly going back upon what, with all its defects, has been the chief agency in keeping alive a spirit of democracy among us—the American public school system.

INDUSTRIAL EDUCATION AND DEMOCRACY

In his recent interesting article, Mr. Miles has raised the question of the "control" of education as it affects the movement for industrial education. According to him, it is a question of whether teachers or business men shall control. It would be hard to find a mode of statement more fitted to befog the real issue, or one better adapted to bring into clear relief the animus of many of those who are interested in establishing segregated schools for the training of their future employes. There is not a city or town in the country, so far as I know, where control of the school system is lodged in teachers. In many cities the superintendent of schools himself is not even a member of the board in control. School boards do not represent either the teachers nor yet "the business men" for whom Mr. Miles is so solicitous. They represent the community as a community in behalf of the community—something considerably wider and more important than the class either of teachers or of business men. The real issue is whether this community control in the interests of the community is to continue, with such developments as changing needs may call for from time to time; or whether this social control is to be abrogated in behalf of a control by business men in the interests of business men.

It may be true, as Mr. Miles intimates, that (in some localities at least) business men have not had sufficient share in the active direction of the policies of the schools. The logic of Mr. Miles's argument is that as long as business men are required to take an interest in education from the standpoint of the well-being of the community as a whole, they will not exert themselves; that only when it is a question of

[First published in *Survey* 29 (1913): 870. For article to which this is a reply, see Appendix 5, this volume.]

specialized education affecting their pecuniary interest as employers of labor will they take an interest in education. Mr. Miles presumes to speak for his fellow "business men"; I should be sorry to make or to believe such an accusation against the public spirit of business men.

CUT-AND-TRY SCHOOL METHODS

My first and in some respects my deepest impression of the evening spent so enjoyably in Edison's laboratory is not directly connected with the educational value of his motion picture scheme. It is rather of the immense advantage a great commercial enterprise has over the greatest of our existing educational institutions in the matter of conducting systematically an experimental development of a new proposal before putting it into general practice.

No intimation was given of the sum of money that is being put into the development of this new undertaking. But it is clear that a large staff is employed to develop "scenarios," to make suggestions and criticisms, and to try out various schemes, in addition to the expense involved in taking the pictures themselves. A large sum of money will have been spent before pecuniary returns begin to come in—a good deal of it on strictly experimental inquiry.

Where is there a school system having at command a sum of money with which to investigate and perfect a scheme experimentally, before putting it into general operation? And can we expect continuous and intelligent progress in school matters until the community adopts a method of procedure which is now a commonplace with every great industrial undertaking? Is not the existing method of introducing reforms into education a relic of an empirical cut-and-try method which has been abandoned in all other great organizations? And is not the failure to provide funds so that experts may work out projects in advance a pennywise and pound foolish performance?

That children will be immensely interested in at least the greater part of the material the Edison people prepare is sufficiently attested by the delight of the adults on the evening of our visit—to say nothing of the hold the nickel "mov-

[First published in *Survey* 30 (1913): 691–92.]

ies" already have upon them. That Mr. Edison has a sound psychologic basis in relying upon the instinctive response of human beings to whatever moves and does something is unquestionable. So is the fact that the deadness of much existing education is due to the absence of anything moving and doing in the schoolroom. Personally I believe that Mr. Edison is in the right in his conviction that children, as well as adults, do best in and learn most from matters in which they are interested; and that there is more discipline, in the sense of actual training of power, where there is interest than where what is done is repulsive and arbitrary.

I was also impressed by the fact that, after all, *seeing* things behave is rather a vicarious form of activity, and that there is some danger of the better becoming an enemy of the best. I mean that a widespread adoption of motion pictures in schools might have a tendency to retard the introduction of occupations in which children themselves actually do things. The more hopeful view, of course, is that the former would pave the way for the latter, affording an intermediate step that in many cases would not be taken directly.

A closely associated danger is that their use will, for a time at least, strengthen the idea, already much too strong, that the end of instruction is the giving of information and the end of learning its absorption. That much more information may be given in many subjects by Mr. Edison's method, that it will be given more efficiently, understandingly, quickly and vividly I have no doubt. Two or three performances may easily make an impression more indelible and more intelligent than weeks of reading about and talking about certain matters—as for example the pictures of the Bessemer process. And the capacity even of children, or perhaps better, especially of children, for absorption of information is immensely greater than is usually supposed. If teachers have sense enough to use the pictures and talk them over in a sensible way, allowing the information to soak in naturally instead of holding up the children to artificial tests of reproduction, perhaps there is no great danger of excessive information being conveyed, though I can but feel that the seeming sanction given to the reigning informational ideal is unfortunate.

Even the limited number of pictures shown proves, however, that some subjects are much better adapted for purposes of conveying information in an intelligent way than others, and that careful discrimination is required. At present there does not seem to be as much provision for expert education as for technical criticism. For example, there are hundreds of schools where the principle of pump action is better taught at present by demonstrations, even without active experimentation and construction on the part of the children, than it was conveyed by the films on that subject. I should say the films on that topic (including the printed statements thrown on the curtain before the picture was shown) gave an example of how not to do it; and that the failure was not accidental, but illustrated a fundamental principle of selection. On the other hand, the filled in geography instruction is almost unlimited, since the material there is not accessible by other and better methods. The same principle applies, though to a less degree, in history, I imagine. In nature study there is no doubt that many operations may be selected for observation which will tend to make children more observing of what is going on around them, and to arouse interest in new problems. For example, children who have seen the films of a fly laying eggs and of the eggs hatching will have a new source of interest, and a new power, in watching real flies. The pictures of movements of the infusoria might very naturally lead to an interest in the use of the microscope.

I hope these suggestions will at least indicate what I mean by the need of a careful expert discrimination, on purely educational grounds, of the appropriateness of various types of subject-matter. There was also a marked tendency in the printed matter preceding the pictures to use a didactic form instead of a questioning form—a mistake that could easily be remedied by consultation with capable teachers.

PROFESSIONAL SPIRIT AMONG TEACHERS

You and I know, we all know, how much time, effort and energy are spent in attempting to develop a professional spirit among teachers. We all know that it is said over and over, and truly said, that if we could achieve a thoroughly professional spirit, permeating the entire corps of teachers and educators, we should have done more to forward the cause of education than can be achieved in any other way. Now it is not my affair to tell of all the ways by which the formation and development of a professional spirit may be promoted or hindered.

It is not my business to attempt even to define very closely just what a professional spirit among teachers is; but I think we would agree that there would be two marked features characterizing the teachers who have a distinctly professional spirit. One of these traits is manifested in the everyday school work with the children, in the questions of instruction and of discipline arising from the teacher's daily contact with the children. It consists in the teacher being possessed by a recognition of the responsibility for the constant study of school room work, the constant study of children, of methods, of subject matter in its various adaptations to pupils. The professional spirit means that the teachers do not think their work done when they have reasonably prepared a certain amount of subject matter and spent a certain number of hours in the school room attempting in a reasonably intelligent way to convey that material to the children. Teachers of a professional spirit would recognize that they still had a problem to deal with. There would be the continued intellectual growth that comes from diverted intellectual interest in the methods and material of the teach-

[Delivered at the organization meeting of the Teachers' League of New York, 28 February 1913. First published in *American Teacher* 2 (1913): 114–16.]

ers' occupation, so that we should have not mere artisans but artists.

The other element in a professional spirit consists, I think, of a recognition of the responsibility of teachers to the general public. It is a commonplace that our young are the chief asset of society, and that their proper protection and their proper nurture is the most fundamental care of society. Now a professional spirit would mean not merely that the teachers would be devoted to the continuous study of the questions of teaching within the school room; but that they would also bear a responsibility as leaders, as directors in the formation of public opinion.

Now I am going to say in passing that it is a somewhat striking fact, and, to one who is himself a teacher, perhaps a somewhat humiliating fact, that in the last of these matters, teachers and professional educators have not been especially active. The larger questions about the protection of childhood, the movements for the abolition of child labor, movements for playgrounds, for recreation centres, even for the adequate use of the school plant, these and the thousand and one problems relative to children that have come forward with the great congestion of population in cities in the last generation—the initiative in the agitation of these questions and the formation of public opinion has to a surprisingly small extent proceeded from the teachers. It has come from social settlements, from philanthropists, from charity workers, from people whose interest was not stimulated by education in a professional way.

Now, why is this? As I said, I have no intention of attempting to go into all the causes. But why is it that there has been so comparatively little done in this latter direction? Why is it that it is necessary to harp so continuously upon the formation of a professional spirit among teachers with respect even to the ordinary affairs, the subject matter, the methods and discipline in the classroom? We do not find, I think, for example, in the medical profession that it is necessary constantly to urge the formation of a professional spirit. We hear more or less about professional ethics; but not of professional spirit in the sense of the duty and responsibility of the physician to study his cases, to inform himself of improvements in methods of diagnosis, methods of surgery and therapeutic methods through the country. It is taken for granted that it is for the physician's own interest to be intellectually growing, intellectually alive, and concerned with these things.

Now, if I am asked for a reply as to the chief cause, not the sole cause, but the chief cause, of the relative backwardness of the formation of professional spirit among teachers and the consequent need of urging them, of preaching to them, and of almost driving them to develop this more enlightened interest in the work and recognition of making contributions to its improvement, my answer would be: the lack of adequate impetus.

It is not enough simply to teach people, and preach to people, and to urge them to do certain things. There must be something in the very nature of the work which makes the thing desirable, makes it their own vital concern.

When teachers have as little to do, as they have at present, with intellectual responsibility for the conduct of the schools; when the teachers who are doing most, if not all, of the teaching have nothing whatsoever to say directly about the formation of the courses of study and very little indirectly; when they have nothing save ways of informal discussion and exchange of experience in teachers' meetings, or very little to say about methods of teaching and discipline; when they have no means for making their experience actually count in practice, the chief motive to the development of professional spirit is lacking. There is not a single body of men and women in the world engaged in any occupation whatsoever among whom the development of professional spirit would not be hampered if they realized that no matter how much experience they got, however much wisdom they acquired, whatever experiments they tried, whatever results they obtained, that experience was not to count beyond the limits of their own immediate activity; that they had no authorized way of transmitting or of communicating it, and of seeing it was taken account of by others.

The situation would be ridiculous if it were not serious: that teachers who come in contact with the students should have nothing to do directly, and so little to do indirectly, with the selection, formation and arrangement of subject matter; that they should find that in printed manuals provided by other people, simply with the instruction to purvey so much of that per year, or per month or per week, or, even in some cases, per day.

Now, either teaching is an intellectual enterprise or it is a routine mechanical exercise. And if it is an intellectual exercise, and the professional spirit means intellectual awakening and enlightenment, there is, I repeat, no way better calculated to retard and discourage the professional spirit than methods which so entirely relieve the teachers from intellectual responsibility as do the present methods.

We hear a good deal about the concentration of responsibility. Now, there is one responsibility that can be concentrated only by distributing it. An intellectual responsibility has got to be distributed to every human being who is concerned in carrying out the work in question, and to attempt to concentrate intellectual responsibility for a work that has to be done, with their brains and their hearts, by hundreds or thousands of people in a dozen or so at the top, no matter how wise and skillful they are, is not to concentrate responsibility—it is to diffuse irresponsibility.

And that describes in the rough the system and organization of schools in the democracy under which we are supposed to be living. I read an article in proof a few days ago—I do not know whether it has come out recently—in which the author says that the question at issue regarding the introduction of industrial education in this country was whether the teachers were to control the new industrial schools, as they, the teachers, controlled all the existing schools; or whether the wide-awake and alert business men were to control these schools. And he pointed out that one reason for the business man's control was the fact that the teachers had made such a mess of the schools of which they are already in control.

Now, I bring to you this happy news—that it is you who are and who have been in control of our public schools. But unfortunately it is only when the schools are to be adversely criticised that the power of the mass of the teachers to control their own work is in evidence.

EDUCATION FROM A SOCIAL PERSPECTIVE*

I

"Society" is a word we hear frequently. Actually, the word covers a variety of concepts. There are *many* societies, not *one* society except in a purely abstract or ideal sense. To consider education from a social perspective, our first step therefore must be to define exactly how we conceive the term "society"; otherwise we risk misleading ourselves, or worse yet, misleading others. As for my own definition, you can understand that I naturally speak from the perspective of the society most familiar to me—that of the United States. But today, the problems of all civilized countries are identical in many respects. The forces that shape them are the same and they pursue the same goals. In the family of modern states, an analysis of education from one country's point of view is likely to apply to some degree in the others. In all of them we find the same democratic aspirations, the same ever-increasing interest in industrial expansion, the same predominance of science among human concerns. In fact, it is precisely these factors whose influence strikes me as decisive in the new educational ideas in the United States.

I do not intend by this, however, to confuse the social and national points of view regarding education. The two can never be completely separated of course: the national point of view necessarily contains some aspects of the social point of view; it is closer to that than to the abstract ideal of individualism in education. To avoid mere formalism, a social ideal must be modeled on the pattern of an existing so-

* Translated from the French by Jo Ann Boydston, revised from her earlier version published in *Educational Theory* 15 (1965): 73–82, 104.

[First published in *L'Année pédagogique* 3 (1913): 32–48. For the original French translation, see Appendix 8 of this volume.]

cial group such as a State. On the other hand, national and social perspectives differ entirely in their principal elements. A short historical note will clarify their respective roles in American education. It will also show us how nationalism and individualism have developed side by side, but under the banner of the latter.

At the beginning of the nineteenth century, nearly all American statesmen conceded that a republican government could maintain itself only through the intellectual cultivation of its citizens. A representative government would be doomed to fail if the members of the State who chose legislators (and from among whom the legislators were chosen) were not sufficiently educated. All centralization was repugnant: "that government governs best, which governs least." The idea of a permanent army that would tend to reinforce the material power of the existing authority was held in national disfavor. For the mass of citizens, the ideal was voluntary obedience to laws voluntarily accepted, an obedience that would be spontaneous rather than imposed by authority. Subsequent experience, however, revealed the utopian nature of this ideal and made it clear that the society had to be built on a foundation of education. Thus it was that education was expected to do everything: there was a naïve belief in the power of schools to provide knowledge and in the absolute power of knowledge to control action. In this manner, social and national perspectives were unconsciously identified. Education was seen as a patriotic necessity, the salvation of the republic. It was expected to suppress crime and misery, to bring forth a generation of loyal and autonomous citizens. Thanks to the geographic and political isolation of the country, this patriotism did not degenerate into rigid nationalism. On the contrary, the republican cause in general and the mission of providing asylum for the oppressed of all nations became—though not without a certain naïveté—identified with one another. Nowhere in the documents of that era will one find expressed a conscious desire to use education to fortify the United States against other countries. The only purpose of education was to assure the existence of the republic through the formation of intelligent and virtuous citizens.

Throughout this period, education had a social character, but that character manifested itself most clearly in the way the school system was organized. The social principle of that organization was to make available to all the means to learn, and in pursuit of this goal, to make the schools accessible to all, to establish a uniform progression from elementary school to the university. There was no thought that the pursuit of this democratic goal implied special programs or types of instruction. To the extent that one may speak of a precise pedagogical doctrine in the early nineteenth century, the dominant doctrine was that of the harmonious development of the individual's abilities (Pestalozzi's ideal). Thus, schooling was what we would call individualistic. There was a need, during the colonial period, for men with initiative, capable of making their own way, of creating careers, of subduing nature. In a new country whose natural resources had not yet been exploited, whose land was not yet settled, it could be assumed that whatever an individual did to assure his personal success would be good for the country.

In his autobiographical sketch, ex-President Roosevelt commented that in his youth the idea that dominated education was "making one's way in the world." Each person would succeed if he applied himself to his task intelligently. There was much talk about self-help and success, and very little about public or social duties. Then that period came to a close: the land was settled, its resources exploited, and a great inequality in the distribution of wealth arose. From that time on, not only did the idea that each person could obtain wealth seem absurd, but also, privileges started to appear, with support in the laws, in the civil administration, and in the courts. Class distinctions and social struggles to which the country had seemed immune became particularly severe. From this period, which we can assign to the last two decades of the last century, arose a new educational philosophy; we were seeking an approach that would be democratic in the social sense of the word, and that would be neither nationalistic nor individualistic.

This historical outline, incomplete as it is, will clarify the comments that follow. Briefly, I will call "the social perspective of education" that particular point of view which is founded on the criticism of traditional doctrines and methods that not only represent the vestiges of past conditions, but which also are opposed to the concept of democracy. This struggle against the content and the goals of traditional education is directed against more than the political and economic individualism to which I referred above. It is directed against teaching methods and approaches as much as against the content of education, and it is particularly aimed against the general notion of culture, the product of a special education reserved for special classes: the educated class and the ruling class.

II

All educational reformers from the nineteenth century to the present day have criticized certain pedagogical traditions, in particular, excessive verbalism, that pure symbol of erudition. But it is a much larger enterprise to attack the very idea that presides over the cult of language, the idea that knowledge is good in and of itself (which assuredly it should be) and is the ultimate good; that training the mind, which makes possible the acquisition and enjoyment of knowledge, is the final goal of any higher education. This ideal, formulated by Aristotle, has since his time always reigned in one form or another. It has had two major sources of support, educational theories being one, the other being those metaphysical systems in which reason is the only reality in the universe, a self-sufficient reality which is self-explanatory, that is to say, basically Divine, and the exercise of such reason, in the joy of knowledge, is considered the only good worthy of man. Clearly, this idea has not always been conceived in as explicit a manner or in as large or noble a sense as it was by the Greeks; in fact, quite the opposite occurred. What persisted is the idea that culture consists of the possession of a large number of ideas, and that consequently it rests on the acquisition of knowledge, sometimes conceived as a mass of information, sometimes as a discipline of certain faculties, the cognitive faculties.

Meanwhile a new task had to be undertaken: education of the masses. It was understood that for the masses usefulness rather than culture should be the aim. But in fact earlier dominant concepts persisted and were transmitted unchanged to the new schools. The only modification imposed in response to the new conditions was to simplify instruction either in its scope or its difficulty, but knowledge was still considered an entity, with inherent origins and limits. The only difference was that, for the education of the masses (which, by definition, must be strictly elementary) lessons of a practical nature were preferred. Obviously, it cannot be said that criticizing traditional concepts of knowledge will produce a social perspective toward education; that would be a misunderstanding. One can hold instruction in low regard and deprecate intelligence but such an attitude hardly conforms to the interests of a truly democratic society. This attitude is quite different from the social perspective, where what is criticized is a certain notion about the nature of education—its origin, its goal, its scope—as expressed in various pedagogical systems. The Aristotelian conception of pure knowledge presents us with something born of reason, a purely theoretical cognitive faculty, something infinitely superior to simple knowledge which is an adaptation created by the necessities of life. The latter exists for a goal; the former exists for itself. Once this concept is renounced, we see that even though knowledge is still highly esteemed, it must, to be rational, be given a new goal and must be put in a different context. This new point of view will entirely modify either our methods of acquiring knowledge or our judgment of the value of different branches of education.

Thus, according to the traditions of the leisure class, the most valuable teaching is that which is furthest from any useful application, even when that application consists of serving the state. Only "pure" learning may be called truly liberal; any other, even that which makes us useful to our fellow-citizens, is seen as servile, vulgar, "mechanical." The idea of an isolated and self-sufficient "reason" is the basis for the traditional division between liberal arts and mechanical arts, with the corresponding distinctions between cultivation that is good in itself and cultivation subordinated to a goal, between pure knowledge and applied or professional knowledge. In continuing recognition of the immense value of education, if we envisage it from the social perspective, we must seek what is most essential to the well-being of the society in those intellectual domains where practical value is the most direct and where usefulness for the shared life within society is most immediate.

I have indicated above how the cult created by traditional education based on verbal symbols stems from a profound belief in their educational value. The rapport between this notion of instruction as purely theoretical and current ideas which place literature at the pinnacle of education is easy to understand. What object would satisfy pure spirit, if not the one presented as the most purely mental? Because of its ideal and non-material character, the mind can only exercise its proper activity on a non-material object. Matter does not have its own end: it has value only through subordination to a goal more elevated than itself. The spirit is therefore debased by contact as soon as it lowers itself to the material. Spirit, pure reason, never grasp direct knowledge of the physical world. They catch a glimpse of it only through the intermediary of the senses, which are themselves material. The physical world will therefore never be an object worthy of the highest science. Idea, thought, pure truth—these are the true manifestations of the spirit and its real nourishment. The primacy of language in education stems from this concept, since language records and preserves ideas and truths as ideas and truths, independent of the physical world.

Undoubtedly, no one goes so far as to proclaim that words constitute a more elevated subject of study than do material objects. But what is certain is that when such a view is engendered by other causes, the concept of pure knowledge is used to justify and sanction it.

Any person who views the study of language and literature as something more noble, more ideal, more harmonious with a liberal education than the study of science, is profoundly influenced, whether consciously or not, by belief in the quasi-divinity of pure spirit. Otherwise, his conviction could only be based on another view, one which finds that the value of literature resides in the services it renders, in the extent and richness of its sphere of application. This proposition is open to discussion: in any event, it clearly substitutes the criterion of social utility for the criterion of the inherent value of pure knowledge.

As I have said, the idea of a social origin and social function of knowledge involves a new conception of the best ways of acquiring an education and a new appreciation of its principal elements. The idea of an intrinsic union between knowledge and reason, that purely cognitive faculty, favored the use of the dialectic method. Universal truths, first principles, ideas and concepts—considered to be innate in the spirit and inherent in the logical relationships by which truths are coordinated—were basic to such a method. Definitions became fetishes, logical divisions and classifications were the temples where one worshipped them. The senses are physical; they are connected to the needs of man; they furnish the stimuli necessary for action. The knowledge they transmit was, then, considered as of an inferior order, as a concession to utility: a necessary concession, of course, since the spirit is joined to a body, but one that had to be kept to a minimum. According to this theory, experimentation also was a method of approaching truths of an inferior order. It involved exterior active use of muscles, of mechanical apparatus, the manipulation of material things. How can all this be compared to pure logic which deduces, through internal means, the consequences of certain first truths? It is an odd state of affairs: methods of observation and experimentation have entirely supplanted the dialectical method in the search for scientific truth but the old methods still reign in the schools! The dominance of these methods helps enhance the esteem in which certain forms of literary expression are held. Literary production is not concerned with observation and experimentation but with ideas and their logical relationships. Ethics, political science, philosophy, even history, have become branches of literature by using its methods of interpretation and exposition.

III

To my regret, I have been obliged from the beginning of this philosophical definition of knowledge to introduce a perspective which is not only somewhat abstract and speculative, but also still contested and controversial. However, it was the best method of establishing clearly the thesis that the social perspective of education does not involve a superficial adaptation of the existing system but a radical change in foundation and aim: a revolution.

From this social perspective, concepts of the origin, the method, and the role of knowledge, of the training of intelligence, become as removed from the concepts that prevail in traditional schools as the logic of Bacon is removed from the scholasticism of the fourteenth century. This social perspective seeks to introduce into education those new methods of investigation which, outside the schools, have revolutionized scientific procedures and have brought a political and industrial revolution in their train. The social perspective tends to show what role in our lives is played by knowledge that comes from everyday life, and that serves to perfect and enrich it.

These views may seem ambitious. But before criticizing them, their scope should be grasped; if not, the objection will be, as it has been too often, that the social movement in education consists of a disdain for science and the subordination of science to practical needs, of polarizing utility and culture in order to sacrifice the latter to the former. If we examine the social perspective of education carefully, we will find that the conflict between science and action, between culture and utility, is simply the consequence of a current dualism. The social reorganization of education will in effect tend to abolish that dualism, not to perpetuate one of its terms at the expense of the other. The basis of the conflict is itself imbedded in a social dualism: the distinction between the working class and the leisure class. The social concept must therefore propose a twofold goal: on the one hand, action, work, must no longer be considered servile and mechanical, but must become liberal and enlightened through their contact with science and history; on the other hand, education must no longer constitute the distinctive mark of a class. It must no longer be seen as a leisure pursuit, an intellectual stimulant, but rather as a necessity for all free and progressive social action.

A few words about some typical teaching will help me to clarify, to make more precise this overly vague and speculative conception of the social goals of education. I have spoken of science a great deal; I may have seemed to value it much more than literature. However, I think that literature and language may well be studied from a social perspective. The present vogue in literary studies certainly relies on the fact that, whatever view one may have about their function, they are connected with and serve to clarify social interests. On the other hand, the natural sciences have also occasionally been taught in an abstract and rationalistic spirit; been disassociated from their human ties, from their origin and their role; science has been taught as if it were a mass of facts and of truths expressing a reciprocal relation between pure spirit, outside of time and space, and a strictly objective world in which no one is alive except by accident, with no links to social aspirations and activities.

The social perspective of education, on the contrary, accentuates the human element that has always been the foundation of linguistic studies. It connects the teaching of science to its historical origins in the need and activity of man. For man, science is among all human concerns the one that aims at the conquest of his environment, and which leads to a life that is freer, more certain, richer. Only when science ceases to be presented as a chaos of particulars, scattered throughout the universe to serve purely theoretical needs of man, will it become alive and beneficial for all, and no longer only for a few specialists. Spencer had a high opinion of science. He reserved the highest place in education for it. This approach was based on the old rationalist concept of knowledge: we must know the universe in order to use it for our benefit. But Spencer did not ask himself how this object of study, which by definition addresses itself only to our purely intellectual faculties, could hold the attention of the mass of students, whose interests are mostly practical. He seems to have thought that all normal infants were budding pedants. Our ideas, our knowledge of facts, could not influence our conduct if they failed to act in concert with our emotional impulses. Doubtless Spencer recognized this at times; however, he seems never to have asked himself by what means science, taught as an object of pure intellectual comprehension, could penetrate the springs of action, could become an integral part of our daily activities.

The social perspective is based on this very different fact: that science is already, by its existence, a predominant element in social activity. What has history shown us above all, for the last 150 years, if not the spectacle of a social evolution, itself brought about by an industrial revolution? In the course of this revolution, we see human activity constantly linked to knowledge of physical forces and their transformation. Doubtless, nothing is simpler than to consider industrial processes in our time as the result of applied science; from the perspective of scientific investigation, this is true. It is no longer true for the community, and especially not for the child, for the youth of our schools. For them, it would be, in effect, reversing the actual order of things if we proposed beginning with science to arrive at its applications. For students, science is seen in all research as suspended in the social phenomenon. It is not science itself they see, abstract and isolated, awaiting application in human action; it is human action, pregnant with the facts and principles of science, which offers itself to their contemplation. Day after day, they see steam and electricity at work, they use the telephone and telegraph. This entire mass of familiar objects constitutes the work of man, which could be realized only through the laws and facts of science. The problem of education thus does not consist of transmitting knowledge of pure and isolated science from which we derive applications to our daily lives; it consists of extracting that science from the human creations where it already manifests its influence.

The accusation of base utilitarianism applied to these views is unfounded. First, it effectively ignores the fact that a school child exempt from the worry of earning his livelihood will look at facts in a completely different way from an adult to whom industry is the source of income. For a child, the utility of the steam engine, the locomotive, the electric motor, the telephone, the reaper, as tools that produce income, is of secondary importance. What he sees are the things that respond to his instincts for activity, to his curiosity, to his need to understand. In all probability, if from infancy this intellectual interest were cultivated and focused on the practical mechanisms of social life, the narrow and utilitarian interests which pervade adult life would gradually be transformed into an attitude more compatible with reason. But separating the cultural point of view from the practical, far from basing the education of the future on a principle that is intrinsic to it, unfortunately imposes on it all the weight of antiquated methods.

A second mistake involved in this accusation of utilitarianism consists of not seeing how the social concept of education approaches the facts of industrial life in the widest social sense. It is not at all a question of isolating economic activities from their social context; on the contrary, its main idea is to study the processes of machinery, of industry, and of commerce, by considering their causes and effects from a three-sided point of view: social, intellectual, and political. All research, all practical application that involves scientific content also embodies the natural expression of the mechanism of social forms. Consequently, education will profit from turning to this research, to these practical applications that emphasize the human significance of all activity.

If we try to define education, we will end by conceiving of it as the power—we might say the acquired habit—of using our imagination to find within things that, taken separately, seem purely technical or professional, a much wider significance, extending to everything in life, to all human enterprise. As long as the sciences are set over against the humanities, they certainly can never aspire to the position they deserve. Only when we have established their human character will we be able to make them universal instruments. As a simple object of study, they can conveniently be separated from the history of their genesis; that has nothing to do with their present character. But educational goals create a different set of priorities: the social conditions that have brought man's attention to certain problems, suggested certain hypotheses, guided certain investigations; circumstances that have created progress in all areas; the influence of these discoveries for man's health, his comfort, the production and distribution of wealth, etc.; and finally, the political transformations engendered by all these—this is what is truly important. All of this envelops pure scientific fact in a humanistic mantle of sorts, and at the same time gives a unique value to linguistic and literary studies, and makes them worthy objects of education.

A look at historical studies is no less convincing. In general, two principal elements predominate here: first, a nationalist tendency that resorts to history to prepare citizens for the State—not for an ideal, theoretical State, but a concrete State as it actually exists; second, a concept on which that tendency vaguely rests—the intellectualist concept, the idea that the accumulation of knowledge has an inherent cultural value capable of instructing and enlightening. The distinction between the nationalist goal and the social goal is very clear: the former sees in the State, as it exists at any given moment, the standard of all its pedagogical values. Now, this State in its actual situation is surrounded by other States that have their own interests, and these diverse interests are very often in opposition, if not actually hostile. And this State is always dominated by a few families, by certain classes, in the conduct of its affairs. In this fashion, the nationalistic goal of education, while it favors the development of patriotism, which assuredly has social value in itself, tends also to accentuate certain divergences, certain specific features that separate each State from the others. By emphasizing historic battles, by celebrating victories and defeats, a latent antagonism is cultivated, ever ready to awake and burst into flame. More or less consciously, the teaching of history is used to eulogize the existing régime. The nation is identified with the method of the government in power. To exalt the former is to idealize the latter. Historicism always leads to conservatism—when it does not degenerate into simply fostering reactionary automatism.

Attitudes in teaching history are altogether different when based on a social perspective. What is important in recalling the past is not the more or less interesting events, not the laws that can be extracted for present use, nor even the examples that stimulate us to act as our fathers acted. In a sense it is true that in addressing history one seeks lessons from it. But these are not lessons in the current sense of the word, models for action or modes of conduct. They are, in final analysis, lessons in method. They show us how the past explains the present with its actions, its tendencies, its imperfections, and its chances of success. The social state we live in is too close to us and too complex for us to grasp. It stimulates us to react more than to reflect. To study it thoughtfully, we must take a spectator's attitude; a certain distance is necessary for perspective. Only the study of history can give us that. Such study describes for us a social mechanism simpler than the infinitely complex one that surrounds us; the first explains the second. By isolating them in their primitive form, historical study reveals certain factors that might have escaped our notice and then develops them along completely different lines from those apparent in our immediate circumstances.

History thus seems to me to be a concrete sociology, awakening the pupil to a practical study of the structure and functioning of the social mechanism. In teaching us about relatively simple social situations, it leads us to understand better the more complex present. If the past were nothing more than the past, education could say to history: "Let the dead bury their dead." Only a few specialists would complain. But so many facts in the past belong not only to the past! So many facts, whose "past" quality is of no interest, but whose immense significance lies in the insights they give us into the mechanism of human behavior and its functioning under the most diverse conditions!

The lessons of history, as we see, are not directly practical. They proceed neither from the ideal, nor from the tyrannical (or sanctified) realm of custom. They are intellectual. They lead us to understand the present through a special preparation of our mental habits, of the instruments of thought. If we cannot hope to reach a perfect understanding of things, it is still indisputable that any progress along the path is a real gain. Tomorrow's act becomes thereby more intelligent. It is, however indirectly, a new force because a more accurate comprehension of social facts is, in itself, a part of the social mechanism of the future.

The most important change that the social concept has introduced into education is probably in the activities known as "manual training" and, at a different level, as "industrial education." As its name indicates, the main goal of manual training is to train students to use their hands, and whenever possible to enlist their motor instincts. Such training is also expected to prepare students for careers that require manual dexterity. But from the social perspective, the work in manual training should be thought of as a veritable embryonic profession, analogous to adult trades that are the basis for social existence. Like these trades, manual training forms a centre around which all our ideas revolve; it raises problems which compel reflection and demand resolution. Like adult work, it too can, when skillfully directed, motivate the student to make a meaningful effort and can provide invaluable experience in social cooperation. What distinguishes this small-scale social "work" of the child from that of adult life is that it is carried on with no consideration of gain, and is thus performed in full freedom of the spirit. It is similar in this respect to play, which in the broadest sense of the word is closely linked to the functioning of the child's instincts, to the ideas evoked by these instincts and not just to ideas of a useful goal and of the exchange value of the object produced.

Beyond the skills acquired, beyond the lessons derived from the intelligent practice of gardening, weaving, woodwork or metalwork, cooking, etc., the habits formed through contact with productive work that has a wide and liberal base cannot fail to stamp the student's work with an eminently human character. I think that a person can get a true social education from any trade, any occupation that has social significance, provided it requires and fosters intellectual effort by those who practice it, and provided it has some economic utility for society. Formerly, in regard to professional education, it was thought that men should be brought up to become farmers, engineers, architects, carpenters, etc. Today the concept is quite different: each person should devote himself to some work that contributes directly or indirectly to the enrichment of community interests, that enlarges the life of the group. If it is important from the social perspective that a specially gifted individual be able to become an astronomer, a painter, etc., it is also necessary that those with a natural talent be prepared to become good farmers, good mechanics, good carpenters, etc. Given the idea that men should be capable of being useful to others through their work, they should be prepared to do so intelligently, with the necessary technical skill, and with that broader intelligence which perceives the relationship between things, and most importantly, between the individual act and the collective interest. As soon as we stop opposing pure knowledge and pure activity, the problem of professional education is transformed. Its goal is no longer to prepare men for an established industrial structure, but to make use of industry, of professional work, as educational endeavors. In this way, we raise the intellectual level of practical activity and, in the end, the established industrial régime itself is transformed.

I hope I have shown in this simple sketch that the social ideal of education, as I conceive it, is not simply a means of modifying the present type of education by adding a few improvements from here and there. It is, rather, a call for the radical reconstruction of pedagogical principles, based on a new concept. As long as learning was the property of the few, and far from freely impregnating the everyday practical life of each of us, as long as the profession of scholar was ranked above all others, an academic and bookish education met prevailing needs. That kind of education was admirable and valuable in its promises if not in its results. It favored the few at the expense of the many, and schools were almost exclusively devoted to it. At the same time, tradition and apprenticeships assumed responsibility for training most citizens for the other occupations that form the foundation of the social edifice. But today the situation has changed. Science has become experimental; industrial processes no longer consist of simple manual skills transmitted from generation to generation—they use the methods of science. The dualism of the past is no longer possible. The price that democratic societies will have to pay for their continuing health is the elimination of an oligarchy—the most exclusive and dangerous of all—that attempts to monopolize the benefits of intelligence and of the best methods for the profit of a few privileged ones, while practical labor, requiring less spiritual effort and less initiative, remains the lot of the great majority. These distinctions will ultimately disappear the day that, under the influence of education, science and practical activity are joined together forever. That is the principle, the law, that dominates the entire social concept of the goal of education, and derives directly from it.

Reviews

A TRENCHANT ATTACK ON LOGIC

Formal Logic: A Scientific and Social Problem
By F. C. S. Schiller. New York: Macmillan Co., 1912.

The reader does not have to go far in Dr. Schiller's *Formal Logic* to discover that the author's purpose is a systematic destructive criticism of what is known as formal logic, not an addition to the almost innumerable textbooks on the subject. "Nonsense fortified by technicality" is his more casual way of referring to it; his more formal statement is that it is "inconsistent, incompetent and meaningless." But we must hasten to add that the book is in no sense adequately characterized by such a selection of abusive epithets. Indirectly, if not directly, the aim of the book is constructive: "to clear the ground for a new logic that will not disdain to reflect upon real thinking, nor confine itself to fictions and falsifications." The book makes its appeal to a narrower, because more technically trained, circle of readers than Schiller's previous books upon humanism. While possessing their lucidity of style, his mode of treatment is more rigorous and more restrained. Probably some academic philosophers who have been offended by his unconventionality and occasional flippancy, and by his disregard of the professional technique for playing the philosophic game, will revise their opinion of Schiller on account of the sobriety, the severe consecutiveness and obvious scholarliness of the present volume.

In substance, the volume (a large octavo of about four hundred pages) is an unrelenting, dogged pursuit of the traditional logic, chapter by chapter, section by section. Not a single doctrine, nor, I think, a single distinction of the official textbooks escapes Schiller's demolishing hand. Those who have forgotten their college logic—which includes all, I imagine, whose fate it has not been to teach it subsequently—would not follow much of the book intelligently unless with a text in hand. Accordingly, I shall make no attempt to summarize its specific contents, as that would take the reader

[First published in *Independent* 73 (1912): 203–5.]

into the far off mysteries of extension and intension of terms, the nature of categories and predicables, the laws of thought and the opposition of propositions, through the syllogism and its rules to the inductive canons and the various kinds of fallacies, formal, semi-logical and material. For purposes of technical students, the value of the book resides in the thorough and detailed way in which Schiller has followed up and criticised all the conceptions of formal logic, never letting up till he has subjected the last one to examination. But, as our author points out, there is a guiding principle of unity that holds together all these detailed criticisms, for there is a single source of the incurable defects of formal logic. And this principle of unity involves a point which concerns any intelligent reader, whatever his lack of interest in the technicalities of formal logic. The difficulties and inconsistencies, the final meaninglessness of formal conceptions, is that formal logic is engaged in the impossible attempt of considering modes of thought "in themselves," apart from their application to actual situations. It is the absurdity of this attempt which deprives formal logic not only of truth, but of meaning. This is the clue that Schiller follows so unrelentingly through the logical labyrinth, and which gives an almost dramatic interest to the driest of the criticisms—dry, because the things criticised are so hopelessly mummified. In every case he shows the abstraction from the concrete conditions of human use of logic, and the fatally paralyzing effect of leaving human application out of account.

Incidentally, one of the most interesting things in the book is the glimpse that it gives, by way of contrast, of a genuine logic which shall report the conditions and aims of actual human thinking. Some of the conceptions which will be fundamental in it and which are totally omitted from formal logic are meaning, truth and error in their concrete difference from each other in a specific case, selection, relevance and risk. Meaning depends upon context, bearing and intention; and formal logic must exclude these from its ideal, for they are human and psychological. While traditional logic has much to say about truth, the truth it talks about is mere formal consistency, since it declines to consider the material application of its premises. Relevance—a fundamental conception of concrete thought—is excluded because it goes with selection, with selection of the *part* that is useful, while formal logic professes an all-inclusive ideal. Selection, moreover, is a voluntary and hence arbitrary act, and so is shut out from a doctrine that acknowledges only what is purely theoretical. Finally, formal logic, with its creed of absolute certitude, abhors the very mention of adventure and risk, the life-blood of actual human thinking, which is aroused by doubts and questions, and proceeds by guesses, hypotheses and experiments, to a decision which is always somewhat arbitrary and subject to the risk of later revision.

A vital and wholesome sense of the realities of actual thinking pervades the whole book; it supplies the background against which the criticisms of formal doctrine are projected. The book should not only attract new readers to Schiller and increase his already enviable reputation, but it should lead some thinkers to reconsider their prejudices against the introduction of psychological—that is, human—factors into logical theory. Mr. Schiller brings out, in case after case, with a cumulative effect which is fairly deadly, that at the crucial point each formal distinction is saved from complete meaninglessness only by an unacknowledged and surreptitious appeal to some matter of context, need, aim and use. Why not, then, frankly recognize the indispensableness of such volitional and emotional factors, and instead of pretending to a logic that excludes them, build up a logic that corresponds to human intellectual endeavor and achievement. It is difficult to see how even the most hardened devotee of a purely theoretical intellectualism can lay down the book without such questions haunting him.

To many it will probably seem that Mr. Schiller exaggerates the importance of the foe which he attacks. He will seem to them to be making too much of what at most is hardly more than a temporary annoyance of some college students. In one respect, I think this feeling is justified. Mr. Schiller is evidently stirred by the educational situation in which he finds himself at Oxford, and to which he wittily refers as follows:

Both logic and science can academically prosper under the delightfully paradoxical regulations of e.g., Oxford, where what is supposed to be the *theory* of science is only taught to those who know nothing of its *practice*, while those who are experts in the practice of science are not allowed to study "a theory of science" which could only delay their progress.

At Oxford, one gathers from many of Schiller's statements and still more from his general tone, formal logic is so deeply entrenched as a subject for study in its traditional form that one runs risk in attacking it. Certainly, it occupies no such consecrated and protected position in American higher education, nor in the esteem of American educational authorities. There would be a general popular willingness to accept the characterization of it as "nonsense (or at least pedantry) fortified by technicalities" without taking the trouble to read the arguments upon which Mr. Schiller bases his description. From our educational point of view, then, there can be no doubt that Mr. Schiller takes the subject-matter of formal logic altogether too seriously. But when one leaves the technical subject-matter and comes to the general conception of the nature of thought and of the intellectual ideals and methods which should operate in life, the same cannot be said. It is impossible to exaggerate the extent of the influence of formal consistency and formal demonstration, and of the notion of an "intellect" working in detachment from need, motive and specific application to a concrete situation. As Mr. James said of a similar matter, the change invoked in passing over to a logical ideal based upon opposite conceptions of the nature of mind and its relation to life, marks a revolution hardly second in importance, with reference to the change indicated in the seat of intellectual authority, to the Protestant Reformation. From this point of view Mr. Schiller's volume, in spite of its technical subject-matter and mode of treatment, is a significant contribution to one of the most fundamental of our social issues. His sub-title, in its reference to a "social problem," is more than justified.

Modern Science and the Illusions of Professor Bergson By Hugh S. R. Elliot, with a preface by Sir Ray Lankester. Longmans, Green, and Co., London and New York, 1912.—pp. xix, 257.

The reader will not go far in this book without discovering that Professor Bergson is, in effect, a symbol—not to say a scapegoat. The sinner is metaphysics, and Professor Bergson serves as an incarnation of the sin. "The attitude maintained throughout this book is that metaphysics is a maze of sesquipedalian verbiage" (p. 6). That is the text in general. "Holding, as I do, that Bergson's metaphysics are a cloud of words, carrying with them no real meaning" (p. 16)—that is the special illustration of the text. So far then as I am concerned, the value of the book lies in its frank, refreshingly frank, exposition of a certain view of the nature of science and of philosophy rather than in its criticism of the alleged scientific aspects of Bergson's philosophy. A competent biological criticism of Bergson from one gifted both with knowledge of biology and with a sympathetic imagination is needed and will doubtless come in time. But Mr. Elliot does not supply the lacuna. It is enough for him to see that metaphors and analogies play a considerable role in the Bergsonian metaphysics in order to emerge in stridently triumphant demonstration that all metaphysics is verbiage and that Bergson is a metaphysician—the Q.E.D. supplies itself. On many a page, one assists at a veritable intellectual Punch and Judy show. "Metaphysics" serves to knock Bergson down, and Bergson's alleged absurdities serve to topple over "metaphysics" if it shows any signs of getting on its feet.

As a presentation from a special point of view of the problem of philosophy in its relation to the problem of science, I nevertheless find a certain kind of instructiveness—though not instruction—in the volume. Nor do I have in mind simply the good old truth in which attacked philosophers may always find consoling refuge: that the ardent devotee

[First published in *Philosophical Review* 21 (1912): 705–7.]

who attacks metaphysics in the name of science generally exhibits himself in flagrant possession of a large assortment of uncriticized metaphysics. Mr. Elliot is no exception to this general rule. Associational psychology and psycho-physical parallelism are to him among the last words of established scientific doctrine. Agnosticism, of a peculiarly *aufgeklärt* sort, is of course not metaphysics, but "science." After imputing to Mr. Bergson a belief in Life as a separate entity, a belief in a pure abstraction as if it were a reality, he disposes of one of the special difficulties that Bergson deals with by remarking: "The protoplasm from which they were derived possessed, I suppose, capacities for evolving in certain directions." He is quite innocent both of the metaphysics lurking in potentiality, and of the fact that he is but stating, in different "verbiage," Bergson's own doctrine. But the really instructive thing is that Mr. Elliot puts in words the attitude of complete disrespect for philosophy undoubtedly entertained, but not explicitly stated, by many men of science. Philosophers, I imagine, are not the obscurantists that Mr. Elliot fancies them. There should be some way for the men of science of wider sympathies than animate Mr. Elliot and the philosophers who are not obscurantists to come to a better understanding of one another's purpose and office. The burden of reaching this understanding rests upon the philosophers. Science, as Mr. Elliot and Mr. Lankester frequently and rightly point out, is justified by its works. Philosophy is thus challenged to show what it has to its credit, either in the way of discovery of fact or in the way of contributing to the well-being of humanity. Philosophy, in my opinion, can say something for itself in reply to this challenge. But to say it effectively it must abandon some of its cherished formulae about rigid demonstrations, and be more willing to recognize its kinship with the play of imaginative vision, and the role of imagination in life.

MODERN PSYCHOLOGISTS

Founders of Modern Psychology
By G. Stanley Hall. New York: D. Appleton & Co., 1912.

President Hall has given us a useful and interesting book. At times, its interest approaches charm—a charm due to the fact that Dr. Hall has been himself a part of the history that he relates, and that he discourses most discursively upon everything—and sundry other things—that his text happens to suggest to him. In the language of psychology itself, the amount of "fringe" in this book in proportion to solid core is very great—and interest is largely dependent upon fringe. Somehow not only the recurring use of unusual and technical words, words used as if they were the commonplace of everyday speech, although they may send even the educated reader to the dictionary, but the shockingly large number of misprints of proper names seem to fall in as a part of this personal discursive intimacy. The personal note is struck in the selection of those dealt with as founders. All six of the names dealt with, Zeller, Lotze, Fechner, Hartmann, Helmholtz, Wundt, are teachers under whom and with whom Dr. Hall himself studied in Germany. It was as a student of philosophy that he worked with the first four, and only with the latter two as interested especially in psychology. This fact is doubtless responsible for the inclusion of Zeller among founders of psychology, as well as for one of the most interesting features of the book: The constant introduction of discussions of the relation of psychology and philosophy, and the development of Dr. Hall's own original views on the matter, and on higher culture in general.

Regarded as a contribution to the history of the development of contemporary scientific psychology, (which the book actually is only in a secondary sense), one of the facts that stand out most prominently is the influence of philosophic interests and prepossessions upon the men, in Germany at

[First published in *New York Times*, Review of Books, 25 August 1912, pp. 457–58.]

least, most responsible for the present standpoint. Leaving Zeller out of account as a historian, not a psychologist, we come to Lotze, whose *Medical Psychology* may be regarded as the first modern contribution to physiological psychology. Dr. Hall's account brings out the fact, often forgotten, that the recent scientific interest in the relations of mind and body took its departure from the heritage of ideas and problems bequeathed to German thought by the transcendental idealism of Kant, Fichte, Schelling, and Hegel. These philosophers had broken down the old dualism of mind and matter by the conception of an "organic unity" between them. They had treated bodily life as an instrumentality for bringing mind to realization, not as a piece of matter in which mind happens to be mysteriously housed. This conception left an aftermath of efforts to treat the specific facts of brain and nerves from the standpoint of their role in expressing spiritual values. By the time Lotze wrote, the scientific reaction against idealism had set in, and scientific men were generally mechanists or materialists. Lotze sympathized sufficiently with the scientific movement to take a critical attitude toward the earlier philosophy. He retained enough of the latter's spirit, however, to declare in what is, probably, his best known sentence, that while the range of mechanism is universal, yet it is everywhere subordinate to values. The service rendered by them to a kingdom of personal values must be recognized in order to reach a philosophy of nature even when nature is viewed as a mechanical system. But it is in the phenomena of psychology that the facts of value come particularly to light. We are feeling and willing beings as well as intellectual ones, and by feeling, (especially the esthetic), and by moral endeavor we penetrate into the supreme realm of values. Such conceptions had a marked influence on all of Lotze's psychological work.

If Lotze may be regarded, without substantial error, as the founder of physiological psychology, Fechner was, along with the physiologist Weber, the founder of psycho-physics, the attempt to measure psychic facts, to introduce quantitative laws into them and to correlate the results with physical laws. Fechner started with science, but his work in psychophysics had a philosophic motif. He was what is now termed a pan-psychist. He believed that matter and mind are everywhere parallel to each other. Consciousness is not the prerogative of man and the higher animals, but is found in however a low and diffused form everywhere in nature. Not only plants and animals are ensouled, but the planets as well. Consciousness is the way in which things appear to themselves; matter is the form in which psychic processes appear to others. Hence there must be some exact correspondence between psychic and physical facts. This was the germinal idea from which sprang his long and laborious experiments on tone and sight sensations to determine the mathematical relation between the physical stimulus and the psychic event. In carrying on these experiments he devised most of the methods which psychologists use to-day in their laboratories, so that even if his own formulation and interpretation of the "psycho-physic law" be rejected, he remains, nevertheless, the founder of experimental psychology.

With von Hartmann we are again frankly in the realm of philosophy, but with a philosophy which has affiliations with the tendencies of many recent psychologists and psychotherapists who make much of unconscious and sub-conscious psychic events. Von Helmholtz, on the contrary, brings us to a figure who was primarily and fundamentally a man of science—probably, with Darwin, the greatest of the nineteenth century. From the first he was interested in both mathematics and physics, and anatomy and physiology. In all of these branches he was a master, a creator, not a mere follower. His contributions to psychological methods and results sprang from his application to physiological problems of the accurate methods of the physical laboratory. He was the first to measure the velocity of the propagation of impulses through the nerves, a demonstration which opened the way for carrying experimental psychology beyond the measurement of sensory phenomena to reaction-times in general, whether of voluntary movements, associations of ideas or judgments, which in turn led to the method recently applied by Jung to criminal psychology, and to therapeutic psychoanalysis. His important contributions to psychological literature proper are contained in his *Sensations of Tone* and his *Physiological Optics*. Of these Dr. Hall says: "They are and will long remain by far the greatest and most original masterpieces in experimental psychology, the study of which should be supremely incumbent upon all who specialize in this field." Helmholtz, man of science as he was, exhibited the philosophic influence of German idealism, especially of Kant, in his psychological interpretations. Kant had taught that space and time are not properties of real objects but forms of perception, forms so universal and necessary that all phenomena of experience must take on their form. In his treatment of visual space perception, Helmholtz regards space as a psychic arrangement of sensations. The theoretic principle of Helmholtz's treatment of visual and auditory perception is that our sensations are not in any way copies of real things, but are signs of real existences. We habitually pass over all those sensations and qualities of sensation which are not of use to us as practical aids in making our adaptations to our environment. Helmholtz applied this conception in his great contribution to musical esthetics, which also reflects Kant's theory that the beautiful object is one whose perception is in accord with the principles inherent in our reason, although without any consciousness on our part of the rational elements. The psychological counterpart of this doctrine in the region of melody and harmony is found in the role of harmonic overtones bearing a definite mathematical relationship to the fundamental. Because their sensations are of no use to us, we are not ordinarily conscious of them, though the ear may be trained to their distinct discernment. But their presence in the whole, felt not perceived, gives musical tone its beauty.

With Wundt (still living and having his eightieth birthday this month) we are in the presence of a characteristically German university professor of our own day. An experimental psychologist by *Fach*, he has written large tomes on ethics, logic, and metaphysics as well. His work has been the systematization of the scattered facts of physiological and experimental psychology into a separate scientific specialty. This he has accomplished by his monumental work, *Physiological Psychology*, and his establishment of a special laboratory, which has served as a model for most of those now existing throughout the world, and where the majority of the leaders in this field received their training. Dr. Hall's treatment of Wundt is noteworthy for its unsympathetic tone as compared with the enthusiasm he devotes to his other subjects, so much so that he gives a foot-note to a more favorable estimate by Prof. Titchener, one of Wundt's most brilliant pupils and followers. In view of all his disparaging comments, the reader does not quite understand why and how Dr. Hall can say "psychology owes to Wundt a debt far greater than to any other man living or dead." Partly, perhaps, on the score of the voluminousness of his writings, for he notes that Wundt has published 16,000 pages, while Spencer and Hegel have only 12,000 and 11,000 respectively to their credit. I have had, of course, to ignore in this review not only Dr. Hall's excursions into fields suggested by his main topic, but any reference to the details of his treatment. Some readers will probably find that to them the most instructive parts of the book are the synopses of various writings. Sometimes, as with Hartmann, there are brief accounts of all the most important writings; sometimes an almost complete epitome of an entire book, as in the case of Wundt, of whose *Physiological Psychology* there is a sixty-page résumé. One gets an attractive picture of the range of President Hall's own studies of men and books.

The psychological expert will hardly make use of this book as an authority for the history of psychology for the period which it covers. Its scope is at once too limited and diffusively extensive to enable it to serve that end, for which, indeed, it was not intended. But even experts will find the technical material with which they are familiar placed in a larger context of culture and human interests. The beginning student of psychology will get not only this, but also much information agreeably conveyed. The general reader, for whom the book is more especially intended, will achieve an insight into some—though not all—of the main currents which have entered into the contemporary study of mind. All readers will get many interesting glimpses of its author's own philosophy of life and education.

Essays in Radical Empiricism
By William James. New York: Longmans, Green, and Co., 1912.

The history of philosophic thought exhibits few more surprising events than the intellectual achievements of William James in the last decade of his life. Careful readers knew that his monumental *Principles of Psychology* carried, scattered through its pages, the essentials of a philosophic attitude. The essays published in 1897, with the title *The Will to Believe*, elaborated many of these points and gave the name of radical empiricism to the attitude. But, none the less, Mr. James's important work and that to which his reputation attached was in the field of psychology. Indeed, among professional philosophers it was rather the fashion to speak in a tone of amused disparagement of his philosophic attempts. The unusual, the almost unique thing is that after having reached an age when most men simply repeat and expand their own past, Mr. James compelled the whole world to take note that a new way of thinking in philosophy had made its appearance. Of course, much of his influence is due to the remarkable vitality and picturesqueness of his style. But literary style alone does not explain the phenomenon. The times were ready; the general state of the imagination had moved so that it was ready and eager for the very ideas that in the earlier days of James's prophetic vision had meant nothing to it.

The words that happen to close the present volume express the general spirit of Prof. James's thought, and help us understand the rapid extension of his influence: "All philosophies are hypotheses to which all our faculties, emotional as well as logical, help us, and the truest of which will at the final integration of things be found in the possession of the men whose faculties on the whole had the best divining power." We are far enough away from any "final integration of things." But every generation must make its own relative

[First published in *New York Times*, Review of Books, 9 June 1912, p. 357.]

integration, and the extraordinary rapidity with which Pragmatism, as the name for a method, and Radical Empiricism, as the name for a system, have made their way is sufficient tribute to the genuineness of Mr. James's divination. That philosophies are hypotheses, rather than mathematical demonstrations; that personal factors, emotional and aesthetic, enter into the formation of these systems; that strictness of logical reasoning is ultimately effective only in the degree in which it works out an original non-logical vision or divination; and that the vision of Mr. James is extraordinarily pertinent to the general trend of contemporary thought—these things the progress of events has proved.

The present volume of *Essays in Radical Empiricism* is the third and presumably the last (unfortunately) of the writings published since Mr. James's all too early death. Taken together, they leave his philosophy incomplete, a sketch and a program, rather than a carefully wrought and enclosed system, like that, for example, of Bergson. While we cannot too much regret that Mr. James is not still with us to give needed developments and explanations, there is still something congenial to Mr. James's personal temperament and to his philosophy in this unfinished state. For there is nothing more characteristic of the substance of his thought than the belief that the world itself has an element of unfinishedness in it and that one of the standing errors of philosophers has been to attribute to reality a completeness which as matter of fact it does not possess.

In the final essay from which we have already quoted, Mr. James gives so precious an expression of this belief that it may well be quoted at length:

> The "through-and-through" universe seems to suffocate me with its infallible impeccable all-pervasiveness. Its necessity, with no possibilities; its relation, with no subjects, makes me feel as if I had entered into a contract with no reserved rights, or rather as if I had to live in a large seaside boarding-house with no private bed-room in which I might take refuge from the society of the place. . . . The "through-and-through" philosophy seems too buttoned-up and white-chokered and clean-shaven a thing to speak for the vast, slow-breathing, unconscious Kosmos, with its dread abysses and its unknown tides. The "freedom" we want to see there is not the freedom, with a string tied to its leg and warranted not to fly away, of that philosophy.

The present volume falls in with his *Meaning of Truth* rather than with his *Pragmatism* or his *Pluralistic Universe*. It is not a volume of spoken lectures addressed to a more or less popular audience, but a series of written essays addressed for the most part to his professional colleagues. This does not mean that Mr. James has parted with his direct and living style of expression: he could never have surrendered that and remained himself. But it does mean that it occupies itself largely with technical matters and is more argumentative, and less purely expository, in expression. It is concerned not so much with setting forth and making vivid and persuasive a certain attitude and method as with applying that method to the consideration of a number of problems mooted among philosophers. As a consequence, it is quite likely that while pragmatism will be popularly identified with the name of James, in professional philosophic circles the considerations presented in this last volume of posthumous essays will be in the end most influential. At all events, as the editor, Prof. Perry, rightly notes in his preface, Prof. James "came toward the end of his life to regard radical empiricism as more fundamental and more important than pragmatism."

What, then, is this "Radical Empiricism"? Empiricism is an old and well-established doctrine, and it is clear that the key to what is distinctive in the Jamesian type of empiricism is to be found in the adjective "radical." Yet of empiricism in its more generic form he gives his own statement, which must be quoted in order that we may understand its radical quality, for even here Mr. James puts the emphasis in a different place than would be expected by those who have learned to identify empiricism with the sensationalism of Hume and the Mills. In the first place, he dwells upon its hypothetical, non-dogmatic character. It is "contented to regard its most assured conclusions regarding matters of fact as hypotheses liable to modification in the course of future experience." And in the second place, it is a postulate of method of procedure in philosophy. This method may be stated as follows:

> Nothing shall be admitted as fact except what can be experienced at some definite time by some experient; and for

every feature of fact ever so experienced, a definite place must be found somewhere in the final system of philosophy. In other words: Everything real must be experienceable somewhere, and every kind of thing experienced must somewhere be real.

Some light is thrown upon part of the significance of this definition by what Mr. James says elsewhere in reply to a critic who asked him if his view precluded the possibility of things beyond experience, acting and being acted upon by experience. "Assuredly not their possibility," replies Prof. James, adding, "yet in my opinion, we should be wise not to consider any thing or action of that nature, and to restrict our universe of philosophic discourse to what is experienced, or, at least, experienceable."

So far, however, we are well within the limits of an empiricism which was held by many thinkers prior to the writings of James. If we read between the lines, the radical quality of this empiricism is at least suggested in that part of the passage quoted where it is said, "Every kind of thing experienced must somewhere be real." Those who have gone by the name of empiricists have been practically unanimous in denying the reality of universals, indeed, of relations generally. They have spent much time and ingenuity in explaining them away; in showing how they are grafted from without upon particulars which alone are real. In short, they have set out with an idea of what experience must be, and have then translated the facts of experience into accord with their prior assumption. In opposition, James holds that if we go to experience itself "we find the relations between things are just as much matters of direct particular experience, neither more so nor less so, than the things themselves."

The development and application of this proposition are contained particularly in the first five essays of the present volume, all of them, however, enforcing the thesis that various problems which have given philosophers all kind of difficulties are simplified and made solvable if we stick to the empirical relations of different sorts which are found among the various items of our experience. The net outcome is that philosophy must regard reality as an "experience-continuum": the doctrine, more elaborately stated, that "though one part of experience may lean upon another part to make it what it is in any one of several aspects in which it may be considered, experience as a whole is self-sustaining and leans upon nothing else."

The first essay applies the conception of empirical relation to the vexed question of the nature of the physical and psychical, things and consciousness. It propounds the radical, almost revolutionary, doctrine of pure experience which is prior to the distinction of mental and physical and wholly neutral as to the distinction. This room, as directly experienced, for example, is not in itself either physical or mental; it is just what it is as experienced; it is an experience. This experience, however, may enter, in its totality, into two different contexts, or may function in two different ways. When it enters into one context, that which we call the history of the house to which the room belongs, it becomes physical; to be taken in this kind of empirical relationship is, indeed, what we mean by physical. As entering into the context of personal biography, it becomes mental or psychical. Taken in this relation, it is what is called consciousness, and it is all that consciousness is or means in experience. Thus the splitting up of experience into thing and mental state is not original, but is added to an experience as that enters into relations in different ways. Or, as Mr. James sums up the doctrine: "Consciousness connotes a kind of external relation, and does not denote a special stuff or way of being."

This doctrine is sufficiently thoroughgoing that it will occupy philosophers a long time while they digest and criticise it. But it has equally revolutionary attachments. Mr. James also holds that concepts, the world thought of, as well as the world perceived, is in its first presentation a matter of pure experience, in itself neither mental nor physical. We do not remember a memory, we do not imagine a fancy, we do not think a thought. We remember, imagine and think realities, bits of pure experience which as directly experienced are perfectly real. Only because of their subsequent history do these realities get split up, some of them forming, say, the world of ideal mathematical relations wholly objective in their ideality, and some the world of our purely mental reveries.

In the fifth essay, called "The Place of Affectional Facts

in a World of Pure Experience," Mr. James makes a very interesting application of the doctrine of a pure experience to the matter of values and of appreciation. Emotions and affections are generally regarded as purely mental and subjective. At the same time naïvely we treat qualities of value as belonging not just to our feelings but to objects. We speak of a precious diamond, a fine day, a beautiful painting, a good man. Those committed to the doctrine of the purely subjective nature of such qualities regard this attribution of value-qualities to objects as a case of transfer or projection, and build up an elaborate machinery for objectifying the subjective. How much simpler and more direct, says in effect Mr. James, to take these qualities of value as realities, just as they are experienced, recognizing that they afterward become subjective or objective according as they act upon their neighbors in experience. The ambiguity of the qualities of appreciation—such qualities as hateful, lovely, good, evil, fine, ugly, precious, trivial—thus becomes a confirmation of the doctrine of pure experience. The doctrine itself saves us from the necessity either of making the values upon which ethics, aesthetics, and logic depend purely subjective and mental, or of calling in some transcendental, unexperienceable principle to give them validity. It would be hard to find a better illustration of the importance which Mr. James attached to the recognition of the complete reality of the empirical relations which the parts of experience bear to one another.

It is impossible to try in passing to give anything more than indications of the meaning of the principle of pure experience. But we cannot close without noting the classification of kinds of relations which is developed in the second and third essays, especially as this affords the systematic basis of the well-known pluralism of Mr. James. The usual procedure of philosophers, facing the problem of relations, has been either (with the empiricists) to deny their reality altogether, or (with the rationalists) to resolve all things into a single closely knit system of relations, or some kind of all-inclusive absolute. Mr. James suggests the simple but almost revolutionary method of sticking to direct experience and recognizing that various types of relations exist which are incapable of resolution into one another, from the comparative externality and mutual indifference of space, mere coexistence, up to the intimacy and mutual interpenetration of our personal strivings. That the world arrived at by such a method is a much more loosely jointed thing than the world of orthodox realism or idealism, empiricism or rationalism, is indeed true. But what stands in the way of accepting the principle save an a priori prejudice that the whole universe must be made on a single uniform plan? It must also be noted that the same essay contains an application of the Jamesian conception of empirical relations to the explanation of the nature of knowledge—a theory which gives the foundation of his pragmatic theory of truth. It would not do to say that an adequate consideration of this foundation would convert Mr. James's critics, but it is not too much to say that it would put the whole controversy on quite a different basis from that on which it is usually conducted.

The review should not close without a recognition of the care and thoroughness with which the editor of the volume, Prof. Perry of Harvard, has done his work—an acknowledgment all the more due since he has kept this work in the background in the most objective way. It is impossible to estimate as yet what the fate of the Jamesian Radical Empiricism is to be. But this review has wholly failed of its purpose if it has not made clear the reviewer's conviction that Mr. James has opened a new road in philosophic discussion. He has compelled philosophers to rethink their conclusions upon many fundamental matters, because he has led them to a new mode of approach. Mr. James left the new philosophy in too undeveloped a state for it to win disciples wholesale; but the contribution of a new organ of vision and criticism is a more precious contribution than that of a complete system based upon any traditional point of view.

The Enjoyment of Poetry
By Max Eastman. New York: Charles Scribner's Sons, 1913.

I read with great pleasure and profit Max Eastman's book on *The Enjoyment of Poetry*. I know of few books that contain so much good sense, wise philosophy, and correct psychology applied to the elucidation of aesthetics in general and literary appreciation in particular. As a scientific foundation for what is usually termed rhetoric it is much superior to anything with which I am acquainted. The style is more than limpid; it is delightful. It exemplifies the principles of art that it professes and so draws students by its own attractiveness to the literature that it discusses—instead of repelling them, as do many works on literary criticism and interpretation. It would be a piece of rare good fortune if this book found its way into general educational use.

[Previously unpublished (?) statement on Max Eastman's *The Enjoyment of Poetry* (New York: Charles Scribner's Sons, 1913), found in the Eastman Papers, Lilly Library, Indiana University at Bloomington.]

Interest and Effort in Education

1. *Unified Versus Divided Activity*

In the educational lawsuit of interest *versus* effort, let us consider the respective briefs of plaintiff and defendant. In behalf of interest it is claimed that it is the sole guarantee of attention; if we can secure interest in a given set of facts or ideas, we may be perfectly sure that the pupil will direct his energies toward mastering them; if we can secure interest in a certain moral train or line of conduct, we are equally safe in assuming that the child's activities are responding in that direction; if we have not secured interest, we have no safeguard as to what will be done in any given case. As a matter of fact, the doctrine of discipline has not succeeded. It is absurd to suppose that a child gets more intellectual or mental discipline when he goes at a matter unwillingly than when he goes at it out of the fullness of his heart. The theory of effort simply says that unwilling attention (doing something disagreeable because it is disagreeable) should take precedence over spontaneous attention.

Practically, the appeal to sheer effort amounts to nothing. When a child feels that his work is a task, it is only under compulsion that he gives himself to it. At every let-up of external pressure his attention, released from constraint, flies to what interests him. The child brought up on the basis of "effort" acquires marvelous skill in appearing to be occupied with an uninteresting subject, while the real heart of his energies is otherwise engaged. Indeed, the theory contradicts itself. It is psychologically impossible to call forth any activity without some interest. The theory of effort simply substitutes one interest for another. It substitutes the impure interest of fear of the teacher or hope of future reward for pure interest in the material presented. The type of character induced is that illustrated by Emerson at the beginning of his essay on Compensation, where he holds up the current doctrine of compensation as implying that, if you only sacrifice yourself enough now, you will be permitted to indulge yourself a great deal more in the future; or, if you are only good now (goodness consisting in attention to what is uninteresting) you will have, at some future time, a great many more pleasing interests—that is, may then be bad.

While the theory of effort is always holding up to us a strong, vigorous character as the outcome of its method of education, practically we do not get such a character. We get either the narrow, bigoted man who is obstinate and irresponsible save in the line of his own preconceived aims and beliefs; or else a character dull, mechanical, unalert, because the vital juice of spontaneous interest has been squeezed out.

We may now hear the defendant's case. Life, says the other theory, is full of things not interesting that have to be faced. Demands are continually made, situations have to be dealt with, which present no features of interest. Unless one has had previous training in devoting himself to uninteresting work, unless habits have been formed of attending to matters simply because they must be attended to irrespective of the personal satisfaction they afford, character will break down or avoid the issue when confronted with the serious matters of life. Life is not a merely pleasant affair, or a continual satisfaction of personal interests. There must be such continual exercise of effort in the performance of tasks as to form the habit of dealing with the real labors of life. Anything else eats out the fibre of character and leaves a wishy-washy, colorless being; a state of moral dependence, with continual demand for amusement and distraction.

Apart from the question of the future, continually to appeal even in childhood days to the principle of interest is eternally to excite, that is, distract the child. Continuity of activity is destroyed. Everything is made play, amusement. This means overstimulation; it means dissipation of energy. Will is never called into action. The reliance is upon external attractions and amusements. Everything is sugar-coated for the child, and he soon learns to turn from everything that is not artificially surrounded with diverting circumstances. The spoiled child who does only what he likes is an inevitable outcome.

The theory is intellectually as well as morally harmful. Attention is never directed to the essential and important facts, but simply to the attractive wrappings with which the facts are surrounded. If a fact is repulsive or uninteresting, it has to be faced in its own naked character sooner or later. Putting a fringe of fictitious interest around it does not bring the child any nearer to it than he was at the outset. The fact that two and two make four is a naked fact which has to be mastered in and of itself. The child gets no greater hold upon the fact by having attached to it amusing stories of birds or dandelions than if the simple naked fact were presented to him. It is self-deception to suppose that the child is being interested in the numerical relation. His attention is going out to and taking in only the amusing images associated with this relation. The theory thus defeats its own end. It would be more straightforward to recognize at the outset that certain facts having little or no interest must be learned and that the only way to deal with them is through effort, the power of putting forth activity independently of any external inducement. In this way only is the discipline, the habit of responding to serious matters, formed which is necessary for the life that lies ahead of the child.

I have attempted to set forth the respective claims of each side of the discussion. A little reflection will convince us that the strong point in each argument lies not so much in what it says in its own behalf as in its attacks on the weak places of the opposite theory. Each theory is strong in its negations rather than in its position. It is not unusual, though somewhat surprising, that there is generally a common principle unconsciously assumed at the basis of two theories which to all outward appearances are the extreme opposites of each other. Such a common principle is found on the theories of effort and interest in the one-sided forms in which they have already been stated.

The common assumption is that of the externality of the object, idea, or end to be mastered to the self. Because the object or end is assumed to be outside self it has to be *made* interesting; to be surrounded with artificial stimuli and with fictitious inducements to attention. Or, because the object lies outside the sphere of self, the sheer power of "will," the putting forth of effort without interest, has to be appealed to. The genuine principle of interest is the principle of the recognized identity of the fact to be learned or the action proposed with the growing self; that it lies in the direction of the agent's own growth, and is, therefore, imperiously demanded, if the agent is to be himself. Let this condition of identification once be secured, and we have neither to appeal to sheer strength of will, nor to occupy ourselves with making things interesting.

The theory of effort means a virtual division of attention and the corresponding disintegration of character, intellectually and morally. The great fallacy of the so-called effort theory is that it identifies the exercise and training of mind with certain external activities and certain external results. It is supposed that, because a child is occupied at some outward task and because he succeeds in exhibiting the required product, he is really putting forth will, and that definite intellectual and moral habits are in process of formation. But, as a matter of fact, the exercise of will is not found in the external assumption of any posture; the formation of moral habit cannot be identified with ability to show up results at the demand of another. The exercise of will is manifest in the direction of attention, and depends upon the spirit, the motive, the disposition in which work is carried on.

A child may externally be entirely occupied with mastering the multiplication table, and be able to reproduce that table when asked to do so by his teacher. The teacher may congratulate himself that the child has been exercising his will power so as to form right habits. Not so, unless right habit be identified with this ability to show certain results when required. The question of educative training has not been touched until we know what the child has been internally occupied with, what the predominating direction of his attention, his feelings, his disposition has been while he has been engaged upon this task. If the task appeals to him merely as a task, it is as certain psychologically, as is the law of action and reaction physically, that the child is simply engaged in acquiring the habit of divided attention; that he is getting the ability to direct eye and ear, lips and mouth, to what is present before him so as to impress those things upon his memory, while at the same time he is setting his thoughts free to work upon matters of real interest to him.

No account of the educative training actually secured is adequate unless it recognizes the division of attention into which the child is being educated, and faces the question of what the worth of such a division may be. External mechanical attention to a task as a task is inevitably accompanied by random mind-wandering along the lines of the pleasurable.

The spontaneous power of the child, his demand for realization of his own impulses, cannot be suppressed. If the external conditions are such that the child cannot put his activity into the work to be done, he learns, in a most miraculous way, the exact amount of attention that has to be given to this external material to satisfy the requirements of the teacher, while saving up the rest of his powers for following out lines of suggestion that appeal to him. I do not say that there is absolutely no moral training involved in forming these habits of external attention, but I say that there is also a question of moral import as to the formation of habits of intellectual dissipation.

While we are congratulating ourselves upon the well-disciplined habits which the pupil is acquiring (judged by his ability to reproduce a lesson when called upon) we forget to commiserate ourselves because his deeper nature has secured no discipline at all, but has been left to follow its own caprices and the disordered suggestions of the moment. I do not see how anyone can deny that the training of habits of imagination and lines of emotional indulgence is at least equally important with the development of certain outward habits of action. For myself, when it comes to the moral question, not merely to that of practical convenience, I think it is infinitely more important. Nor do I see how anyone at all familiar with the great mass of existing school work can deny that the greater part of the pupils are gradually forming habits of divided attention. If the teacher is skillful and wide-awake, if she is what is termed a good disciplinarian, the child will indeed learn to keep his senses intent in certain ways, but he will also learn to direct his thoughts, which should be concentrated upon subject matter if the latter is to be significant, in quite other directions. It would not be wholly palatable if we had to face the actual condition of the majority of pupils that leave our schools. We should find this division of attention and the resulting disintegration so great that we might cease teaching in sheer disgust. None the less, it is well for us to recognize that this state of things exists, and that it is the inevitable outcome of those conditions which exact the simulation of attention without securing its essence.

The principle of "making" objects and ideas interesting implies the same divorce between object and self. When things have to be *made* interesting, it is because interest itself is wanting. Moreover, the phrase is a misnomer. The thing, the object, is no more interesting than it was before. The appeal is simply made to the child's love of something else. He is excited in a given direction, with the hope that somehow or other during this excitation he will assimilate something otherwise repulsive. There are two types of pleasure. One is the accompaniment of activity. It is found wherever there is successful achievement, mastery, getting on. It is the personal phase of an outgoing energy. This sort of pleasure is always absorbed in the activity itself. It has no separate existence. This is the type of pleasure found in legitimate interest. Its source lies in meeting the needs of the organism. The other sort of pleasure arises from contact. It marks receptivity. Its stimuli are external. It exists by itself as a pleasure, not as the pleasure of activity. Being merely excited by some external stimulus, it is not a quality of any act in which an external object is constructively dealt with.

When objects are made interesting, this latter type of pleasure comes into play. Advantage is taken of the fact that a certain amount of excitation of any organ is pleasurable. The pleasure arising is employed to cover the gap between self and some fact not in itself having interest.

The result is division of energies. In the case of disagreeable effort the division is simultaneous. In this case, it is successive. Instead of having a mechanical, external activity and a random internal activity at the same time, there is oscillation of excitement and apathy. The child alternates between periods of overstimulation and of inertness, as is seen in some so-called kindergartens. Moreover, this excitation of any particular organ, as eye or ear, by itself, creates a further demand for more stimulation of the same sort. It is as possible to create an appetite on the part of the eye or the ear for pleasurable stimulation as it is on the part of taste. Some children are as dependent upon the recurrent presence of bright colors or agreeable sounds as the drunkard is upon his dram. It is this which accounts for the distraction and dissipation of energy characteristic of such children, for their dependence upon external suggestion, and their lack of resources when left to themselves.

The discussion up to this point may be summarized as follows: Genuine interest is the accompaniment of the identification, through action, of the self with some object or idea, because of the necessity of that object or idea for the maintenance of a self-initiated activity. Effort, in the sense in which it may be opposed to interest, implies a separation between the self and the fact to be mastered or task to be performed, and sets up an habitual division of activities. Externally, we have mechanical habits with no mental end or value. Internally, we have random energy or mind-wandering, a sequence of ideas with no end at all, because they are not brought to a focus in action. Interest, in the sense in which it is opposed to effort, means simply an excitation of the sense organ to give pleasure, resulting in strain on one side and listlessness on the other.

But when we recognize there are certain powers within the child urgent for development, needing to be acted out in order to secure their own efficiency and discipline, we have a firm basis upon which to build. Effort arises normally in the attempt to give full operation, and thus growth and completion, to these powers. Adequately to act upon these impulses involves seriousness, absorption, definiteness of purpose; it results in formation of steadiness and persistent habit in the service of worthy ends. But this effort never degenerates into drudgery, or mere strain of dead lift, because interest abides—*the self is concerned throughout. Our first conclusion is that interest means a unified activity.*

2. *Interest As Direct and Indirect*

We now come to our second main topic, the psychology of interest. I begin with a brief descriptive account. Interest is first active, projective, or propulsive. We *take* interest. To be interested in any matter is to be actively concerned with it. Mere feeling regarding a subject may be static or inert, but interest is dynamic. Second, it is objective. We say a man has many interests to care for or look after. We talk about the range of a man's interests, his business interests, local interests, etc. We identify interests with concerns or affairs. Interest does not end simply in itself, as bare feelings may, but is embodied in an object of regard. Third, interest is personal; it signifies a direct concern; a recognition of something at stake, something whose outcome is important for the individual. It has its emotional as well as its active and objective sides. Patent law or electric inventions or politics may be a man's chief interest; but this implies that his personal well-being and satisfaction is somehow bound up with the prosperity of these affairs.

These are the various meanings in which common sense employs the term interest. The root idea of the term seems to be that of being engaged, engrossed, or entirely taken up with some activity because of its recognized worth. The etymology of the term *inter-esse*, "to be between," points in the same direction. Interest marks the annihilation of the distance between the person and the materials and results of his action; it is the sign of their organic union.[1]

1. It is true that the term interest is also used in a definitely disparaging sense. We speak of interest as opposed to principle, of self-interest as a motive to action which regards only one's

1. The active or propulsive phase of interest takes us back to the consideration of impulse and the spontaneous urgencies or tendencies of activity. There is no such thing as absolutely diffuse impartial impulse. Impulse is always differentiated along some more or less specific channel. Impulse has its own special lines of discharge. The old puzzle about the ass between two bundles of hay is only too familiar, but the recognition of its fundamental fallacy is not so common. If the self were purely passive or purely indifferent, waiting upon stimulation from without, then the self illustrated in this supposed example would remain forever helpless, starving to death, because of its equipoise between two sources of food. The error lies in assuming any such passive condition. One is always already doing something, intent on something urgent. And this ongoing activity always gives a bent in one direction rather than another. The ass, in other words, is always already moving toward one bundle rather than the other. No amount of physical cross-eyedness could induce such mental cross-eyedness that the animal would be in a condition of equal stimulation from both sides. Wherever there is life there is activity, an activity having some tendency or direction of its own.

In this primitive condition of spontaneous, impulsive activity we have the basis of natural interest. Interest is no more passively waiting around to be excited from the outside than is impulse. In the selective or preferential quality of impulse we have the fact that at any given time, if we are awake at all, we are always interested in one direction rather than another. The condition either of total lack of interest, or of impartially distributed interest, is as mythical as the story of the ass in scholastic ethics.

2. The objective side of interest. Every interest, as already said, attaches itself to an object. The artist is interested in his brushes, in his colors, in his technique. The

personal advantage; but these are neither the only nor the controlling senses in which the term is used. It may fairly be questioned whether this is anything but a narrowing or degrading of the legitimate sense of the term. However that may be, it appears certain that controversy regarding the use of interest arises because one party is using the term in the larger, objective sense of recognized value or engrossing activity, while the other is using it as equivalent to a selfish motive.

business man is interested in the play of supply and demand, in the movement of markets, etc. Take whatever instance of interest we choose, and we shall find that, if we cut out an object about which interest clusters, interest itself disappears relapsing into empty feeling.

Error begins in supposing the object already there, and then calling the activity into being. Canvas, brushes, and paints interest the artist, for example, because they help him discover and promote his existing artistic capacity. There is nothing in a wheel and a piece of string to arouse a child's activity save as they appeal to some instinct or impulse already active, and supply it with means of execution. The number twelve is uninteresting when it is a bare, external fact; it has interest (just as has the top or wheelbarrow or toy locomotive) when it presents itself as an instrument of carrying into effect some dawning energy or desire—making a box, measuring one's height, etc. And in its difference of degree exactly the same principle holds of the most technical items of scientific or historic knowledge—whatever furthers action, helps mental movement, is of interest.

3. We now come to the emotional phase. Value is not only objective but also subjective. There is not only the thing which is projected as valuable or worth while, but there is also appreciation of its worth.

The gist of the psychology of interest may, accordingly, be stated as follows: An interest is primarily a form of self-expressive activity—that is, of growth that comes through acting upon nascent tendencies. If we examine this activity on the side of what is done, we get its objective features, the ideas, objects, etc., to which the interest is attached, about which it clusters. If we take into account that it is *self*-development, that self finds itself in this content, we get its emotional or appreciative side. Any account of genuine interest must, therefore, grasp it as outgoing activity holding within its grasp an object of direct value.

There are cases where action is direct and immediate. It puts itself forth with no thought of anything beyond. It satisfies in and of itself. The end *is* the present activity, and so there is no gap in the mind between means and end. All play is of this immediate character. Purely aesthetic appreciation approximates this type. The existing experience holds us for its own sake, and we do not demand that it take us into something beyond itself. With the child and his ball, the amateur and the hearing of a symphony, the present object engrosses. Its value is there, and is there in what is directly present.

On the other hand, we have cases of indirect, transferred, or technically speaking, mediated interest. Things indifferent or even repulsive in themselves often become of interest because of assuming relationships and connections of which we were previously unaware. Many a student, of so-called practical make-up, has found mathematical theory, once repellent, lit up by great attractiveness after studying some form of engineering in which this theory was a necessary tool. The musical score and the technique of fingering, in which the child finds no interest when it is presented as an end in itself, when it is isolated, becomes fascinating when the child realizes its place and bearings in helping him give better and fuller utterance to his love of song. Whether it appeals or fails to appeal is a question of relationship. While the little child takes only a near view of things, as he grows in experience he becomes capable of extending his range, and seeing an act, or a thing, or a fact not by itself, but as part of a larger whole. If this whole belongs to him, if it is a mode of his own movement, then the thing or act which it includes gains interest too.

Here, and here only, have we the reality of the idea of "making things interesting." I know of no more demoralizing doctrine—when taken literally—than the assertion of some of the opponents of interest that *after* subject-matter has been selected, *then* the teacher should make it interesting. This combines in itself two thoroughgoing errors. On one side, it makes the selection of subject-matter a matter quite independent of the question of interest—that is to say of the child's native urgencies and needs; and, further, it reduces method in instruction to more or less external and artificial devices for dressing up the unrelated materials, so that they will get some hold upon attention. In reality, the principle of "making things interesting" means that subjects be selected in relation to the child's present experience, powers, and needs; and that (in case he does not perceive or appreciate this relevancy) the new material be presented in such a way as to enable the child to appreciate its bearings, its relationships, its value in connection with what already has significance for him. It is *this bringing to consciousness of the bearings of the new material* which constitutes the reality, so often perverted both by friend and foe, in "making things interesting."

In other words, the problem is one of *intrinsic* connection as a motive for attention. The teacher who tells the child he will be kept after school if he doesn't recite his geography lesson better[2] is appealing to the psychology of mediate interest. The old English method of rapping knuckles for false Latin quantities is one way of arousing interest in the intricacies of Latin. To offer a child a bribe, or a promise of teacher's affection, or promotion to the next grade, or ability to make money, or to take a position in society, are other modes. They are cases of transferred interest. But the criterion for judging them lies just here: How far is one interest externally attached to another, or substituted for another? How far does the new appeal, the new motive, serve to interpret, to bring out, to *relate* the material otherwise without interest? It is a question, again, of *inter-esse*. The problem may be stated as one of the relations of means and end. Anything indifferent or repellent becomes of interest when seen as a means to an end already commanding attention; or seen as an end that will allow means already under control to secure further movement and outlet. But, in normal growth the interest in means is not externally tied on to the interest in an end; it suffuses, saturates, and thus transforms it. It interprets or revalues it—gives it a new significance. The man who has a wife and family has thereby a new motive for his daily work—he sees a new meaning in

2. I have heard it argued in all seriousness that a child kept after school to study has often acquired an interest in arithmetic or grammar which he didn't have before, as if this proved the efficacy of "discipline" *versus* interest. Of course, the reality is that the greater leisure, the opportunity for individual explanation afforded, served to bring the material into its proper relations in the child's mind—he "got a hold" of it.

it, and takes into it a steadiness and enthusiasm previously lacking. But when he does his day's work as a thing intrinsically disagreeable, as drudgery, simply for the sake of the final wage-reward, the case is quite different. Means and end remain remote; they do not permeate one another. The person is no more really interested in his work than he was before; in itself, it is a hardship to be escaped from. Hence he cannot give full attention to it; he cannot put himself unreservedly into it. But to the other man every stroke of work may literally mean his wife and baby. Externally, physically, they are remote; mentally, with respect to his plan of living, they are one; they have the same value. In drudgery on the contrary means and end remain as separate in consciousness as they are in space and time. What is true of this is true of every attempt in teaching to "create interest" by appeal to external motives.

At the opposite scale, take a case of artistic construction. The sculptor has his end, his ideal, in view. To realize that end he must go through a series of intervening steps which are not, on their face, equivalent to the end. He must model and mold and chisel; perform a series of particular acts, no one of which exhibits or *is* the beautiful form he has in mind, and every one of which represents the putting forth of personal energy. But because these are necessary means in the achieving of his activity, the meaning of the finished form is transferred over into these special acts. Each molding of the clay, each stroke of the chisel, is for him at the time the whole end in process of realization. Whatever interest or value attaches to the end attaches to each of these steps. He is as much absorbed in one as in the other. Any failure in this complete identification means an inartistic product, means that he is not really interested in his ideal. Upon the other hand, his interest is in the end regarded as an end *of* the particular processes which are its means. Interest attaches to it because of its place in the active process of what it is but the culmination. He may also regret the approach of the day that will put an end to such an interesting piece of work. At all events, it is not the mere external *product* that holds him.

We have spoken freely of means and ends because these

terms are in common use. We must, however, analyze them somewhat to make sure they are not misunderstood. *The terms "means" and "end" apply primarily to the position occupied by acts as stages of a single developing activity*, and only secondarily to things or objects. The end really means the final stage of an activity, its last or terminal period; the means are the earlier phases, those gone through before the activity reaches its termination. This is plainly seen in, say, the leisurely eating of a meal, as distinct from rushing through it to have it over as soon as possible; in the playing of the game of ball, in listening to a musical theme. In each case there is a definite outcome; after the meal is eaten, there is a certain amount of food in the system; when the nine innings of the game of baseball are ended, one side or the other has won. Henceforth—afterwards—it is possible to separate the external result from the process, from the continuous activity which led up to it. *Afterwards* we tend to separate the result from the process; to regard the result of the process as the end and the whole process as simply a means to the external result. But in civilized society, eating is not merely a means to getting so much food-power into the system; it is a social process, a time of family and friendly reunion; moreover, each course of the meal has its own enjoyment just as a matter of *partaking* of food, that is, of an active continuing process. Division into means and end hardly has any meaning. Each stage of the entire process has its own adequate significance or interest; the earlier quite as much as the latter. Even here, however, there is a tendency to keep the best till the last—the dessert comes at the end. That is, there is a tendency to make the *last* stage a *fulfilling* or consummating stage.

In the hearing of the musical theme, the earlier stages are far from being mere means to the later; they give the mind a certain set and dispose it to anticipate later developments. So the end, the conclusion, is not a mere last thing in time; it *completes* what has gone before; it settles, so to speak, the character of the theme as a whole. In the ball game, the interest may intensify with every passing stage of the game; the last inning *finally* settles who wins and who loses, a matter which up to that time has been in suspense or doubt. In the game, the last stage is not only the last in time, but also settles the character of the entire game, and so gives meaning to all that has preceded. Nevertheless the earlier parts of the game are true parts of the game; they are not mere means for reaching a last inning.

In these illustrations we have seen how the last stage may be the fulfilling, the completing, or consummating of all that has gone before, and may thus decide the nature of the activity as a whole. In no case, however, is the end equivalent simply to an external result. The mere fact that one side won —the external result or object—is of no significance apart from the game whose conclusion it marks. Just so, we may say that the value of x in an algebraic equation is 5. But to say in general that x equals 5 is nonsense. This result is significant only as the outcome of a particular process of solving a particular equation. If, however, the mathematical inquiry is carried on to deal with other connected equations, it is possible to separate the result, 5, from what led up to it, and in further calculating to use 5 independently of the equation whose solution it was. This fact introduces a further complication.

Many, most, of our activities, are interconnected. We not only have the process of eating the meal, but we have the further use of the food eaten—its assimilation and transformation into energy for new operations. The musical theme heard may represent a step in a more continuous process of musical education. The outcome of the game may be a factor in determining the relative standing of two clubs in a series of contests. An inventor of a new telephonic device is preoccupied with the different steps of the process; but when the invention is completed, it becomes a factor in a different set of activities. When the artist has finished his picture, his question may be how to sell that picture so as to get a living for his family. This fact of the employment of the result of one course of action as a ready-made factor in some other course leads us to think of means and ends as fixed things external to an activity, and to think of the whole activity as a mere means to an external product. The ball game is thus thought of as a mere means to winning, and that winning in turn as a mere means to winning a series. Winning the series may in turn be regarded as a mere means of getting a sum of money or a certain amount of glory, and so on indefinitely. Unless discussion is to get confused, we must therefore carefully distinguish between two senses of the term end. While the activity is in progress, "end" simply means an object as standing for the culminating stage of the whole process; it represents the need of looking ahead and considering what we are now doing so that it will lead as simply and effectively as possible into what is to be done later. *After* the activity has come to its conclusion, "end" means the product accomplished as a fixed thing. The same considerations apply to the term "means." During the activity it signifies simply the materials or ways of acting involved in the successive stages of the growth of an activity up to its fulfillment. After the activity is accomplished, its product as detached from the action that led up to it may be used as a means for achieving something else.

This distinction is not a merely theoretical one, but one that affects the whole scope and significance of interest in teaching. The purely adventitious interests we have discussed —making a thing interesting by the sugar-coating method—assumes a certain ready subject-matter—a subject-matter existing wholly independently of the pupil's own activity. It then asks how this alien subject-matter may be introduced into the pupil's mind; how his attention may be drawn away from the things with which it is naturally concerned and drawn to this indifferent, ready-made external material. Some interest, some bond of connection, must be found. Prevalent practices and the training and disposition of the teacher will decide whether the methods of "hard" or of "soft" pedagogy shall be resorted to; whether we shall have a "soup-kitchen" type of teaching or a "penitentiary" type. Shall the indifferent thing (indifferent because lying outside of the individual's scheme of activities) be made interesting—by clothing it with adventitious traits that are agreeable; or by methods of threats—by making attention to it less disagreeable than the consequences of non-attention so that study is a choice of the lesser of two evils?

Both of these methods, however, represent failure to ask the right question and to seek for the right method of solution. What course of activity exists already (by native endowment or by past achievement) operative in the pupil's experience *with respect to which the thing to be learned, the mode of skill to be acquired, is either a means or an end?* What line of action is there, that is to say, which can be carried forward to its appropriate termination better by noting and using the subject-matter? Or what line of action is there, which can be directed so that when carried to its completion it will naturally terminate in the things to be learned? The mistake, once more, consists in overlooking the activities in which the child is already engaged, or in assuming that they are so trivial or so irrelevant that they have no significance for education. When they are duly taken into account the new subject-matter is interesting on its own account in the degree in which it enters into their operation. The mistake lies in treating these existing activities as if they had reached their limit of growth; as if they were satisfactory in their present shape and simply something to be excited; or else just unsatisfactory and something to be repressed.

The distinction between means and ends external to a process of action and those intrinsic to it enables us to understand the difference between pleasures and happiness. In the degree in which anybody externally happens to fall upon anything and to be excited agreeably by it, pleasure results. The question of pleasure is a question of the immediate or momentary reaction. Happiness differs in quality from both a pleasure and a series of pleasures. Children are almost always happy, joyous—and so are grown people—when engaged consecutively in any unconstrained mode of activity—when they are occupied, busy. The emotional accompaniment of the progressive growth of a course of action, a continual movement of expansion and of achievement, is happiness;—mental content or peace, which when emphatic, is called joy, delight. Persons, children or adults, are interested in what they can do successfully, in what they approach with confidence and engage in with a sense of accomplishment. Such happiness or interest is not self-conscious or selfish; it is a sign of developing power and of absorption in what is being done. Only when an activity is monotonous does happiness cease to attend its performance, and monotony means that growth, development, have ceased; nothing new is entering in to carry an activity forward. On the other hand, lack of normal occupations brings uneasiness, irritability, and demand for any kind of stimulation which will arouse activity —a state that easily passes into a longing for excitement for its own sake. Healthy children in a healthy family or social environment do not ask, "What pleasure can I have now?" but "What can I *do* now?" The demand is for a growing activity, an occupation, an interest. Given that, happiness will take care of itself.

There is no rigid, insurmountable line between direct and indirect interest. As an activity grows more complex, it involves more factors. A child who is simply building with blocks has an activity of very short time span; his end is *just* ahead of what he is doing at the moment—namely, to keep on building so that his pile grows higher—does not tumble down. It makes no difference to him just what he makes, as long as it stands up. When the pile tumbles, he is content to start over again. But when he aims at something more complicated, the erection of a certain kind of structure with his blocks, the increased complexity of the end gives the cycle of his actions a longer time span; arrival at its end is postponed. He must do more things before he reaches his result, and accordingly he must carry that result in mind for a longer time as a control of his actions from moment to moment. Gradually this situation passes over into one where an immediate activity would make no appeal at all were it not for some more remote end which is valuable and for the sake of which intervening means, not of themselves of concern, are important. With trained adults an end in the distant future, a result to be reached only after a term of years, may stimulate and regulate a long series of difficult intervening steps which, in isolation from the thought of the end, would be matters of total indifference, or even repellent. From this side, then, the development of indirect interests is simply a sign of the growth or expansion of simple activities into more complex ones, requiring longer and longer periods of time for their execution, and consequently involving postponement of achieving the end which gives decisive meaning and full worth to the intervening steps.

Not only, however, does the direct interest in an object pass thus gradually and naturally into indirect interest as the scope of action is prolonged, but the reverse process takes place. Indirect values become direct. Everybody has heard of the man who at first is interested in an acquisition of money because of what he can do with it and who finally becomes so absorbed in the mere possessing of gold that he gloats over it. This clearly expresses an undesirable instance of the change of means into end. But normal and desirable changes of the same kind are frequent. Pupils who are first interested in, say, number relations, because of what they can do with these relations in making something else (at first interested, that is, in a branch of arithmetic simply as a means or tool), may become fascinated by what they can do with number on its own account.[3]

Boys who are at first interested in skill in playing marbles or ball, simply because it is a factor in a game which interests them, become interested in practicing the acts of shooting at a mark, of throwing, catching, etc., and so arduously devote themselves to the perfecting of skill. The technical exercises that give skill in the game become themselves a sort of a game. Girls who are interested in making clothes for a doll, simply for the sake of the interest in playing with dolls, may develop an interest in making clothes till the doll itself becomes simply a sort of an excuse, or at least just a stimulus, for making clothes.

If the reader will reflect upon his own course of life over a certain period of time, he will find that the sort of thing which is somewhat trivially illustrated in these examples is of constant occurrence. He will find that wherever his activities have grown in extent and range of meaning (instead of becoming petrified and fossilized), one or other (or both) of two things has been going on. On the one hand, narrower and simpler types of interest (requiring a shorter time for their realization) have been expanding to cover a longer time. With this change they have grown richer and fuller. They have grown to include many things previously indiffer-

3. In our usual terminology interest in "concrete" number passes into an interest in "abstract" number.

ent or even repulsive as the value of the end now takes up into itself the value of whatever is involved in the process of achieving it. On the other hand, many things, that were first of significance only because they were needed as parts of an activity of interest only as a whole, have become valued on their own account. Sometimes it will even be found that they have displaced entirely the type of activity in connection with which they originally grew up. This is just what happens when children outgrow interests that have previously held them; as when boys feel it is now beneath them to play marbles and girls find themselves no longer interested in their dolls. Looked at superficially, the original interest seems simply to have been crowded out or left behind. Examined more carefully, it will be found that activities and objects at first esteemed simply because of their place within the original activity have grown to be of more account than that for the sake of which they were at first entertained. In many cases, unless the simpler and seemingly more trivial interest had had sway at the proper time, the later more important and specialized activity would not have arisen. And this same process can be verified in adult development as well, *as long as development goes on.* When it ceases, arrest of growth sets in.

We are now in a position to restate, in a more significant way, the true and the false ways of understanding the function of interest in education, and to formulate a criterion for judging whether the principle of interest is being rightly or wrongly employed. *Interest is normal and reliance upon it educationally legitimate in the degree in which the activity in question involves growth or development. Interest is illegitimately used in the degree in which it is either a symptom or a cause of arrested development in an activity.*

These formulae are of course abtract and far from self-explanatory. But in the light of our prior discussion their significance should be obvious. When interest is objected to as merely amusement or fooling or a temporary excitation (or when in educational practice it does mean simply such things), it will be found that the interest in question is something which attaches merely to a momentary activity *apart from its place in an enduring activity*—an activity that develops through a period of time. When this happens, the object that arouses (what is called) interest is esteemed just on the basis of the momentary reaction it calls out, the immediate pleasure it excites. "Interest" so created is abnormal, for it is a sign of the dissipation of energy; it is a symptom that life is being cut up into a series of disconnected reactions, each one of which is esteemed by itself apart from what it does in carrying forward (or developing) a consecutive activity. As we have already seen, it is one thing to make, say, number interesting by merely attaching to it other things that happen to call out a pleasurable reaction; it is a radically different sort of thing to make it interesting by introducing it so that it functions as a genuine means of carrying on a more inclusive activity. In the latter case, interest does not mean the excitation due to the association of some other thing irrelevant to number; it means that number is of interest because it has a function in the furtherance of a continuous or enduring line of activity.

Our conclusion, then, is not simply that some interests are good while others are bad; but that true interests are signs that some material, object, mode of skill (or whatever) is appreciated on the basis of what it actually does in carrying to fulfillment some mode of action with which a person has identified himself. Genuine interest, in short, simply means that a person has identified himself with, or has found himself in, a certain course of action. Consequently he is identified with whatever objects and forms of skill are involved in the successful prosecution of that course. This course of action may cover greater or shorter time according to circumstances, particularly according to the experience and maturity of the person concerned. It is absurd to expect a young child to be engaged in an activity as complex as that of an older child, or the older child as in that of an adult. But some expansion, enduring through some length of time, is entailed. Even a baby interested in hitting a saucer with a spoon is not concerned with a purely momentary reaction and excitation. The hitting is connected with the sound to follow, and has interest on that account; and the resulting sound has interest not in its isolation, but as a consequence of the striking. An activity of such a short span forms a direct interest, and spontaneous play activities in general are of this sort. For (to repeat what has already been said) in such cases it is not necessary to bear the later and fulfilling activities in mind in order to keep the earlier activities agoing and to direct their manner of performance and their order or sequence. But the more elaborate the action, the longer the time required by the activity; the longer the time, the more the consummating or fulfilling stage is postponed; and the longer the postponement, the greater the opportunity for the interest in the end to come into conflict with interest in intervening steps.

The next step in the discussion consists in seeing that effort comes into play in the degree in which achievement of an activity is postponed or remote; and that the significance of situations demanding effort is their connection with thought.

3. *Effort, Thinking, and Motivation*

What is it that we really prize under the name of effort? What is it that we are really trying to secure when we regard increase in ability to put forth effort as an aim of education? Taken practically, there is no great difficulty in answering. What we are after is *persistency, consecutiveness,* of activity: endurance against obstacles and through hindrances. Effort regarded as mere increase of strain in the expenditure of energy is not in itself a thing we esteem. Barely in itself it is a thing we would avoid. A child is lifting a weight that is too heavy for him. It takes an increasing amount of effort, involving increase of strain which is increasingly painful, to lift it higher and higher. The wise parent tries to protect the child from mere strain; from the danger of excessive fatigue, of damaging the structures of the body, of getting bruises. Effort as mere strained activity is thus not what we prize. On the other hand, a judicious parent will not like to see a child too easily discouraged by meeting obstacles. If the child is physically healthy, surrender of a course of action, or diversion of energy to some easier line of action, is a bad symptom if it shows itself at the first sign of resistance. The demand for effort is a demand for *continuity* in the face of difficulties.

This account of the matter is so obvious as to lie upon the surface. When we examine into it further, however, we find it only repeats what we have already learned in connection with interest as an accompaniment of an *expanding* activity. Effort, like interest, is significant only in connection with a *course* of action, an action that takes time for its completion since it develops through a succession of stages. Apart from an end to be reached, effort would never be anything more than a momentary strain or a succession of such strains. It would be a thing to be avoided, not so much for its disagreeableness as because nothing comes of it save exposure to dangers of exhaustion and accident. But where the action is a developing or growing one, effort, willingness to put forth energy at any point of the entire activity, measures the hold which the activity, as one whole affair, has upon a person. It shows how much he really cares for it. We never (if we are sensible) take, in ourselves or in somebody else, the "will for the deed" unless there is evidence that there really *was* a will, a purpose; and the sole evidence is some *striving* to realize the purpose, the putting forth of effort. If conditions forbid all effort, it is not a question of "will" at all, but simply of a sympathetic wish.

This does not mean, of course, that effort is always desirable under such conditions. On the contrary, the game may not be worth the candle; the end to be reached may not be of sufficient importance to justify the expenditure of so much energy, or of running the risks of excessive strain. Judgment comes in to decide such matters, and speaking generally it is as much a sign of bad judgment to keep on at *all* costs in an activity once entered upon, as it is a sign of weakness to be turned from it at the first evidence of difficulties. The principle laid down shows that effort is significant not as *bare* effort, or strain, but in connection with carrying forward an activity to its fulfillment: it all depends, as we say, upon the end.

Two considerations follow. (1) On the one hand, when an activity persists in spite of its temporary blocking by an obstacle, there is a situation of *mental* stress: a peculiar emotional condition of combined desire and aversion. The end continues to make an appeal, and to hold one to the activity in spite of its interruption by difficulties. This continued forward appeal gives desire. The obstacle, on the other hand, in the degree in which it arrests or thwarts progress ahead, inhibits action, and tends to divert it into some other channel—to avert action, in other words, from the original end. This gives aversion. Effort, as a mental experience, is precisely this *peculiar combination of conflicting tendencies*—tendencies away from and tendencies towards: dislike and longing.

(2) The other consideration is even more important, for it decides what happens. The emotion of effort, or of stress, is a warning to *think*, to consider, to reflect, to inquire, to look into the matter. Is the end worth while under the circumstances? Is there not some other course which, under the circumstances, is better? So far as this reconsideration takes place, the situation is quite different from that of a person merely giving up as soon as an obstacle shows itself. Even if the final decision is to give up, the case is radically different from the case of giving up from mere instability of purpose. The giving up now involves an appeal to reason, and may be quite consistent with tenacity of purpose or "strength of will." However, reflection may take quite another course: it may lead not to reconsideration of ends, but to seeking for *new* means; in short, to discovery and invention also. The child who cannot carry the stone that he wishes may neither keep on in a fruitless struggle to achieve the impossible, nor yet surrender his purpose; he may be led to think of some other way of getting the stone into motion; he may try prying it along with a bar. "Necessity is the mother of invention."

In the latter case, the obstacle has, indeed, diverted energy; but the significant thing is that energy is *diverted into thinking*; into an intelligent consideration of the situation and of available ways and means. The really important matter in the experience of effort concerns its connection with thought. The question is not the amount of sheer strain involved, but the way in which the *thought of an end* persists in spite of difficulties, and induces a person to reflect upon the nature of the obstacles and the available resources by which they may be dealt with.

A person, child or adult, comes, in the course of an activity, up against some obstacle or difficulty. This experience of resistance has a double effect;—though in a given case one effect may predominate and obscure the other. One effect is weakening of the impetus in the forward direction; the existing line of action becomes more or less uncongenial because of the strain required to overcome difficulties. As a consequence, the tendency is to give up this line of action and to divert energy into some other channel. On the other hand, meeting an obstacle may enhance a person's perception of an end; may make him realize more clearly than ever he did before how much it means to him; and accordingly may brace him, invigorate him in his effort to achieve the end. Within certain limits, resistance only arouses energy; it acts as a stimulus. Only a spoiled child or pampered adult is dismayed or discouraged and turned aside, instead of being aroused, by lions in the path—unless the lions are very fierce and threatening. It is not too much to say that a normal person *demands* a certain amount of difficulty to surmount in order that he may have a full and vivid sense of what he is about, and hence have a lively interest in what he is doing.

Meeting obstacles makes a person project more definitely to himself the later and consummating period of his activity; it brings the end of his course of action *to consciousness*. He now *thinks* of what he is doing, instead of doing it blindly from instinct or habit. The result becomes a conscious aim, a guiding and inspiring purpose. In being an object of desire, it is also an object of endeavor.

This arousing and guiding function is exercised in two ways. Endeavor is steadied and made more persistent when its outcome is regarded as something to be achieved; and thought is stimulated to discover the best methods of dealing with the situation. The person who keeps on blindly pushing against an obstacle, trying to break through by main strength, is the one who acts unintelligently; the one who does not present to himself the nature of the end to be reached. He remains on the level of a struggling animal, who by mere quantity of brute strength tries to break down resistance and win to his goal. The true function of the conditions that call forth effort is, then, first, to make an individual more *conscious of the end and purpose of his actions*; secondly, to *turn his energy from blind, or thoughtless, struggle into reflective judgment*. These two phases of thought are interdependent. The thought of the result, the end as a conscious guiding purpose, leads to the search for means of achievement; it suggests appropriate courses of action to be tried. These means as considered and attempted supply a fuller content to the thought of the end. A boy starts somewhat blindly to make a kite; in the course of his operations he comes across unexpected difficulties; his kite doesn't hold together, or it won't balance. Unless his activity has a slight hold upon him, he is thereby made aware more definitely of just what he intends to make; he conceives the object and end of his actions more distinctly and fully. His end is now not just *a* kite, but some special kind of a kite. Then he inquires what is the matter, what is the trouble, with his existing construction, and searches for remedial measures. As he does this, his thought of the kite as a complete whole becomes more adequate; then he sees his way more clearly what to do to make the kite, and so on.

We are now in possession of a criterion for estimating the place in an educative development of difficulties and of effort. If one mean by a task simply an undertaking involving difficulties that have to be overcome, then children, youth, and adults alike require tasks in order that there may be continued development. But if one mean by a task something that has no interest, makes no appeal, that is wholly alien and hence uncongenial, the matter is quite different. Tasks in the former sense are educative because they supply an indispensable stimulus to thinking, to reflective inquiry. Tasks in the latter sense signify nothing but sheer strain, constraint, and the need of some external motivation for keeping at them. They are *un*educative because they fail to introduce a clearer consciousness of ends and a search for proper means of realization. They are *mis*educative, because they deaden and stupefy; they lead to that confused and dulled state of mind that always attends an action carried on without a realizing sense of what it is all about. They are also miseducative because they lead to dependence upon external ends; the child works simply because of the pressure of the taskmaster, and diverts his energies just in the degree in which this pressure is relaxed; or he works because of some alien inducement—to get some reward that has no intrinsic connection with what he is doing.

The question to be borne in mind is, then, twofold: Is this person doing something too easy for him—something which has not a sufficient element of resistance to arouse his energies, especially his energies of thinking? Or is the work assigned so difficult that he has not the resources required in order to cope with it—so alien to his experience and his acquired habits that he does not know where or how to take hold? Between these two questions lies the teacher's task—for the teacher has a problem as well as the pupil. How shall the activities of pupils be progressively complicated by the introduction of difficulties, and yet these difficulties be of a nature to stimulate instead of dulling and merely discouraging? The judgment, the tact, the intellectual sympathy of instructors is taxed to the uttermost in answering these questions in the concrete with respect to the various subjects of study.

When an activity is too easy and simple, a person either engages in it because of the immediate pleasurable excitement it awakens, or he puts just enough of his powers upon it—their purely mechanical and physical side—to perform what is required in a perfunctory way, while he lets his mind wander to other things where there is at least enough novelty to keep his fancies going. Strange as it may seem to say it, one of the chief objections both to mechanical drill work and to the assigning of subject-matter too difficult for pupils is that the only activity to which they actually incite the pupils is in lines too *easy* for them. Only the powers already formed, the habits already fixed, are called into play; the mind—the power of thinking—is not called into action. Hence apathy in children naturally sluggish, or mind-wandering in children of a more imaginative nature. What happens when work too difficult, work beyond the limits of capacity, is insisted upon? If the teacher is professionally skilled, a pupil will not be able entirely to shirk or to escape. He must keep up the *form* of attentive study, and produce a result as evidence of having been occupied. Naturally he seeks short cuts; he does what he can do without recourse to processes of thinking that are beyond him. Any external and routine device is employed to "get the answer"—possibly surreptitious aid from others or downright cheating. Any way, he does what is already easiest for him to do; he follows the line of least resistance. The sole alternative is the use of initiative in thinking out the conditions of the problem and the way to go at it. And this alternative is within his reach only when the work to be done is of a nature to make an appeal to him, or to enlist his powers; and when the difficulties are such as to stimulate instead of depressing.

Good teaching, in other words, is teaching that appeals to established powers while it includes such *new* material as will demand their redirection for a new end, this redirection requiring thought—intelligent effort. In every case, the educational significance of effort, its value for an educative growth, resides in its connection with a stimulation of greater *thoughtfulness*, not in the greater strain it imposes. Educative effort is a sign of the transformation of a comparatively blind activity (whether impulsive or habitual) into a more consciously reflective one.

For the sake of completeness of statement, we will say (what hardly should now require statement on its own account) that such effort is in no sense a foe of interest. It is a part of the process of growth of activity from direct interest to indirect. In our previous section, we considered this development as meaning an increase of the complexity of an activity (that is, of the number of factors involved), and the increased importance of its outcome as a motive, in spite of contrary appeals, for devotion to intervening means. In this section, we have brought out more emphatically the fact that along with this increasing remoteness of the end (the longer period required for the consummation of an activity) goes a greater number of difficulties to be overcome, and the consequent need of effort. And our conclusion has been that the effort needed is secured when the activity in question is of such positive and abiding interest as to arouse the person to clearer recognition of purpose and to a more thoughtful consideration of means of accomplishment. The educator who associates difficulties and effort with *increased depth and scope of thinking* will never go far wrong. The one who associates it with sheer strain, sheer dead lift of energy, will never understand either how to secure the needed effort when it is needed nor the best way to utilize the energy aroused.

It remains to apply what has been said to the question of motivation. "Motive" is the name for the end or aim in respect to its hold on *action*, its power to *move*. It is one thing to speculate idly upon possible results, to keep them before the mind in a purely theoretical way. It is another thing for the results contemplated or projected to be so desired that the thought of them stirs endeavor. "Motive" is a name for the end in its active or dynamic capacity. It would be mere repetition of our previous analysis to show that this moving power expresses the extent to which the end foreseen is bound up with an activity with which the self is identified. It is enough to note that the motive force of an end and the interest that the end possesses are equivalent expressions of the vitality and depth of a proposed course of activity.

A word of warning may be in place against taking the idea of motivation in too *personal* a sense, in a sense too detached, that is, from the object or end in view. In the theory of instruction, as distinct from its practice, the need of motivation was for a long time overlooked or even denied. It was assumed that sheer force of will, arbitrary effort, was alone required. In practice this meant (as we have seen) appeal to extraneous sources of motivation: to reverence for the authority of teacher or text; to fear of punishment or the displeasure of others; to regard for success in adult life; to winning a prize; to standing higher than one's fellows; to fear of not being promoted, etc. The next step was taken when some educators recognized the ineffective hold of such motives upon many pupils—their lack of adequate motivating force in the concrete. They looked for motives which would have more weight with the average pupil. But too often they still conceived the motive as outside the subject-matter, something existing purely in the feelings, and giving a reason for attention to a matter that in itself would not provide a motive. They looked *for* a motive for the study or the lesson, instead of a motive *in* it. Some reason must be found in the *person*, apart from the arithmetic or the geography or the manual activity, that might be attached to the lesson material so as to give it a leverage, or moving force.

One effect was to substitute a discussion of "motives" in the abstract for a consideration of subject-matter in the concrete. The tendency was to make out a list of motives or "interests" by which children in general or children of a given age are supposed to be actuated, and then to consider how these might be linked up with the various lessons so as to impart efficacy to the latter. The important question, however, is what specific subject-matter is so connected with the growth of the child's existing concrete capabilities as to give it a moving force. What is needed is not an inventory of personal motives which we suppose children to have, but a consideration of their *powers*, their tendencies in action, and the ways in which these can be carried forward by a given subject-matter.

If a child has, for example, an artistic capacity in the direction of music or drawing, it is not necessary to find a motive for its exercise. The problem is not to find a motive, but to find material of and conditions for its exercise. Any material that appeals to this capacity has by that very fact motivating force. The end or object in its vital connection with the person's activities *is* a motive.

Another consequence of a too personal conception of motivation is a narrow and external conception of use and function. It is justifiable to ask for the utility of any educational subject-matter. But use may be estimated from different standpoints. We may have a ready-made conception of use or function, and try the value of what is learned by its conformity to this standard. In this case we shall not regard any pursuit as properly motivated, unless we see that it performs some special office that we have laid down as useful or practical. But if we start from the standpoint of the active powers of the children concerned, we shall measure the utility of new subject-matter and new modes of skill by the way in which they promote the growth of these powers. We shall not insist upon tangible material products, nor upon what is learned being put to further use at once in some visible way, nor even demand evidence that the children have become morally improved in some respect: save as the growth of powers is itself a moral gain.

4. Types of Educative Interest

The clue we have followed in our discussion of interest is its connection with an activity engaging a person in a whole-hearted way. Interest is not some one thing; it is a name for the fact that a course of action, an occupation, or pursuit absorbs the powers of an individual in a thoroughgoing way. But an activity cannot go on in a void. It requires material, subject-matter, conditions upon which to operate. On the other hand, it requires certain tendencies, habits, powers on the part of the self. Wherever there is genuine interest, there is an identification of these two things. The person acting finds his own well-being bound up with the development of an object to its own issue. If the activity goes a certain way, then a subject-matter is carried to a certain result, and a person achieves a certain satisfaction.

There is nothing new or striking in the conception of activity as an important educational principle. In the form of the idea of "self-activity" in particular, it has long been a name for the ultimate educational ideal. But activity has often been interpreted in too formal and too internal a sense, and hence has remained a barren ideal without influence on practice; sometimes it becomes a mere phrase, receiving the homage of the lips only. To make the idea of activity effective, we must take it broadly enough to cover all the doings that involve growth of power—especially of power to realize the *meaning* of what is done. This excludes action done under external constraint or dictation, for this has no significance for the mind of him who performs it. It excludes also mere random reaction to an excitation that is finished when the momentary act has ceased—which does not, in other words, carry the person acting into future broader fields. It also excludes action so habitual that it has become routine or mechanical. Unfortunately action from external constraint, for mere love of excitement, and from mechanical force of habit are so common that these exceptions cover much ground. But the ground lying within these excepted fields is the ground where an educative process is *not* going on.

The kinds of activity remaining as true educative interests vary indefinitely with age, with individual native endowments, with prior experience, with social opportunities. It is out of the question to try to catalogue them. But we may discriminate some of their more general aspects, and thereby, perhaps, make the connection of interest with educational practice somewhat more concretely obvious. Since one of the main reasons for taking self-activity in a formal sense was ignoring the importance of the body and of bodily instinct, we may well begin with interest in activity in this most direct and literal sense.

1. It is an old story that the human young have to *learn* most of the things that the young of other animals do instinctively or else with a slight amount of trying. Reflection on this fact shows that in learning these things human offspring are brought to the need of learning other things, and also to acquiring a habit of learning—a love of learning. While these considerations are fairly familiar, we often overlook their bearing upon the fact of physical activities. It follows from them at once that in so far as a physical activity has to be *learned*, it is not merely physical, but is mental, intellectual, in quality. The first problem set the human young is learning to use the organs of sense—the eye, ear, touch, etc.—and of movement—the muscles—in connection with one another. Of course, some of the mastery achieved does not involve much mental experimentation, but is due to the ripening of physiological connections. But nevertheless there is a genuinely intellectual factor when the child learns that one kind of eye-activity means a certain kind of moving of the arm, clasping of the fingers, etc., and that this in turn entails a certain kind of exploring with the fingers, resulting in experience of smoothness, etc. In such cases, there is not simply an acquisition of a new physical capacity; there is also learning in the mental sense; something has been found out. The rapidity of mental development in the first year and

a half of infancy, the whole-hearted intentness and absorption of the growing baby in his activities, the joy that accompanies his increase of ability to control his movements—all of these things are object-lessons, writ large, as to the nature of interest, and the intellectual significance of actions that (externally judged) are physical.

This period of growth occurs, of course, before children go to school; at least before they go to anything called school. But the amount and the mode of learning in this school of action is most significant in revealing the importance of types of occupation within the school involving the exercise of senses and movement. One of the reasons (as already indicated) for the slight advance made in putting in practice the doctrine of self-activity (with its recommendation of mental initiative and intellectual self-reliance, and its attacks upon the idea of pouring in and passive absorption) is precisely that it was supposed that self-activity could be secured purely internally, without the cooperation of bodily action through play, construction of objects, and manipulation of materials and tools. Only with children having specialized intellectual abilities is it possible to secure mental activity without participation of the organs of sense and the muscles. Yet how much of elementary schooling has consisted in the imposition of forms of discipline intended to *repress* all activity of the body! Under such a régime it is not surprising that children are found to be naturally averse to learning, or that intellectual activity is found to be so foreign to their nature that they have to be coerced or cunningly coaxed to engage in it! So educators blamed the children or the perverseness of human nature, instead of attacking the conditions which, by divorcing learning from use of the natural organs of action, made learning both difficult and onerous.

The teachings of Pestalozzi and of the sense-training and object-lesson schools in pedagogy were the first important influence in challenging the supremacy of a purely formal, because inner and abstract, conception of self-activity. But, unfortunately, the psychology of the times was still associated with a false physiology and a false philosophy of the relations of mind and body. The senses were supposed to be the inlets, the avenues, the gateways, of knowledge, or at least of the raw materials of knowledge. It was not known that the sense-organs are simply the pathways of *stimuli to motor-responses*, and that it is only through these motor-responses, and especially through consideration of the adapting of sense-stimulus and motor-response to each other that growth of knowledge occurs. The sense-qualities of color, sound, contact, etc., are important not in their mere reception and storage, but in their connection with the various forms of behavior that secure intelligent control. The baby would not arrive even at the knowledge of individual things,—hat, chair, orange, stone, tree,—were it not for the active responses through which various qualities are made mutually significant of one another, and thereby knit into coherent wholes. Even in the ordinary hard-and-fast school, where it is thought to be a main duty to suppress all forms of motor-activity, the physical activities that are still allowed under the circumstances, such as moving the eyes, lips, etc., in reading to one's self; the physical adjustments of reading aloud, figuring, writing, reciting, are much more important than is generally recognized in holding attention. The outlet in action is so scanty and so accidental, however, that much energy remains unutilized and hence ready to break forth in mischief or worse; while mind takes flights of uncontrolled fancy, day-dreaming and wandering to all sorts of subjects.

The next great advance in the development of a more real, less arbitrary conception of activity, came with Froebel and the kindergarten movement. Plays, games, occupations of a consecutive sort, requiring both construction and manipulation, were recognized, practically for the first time since Plato, as of essential educational importance. The place of the exercise of bodily functions in the growth of mind was practically acknowledged. But the use of the principle was still hampered and distorted by a false physiology and psychology. The *direct* contribution to growth made by the free and full control of bodily organs, of physical materials and appliances in the realization of purposes, was not understood. Hence the value of the physical side of play, games, occupations, the use of gifts, etc., was explained by recourse to *indirect* consideration—by symbolism. It was supposed that the educative development was not on account of what was directly done, but because of certain ultimate philosophical and spiritual principles which the activities somehow symbolically stood for. Save for the danger of introducing an element of unreality and so of sentimentality, this misinterpretation of the source of value in the kindergarten activities would not have been so serious had it not reacted very decisively upon the selection and organization of materials and activities. The disciples of Froebel were not free to take plays and modes of occupation upon their own merits; they had to select and arrange them in accordance with certain alleged principles of symbolism, as related to a supposed law of the unfolding of an enfolded Absolute Whole. Certain raw materials and lines of action shown by experience outside the school to be of great value were excluded because the principles of symbolic interpretation did not apply to them. These same principles led, moreover, to an exaggerated preference for geometrically abstract forms, and to insistence upon rigid adherence to a highly elaborate technique for dealing with them. Only within the last generation have the advances of science and philosophy brought about recognition of the direct value of actions and a freer utilization of play and occupational activities. Conceived in this freer and more scientific way, the principles of Froebel undoubtedly represent the greatest advance yet made in the recognition of the possibilities of bodily action in educative growth. The methods of Montessori are based on a like recognition, with the advantage of additional technical knowledge; and if the tendency to reduce them to isolated mechanical exercises (a tendency unfortunately attendant upon the spread of every definitely formulated system) can be resisted or overcome, they undoubtedly suggest further resources that can be utilized with younger children, or with older children whose sensori-motor development has been retarded.

2. In this discussion of physical activity I have had in mind for the most part that of the organs of the body, especially the hands, as employed directly with simple materials, or at most such simple appliances as a pencil, a brush, etc. A higher form of activity involving the sensori-motor apparatus of the body is found when the control over external objects is achieved by means of tools of some sort, or by the

application of one material to another. The use of a saw, a gimlet, a plane, of modeling-sticks, etc., illustrates the intervention of tools. The use of a thread in sewing, the application of heat and moisture in cooking or other simple experimentations, illustrate the use of one thing (or mode of energy) to bring about a change in another thing. There is, of course, no sharp distinction, either in practice or in principle, between this form of activity and the more direct kind just discussed. The organs of the body—especially the hands—may be regarded as a kind of tools whose use is to be learned by trying and thinking. Tools may be regarded as a sort of extension of the bodily organs. But the growing use of the latter opens a new line of development so important in its consequences that it is worth while to give it distinctive recognition. It is the *discovery and use of extra-organic tools which has made possible, both in the history of the race and of the individual, complicated activities of a long duration*—that is, with results that are long postponed. And, as we have already seen, it is this prolongation and postponement which requires an increasing use of intelligence. The use of tools and appliances (in the broad sense) also demands a greater degree of technical skill than does mastery of the use of the natural organs—or rather, it involves the problem of a progressively more complicated use of the latter—and hence stimulates a new line of development.

Roughly speaking, the use of such intervening appliances marks off games and work on one side, from play on the other. For a time children are satisfied with such changes as they can bring about with their hands and by locomotion and transportation. Other changes which they cannot so effect they are satisfied to *imagine*, without an actual physical modification. Let us "play"—let us "make-believe" that things are so and so, suffices. One thing may be made to stand for another, irrespective of its actual fitness. Thus leaves become dishes, bright stones articles of food, splinters of wood knives and forks, when children are playing at setting a table. In free play things are plastic to alter their nature as mood or passing need dictates; chairs now serve as wagons, now as a train of cars, now as boats, etc. In games, however, there are rules to be followed; so that things have to be used in *definite* ways, since they are means for accomplishing definite ends, as a club is a bat for hitting a ball. In similar fashion, children as their powers mature want real dishes, real articles of food; and are better satisfied if they can actually make a fire and cook. They want to use the things that are fitted to their purposes and that will really accomplish certain results, instead of effecting them only in fancy. It will be found that the change comes with ability to carry a purpose in mind for a longer time. The little child is impatient, as we say, for immediate returns. He cannot wait to get the appropriate means and use them in the appropriate way to achieve the end: not because he is physically more impatient than older persons, but because an end that is not achieved almost at once gets away from his mind. To execute his purpose he makes his "means" realize his ideas at one stroke of the magic wand of imagination. But as ideas persist for a longer time they can be employed to effect an actual transformation of conditions—a process that almost always requires the intervention of tools, or the use of intervening appliances.

There seems to be no better name for the acts of using *intermediate* means, or appliances, to reach ends than *work*. When employed in this way, however, work must be distinguished from labor and from toil and drudgery. Labor means a form of work in which the direct result accomplished is of value only as a means of exchange for something else. It is an *economic* term, being applied to that form of work where the product is paid for, and the money paid is used for objects of more direct values. Toil implies unusual arduousness in a task, involving fatigue. Drudgery is an activity which in itself is quite disagreeable, performed under the constraint of some quite extraneous need. Play and work cannot, therefore, be distinguished from one another according to the presence or absence of direct interest in what is doing. A child engaged in making something with tools, say, a boat, may be just as immediately interested in what he is doing as if he were sailing the boat. He is not doing what he does for the mere sake of an external result—the boat—nor for the mere sake of sailing it later. The thought of the finished product and of the use to which it is to be put may come to his mind, but so as to enhance his immediate activity of construction. In this case, his interest is free. He has a play-motive; his activity is essentially artistic in principle. What differentiates it from more spontaneous play is an *intellectual* quality; a remoter end in time serves to suggest and regulate a series of acts. Not to introduce an element of work *in this sense* when the child is ready for it is simply arbitrarily to arrest his development, and to force his activities to a level of sense-excitation after he is prepared to act upon the basis of an idea. A mode of activity that was quite normal in its own period becomes disintegrating when persisted in after a person is ripe for an activity involving more thought. We must also remember that the change from an activity with an end near by to one with an end farther off does not come all at once, nor at the same time with respect to all things. A child may be ready for occupation with tools like scissors, paint and brush, for setting a table, cooking, etc., while with respect to other activities he is still unable to plan and arrange ahead. Thus there is no ground for the assumption that children of kindergarten age are capable only of make-believe play, while children of the primary grades should be held to all work and no play. Only the false idea about symbolism leads to the former conclusion; and only a false identification of interest and play with trivial amusement leads to the latter conclusion. It has been said that man is man only as he plays; to say this involves some change from the meaning in which play has just been used. But in the broader sense of whole-hearted identification with what one is doing—in the sense of completeness of interest, it is so true that it should be a truism.

Work in the sense in which it has been defined covers all activities involving the use of intervening materials, appliances, and forms of skill consciously used in achieving results. It covers all forms of expression and construction with tools and materials, all forms of artistic and manual activity so far as they involve the conscious or thoughtful endeavor to achieve an end. They include, that is, painting, drawing, clay modeling, singing so far as there is any conscious attention to means—to the technique of execution. They comprehend the various forms of manual training, work with wood, metal, textiles, cooking, sewing, etc., so far as these involve an idea of the result to be accomplished (instead of working from dictation or an external model which does away with the need for thought). They cover also the manual side of scientific inquiry, the collection of materials for study, the management of apparatus, the sequence of acts required in carrying on and in recording experiments.

3. So far as this latter interest—the interest in discovery or in finding out what happens under given circumstances—gains in importance, there develops a third type of interest—the distinctively intellectual interest. Our wording should be carefully noted. The intellectual interest is not a new thing, now showing itself for the first time. Our discussion of the development of the so-called physical activities of a baby, and of the constructive work of children, youth, and adults has been intended to show that intelligence, in the form of clear perception of the result of an activity and search for and adaptation of means, should be an integral part of such activities. But it is possible for this intellectual interest to be subordinate, to be subsidiary, to the accomplishment of a process. But it is also possible for it to become a dominating interest, so that instead of thinking things out and discovering them for the sake of the successful achievement of an activity, we institute the activity for the sake of finding out something. Then the distinctively intellectual, or theoretical, interest shows itself.

As there is no sharp line of division in theory, so there is none in practice. Planning ahead, taking notice of what happens, relating this to what is attempted, are parts of all intelligent or purposive activities. It is the business of educators to see that the conditions of expression of the practical interests are such as to encourage the developing of these intellectual phases of an activity, and thereby evoke a gradual transition to the theoretical type. It is a commonplace that the fundamental principle of science is connected with the relation of cause and effect. Interest in this relation begins on the practical side. Some effect is aimed at, is desired and worked for, and attention is given to the conditions for producing it. At first the interest in the achievement of the end predominates; but in the degree in which this interest is bound up with *thoughtful* effort, interest in the end or effect is of necessity transferred to the interest in the means —the causes—which bring it about. Where work with tools, gardening, cooking, etc., is intelligently carried on, it is comparatively a simple matter to secure a transfer of interest from the practical side to experimentation for the sake of discovery. When any one becomes interested in a problem as a problem and in inquiry and learning for the sake of solving the problem, interest is distinctively intellectual.

4. Social interest, interest in persons, is a strong special interest, and also one which intertwines with those already named. Small children's concern with persons is remarkably intense. Their dependence upon others for support and guidance, if nothing else, provides a natural basis for attention to people and for a wish to enter into intimate connections with them. Then distinctively social instincts, such as sympathy, imitation, love of approval, etc., come in. Children's contact with other persons is continuous; and there are practically no activities of a child that are isolated. His own activities are so bound up with others, and what others do touches him so deeply and in so many ways, that it is only at rare moments, perhaps of a clash of wills, that a child draws a sharp line between other peoples' affairs as definitely theirs and his own as exclusively his. His father and mother, his brothers and sisters, his home, his friends are *his*; they belong to his idea of himself. If they were cut away from his thought of himself, and from his hopes, desires, plans, and experiences, the latter would lose pretty much all their contents. Because of limitations of experience and of intelligence, there are many affairs of others that a child cannot make his own; but within these limits a child's identification of his own concerns with those of others is naturally even more intense than that of grown persons. He has not come into business rivalries with them; the number of people whom he meets who are not sympathetic with his concerns is small; it is through entering into the actions of others, directly and imaginatively, that he finds the most significant and the most rewarding of all his experiences. In these regards, a child is likely to be more social in his interests than the average adult.

This social interest not only, then, interfuses and permeates his interest in his own actions and sufferings, but it also suffuses his interest in *things*. Adults are so accustomed to making a sharp distinction between their relations to things and to other persons; their pursuits in life are so largely specialized along the line of having to do with things just as things, that it is difficult for them, practically impossible, to realize the extent to which children are concerned with things only as they enter into and affect the concerns of persons, and the extent to which a personal-social interest radiates upon objects and gives them their meaning and worth. A moment's consideration of children's plays shows how largely they are sympathetic and dramatic reproductions of social activities; and thereby affords a clue to the extent in which interest in things is borrowed from their ideas of what people do to and with things. Much of the so-called animistic tendency of children, their tendency to personify natural objects and events, is at bottom nothing but an overflow of their social interests. It is not so much that they literally conceive things to be alive, as that things are of interest to them only when they are encompassed with the interests they see exemplified in persons; otherwise things are, at first, more or less matters of indifference to them.

No doubt some of the repulsiveness of purely abstract intellectual studies to many children is simply the reflex of the fact that the things—the facts and truths—presented to them have been isolated from their human context. This does not mean, of course, that a mythological or fanciful human character should be attributed to inanimate things; but it does mean that impersonal material should be presented so far as possible in the role it actually plays in life. Children generally begin the study of geography, for example, with a social interest so strong that it is fairly romantic. Their imaginations are fired by the thought of learning how strange and far-away peoples live and fare. Then they are fed on abstract definitions and classifications; or, what is almost as deadening, upon bare physical facts about the forms of land and water, the structure of continents, etc. Then there are complaints that children have so little interest in the study—simply because they have not been touched where they are at home. In such sciences as physics and chemistry there are enough facts and principles which are associated with human concerns to supply adequate material for thorough grounding in the methods of those sciences.

It is not necessary to do more than to allude to the close connection between social and moral interests.[1] In those cases where direct interest points one way and obligation another, no reinforcement of the demand of duty is as strong as that furnished by a realization of the interests of others that are bound up with it. The abstract idea of duty, like other abstract ideas, has naturally little motivating force. Social interests have a powerful hold, which, by association, is transferred to what is morally required. Thus a strong indirect interest resists the contrary pull of immediate inclination. The only other moral point that need be mentioned here is that the conception of interest as naturally a selfish or egoistic principle is wholly irreconcilable with the facts of the case. All interest is naturally in *objects* that carry an activity forward or in *objects* that mark its fulfillment; hence the character of the interest depends upon the nature of these objects. If they are low, or unworthy, or purely selfish, then so is the interest, but not otherwise. The strength of the interest in other persons and in their activities and aims is a natural resource for making activities broad, generous, and enlightened in scope; while the physical, manual, and scientific interests in their identification with *objects* make for a broadening of the self.

5. *The Place of Interest in the Theory of Education*

We conclude with a brief restatement setting forth the importance of the idea of interest for educational theory. Interests, as we have noted, are very varied; every impulse and habit that generates a purpose having sufficient force to move a person to strive for its realization becomes an interest. But in spite of this diversity, interests are one in principle. They all mark an identification in action, and

1. See *Moral Principles in Education* [*Middle Works* 4:265–91].

hence in desire, effort, and thought, of self with objects; with, namely, the objects in which the activity terminates (ends) and with the objects by which it is carried forward to its end (means). Interest, in the emotional sense of the word, is the evidence of the way in which the self is engaged, occupied, taken up with, concerned in, absorbed by, carried away by, this objective subject-matter. At bottom all misconceptions of interest, whether in practice or in theory, come from ignoring or excluding its *moving, developing* nature; they bring an activity to a standstill, cut up its progressive growth into a series of static cross-sections. When this happens, nothing remains but to identify interest with the momentary excitation an object arouses. Such a relation of object and self is not only *not* educative, but it is worse than nothing. It dissipates energy, and forms a habit of dependence upon such meaningless excitations, a habit most adverse to sustained thought and endeavor. Wherever such practices are resorted to in the name of interest, they very properly bring it into disrepute. It is not enough to *catch* attention; it must be *held*. It does not suffice to arouse energy; the *course* that energy takes, the results that it effects are the important matters.

But since activities, even those originally impulsive, are more or less continuous or enduring, such static, non-developing excitements represent not interest, but an abnormal set of conditions. The positive contributions of the idea of interest to pedagogic theory are twofold. In the first place, it protects us from a merely *internal* conception of mind; and, in the second place, from a merely *external* conception of subject-matter.

(1) Any one who has grasped the conception of an interest as an activity that moves toward an end, developing as it proceeds thought of this end and search for means, will never fall into the error of thinking of mind (or of the self) as an isolated inner world by itself. It will be apparent that mind is one with intelligent or purposeful activity—with an activity that *means* something and in which the meaning counts as a factor in the development of an activity. There is a sense in which mind is measured by growth of power of abstraction, and a very important sense this is. There is

another sense in which it can be truly said that abstractness is the worst evil that infests education. The false sense of abstraction is connected with thinking of mental activity as something that can go on wholly by itself, apart from objects or from the world of persons and things. Real subject-matter being removed, something else has to be supplied in its place for the mind to occupy itself with. This something else must of necessity be mere symbols; that is to say things that are not signs *of* anything, because the first-hand subject-matter which gives them meaning has been excluded or at least neglected. Or when objects—concrete facts, etc.—are introduced, it is as mere occasions for the mind to exercise its own separate powers—just as dumb-bells or pulleys and weights are a mere occasion for exercising the muscles. The world of studies then becomes a strange and peculiar world, because a world cut off from—abstracted from—the world in which pupils as human beings live and act and suffer. Lack of "interest," lack of power to hold attention and stir thought, are a necessary consequence of the unreality attendant upon such a realm for study. Then it is concluded that the "minds" of children or of people in general are averse to learning, are indifferent to the concerns of intelligence. But such indifference and aversion are always evidence—either directly or as a consequence of previous bad conditions—that the appropriate conditions for the exercise of mind are not there: —that they are excluded because there has been no provision of situations in which things have to be intelligently dealt with. Everything that is disparaging in the common use of the terms academic, abstract, formal, theoretical, has its roots here.[1]

(2) The supposed externality of subject-matter is but the counterpart phase of the alleged internal isolation of mind. If mind means certain powers or faculties existing in themselves and needing only to be exercised *by* and *upon* presented subject-matter, the presented subject-matter must mean something complete in its ready-made and fixed sepa-

1. Of course, nothing that is said here is meant to depreciate the wonderful possibilities involved in an *imaginative experimentation* with things, *after* the conditions of more direct transactions with them have been met.

rateness. Objects, facts, truths of geography, history, and science not being conceived as means and ends for the intelligent development of experience, are thought of just as stuff to be learned. Reading, writing, figuring are mere external forms of skill to be mastered. Even the arts—drawing, singing—are thought of as meaning so many ready-made things, pictures, songs, that are to be externally produced and reproduced. Then we have the situation described in the early portion of this essay: Some means must be found to overcome the separation of mind and subject-matter; problems of method in teaching are reduced to various ways of overcoming a gap which exists only because a radically *wrong method* had already been entered upon. The doctrine of interest is not a short cut to "methods" of this sort. On the contrary, it is a warning to furnish conditions such that the natural impulses and acquired habits, as far as they are desirable, *shall obtain subject-matter and modes of skill* in order to develop to their natural ends of achievement and efficiency. Interest, the identification of mind with the material and methods of a developing activity, is the inevitable result of the presence of such situations.

Hence it follows that little can be accomplished by setting up "interest" as an end or a method by itself. Interest is obtained not by thinking about it and consciously aiming at it, *but by considering and aiming at the conditions* that lie back of it, and compel it. If we can discover a child's urgent needs and powers, and if we can supply an environment of materials, appliances, and resources—physical, social, and intellectual—to direct their adequate operation, we shall not have to think about interest. It will take care of itself. For mind will have met with what it needs in order to *be* mind. The problem of educators, teachers, parents, the state, is to provide the environment that induces educative or developing activities, and where these are found the one thing needful in education is secured.

Miscellany

INTRODUCTION TO *A CONTRIBUTION TO A BIBLIOGRAPHY OF HENRI BERGSON*

Henri Bergson's books are fortunately now accessible to the public in an English dress. For this reason and because it seems desirable to have Professor Bergson speak for himself as to his fundamental doctrines, no synopses of the books are given in the following pages. A few words—derived as far as possible from Mr. Bergson himself—are, however, prefixed regarding the more general features of his philosophy. And first as to Intuition, an idea that plays, as everybody knows, a large role in his conception of philosophic method. It happens that in English thought the associations that cluster about the word are mainly derived from Platonic transcendentalism, and from the theories of the Scotch School and the super-scientific regarding an organ of knowledge that is independent of experience and superior to the sciences. These associations with the *a priori* are quite foreign to the use of the term in the Bergsonian philosophy; and no one has deprecated their introduction into it more vigorously than Professor Bergson himself. He has said:

> The method that I propose does not consist in extracting from reality a simple concept in order that it may then be submitted to dialectic elaboration. On the contrary, my method demands uninterrupted contact with reality. It consists in following reality in all its sinuosities. It demands that our faculties of observation even stretch themselves at times to surpass themselves. It is made of corrections, retouchings, gradual complications. It aspires to constitute metaphysics as certain and as universally recognized as any of the other sciences.

And again he has said:

> Let us accept science in all its concrete complexity; then let us recommence, with this new science as its material, a task like

[First published as the Introduction to Isadore Gilbert Mudge's *A Contribution to a Bibliography of Henri Bergson* (New York: Columbia University Press, 1913), ix–xiii.]

that which ancient metaphysicians undertook with the simpler science of their day. We must break the mathematical framework, take account of biological, psychological and sociological sciences, and upon this larger base erect a metaphysics capable of going higher and higher by means of the continuous, progressive and organized effort of all philosophers who are associated in the same respect for experience.

Again he says:

I have never claimed that intelligence should be replaced by something else, or that instinct should be preferred to it. I have simply tried to show that when we leave the realm of mathematical and physical objects to enter that of life and consciousness, we need to appeal to a certain sense of life that encroaches upon pure understanding and that has its origin in the same vital impetus as instinct—although, strictly speaking, instinct is something wholly different.

Finally:

There is nothing mysterious in this faculty. Every one of us has had occasion to exercise it to a certain extent. Any one of us, for example, who has attempted literary composition, knows that after the subject has long been studied, materials collected and notes made, something is still needed to set up the work of composition itself; namely, an effort, often quite painful, to place ourselves at the very heart of the subject, to seek there, as deeply as possible, an impulse after which we need only let ourselves go. . . . Metaphysical intuition seems to be something of the same kind. The sum of observations and experiments gathered together by physical science corresponds in metaphysics to the documents and notes of literary composition. We do not secure an intuition of reality—that is, *an intellectual sympathy with the most intimate part of it*—unless we have won its confidence by long companionship with its outer manifestations.

Turning from method to subject-matter, the following passage seems to be highly significant for an understanding of Bergson's treatment of the two problems which form the themes of his *Matter and Memory* and his *Creative Evolution*—a passage composed, it should be added, in 1901, namely, after the publication of the former book and considerably prior to the appearance of the latter:

I cannot envisage general evolution and the progress of life in the totality of the organic world, the coordination and subordination of vital organs to one another in a single living being, the relations which physiology and psychology seem to have established between cerebral activity and thought in man, without arriving at the conclusion that life is an immense effort put forth by thought to obtain from matter something that matter is unwilling to give. Matter is inert; it is the seat of necessity; it proceeds mechanically. It seems as if thought seeks to profit by this mechanical attitude of matter, to utilize it for *actions*; and thus to convert into contingent movements in space and unforeseeable events in time all the creative energy that thought carries within itself—at least all that is capable of being brought into play and externalized. Cunningly and laboriously it piles complication on complication in order to make liberty out of necessity, to arrange a matter so subtle, so mobile, that, by a veritable physical paradox and grace to an effort which can not long endure, liberty may hold itself in equilibrium on this very mobility. But thought is caught in the net. The vortex upon which it has placed itself seizes and holds it. It becomes a prisoner of the mechanisms which it has climbed. Automatism captures it, and by an inevitable forgetfulness of the end that it had set for itself, life, which should be only a means for a higher end, consumes itself in the effort at simple self-conservation. From the humblest of organic beings to the higher vertebrates which just antecede man we are watching an endeavor always missing success, always reundertaken with an increasingly wise art. Man has triumphed—but with difficulty and so partially that it needs only a moment of relaxation or inattention for automatism to recapture him. Nevertheless he has triumphed, thanks to that marvellous mechanism, the human brain. The superiority of this instrument seems to me to depend wholly upon the indefinite latitude it permits of surmounting the mechanisms that have given pause to other animals. It forms, not once for all but continuously, motor habitudes whose exercise it delegates to lower centres. . . . In a general way, the superiority of our brain resides in the power of liberation which it gives us in regard to bodily automatisms through permitting us incessantly to form new habits which absorb old ones or hold them in subordination. In this sense there is nothing to be found in the brain corresponding to the operation of thought in its strict sense. Nevertheless it is the brain that has rendered human thought possible. Without it the higher powers of thought could not turn toward the material world without being captured by automatism and drowned in unconsciousness.

No one needs to be told how thoroughly Professor Bergson has exemplified in his own method of thinking and writing the intellectual sympathy which he has so well described—how after gathering together and absorbing all available scientific material he has found a point of synoptic vision from which to envisage the multiplicity of details. Nor does any one who has followed the development of contemporary philosophy need to be reminded that in so doing Professor Bergson has, in his successive books, placed in a new light the old and oft shop-worn questions of the nature of human intelligence, its relation to the brain and to matter and to evolution. Perhaps only the more professional students of philosophy can adequately realize the debt under which he has placed all workers in this field by centering attention in such an illuminating and rewarding way upon the nature of time, and the fundamental character of the problem of time for theories of reality, of mental life, of freedom and evolution. No philosophic problem will ever exhibit just the same face and aspect that it presented before Professor Bergson invited us to look at it in its connexions with duration as a real and fundamental fact.

It is the object of the following bibliographical pages to help to bring an even wider audience in touch with the vital influences that radiate from Professor Bergson's thought. They should facilitate a more intelligent understanding of his lectures, and enable those interested to follow up, by more leisurely reading, the desire for further knowledge that will spring from them. It has been my privilege, in these prefatory words, to indicate the place of this Bibliography in the intellectual and personal welcome that Columbia University in general and its Department of Philosophy in particular extends to our colleague for the time being, Professor Henri Bergson.

INTRODUCTION TO *DIRECTORY OF THE TRADES AND OCCUPATIONS TAUGHT AT THE DAY AND EVENING SCHOOLS IN GREATER NEW YORK*

The educational question faced by the City of New York, as by every other great industrial centre, is whether the community as a whole shall care for the education of the children or whether the education of the largest number shall be left to the unregulated conditions of factory life. Child labor laws have, upon the whole, approached the question from the negative side. They have kept the children out of industrial pursuits until they have reached a certain age, and have presumably secured a certain amount of schooling. The problem will not be adequately dealt with on its positive and constructive side until the community furnishes to the large number of boys and girls, who are about to become wage-earners, educational facilities that equip them intellectually and morally for their callings in life; and until continuation schools, in some form or other, are provided for at least all children between fourteen and sixteen who are engaged in factory work. The new Child Labor Law of the State of New York, while more stringent as a preventive measure than the older law (since it requires the boys and girls to have attained the Grade of 6B or the age of sixteen years) actually increases the demand for more schools and courses of study better adapted to the needs of those going into industrial pursuits. Naturally, it is the duller children who, not reaching the 6B grade, have to remain in school till they are sixteen years old. To a large extent, these children, backward in book studies, are just the ones to whom instructions that use the hands and the motor energies would appeal. Meantime, they are kept out of industry, and yet are not adequately prepared for any useful activity in life.

[First published as the Introduction to the Henry Street Settlement's *Directory of the Trades and Occupations Taught at the Day and Evening Schools in Greater New York* (New York, 1913), 2–3.]

The public is indebted to the Henry Street Settlement for the thoroughgoing pains taken in the preparation of this Directory, which places before those interested an exhibit of existing facilities for industrial and trade education in Greater New York. The Settlement maintains a system of scholarships for the benefit of those boys and girls who might otherwise leave school and go to work at fourteen. The purpose of the scholarships is to give as many children as possible two years of further education and vocational training during that period which has been called the "two wasted years." The giving of scholarships to the comparatively few children fortunate enough to secure this protection, and the supervision of their education, keep the committee in close touch with the educational agencies throughout the city. While we must rejoice that the showing is as good as it is, and that such excellent work is done by these schools, nevertheless we must confess that the showing is a meagre and inadequate one. When one considers the thousands and thousands of children destined to wage-earning pursuits, the obvious conclusion from the exhibit found in this Directory is that neither by public activity nor by voluntary agencies has the City of New York as yet made more than a bare beginning. The Directory should thus serve a double purpose, in that it gives information—otherwise very difficult to procure—regarding existing facilities, and in that it makes evident the immense work that remains to be done.

Contributions to *A Cyclopedia of Education* Volumes 3, 4, and 5

GENERALIZATION.—The process by which a principle or law is reached; the term is also used to denote the product. The term expresses the use or function of induction, which endeavors, beginning with a number of scattered details, to arrive at a general statement. Generalization expresses the natural goal of instruction in any topic, for it works a measure of economy and efficiency from the standpoints alike of observation, memory, and thought. The number of particulars that can be obtained is limited. When, however, different cases are brought together,—and this bringing together is expressed in a general principle,—a great variety of cases are practically reduced to one case, and further observation is freed to attack new particular things and qualities not yet systematized. Exactly the same holds good for memory. There are a few prodigies who can carry in mind an indefinite number of unrelated details; but most persons need the help of generalizations in order to retain special facts and to recall them when needed. Logically, a principle not only sums up and registers the net intellectual outcome of a great many different experiences which have been undergone at diverse times and places, but is an illuminating and clarifying means of interpreting new cases that without it could not be understood.

Because the older deductive, classificatory schemes of instruction began with a statement of the law or principle, educational reformers who were influenced by the scientific movement toward induction were compelled to emphasize the later and derived place occupied by generalization in the intellectual life. Zealots for the new method sometimes swung to the extreme of reaction against universals, and, treating observation and imagination of particulars as an end

[First published in *A Cyclopedia of Education*, ed. Paul Monroe (New York: Macmillan Co., 1912–13), Vols. 3, 4, and 5.]

in itself, neglected the importance of generalization as a normal terminus of study. Another educational error is to suppose that generalization is a single and separate act coming by itself, *after* the mind has been exclusively preoccupied with particular facts and events. To the contrary, generalization is a continuous, gradual movement away from mere isolated particulars toward a connecting principle. A necessary part of the work of instruction is, therefore, to make the conditions such that the mind will move in the direction of a fruitful generalization as soon as it begins to deal with and to collect particulars. The resulting generalization will, of course, be crude, vague, and inadequate, but, if formed under proper conditions, it will serve at once to direct and vitalize further observations and recollections, and will be built out and tested in the application to new particulars. This suggests the final educational principle: A generalization or law is such not in virtue of its structure or bare content, but because of its use or function. We do not first have a principle and then apply it; an idea becomes general (or a principle) in process of fruitful application to the interpretation, comprehension, and prevision of the particular facts of experience.

See Abstract and Concrete; Concept; Empirical.

HARMONY, HARMONIOUS DEVELOPMENT.—The social philosophy of the later eighteenth century was cosmopolitan, not nationalistic, in tenor. It regarded the divisions of mankind into different political states as arbitrary or artificial, and took Humanity as its ideal object of endeavor. Man was more than the citizen. Consequently the educational systems that had national, or any particularistic political or religious, ends were looked upon with hostility. In opposition to them were urged the superior claims of an education which should develop the individual as a member of humanity. The motto of such an education was the harmonious development of all the faculties of the individual, as against the partial and narrowing tendencies attributed to national and confessional systems of education. The conception of harmony of development was strengthened by the tendency toward "Hellenism"—that is, to regard the Greek personality as the normal expression of human powers. (See CULTURE.) It was also associated with the popular objective and absolute idealisms of the time, which regarded the individual as universal mind in miniature, and which treated development as the process of actualizing the latent or potential universality. Under this influence the idea of harmony took in some cases (as in that of Froebel) a romantic or even mystical turn, instead of the classic form characteristic of the Hellenic ideal.

See DEVELOPMENT; FROEBEL; GOETHE; HERBART; LESSING; NEO-HUMANISM; PESTALOZZI; ROMANTICISM; VOLTAIRE.

HEDONISM (ἡδονή pleasure).—A term used to denote theories that make pleasure either the end, or the standard of intentional or conscious activity, moral behavior included. The ancient and the modern theories grouped under that name are, however, more widely different from each other than their common name would indicate. Ancient hedonism is associated with Epicureanism. Its chief motivation was revolt, on the one hand, against the moral theories which made virtue consist in fitting into the existing social order by performing the duties appropriate to the status in which a person found himself; and, on the other hand, against the theories which gave morals a purely rationalistic cast, basis, and aim. As against the first, Epicurean hedonism taught the advisability of abstinence, as far as possible, from civic life, and the cultivation of voluntary associations based on congeniality and friendship. As against the second, it emphasized the importance of the feelings, and of cultivating the various types of enjoyment naturally accessible to the individual. Contrary to the usual belief, it taught not surrender to appetite, but moderation of desire, on the ground that excessive desire was fatal to happiness. Ancient, like modern, hedonism was naturalistic in tone; but here again the motive was different, ancient hedonism being convinced that supernaturalism tended to fear of death and of the intervention of the gods, and hence was detrimental to a life of serenity and contentment.

Modern hedonism, in its influential forms, has been associated with an empirical philosophy and with utilitarianism. Its chief object has been to set up a concrete standard for measuring the worth of acts: their consequences in the way of pleasures and pains produced. Its interest was not in outlining an agreeable mode of life, remote from strife and disturbance, but the discovery of a scientific mode of estimating right and wrong methods of action. Of the conscious search for pleasure it has made little, generally holding, in fact, that happiness is best attained when not consciously aimed at—the so-called hedonistic paradox. In its most important representatives—as Bentham and the Mills—it has been more interested in the development of methods for judging the effects of legislation and administration, civil and penal, by tracing their effect among the pleasures produced and the pains entailed upon the masses affected by them, than in elaborating a code for right action in private life.

As a moral system, hedonism has had little direct influence upon educational theory or practice. Matters of pleasure and pain are, however, so closely connected with the motivation of conduct that it would not be difficult to trace an implicit hedonism in the use made of rewards promised and punishments threatened as motives to studious behavior. Asceticism, moreover, is a kind of inverted hedonism, involving the notion that man is so naturally prone to pleasure-seeking that the agreeable must be shunned as a temptation to evil. Ascetic notions underlie many educational ideas and procedures, especially those that cluster about the notion that there is something disciplinary and moralizing in tasks and exercises in the degree in which they are disagreeable (see FORMAL DISCIPLINE).

See UTILITARIANISM.

References:—

ALEXANDER, S. *Moral Order and Progress.* (London, 1889.)
BAIN, A. *Emotion and Will.* (London, 1875.)
DEWEY, J., and TUFTS, J. H. *Ethics.* (New York, 1908.)
GREEN, T. *Prolegomena to Ethics.* (Oxford, 1889.)
JAMES, W. *Principles of Psychology.* (New York, 1899.)
MACKENZIE, J. S. *Manual of Ethics.* (London, 1900.)
MUIRHEAD, J. H. *Elements of Ethics.* (New York, 1892.)

PATER, W. *Marius the Epicurean.*
PLATO. *Gorgias.*
RICKABY, J. *Moral Philosophy.* (London, 1888.)
SIDGWICK, H. *History of Ethics.* (London, 1892.)
Methods of Ethics. (London, 1901.)
WATSON, J. *Hedonistic Theories from Aristippus to Spencer.* (Glasgow, 1895.)
See also Baldwin, J. M. *Dictionary of Philosophy and Psychology,* Vol. III, pt. II, pp. 899–901, for articles in current magazines.

HUMANISM AND NATURALISM.—In educational literature, humanism has usually a specific meaning, indicating a distinctive intellectual tendency that marked the revival of learning in the fifteenth and sixteenth centuries. For that aspect of humanism, see RENAISSANCE AND EDUCATION.

Under the present caption, only a somewhat rarer and also looser signification of the term, belonging to certain problems in the philosophy of education, receives consideration. From the side of educational practices, this philosophical question originated in the just mentioned historic sense of humanism. As a consequence of the revival of learning (along with the backward state of the natural sciences), linguistic and literary culture succeeded theology as the controlling factor in higher education. By the nineteenth century, however, natural science had made such extraordinary advances that its representatives were naturally restive, and even rebellious. They challenged the practical supremacy of language and literature, and attacked on intellectual grounds the theories that were advanced in justification of this supremacy. Upon the practical side, the case was decided in favor of the claims of the natural sciences—not, of course, that the humanistic studies were excluded, but that the claims of scientific study were admitted upon substantially equal footing, whether by insertion of some natural science into the old classical course or by affording students an option between a literary and a scientific course. The adjustment thus far reached represents, however, a working compromise through concession to forces strong enough to force recognition, rather than a solution based upon any generally recognized philosophy of the relations of man and nature to each other. As ideals humanism and naturalism are perhaps more sharply opposed to each other now than at any previous period.

Humanism may be defined as the conviction that spiritual and ideal values are of supreme rank in the make-up of reality, and that these values are most adequately expressed in the great or classic achievements of humanity in literature and art—especially literature. Naturalism rests upon the conviction that, negatively, humanism is a survival of the geocentric medieval philosophy, with its false conception of the place of the earth and of man in the universal scheme, and with its exaggerated teleological interpretation of things; positively, that man and his affairs are a subordinate part of nature, seen in their true place only when nature is made the chief and primary object of study. Incidentally, naturalism almost always has as one of its implications that language and literature are too artificial, factitious, and, as it were, ornamental, to be a sound basis for education. Science, it is urged, presents mankind with truths concerning realities of existence; language and literature with man's accidental and fanciful reactions to these realities.

Philosophically viewed, the controversy is a reflection of the time-worn discussion of the relations of spirit and matter, mind and nature, subject and object; and the supposed antagonism of naturalism and humanism originates in dualism (*q.v.*) respecting these concepts. Greek classic philosophy presents, upon the whole, a view of things in which there is a balance between naturalism and humanism. From one standpoint, that of value, a humanistic idealism dominates; the life of reason as exhibited in the realization of distinctively human functions is the supreme moral good, and hence the ultimate measure of worth in education. This conception was embodied in the Aristotelian conception of a *liberal* education and in the notion of the liberal as distinct from the mechanical and industrial arts. But reason is not a peculiar and isolated property, much less creation, of man. On the contrary, nature, in virtue of its orderliness, and especially in view of the fact that its order shows itself in the tendency to achieve specific ends, is itself rational, and the attainment of rationality by man is nothing but the realization in conscious thought of the relations immanent in nature. From the side of conditions or efficient means nature also, not man, is supreme. The values, or goods, of life are absolutely dependent for their achievement upon the efficacious workings of physical conditions; even the contribution of human deliberation and effort, regarded as a causal factor, falls within the scope of nature. Or, as Aristotle puts it, mind is the actualizing, the complete energizing, of the body, a view which makes it impossible to regard mind as a separate independent causal force. In short, classic Greek idealism was idealistic in the sense that it had a teleological view of nature. Nature and mind were not regarded as two forces working either together or against each other, but as means and end, causal conditions and final values, potentiality and actuality.

Medieval philosophy, even when professedly following Aristotle, introduced two profound modifications into this view. On the one hand, nature as it now exists is fallen or corrupted, being implicated in "an aboriginal catastrophe," the denial by the first man of God's will as law, and the substitution for it of human inclination. This profound perversion of reality affected all physical nature, in itself completely good, as well as human nature. The inevitable result (taken of course in connection with the barbarous state of society) was a depreciatory attitude toward all knowledge of a natural kind, in contrast with knowledge having to do with man's redemption—the subordination, both in philosophic theory and educational practice, of natural knowledge to supernaturally revealed science, or theology. Medieval philosophy also inverted the relation between mind and nature, for it regarded mind as the sole ultimate *efficient* cause of natural existence, instead of conceiving mind as the *final* cause, or good, of natural things. Thereby a metaphysical dualism of spirit and matter was superadded to moral dualism of the first state and ultimate destiny of man as contrasted with the present state of nature.

Renaissance philosophy was humanistic in both the narrower and the wider sense of that term. It found in the revival of Greek philosophic thought a means of justifying the growing interest in the phenomena of physical and human nature. Like Greek thought, it rested in a conception which united humanism and naturalism. Naturalism was opposed to supernaturalism, and hence represented the means of satisfying distinctively human, instead of theological, potentialities and aims. The prevailing way of conceiving the relation of man and nature was that of a microcosm to a macrocosm. Man was in small edition that which the universe was in large. As Windelband truly says, the natural science of the seventeenth century was the daughter of the humanism of the sixteenth century.

This union, resting upon the use of Greek thought and the emulation of the free Greek spirit to justify a free and full satisfaction of human capacity through natural conditions, was, however, soon undermined from both sides. Humanism became more technical, more literary and philological, and less philosophical. Moreover, the rise of the Protestant-Catholic controversy diverted the study of language and literature from social and aesthetic channels, and made its use a weapon of religious dispute. As natural science worked itself free from the earlier mystical and imaginative traits, it became more and more purely mechanical, more and more indifferent to teleological considerations. Nature mechanically viewed is indifferent to mind, or even opposed to it, since the chief mark of mind is its purposiveness. This tendency of natural science toward dualism was reenforced by the growing moral and political interest in the self or ego, and by the development of the idea that the final source of certain knowledge (as against the authoritative impositions of dogmatic beliefs) was to be sought simply within the inner self, the field of personal consciousness. These two latter factors conspired with the discovery of the "inner world" as a field for literary exploitation to mark off mind, reason, as a realm by itself, sharply contrasted with nature. Natural and mechanical science was concerned with the "object," and over against the object stands the "subject," defined and described in terms exactly antithetical to those applicable to nature, or the object. The resulting dualism motivates directly all the philosophic problems of the seventeenth century, and supplies the background of the controversy between naturalism and humanism in education.

The difficulties and problems that arise in rigid philosophic dualism are paralleled in educational controversy. By assumption, there are two separate words, and yet both of them are necessary to make up the whole account of our real experience. The result is, inevitably, whether in pure theory or in educational, a mechanical compromise assigning one isolated region to mind and humanistic study and another to matter and to naturalistic studies. The same forces, however, that have tended to break down the rigid dualism of mind and matter have operated, though independently, to render questionable the division of studies into exclusively human and exclusively physical. The rapid development of the historical, anthropological, economic, and other social sciences has introduced a large and important body of material that will not fit easily into either of the older rubrics. Obviously humanistic in matter and import, it also emphasizes both in its subject matter and its methods of explanation processes that connect man's life with natural conditions. The theory of evolution when applied to humanistic subject matter tends also to bring out its continuity with natural conditions. Industrial conditions are seen to have the most intimate bearing upon human affairs, and they also are bound up with the natural sciences. As long as economic affairs were regarded as out of the pale of serious concern by all those occupied with man's higher interests, it was an easy matter to sidetrack them intellectually and educationally. Now that the close connection of economic conditions with success in attaining the highest political and moral status of society is generally recognized, the thinness and superficiality of a humanism that excludes from attention all reference to industry, commerce, and applied science become increasingly obvious. As a consequence, contemporary philosophy and contemporary educational theory may be said to be confronted with a common problem: The discovery of the common background or matrix in which humanistic and naturalistic interests are united; and the tracing of their respective differentiations from this community of origin,—a differentiation, however, which should not become a separation, and which, accordingly, secures the possibility of fruitful interaction between them whenever desired.

See Idealism and Realism in Education; Nature.

HUMANITIES, THE.—This term came into use in the fifteenth and sixteenth centuries as an English equivalent of the Latin *literae humaniores*, meaning in effect literary culture, "letters." The sense of the term was probably influenced by reminiscence of the use of the word *Humanitas* by Aulus Gellius and Cicero to denote the liberal culture befitting a man as a man. It was influenced by a differentiation from "divinity," so as to designate the studies of human interest as distinct from the theological studies which had dominated medieval education—especially to designate secular instead of "sacred" rhetoric, poesy, and grammar. This wider sense of the term shaded naturally into a narrower one. Since as a matter of fact the material of literary secular culture was at first the Latin, and then the Greek languages and literatures, the term "humanities" came to mean almost exclusively the study of Latin and Greek. Humanity is still in use in the Scottish universities as a technical term for the study of Latin; and at Oxford the classical studies are known as *literae humaniores*. Generally speaking, in the seventeenth century a humanist meant a grammarian or philologist. In the nineteenth century the use of the term was influenced by the conflict in higher education between the classical studies and the sciences of nature. In the course of the controversy, the term tended to broaden its meaning, and to revert to designating whatever concerns man as distinct from physical nature.

See HUMANISM AND NATURALISM; LIBERAL EDUCATION; NEO-HUMANISM; RENAISSANCE AND EDUCATION.

References:—

FARRAR, F. W. *Essays on a Liberal Education.* (London, 1867.)
FINDLAY, J. J. *Principles of Class Teaching.* (London, 1902.)
GOODSELL, W. *Conflict of Naturalism and Humanism.* (New York, 1910.)

HYPOTHESIS.—A supposition, a theory, or a mode of explanation held tentatively pending further inquiry, because of its value in the organization of knowledge and in direction of inquiry. The increased importance attached, in the development of modern science, to making and using hypotheses is a necessary part of the evolution of inductive and experimental science. It marks the attainment of a genuinely critical reflective attitude, and provides the working method for dealing with the otherwise insoluble antagonism of dogmatism and skepticism. The older and classic scientific attitude (commonly called deductive, but better termed subsumptive or authoritative) assumed that science was possible only where there existed a body of absolutely certain and definite fixed principles or "truths," under which empirical or observable data might be brought. Only as the body of experienced data was subsumed under the absolute first principles did the former acquire logical systematization and rational justification, that is, the characteristic traits of a science. These first principles were themselves, accordingly, of a radically different nature from that of the facts of experience. The former were universal and necessary; self-evident truths of reasons or rational intuitions, innate ideas, *a priori* to all experience. The latter were *a posteriori*, the result of sensations and imagination, contingent, fluctuating, particular. When acceptance of ultimate rational principles was made the foundation of all science, doubt and denial of their existence led to skepticism regarding the possibility of knowledge. Dogmatism and skepticism thus exhausted the philosophies of knowledge.

The modern scientific movement began when men gave up the notion that science consisted in defining and classifying existences just as they were found and substituted the search for processes and energies which made the objects, or brought them into existence. The latter point of view necessarily involved the use of imaginative conceptions of *possible* causes. The speculative danger latent in the new method was checked by insistence that the imaginative conceptions, or hypotheses, must lend themselves to mathematical statement, deduction, and to corroboration by the results of experimental observations. Descartes's theory of knowledge marks the transition from the older to the newer, or scientific, logic. He retained the notion that science begins with truths or concepts of pure reason, and that what was needed was concentric deduction from these universals, until the phenomena revealed to sense observation were approximated. At the same time he insisted upon the necessity of definite and accurate (mathematical) formulation of these ultimate notions and upon methodic procedure, a series of intermediate steps from the universal to the particulars. When the Cartesians called these ultimate principles "hypotheses," they did not mean to imply their doubtful character, but rather that they were "placed under" all the particular facts of existence and of science. When Newton said that he did not make hypotheses (*non fingo hypotheses*), he did not mean (as is sometimes stated) that he did not gratuitously invent them, but that he did not employ them in the Cartesian way. In the modern sense, no one invented or used hypotheses more freely than Newton; but, as against the Cartesian theory of the world, he held that general interpreting principles must not be derived from pure thought, but be suggested by experience and then transferred by analogy to other phenomena, their verification existing in the suggestion of new or experimental observations exactly confirming the deductive results. In Kant, we find again an inconsistent compromise of the old and the new logics. He recognizes that science does not consist in the mere accumulation and classification of facts, since it requires conceptions which the mind, from its own initiative, uses to cross-examine existing observations and employs also as methods of undertaking new experimental constructions. To quote his own words: "When Galileo caused balls which he had carefully weighed to roll down an inclined plane, or Torricelli made the air bear up a weight which he knew beforehand to be equal to a standard column of water, a new light broke on the mind of the scientific discoverer. It was seen that reason has insight only into that which it produces after a plan of its own, and that it must itself lead the way with principles of judgment and force nature to answer its questions." But in his general philosophic formulation of this insight, Kant overlooked the fact that the "principles of judgment" with which thought approaches objects are purely hypothetical in character and are approved or rejected according as they work out in experimental construction of objects. Accordingly, his philosophy, though called critical, was at bottom a revival of dogmatic rationalism, since he held that knowledge requires a fixed stock of *a priori* concepts that are imposed once for all upon objects. The inherent difficulties in this position conspired with the constantly increasing emphasis upon experimental verification to discredit the older empiricism and rationalism alike, and led to the formulation of the doctrine that all general ideas, or concepts, are originally purely hypothetical, gaining certainty as they work successfully to interpret and organize observations and to direct further fruitful experiments. In placing the standard of value for concepts in their use, instead of their structure, the resulting functional empiricism becomes truly critical, assigning a distinctive important role to concepts, a role not capable of being played by facts and observations by themselves, but insisting also upon the need of experimental test.

See CONCEPT; IDEA; JUDGMENT; KNOWLEDGE; METHOD; PRAGMATISM.

IDEA AND IDEATION.—Ideation denotes either the act of thinking or the course, the stream, of ideas, according as ideas are regarded as manifestations of a soul substance or spiritual entity, or as mental contents which in their associations and sequences make up the mind. Upon a third view, it expresses the function exercised by ideas, the results they effect in subsequent experience. So far accordingly as the word is not a synonym for the process of thinking (*q.v.*), its meaning depends upon that assigned to the term "idea."

Historically, the term "idea" dates from the Platonic philosophy. With him, it means an absolute, unchanging, immaterial archetype, standard, or pattern, which the manifold changing particulars of sense that are called by the same name partially share in and represent. It was the form, the nature, the essential character of a set of particular existences. It was their universal, generic, and also their end, their completion, or perfect reality. Through its presence, and only through its presence, are changes controlled, or made other than an aimless, chaotic flux which as a flux is unknowable because not enduring long enough to have any assignable character. Within the world of physical change or becoming, these ultimate immaterial essences appear as mathematical forms. Mathematical relations supply nature with all its regularity and recurrence, with whatever is constant, or resembles constancy, amid the scene of change. They also supply the only conditions through which nature may be, in any genuine sense, known, be matter of science. The usual charge against the Platonic theory of ideas is that it confused mental concepts with things. If the charge means that Plato began with psychical existences or even with logical abstractions and ended with hypostatizing them, it quite misses the method and object of Plato. He began with changing objects, acts, and beliefs, and concluded that self-consistent beliefs, stable modes of behavior (individual and social), permanently real objects (and no object not permanently real can be truly real at all) all imply unified eternal essences, which as unified and eternal must be immaterial. This meaning of the term (or of its Latin transliteration of the Aristotelian *eidos*, species, namely) lasted through the entire scholastic period, nominalism alone denying the objective existence of archetypal standards of action and belief. Moreover, through the use of final causes in the medieval science of nature, these standard patterns, in the form of the ends for the sake of which events occur, were assumed also to be the keys to the natural sphere. Even today, any one who believes in absolute eternal objective standards or types of justice, truth, law (whether natural or moral), etc., to which particular sets and events tend to conform (or should conform) accepts the essentials of the Platonic doctrine of ideas.

Quite early in modern thought, however, the term "idea" began to change its signification, taking on a more distinctively mental coloring. The notion of objective pattern shaded over into that of internal design, a mental copy according to which an action is carried on; the notion of objective end similarly shades into that of *conscious* intent, purpose as a mental copy of some result to be accomplished. In this way, the term "idea" came to designate any object so far as that object was held in mind, whether for purposes of action or thought. According to the scholastic theory of knowledge, the *species*, the kind, was always the real object of knowledge, even in dealing with a particular thing; that is, in *this* table the table-character is what is grasped by intelligence; whatever does not take the form of such a universal is incognizable. John Locke also called the immediate object of the mind in knowledge an idea, but according to him general characters are never directly apprehended objects or simple ideas. On the contrary, sensible qualities, red, hard, loud, sweet, etc., are the forms, the ideas, which mind grasps or "knows" directly. But Locke also accepted the notion that many of these qualities exist only in *mind*, and so he tended (though with some ambiguities) to hold that the objects of the mind in knowledge are mental objects only. Locke's influence practically determined, accordingly, the subsequent sense of the term "idea"—namely, mental event, occurrence, existence, especially if any cognitive force is attached to the mental existence. However, even this restriction was not always observed; idea was often used to designate any mode of so-called psychic existence, such as a feeling, desire, etc. (The word "thought" has also been used in the same loose style.) On the other hand, some surviving flavor of the earlier intellectual connotation clung to the term, so that, following Hume, many psychologists reserved the term for secondary or revived mental events, keeping the terms "sensation," "feeling," "impression" for the primary.

The significance of the term is still further confused by the fact that it has developed a sense intermediate between the original Platonic objective one and the modern psychic one: a logical usage to denote meaning (*what* is meant), conception (*what* is conceived), the object of intellectual reference as distinct from the act of referring. The fundamental importance of meanings in mathematics, the fruitful way in which these meanings interact for the production of new meanings which no inspection of the original meanings could have revealed, the objective coherence of the resulting systems, have led to the formation of a school of Neo-realism which insists that the science of mathematics proves the independent existence of intellectual essences, not subject to the flux of time and non-physical in character. Moreover, many critics have pointed out that the psychical school confused ideas as meanings with ideas as private, psychic existences, thus making knowledge impossible, since knowledge requires that sensation, image, idea, have a stable reference beyond its own existence. The use of hypothetical meanings as tools of inquiry has meantime suggested still another sense for the term "idea"—that of tentative hypothesis, suggestion, theory. This interpretation mediates between the two conceptions of meaning as pure objective essence and idea as mere psychic existence. As uncertain and tentatively used, the hypothesis or suggestion is mental; in its application and possible outcome, if confirmed, it is subjective.

See CONCEPTION; HYPOTHESIS; METHOD; THINKING; also ASSOCIATION OF IDEAS.

IDEALISM.—In the history of thought, idealism covers two things very different from one another, each kind including many varieties and both distinct from the meaning of the term "idealism" as employed in life. In the latter sense, idealism means a praiseworthy *moral* attitude, consisting in devotion to high aims, to ideals, even at the expense of personal loss in material comfort and financial gain. In its technical philosophical meaning, the two types of idealism are characteristic of ancient and modern thought, respectively. The former is primarily a teleological theory of the cosmos, of nature; the latter is primarily an assimilation of nature to consciousness. Classic idealism was a systematized method of interpreting nature from the standpoint of final cause (see CAUSE). It held that nature exists for the sake of realizing purpose, the ultimate purpose being the Good. The degree of reality possessed by any temporal or phenomenal form of existence is accordingly measured on the scale of the degree in which it embodies or realizes the End, the Good. Reason, intelligence, was conceived as either the highest, the final, good of existence or at least as an indispensable element in the culminating end. It was not conceived, however, as either the efficient cause of nature or as the stuff out of which apparently physical things are made. Nor was the proof of idealism sought in psychological or epistemological grounds. On the contrary, the theory of knowledge was such as would now be termed realistic. It held that the human knower, the individual mind, became intelligent or rational through the process of knowing objects that exist independently of it, by means of appropriating to itself the amount and kind of ultimate reality embodied in them. In the phraseology of Aristotle, sensation is a realization of the sensible qualities of objects; imagination of their form so far as still immersed in particular cases; reason of their universal form, free from particular limitations. And while Plato and Aristotle, the two great names of classic idealism, disagreed in many respects, they were at one in holding that our mental operations are to be viewed and explained from the standpoint of objective reality, not objective reality from the standpoint of our operations of knowing. Consequently, while much is made of reason as explaining the order, the harmony, and proportion found in nature, little is made of the chief concept of modern idealism, consciousness, so that the term hardly appears as a significant conception.

Modern idealism may be said to have found its points of departure in two convictions: (*a*) The most certain, the best known, thing is an individual's own inner life, his play of emotions, hopes, fears, pleasures, pains, ideas, memories, etc., what was later termed consciousness, or the psychic; (*b*) all objects as known are relative to the processes of sense-perception and judgment that are involved in knowing them. (1) From the feeling that the surest, the most accessible region, in fact the only directly accessible and absolutely sure thing, is the individual's own inner life, it was but a step to the conclusion that the sole escape from skepticism as to the possibility of scientific knowledge of the world, as well as the sole way of explaining how a physical world can interact with a mental world, is to resolve that external world itself into psychic material. The assimilation of the objective to the subjective has been the characteristic trait of every form of modern idealism. (2) The conviction that sense qualities are relative to the individual percipient had been held by some of the sophists in antiquity. Under the prevailing conditions of science at that time, however, such a theory could issue only in intellectual nihilism, the denial of all stable knowledge. The case was quite otherwise with the beginnings of modern science. All those interested in removing from science the incubus of explanation through final causes fastened upon it by scholasticism, and in substituting a mechanical mode of explanation, were interested in reducing physical nature to a homogeneous medium, to mass, motion, space, and time capable of interchangeable statement in terms of one another. The most obvious obstacle to the accomplishment of this ideal was the diversity of static qualities presented by natural objects. By the simple device of relegating color, sound, smells, tastes, to the mind of the percipient, this obstacle was overcome, and the residual "real" object was left with only properties that lent themselves to mathematical formulation and mechanical explanation. Hence, it was those most interested in the progress of physical science that were most emphatic in declaring the purely mental nature of the "secondary" qualities. Galileo, Descartes, Hobbes, all taught that they are "effects" produced by the real object on the sentient mind, useful as signs to point to powers in the object, but having a purely mental status.

It was the work of Berkeley (*q.v.*) to carry this line of argument into a thoroughgoing idealism. With acumen and vigor he pointed out that to common sense, to the plain man, the real object and the perceived object are identical; that as a matter of fact the so-called primary qualities (extension, resistance, and the spatial-mathematical properties generally) are inseparably bound up with the visible and tangible qualities, and hence that the so-called material real object was but an "abstract" idea. Hence the entire world of known and knowable objects was mental: *esse* equals *percipi*. Berkeley, as a theologian, had no difficulty in attributing the permanent and orderly relations manifested in the world of perceived objects—their "laws"—to the work of divine mind, leading us to expect, in regular and reliable ways, one perception to follow upon another. Hume (*q.v.*), with his antitheological bias, had no difficulty in showing that upon Berkeley's own principles, God, being unperceivable, has no valid status, and that mind itself must be resolved into the simple flux or stream of changing perceptions.

Since his time, idealism has flowed in two separate channels. Empirical, psychological, or subjective idealism has stood for the Berkeleyan resolution of existence into perceptions and their associations, simultaneous and successive—minus, of course, his assumption of spiritual soul substance, divine and human. But since one school of philosophic theory, and upon the whole, the orthodox one, had always attributed slight, or even negative, importance to perceptions as compared with conceptions, in determining the framework of knowledge and in giving certainty, there arose another type of idealism which identified "Reality" with conceptual, or rational, contents, whose motto was *esse* equals *intelligi.* This school of rational idealism is also termed objective realism, because it has taught that thought relations constitute objects independently of relation to any individual percipient, which, as merely individual, is only sentient and hence incapable of general (scientific) knowledge except as it is informed by the same *a priori* or objective reason that constitutes the objective world itself. Its chief motif has been the necessity of permanent and universal relations for the existence of objects of scientific and systematized knowledge, and the identification of these relations with the various functions of rational thought. This type of idealism was introduced by Kant and was carried to its culmination by Hegel, who, however, introduced another and independent conception: that the objective manifestation of mind is found more adequately presented in social life, in the state, and in the historic phenomena of politics, art, and religion than in nature. Schopenhauer, in turn, gave idealism a further distinctive turn by finding the clue to the nature of existence in will rather than in rational thought.

It may almost be said that, barring materialistic and agnostic philosophies, these two types of idealism divided the field between them for a century after Kant. At present, there are many signs that the idealistic movement has, temporarily at least, spent its force. At least, there is a strong realistic tendency in active progress. This movement is too recent and too close to permit of any accurate and just assignment of causes. Some of the main reasons for it are, however, obvious. One is the exhaustion of interests in the type of problems that gave idealism its original impetus. Another is a number of inherent inconsistencies that no type of idealism has completely overcome. Allied to this is the seeming deadlock between the two kinds of idealism. Moreover, there is a growing feeling that the complete resolution of everything into psychical existence, whether sentient or rational or a fusion of them both (as in Bradley and Royce) in breaking down all distinction between mind and anything else, defeats its own end—that of attributing some distinctive, significant place and efficacy to intelligence in the scheme of existence. Concretely, the most influential force has probably been the development of the doctrine of biological evolution and its evidence that mind, instead of being the sole monopolistic existence, is itself an expression of life, and the means by which life secures its most effective control of the environment in the furtherance of its own active processes. At present, the realistic movement has both a pragmatic and an intellectualistic form, the two agreeing in their common opposition to traditional idealistic systems rather than in a positive body of convictions.

References:—

BERKELEY, G. *Works.* (Oxford, 1901.)

BRADLEY, F. H. *Appearance and Reality.* (London, 1897.)

CAIRD, E. *Critical Philosophy of Immanuel Kant.* (Glasgow, 1889.)

FICHTE, J. G. *Grundlage der gesammten Wissenschaftslehre.* (Tübingen, 1802.)

FOUILLÉE, A. *Le Mouvement idéaliste et la Réaction contre la Science.* (Paris, 1896.)

HERBERT, T. M. *The Realistic Assumption of Modern Science.* (London, 1879.)

HÖFFDING, H. *History of Modern Philosophy.* (London, 1908.)

HUME, D. *Philosophical Works.* (London, 1875.)

KANT, I. *Kritik der reinen Vernunft.* (Riga, 1787.)

LADD, G. T. *A Theory of Reality.* (New York, 1899.)

ORMOND, A. T. *Foundations of Knowledge.* (London, 1900.)

ROYCE, J. *Spirit of Modern Philosophy.* (Boston, 1892.)

The World and the Individual. (New York, 1900–1901.)

SCHOPENHAUER, A. *Works.* (Leipzig, 1891.)

TAINE, H. *L'Idéalisme Anglais.* (Paris, 1864.)

WATSON, J. *Christianity and Idealism.* (London, 1897.)

See also BALDWIN, J. M. *Dictionary of Philosophy and Psychology.* Vol. III, Pt. II, pp. 615–620, for articles in current magazines, etc.

IDEALISM AND REALISM IN EDUCATION.—Two idealistic systems of philosophy have had a peculiarly intimate connection with the theory of education, the Socratic-Platonic movement in antiquity and that of German transcendentalism in recent times. They have also exercised a significant influence upon educational practice. The effect upon practice has not been so much direct as reflex, consisting chiefly in affording a supposed intellectual justification for procedures that originated independently of philosophy. The Platonic idealism, so far as it affected education, was a development of the method pursued by Socrates in his endeavor to arrive at fundamental principles and standards of action. Socrates urged that since no man would voluntarily do violence to his own being or deliberately seek his own harm, ignorance of his own real nature and its proper end, or good, was the source of all evil-doing. Moreover, ignorance was the cause of the divisions, the struggles and factions, of civil life. Wherever there is knowledge or true understanding, dispute is impossible; agreement and knowledge are equivalent. The search for knowledge, the process of learning, is, therefore, of necessity a search for that which all men have in common, and which, accordingly, they have a mutual interest in reaching. Argumentative dispute, the desire to conquer in argument, is *ipso facto* evidence of lack of love of wisdom or knowledge. Its opposite, comparison of ideas with a view to discovering their common basis and intent, Socrates called dialectic. Since opinions and beliefs could differ only if they meant to refer to the same thing, a common underlying reality was implied in them.

In the dialectic method there were accordingly three elements: (*a*) The presupposition of an objective universal as the proper subject matter of knowledge; (*b*) the implication of this universal in all particular opinions and beliefs; (*c*) the possibility of its discovery by systematic comparison of particulars. The resultant discovery formed the concept or definition of the object in question—justice or whatever ethical reality might be the object of search. Unless there were such objective universals, the moral anarchy of subjectivism was inevitable; anything was good or right that seemed to be right or good to an individual at any particular moment. The further consequence was social discord and strife, for only an objective universal gave anything common, that is, supplied a basis of unity.

Plato extended the Socratic method from moral realities and knowledge of them to all realities and the proper method of knowing them. Knowledge as distinct from private shifting opinions is possible only by virtue of unchangeable substantial universals in which all the particulars of a class participate and through reference to which they can be defined and understood. These objective universals were the Platonic Ideas (*q.v.*) or Forms. Moreover, since all particulars were changing, they were capable of order and uniformity only in the degree in which their changes tended toward their universal. It was then their end, their good, or perfection. Hence true or dialectical knowledge consists in knowing the ends for which natural things exist; a thing without an end is a mere monstrosity.

There are many phases of the Platonic idealism that are reflected in his own educational theory. In fact, education was of central importance in his philosophy, since it was only by a proper method of education that men could become skilled in the use of the dialectic method and be enabled to turn the eye of the soul from the sense appetites and opinions, that correspond to mutable particulars, upon the eternal universal. But a more important consideration for our present purpose is the fact that while the details of the Platonic scheme remained practically without influence, the two chief aspects of his method became firmly embedded in all higher education. These were the setting of dialectical above physical inquiry, and of discussion of final causes above search for efficient causes. Physical science dealt with just the particular and changing things which, according to this philosophy, were relatively unreal; they corresponded only to sense knowledge and mere probability, or opinion. More important was the elaborating and comparing of ideas and beliefs; matters of classification and definition, rather than of observation and experiment. Knowledge of antecedent conditions and constituent (physical) elements was, moreover, held in contempt compared with knowledge of the end or purpose for which things existed. And this latter was a matter of development of meanings rather than of external observation of facts.

That for over fifteen hundred years education followed

these lines is too well known to need recording. There is also no need to say that causes quite independent of the Platonic idealism were responsible for the neglect of the physical sciences and mechanical methods of analysis. But the Platonic dialectic as elaborated through the Aristotelian logic furnished the intellectual tools for the entire patristic and scholastic system of education, and the philosophic ideas through which the leading ideas were defended and systematized. Even in the humanistic educational ideal, the feeling that preoccupation with ideas and beliefs is intrinsically more worthy than inquiry into natural existences is to a considerable extent a survival of the dialectic side of classic idealism.

In the general sense of the term, accordingly, Realism in education began with the reaction of the Renaissance period against the supremacy of those forms of subject matter that could be dealt with by pure logic. It contended that such subject matter consisted simply of abstractions at its best, and at worst simply of words. Moreover, since only ideas and beliefs that were already in the mind, or that were already current, could be analyzed, defined, and systematized by purely dialectic method, this method confined men to tradition and authority. In the interest, then, of both reality and mental emancipation, the Realism of the sixteenth and seventeenth centuries called men from ideas to things. Francis Bacon is the great representative of this movement, philosophically; so far as philosophic Realism influenced education it was chiefly through his work. The older methods were, however, too deeply entrenched to undergo much more than slight transformations in externals. The Baconian Realism was but prophetic; there were no well-developed methods of inquiring into fact and no organized subject matter available for educational purposes.

The transcendental idealism of the later eighteenth and early nineteenth century had a symbolic and an institutional form, the former represented in education by Froebel, the latter by Hegel. Both are dominated by the idea of a progressive development or unfolding of a spiritual self-consciousness (which is the principle of totality) in and through the particulars of nature and human experience.

According to romantic (or symbolic) idealism, particulars (especially those approximating mathematical form) are suggestive, illustrative, allegorically symbolic of the absolute truth. Accordingly they may be employed to awaken in the mind of infancy the absolute truth or reality already implicit or latent in it. Froebel's great natural aptitude for perceiving the educative force of plays and games, and modes of occupation, was accordingly utilized by him in the interest of a religious, quasi-mystic, quasi-mathematical formalism, the formalism being explained and sanctioned by its supposed correspondence in the realm of feeling and sense with spiritual essence and law in the absolute sphere.

Hegel's idealism was substantially an outgrowth of his opposition to the subjective idealism he attributed to Kant and Fichte. According to him, absolute mind is externalized in physical nature, but truly objectified in social institutions and history. The state is objective reason and will. Only by participating in this realized spirit can the potential mind, latent in individuals, get rational substance or body for what otherwise is a mere empty capacity for consciousness. The unqualified necessity of social institutions as the agencies through which the latent rationality of individuals is to be awakened and developed or brought to full reality, was thus the final lesson of the Hegelian idealism. The accomplishing of this end constitutes education.

Remarkably enough, the great metaphysical realist, Herbart, reached essentially the same conclusion by an opposed route. According to him, there is no one final, all-embracing, absolute reality; there is a plurality of reals. Moreover, there is no intrinsic tendency in the individual mind to evolve according to its own inner law into realization of supreme reason or spirit. There is only the capacity to react in a characteristic way to every contact with a real. Education is thus not the growth or development of the mind in accord with its own inner nature; it is a forming or shaping of mind through the presentation of the external reals which operate upon it. The earlier reactions persist as ideas and form the mental material through which all later presentative reactions are received and organized. By controlling the earlier presentations, in terms of which the later are "apperceived" and made effective, we can accordingly control the formation of mind and character, this latter being, indeed, but the complex of patterns formed by past contents as they operate in determining the reception and organization of new contents. In deciding, however, the order and sequence of the presentation of materials, Herbart was almost wholly under the influence of the notion of recapitulation of the culture of the past. As the earlier contents in the history of the individual dominate the assimilation of the later, so these earlier contents are to be assimilated to the culture products of the earlier stages of civilized mankind. Thus, in spite of their radically diverging bases, the Hegelian and the Herbartian systems, as applied to education, agree in the primacy of social material, the former emphasizing the value of institutions, the latter of culture products.

It is out of the question in a matter involving as many important considerations and issues as the idealistic-realistic controversy to do more than point out some of the chief points involved in passing judgment upon it. From the earlier historic division it appears that the question concerns the respective places of meanings and of natural existences in the scheme of experience. From the latter discussion, the issue is seen to have to do with the respective functions of inner development and outer control. If one commenced the investigation of the problem with educational interests uppermost, one's most probable conclusion would be that existence and meaning, internal growth and outer direction, are mutually complementary, not exclusive rivals. As matter of fact, the beliefs of the greatest number of men have always been dualistic rather than exclusively idealistic or realistic. But, again, from the standpoint of that direction of growth of character and intelligence that we call education, what is needed is not a division of the field into separate regions, or into two disconnected kinds of force, but a cooperation of two distinctions which are both relative to the evolution of life and experience. In short, from the standpoint of education, the need is for a philosophy which translates the static divisions of mind and world, inner and outer, that characterize traditional dualisms into dynamic interacting factors of growth, thereby going beyond both traditional idealism and realism.

See Dualism; Humanism and Naturalism.

IMITATION . . . Imitation in Education.—Large reliance upon imitation in education has been defended upon two grounds, one psychological, the other sociological. Psychologically, it is claimed that out-of-school experience shows that the child acquires the larger part of his skill in various directions by imitation, so that economy and efficiency require that it be the chief resource for learning in school. Socially, it is contended that the chief distinguishing feature of social life is identity of mental contents, especially of thought and beliefs, on the part of the various individuals who constitute society, and that this identity is secured by imitation. Largely under the influence of Tarde, older biological theories of society were replaced by "psychological" conceptions of society, and imitation was made the chief, if not the sole, category of social psychology. If this doctrine be accepted, appeal to imitation is not merely a valuable psychological expedient, but is an ethical necessity.

Both of these conceptions are questionable. A common fallacy seems to underlie them both. Wherever there is a social group, people are found doing the same sort of things; and, what is even more important, believing the same sort of things and using the same standards of valuation. Since it is demonstrable that this similarity is acquired, and since it is certain that the younger members of society have learned from the older, it is an easy conclusion that the likeness is due to imitation. But this explanation hardly does more than to take a result and then give it the name of a cause or force. The certain fact that persons do, externally viewed, imitate one another, that is, do alike and think alike, and that this community is essential to society is translated over into a belief that imitation is a natural internal force, working to bring about the likeness. Closer inquiry shows, however, that other causes are chiefly responsible, and that so far as there is a distinctive psychological tendency to imitate, it works effectively only in subordination to these other factors.

Upon the personal side, the initial factor is the tendency of native impulses and acquired habits to complete or realize themselves in some external form. The child spontaneously, naturally or instinctively as we say, tries to effect something, urged on by the force of his own impulsive tendency. He reaches out his hand, makes babbling noises, tries to throw a ball, to walk, etc. Intent upon his end, he unconsciously selects and adapts anything he notes that might help him. He does what he sees others do in the same situation, not in order to imitate them,—a matter of which he may be quite unconscious,—but as a way of executing his own inchoate tendency. The mere imitation of others, apart from selective use, is found in imbeciles, in the less intelligent children, and in the more mechanical and empty moments of intelligent children. When reliance upon imitation is urged in teaching, the essential thing in the natural situation, personal initiative in a certain direction, is forgotten, and there is substituted for it a servile dependence upon the ends of others. Since the process of selecting and adapting the observed actions of others to one's own results involves intelligence, while taking the acts of others as one's ends abrogates judgment, it is not surprising that objection is made out of school to the latter process.

Further examination shows that imitation, even in its subordinate role, is properly called such from without, not from within. Psychologically what occurs is a case of the wider principle of sensori-motor adaptation. While the human infant is not limited to predetermined coordinations of sensory stimulus and motor response, as are the young of lower animals, the necessities of life require that there be some preference for certain forms of behavior in connection with certain modes of excitation. A stimulus of light, for example, at once induces movement of the eyes in fixing and following it. This act operates in turn as stimulus to the body to throw itself into a certain posture, to the arm and hand to reach, and, at times, to follow by tracing the movements of the light. Persons watching a runner, a baseball batter, or one performing a gymnastic feat, unintentionally sway the body sympathetically. Externally viewed, there is acceptance of another as a model for copy; psychologically viewed, there is only the completion of the sensori-motor coordination involved in every act of perception. Accordingly, from the side of individual development, "imitation" is but a species of a wider genus. Persons act much alike and think much alike because they are subject to the same stimuli and are urged on by the same needs.

The case works out in a similar way from the social side. Mere imitation would never even make a beginning of a society, because it would only give a number of persons doing the same thing at the same time. A society involves diversity of activities on the part of different persons (division of labor, in a wide sense of that term) and cooperation of different acts to a common end. But in addition to this coadaptation of different acts to a single result (which is found in machinery), there must be also an intellectual and emotional appreciation of the common end and of the relation of the diverse individuals to it. This fact has been partially recognized in Baldwin's version of Tarde's theory, for he criticizes Tarde on the ground that his doctrine would apply equally well to a collection of tuning forks where one vibrates in response to another. Consequently he amends the conception to read imitation of *thoughts*, or *mental contents*, not of acts. In effect, this is to surrender the idea of imitation and keep merely the name, for thoughts or mental contents as such, cannot possibly be imitated, being invisible and unobservable. And the details of Baldwin's account show that what he really is dealing with is the various processes by which one person *arrives* at community of beliefs and ideas with others. This confirms our statement that the so-called "imitation" is simply a name for the fact that different persons do, in the same community, think alike, that likeness of thought being necessary to social life, but that it is not a causal factor by which this community of ideas and emotions is brought about.

Educationally, the emphasis upon imitation as the essential fact about society not only fails to throw light upon the causal forces by which social direction is brought about, but in a progressive society sets up a false ethical ideal. It makes identity of belief a good, and the supreme social good, just by itself. Such a standard obtains only in static communities, controlled by conformity to custom, and it is a symptom and a cause of their stationary nature. The intellectual and moral progress of the human race has come through first tolerating and then encouraging divergencies and diversities of thought,—the essence of individuality,—and through the conception that mere identity of thoughts is not an end in itself, but an incident of the accomplishment of other ends. More specifically, it is quite contrary to the spirit of a democratic and progressive society to set up as a conscious end the idea that one, even if he be only an immature child, shall repeat the acts of another so as to arrive at a state of passive acquiescence in the ideas of others. Whether as a psychological method or as a social standard, imitation occupies a subordinate position.

References:—

BALDWIN, J. M. *Mental Development in the Child and Race.* (New York, 1897.)

Social and Ethical Interpretations. (New York, 1897.)

MCDOUGALL, W. *Social Psychology.* (London, 1908.)

ROYCE, J. *Century Magazine*, May, 1894; *Psych. Review*, Vol. II, 1895.

TARDE, G. *Les lois de l'imitation* (Paris, 1890); tr. by E. C. Parsons (New York, 1903).

INDIVIDUALITY.—The idea and fact of individuality are among the most familiar and best known things in experience. They are also among the most difficult to describe and define. Individuality is such a fundamental matter that it can hardly be defined without presupposing itself or giving a purely verbal equivalent, such as the unique, the distinctive to the point of the irreplaceable. An indication of its meaning is given by its logical usage, where it always implies contrast with a kind, sort, or *class.* This implied contrast also gives an indication of the place where the conception of individuality is important for educational philosophy. School administration and instruction require a certain uniformity of rule and method; these in turn presuppose sameness of character in those dealt with. In so far individuals are regarded as members, specimens of a class, distinguished from one another by purely external and physical traits. Since, as a matter of fact, there are intrinsic mental and moral differences, the purely uniform, or class, standpoint leaves out of consideration conditions that cannot safely be ignored. The idea of individuality serves as a reminder of these outstanding conditions. It calls attention to those traits which are unique, non-repeatable, which are differential, and which accordingly require special treatment, particular re-adaptation of general or class methods and standards.

History shows a continual, even if irregular, movement toward individuation; the recognition of the increasing importance of individually distinctive traits. In savage societies, the individual is also lost in the group—in the clan or tribe. Not till a comparatively recent point of historic development do we find individuals possessing rights on their own account in contradistinction from their status as members of a family, guild, class, caste, etc. Their rise from submergence in a class is a part of the growth of democracy as a social principle. From the scientific side, the appearance of the doctrine of evolution has emphasized the importance of individual differences and variations, as against the older notion of the fixed species within which the individual was placed and which exhausted his important or essential nature.

One of the most fundamental of all philosophic cleavages centres in the question of the method of valuing the facts of individuality. Professor James has divided philosophies into those which tend to assume the priority of the whole and to derive the individuals from the whole as its constituent parts or specimen instances; and those which assume the priority of the parts, the individuals, and make the whole secondary, dependent upon the arrangements reached among the individuals. The former philosophies approximate monism in substance and rationalism in method, the latter are pluralistic and empirical. The prominence of the concept of the organic in nineteenth-century idealism is owing to the fact that it seemed to yield a conception for reconciling the otherwise opposed ideas of individual and universal, whole and part. It may be questioned, however, whether the notion of the organic is a solution or only a peculiarly vivid presentation of the terms of the problem. The proper method of dealing with the question is probably suggested by the connection that exists between the common, generic, or class-universal and the facts of stability, order, conservation on one hand, and between individuality and variability, freedom, progress on the other. In a static and finished world, individuality would have no meaning; while a world lacking in universal characters, in characters that make things capable of reduction to classes, would not present any signs of law, permanence, and conservation. For the further educational significance of the term, see EDUCATION; and PHILOSOPHY OF EDUCATION.

INDUCTION AND DEDUCTION.—There are two complementary movements of thinking involved in directing inquiry to a well-grounded conclusion. When a perplexity occurs or a problem presents itself, the first step is to clarify the obscure situation. This consists in such analysis of the situation as indicates a principle, law, or relation. Induction always terminates in an idea or proposition which is general because a statement of a relation, a universal. Deduction is the application of the generic factor to the interpretation, explanation, and organization of specific data. The two movements are complementary because induction terminates in the universal with which deduction sets out, while the validity and scope of the universal is determined by its application, under test conditions, to new facts—this application being deduction.

In Aristotelian logic, syllogism and demonstration correspond to what is now called deduction. The term which was translated into Latin as *deductio* designated simply the method of *reductio ad absurdum*, or the indirect proof of a proposition by showing that its contradictory proposition involved a logical absurdity or self-contradiction. Induction was a method of collecting instances or particular cases, and was perfect when all cases agreed, and formed, therefore, a class as it was imperfect when a number of cases (not all) agreed, so that the most that could be said was that some S is P, or that usually S is P. Perfect induction was known as induction by simple enumeration. After the rise of modern methods of induction, many logicians denied that the method of enumeration was a true case of reasoning, on the ground that it merely summed up in a single statement what was already known, instead of discovering any new truth.

In the sixteenth and seventeenth centuries attacks upon syllogistic logic because of its barrenness and verbal character were widespread. Interest centered in a logic that could be employed to wrest nature's secrets from her, while the syllogism was fitted, as Bacon said, only for argumentation. Agreed in their opposition to the old organon of thought, the new logicians at once divided among themselves. Some, Descartes and his followers, sought the new method in a new type of deduction; others, the British empiricists, in a new form of induction. According to the former school, we should begin by making a *tabula rasa* of all traditional beliefs, and seek for some concepts that are so inherently clear and certain that their meaning cannot be disputed nor their truth doubted. From these most general truths, by combination, further truths were to be established, proceeding by graded steps, so that at no time should any new factor be introduced which was not clearly defined and certain. In this way, reason was to proceed until reaching particular phenomena or concrete events, in space and time. These deduced phenomena would be approximated by actual sensible phenomena, and would constitute the rationality or explanation of the latter. Descartes even went so far as to offer a system of (to him) self-evident first principles, from which, given an original chaotic state of nature, the whole existing order of the world might be rationally deduced. Stated in the above fashion, the method appears as formal and as fruitless as ever the syllogistic logic had been; but, as matter of content, the whole scheme was conceived in mathematical terms. In effect it was a plea for the application of mathematics to nature. Toward the development of a mathematical science of nature, Descartes himself took the first step by his invention of analytic geometry. And for succeeding men of science—however it may have been with philosophers—deduction has meant mathematical procedure, which, entering upon a brilliant career, became a chief tool of scientific exploration and formulation.

Francis Bacon is popularly reckoned the father of modern induction—an attribution for which Macaulay is probably largely responsible. As a matter of fact, while he made much of induction, the method he proffered under that name is a confused mixture of the older method of cataloguing and the newer method of analysis. Sir Isaac Newton was both the practitioner and the formulator of induction proper, Locke's influence on the philosophic side blending with Newton's. According to Newton, the beginning must always be made with observations; these observations by analogy suggest some force or principle, known on other grounds to exist in nature, though not previously known to be concerned in the phenomena in question. This principle is then to be treated deductively, or mathematically, and thereby phenomena predicted which have not been previously observed, but which must be found if the theory is true. Further observation must then be resorted to to see whether the indicated phenomena do exist. If the actual phenomena agreed precisely with the deduced phenomena, the theory should be accepted until contrary evidence is discovered. So consistent was Newton in his demand for precise corroboration that when the observed astronomical data did not exactly agree with the results he calculated on the basis of his theory, he held the theory of gravitation in suspense until new data enabled him to revise his calculations. For a time the Newtonian and the Cartesian theories of the constitution of the solar system were rivals, but as the immense superiorities of Newton's explanation became more and more evident, the inductive-observational method was as firmly established in the natural sciences of facts, as the deductive in the mathematical.

No important developments in the theory of induction took place after Newton's time until toward the middle of the nineteenth century, when suggestions by Whewell and Herschel were taken up by John Stuart Mill, whose *System of Logic* is almost as classic a statement of an empirical inductive logic, as Aristotle's had been of a syllogistic logic. According to Mill, we reason or infer, originally, from particular to particular, from one case to another. This is due to an inherent propensity to generalize, or to assume that what happens in one case will also happen in other cases. The sole scientific warrant for this belief is the uniformity of nature, which is itself an induction from a vast, literally countless, number of particular observations, where not a single contrary or negating instance is found. This widest of all inductions is, then, the logical ground upon which all other inductions rest.

In the development of his system Mill alternates between two different definitions and treatments of induction, one conventional and rather sterile, the other based on the actual procedure of experimental science. According to the former, induction is the process of inferring that what has been observed to happen in a certain number of observed cases will always happen in cases resembling them. Evidently such a statement is vague. It raises the questions: How great must the number of observed cases be? What is it that really happens in the original cases—no easy matter to determine because of the complexity of natural events. Just what degree of resemblance must exist to warrant belief in the same thing happening in other cases? And how shall we make sure that the required kind of similarity exists? In dealing with such questions, Mill passed over to the idea that the crux of induction is found in the various methods that analyze the observed cases and bring to light within them some unvarying coexistence or sequence of elements. Induction is thus the method of finding *in* the phenomena some relation which is not directly observable.

Mill never clearly apprehended, however, the transformation which he himself effected in the notion of induction. According to his first and official views, induction simply extends to all cases what is found in some cases. According to the later, his *working,* though not professed, view, it consists in finding out what *really* happens or exists in "some cases." The emphasis has shifted from the mere quantitative collection and mechanical comparison of instances to the qualitative and experimental analysis of the one typical case, or to the few carefully selected cases. Empirical collection of a great number of cases remains indeed of great importance, but as an assistance and safeguard in the selection and analysis of a typical case and in testing the resulting hypothesis, not as furnishing the original premises of an inductive inference.

Educational methods have reflected and have suffered from the divorce of the deductive and inductive phases of reflective inquiry characteristic of the history of logic. The chief error upon the side of the inductive movement is in supposing that the mind begins with a lot of separate, independent objects, such as this, that, and the other river, and then proceeds by mechanical comparison to select the things they statically have in common, and to reject the qualities not found in them all. As a matter of fact, induction consists in grasping what is *significant*, what is intellectually important, in any one river. Comparison and contrast with other rivers is of value, not in pointing out external likenesses and differences, but in helping to weigh the relative importance of qualities, and to seize upon and to emphasize any property that gives a clue to understanding other features. The trait of generalization found in induction does not primarily have to do with what is common to a number of cases, but with the *law or relation* which is significant in *any* case.

Educationally, this means that it is important to deal with a *single* river basin as a typical case, so as to get an idea of what is important in it, rather than to deal superficially with a large number of river systems. Moreover, the *importance* of any feature means its power to explain other features. Hence what should be emphasized in inductive study is the *causal*, the productive or dynamic factors. These can best be brought out by a thorough study of a river system treated as a type, while comparing a large number of cases without careful analysis of any one case brings into relief only static properties, effects, not causes.

It will be noted that when the inductive method of instruction takes as its object the discovery of causal or explanatory features, it is organically connected with deduction, since the motive of discovering these basic features is to get a principle which may be applied to interpreting and organizing the other facts characteristic of rivers. This application is deductive. On the other hand, the mere selection of properties common to a number of objects throws no light upon *why* they are common, nor does it help explain the traits which, being dissimilar, are eliminated. Hence induction is arbitrarily separated from deduction.

Other errors in the method of instruction due to this

mechanical division of induction and deduction are the following: (1) Teaching any subject so that isolated facts are amassed, without using them so that there is gained a view of some inclusive situation in which the different clues are connected and hence significant. (2) Or, when the weakness of this method is perceived, the teacher is content to leave the pupils with only a vague notion of the whole to which the details belong. This vagueness can be expelled (and the special facts made really significant) only as the mind realizes *how* the particulars go together to make up the inclusive whole.

It goes without saying that when induction is isolated from deduction, the latter must also be isolated and hence fail to exercise its proper function. Educational errors of method flowing from this isolation are the following: (1) Beginning with definitions, rules, principles, laws. It may sometimes be pedagogically advisable to *present* a definition or law at the outset, especially with older students, but in all cases it should be recognized that this is a psychological device for directing attention to a *problem*, not a statement of a true logical principle. Logically, the general principle or law has no meaning until in the course of dealing with some individual complex situation need has arisen for explaining various particulars by binding them together into a more coherent system. (2) Even when the explanatory principle has been properly reached, there may be failure in the proper use of deduction through not securing its *application* to *new* cases. It is at this point, not at the outset, that the reference to a number of cases becomes most important. When, by a study of a type case, the pupil has become possessed of its principle, or generic nature, this principle must be expanded, clinched, and tested by application to a variety of other cases not previously studied. So far as possible this application should involve not only new observations, but also a factor of experimentation (*q.v.*). Mathematics, primarily a deductive study, suffers particularly in education from lack of application of its general principles to concrete empirical situation. The application of a mathematical conception simply to other mathematical cases, however adequate in abstract theory, is, pedagogically, simply an elaboration of the principle, not a deductive testing of its meaning.

The prior discussion may be summed up by saying that educational method has lagged behind the development of scientific method. It has tended to remain at the plane of the earlier scientific practices in which induction as dealing with particulars, and deduction as dealing with universals, were separated from each other. Educational method should adapt itself to the change in scientific method, in accord with which reflective inquiry is concerned with complex objects and situations, in which induction serves to discover, by analysis, a relation or principle, while deduction employs that principle synthetically to reconnect particulars into a more comprehensive situation or object.

See Abstraction; Analysis and Synthesis; Conception; Generalization; Hypothesis; Knowledge; Method.

References:—

Colvin, S. S. *The Learning Process.* (New York, 1911.)

Dewey, John. *How We Think.* (Boston, 1911.)

Studies in Logical Theory. (Chicago, 1903.)

Lotze, H. *Logik.* (Leipzig, 1880.)

Mill, J. S. *A System of Logic.* (New York, 1900.)

Miller, I. E. *Psychology of Thinking.* (New York, 1909.)

Sigwart, C. von. *Logic.* Tr. by H. Dandy. (London, 1895.)

Venn, J. *Principles of Empirical or Inductive Logic.* (London, 1889.)

INFANCY, THEORY OF, IN EDUCATION.—Infancy denotes, biologically, the phase of immaturity in the development of a function or organ of an organism. It is a more or less relative term, since some one function may be quite undeveloped while others are fully operative. The conception of infancy in contemporary educational theory is also colored by its legal, or better, social sense. Infancy means the period of minority, the period when an individual is legally represented by an adult and is under special protection and supervision. By a natural extension of this meaning, infancy, in education, signifies the entire period in which individuals are protected from the assumption of the full duties of adult life, especially those of economic self-support. So considered, infancy consists of those years in which children are shielded against the impact of economic conditions, in order that their time and energies may be devoted to adequate growth; in other words, the years in which the chief interest is education. Quite obviously, the biological and economic phases of infancy go together. The immaturity of capacity is the cause of economic dependence, while the period of economic dependence preserves the plasticity of organs that is favorable to continuous educational growth. Thus the conditions favorable to education have been identified with "the prolongation of infancy."

John Fiske is the author of the doctrine of the importance of prolonged infancy. He seized upon the fact that early perfection and high specialization of function are unfavorable to further development, and that they render practically impossible the acquisition of *new* powers. In some sense, the early perfection of animal instincts and powers is the barrier that precludes learning, and hence development. On the other hand, the incompetency for specialized acts of the human young means a plasticity (*q.v.*) which permits and demands learning—adaptation of capacities to new conditions as these show themselves. Consequently, infancy (of some organ) remains as long as genuine growth, transformation, is possible to a human being. Its opposite is not so much competency of action as arrest of growth, exhaustion of potentiality, of possible assumption of new directions of thought and action.

It follows that infancy is to be conceived positively, rather than negatively; it marks the presence of a powerful and significant resource rather than the mere absence of capacities. Our tendency to conceive infancy in terms of lack, deprivation, impotency, is due to our taking certain specialized adult forms of capacity as our standard; the lack and impotency are purely relative and comparative. If we emphasize the limit of growth which characterizes adult specialized powers (the fact that they evidence the formation of habits that resist readaptation), adult powers are a sign of defect as compared with the mobile, alert ease of adaptation to the new that characterizes infancy. Viewed absolutely, infancy is a power, not an impotency. It is power of growth. Viewed statically, crosswise as it were, immaturity is mere deficiency of development; and till the rise of the biological sciences and of the theory of evolution, it was almost universal to conceive childhood in this negative fashion. Children were simply partial, incomplete adults; the object of education was to hurry them through this period of lack into the full competency of adulthood. Put otherwise, education was a preparation for a future which alone was fully real and significant. But the theory of education substitutes a lengthwise view for this crosswise interpretation; it reveals immaturity as the essence of life itself, the power of continuing development, of renewal, of readaptation to the changing. It represents, so to speak, the evolutionary impetus itself, as against the fixations of capacity for adaptation indicated by matured organs.

The importance of the idea of infancy for educational purposes requires that we note the reflex influence of prolonged infancy upon the social conditions of adult life. It is hardly too much to say, as Mr. Fiske (*q.v.*) also first pointed out, that the helplessness of infancy has probably been the chief force in socializing the human race in its progress out of an animal condition. Mutual defense and economic efficiency have been powerful forces in bringing about associations of human beings. Relations of sex have brought about even more intimate and intense associations. But combinations brought about by these forces are relatively transitory and instinctive as compared with those due to the need of the continued care of the young. Although the young of savage peoples are more precocious than those of civilized races, the years in which their dependence demands continued close association are relatively long in contrast with the weeks, days, or hours during which economic and sexual needs hold people together. It is generally admitted, for example, that the change of the marriage relation from a temporary to an enduring form has been chiefly effected by the presence of children, with their long-continued need for support. And this latter motive can hardly have failed to react into industry, changing it from a predatory immediate satisfaction of physical wants as they became urgent into systematized, cooperative, and sustained modes of action. And this is only to say, with respect both to family and industry, that the presence of the dependent young has been a powerful factor in transforming instincts into conscious affections and thoughts. The continued care of children tends to change passionate attraction into tender emotions, into sympathy, into affectionate interest. It also involves foresight, planning ahead, taking into consideration matters broader and longer than the immediate satisfaction of organic appetite. An interesting light upon the education of adults through the necessities due to the presence of children is shed by the role which the need of instruction has played in the organization of science. Desire to get knowledge into a form in which it would be available and effective in the training of the less advanced has been an infinitely more powerful motive in bringing together and systematizing knowledge and beliefs than all purely logical motives put together. The need of education has been the chief cause of a survey of experience wider than that required by the narrow immediate personal exigencies of appetite and circumstance. This fact is illustrative of the fundamental intellectual and moral influence due to the presence of infants—that is, of the relatively helpless. In the narrower psychological sense of the term, applying to the period from birth to the end of the third year, the subject is discussed in the preceding article on INFANT EDUCATION.

See EDUCATION; GROWTH; also CHILD LABOR; CHILD PSYCHOLOGY; CHILD STUDY; CHILDHOOD, LEGISLATION FOR THE CONSERVATION OF.

References:—

BUTLER, N. M. *The Meaning of Education.* (New York, 1905.)
CHAMBERLAIN, A. F. *The Child*, ch. 1. (London, 1900.)
FISKE, J. *The Meaning of Infancy.* (Boston, 1909.)
HALL, G. S. *Adolescence.* (New York, 1907.)
Youth. (New York, 1906.)
HENDERSON, E. N. *Text-Book in the Principles of Education*, ch. 2. (New York, 1911.)
KIRKPATRICK, E. A. *Fundamentals of Child Study*, ch. 1. (New York, 1903.)

INFERENCE.—The process of thinking or reasoning, in so far as it arrives at new facts, conceptions, or truths. It is practically synonymous with going from the known to the unknown, from the uncertain to the established. In its widest use, it covers the entire process of reflection so far as that terminates in discovery. Sometimes, however, the emphasis falls so sharply on discovery that inference and proof are treated as the two antithetical functions of thinking—inference making the leap to the new, the hitherto unknown, while proof tests and validates what is inferred. As demonstrative proof and deduction are usually identified, this limited meaning identifies inference with induction (*q.v.*).

See PROOF.

INFORMATION.—That phase or branch of knowledge (*q.v.*) which consists of facts and ideas that have been communicated or transmitted by others; and that are accepted, partially at least, on the credit and authority of others; that branch of learning (*q.v.*) that concerns the materials learned from other persons, orally or through books. As will be seen from the definition, information has two marks: a body of cognitive material existing irrespective of its original acquisition and utilization—a ready-made character; and dependence upon social transmission. Obviously the two traits belong together. The ready-made character of information is due to its being carried along in the social medium; while by means of the social processes of communication, facts and ideas discovered by any individual are taken up into the general body of knowledge, independently of the conditions of the original discovery.

Without the funding of personal experiences into information capable of separation from the experiences in which it originated, so that it may be acquired by others without the necessity of their repeating the original experience, every generation would be obliged to rediscover everything by its own observations and reflections—which means of course that mankind would be forever engaged in a hopeless struggle to emerge from savagery. Since language is the medium of deposit and transmission, it is natural that language as the store-house and vehicle of information should be, upon the whole, the chief concern of schooling, and that teaching should be largely identified with the processes of purveying information. On the other hand, the attacks which educational reformers have always found it necessary to make against the domination of schooling by language give evidence of certain dangers lurking in the dependence of individual intelligence upon social acquisitions. The material, not originating in personal initiative and motivation, may easily become a foreign dead load, carried by memory, but not entering in a vital way into personal observations, thoughts, and acts. Such an external second-handed body of information is not only useless, but positively harmful. It weighs down native active tendencies, crushing them, and comes between a person and his use of his natural judgment.

There is, therefore, no problem in education more pressing than the right adaptation of information, as socially communicated knowledge, with these modes of knowledge whose achievement involves active personal response. Without the material of information, individual experience is raw, crude, narrow, untrained. But without the organic assimilation of this material, knowledge tends to be useless pedantry, or learning displayed simply for impressing others by its sheer mass. In the degree in which the body of information remains a special isolated set of facts and ideas not entering freely into everyday direct experiences, it fails wholly of its proper enlightening and directive function. It is suggestive to note that we distinguish between a person of much information and an informed person. The latter is not one who is possessed of a large bulk of second-hand knowledge, but one who is wise, posted, equipped to deal with the matters that concern him. In order that information should be really informing, it is necessary that it be communicated in connection with an active direct experience, not simply in association with other information. It is also necessary that it be applied to use in some direct activity. For example, scientific information communicated in connection with the undertaking of a laboratory inquiry so as to clarify the question at issue and to direct the experiment intelligently is much more likely to be assimilated into effective knowledge (or "wisdom") than exactly the same material conveyed as just so much matter to be learned by itself. The same may be said about the connection of, say, geographical material with the taking of excursions; there is very much important knowledge about the world that pupils cannot possibly acquire by themselves, but this transmitted material is likely to be fruitful in just the degree in which it is conveyed in connection with those activities in which pupils acquire something through their own observations and reflections. In the latter case, the two modes of knowledge blend and reenforce each other; in the former they remain in mechanical juxtaposition, and their isolation prevents the due efficiency of both.

See KNOWLEDGE.

INITIATIVE.—A term denoting originality and independent force as factors to be maintained and secured in education. Initiative is etymologically connected with the word "initial"; namely, something at the beginning or outset. It thus refers to ability to originate, to undertake independently, some desired line of action. It is opposed to mere docility, passiveness, imitativeness, and other conceptions that denote dependence upon others in entering upon a new course of action. The demand for initiative as an indispensable part of the educational aim is coincident practically with the growth of democracy (*q.v.*). In a feudalistic society personal initiative is undesired with respect to the masses of men; what is wanted is that they should readily subordinate themselves to the carrying out of the demands and ideas of others. The proper adjustment of the personal initiative required by a democracy on its social and political sides to the conditions of industrial employment and wage-earning involved in the capitalistic régime is a problem still to be solved, or even seriously considered, yet it is the heart of the question of industrial education.

See ACTIVITY; INDIVIDUALITY; FREEDOM.

INNATE IDEA.—The rationalistic school has always attributed to thought or reason a certain inherent content of its own, irrespective of the processes of experience. It has insisted that without this original equipment experience itself would be a floating, unorganized mass of particulars, incapable of delivering any general or scientific knowledge. The particular mode in which this inherent endowment was conceived varied from time to time according to conditions. In the seventeenth century the supposed rational stock was quite commonly spoken of as ideas or conceptions which the individual immaterial soul brought with it to its union with the body as inborn ideas. In the interests of empiricism, Locke attacked this whole theory, contending that none of the tests relied upon by the innate school bore out their contention; that the origin of all ideas could be traced in experience itself, and that the belief in innateness, instead of being favorable to the advance of science, tended to block inquiry by consecrating as unquestionable principles any long-standing prejudice, especially if class interests were concerned in its maintenance. Locke's onslaught was substantially successful against the doctrine which he attacked. But, as Locke himself held to certain innate powers (such as comparing, combining, discerning, abstracting) of the mind, it was not difficult for the rationalistic school to regather its forces. The modified form of the conception found its classical expression in Kant, who, denying the existence of ideas, or mental contents, conceptions, beliefs, prior to sense experience, nevertheless held that the mind brought with it certain *a priori* forms and categories to the reception and organization of the materials of sense. The universal and necessary action of these *a priori* forms alone made experience capable of delivering coherent and instructive judgments.

See INTUITION.

INTEREST.—The "doctrine of interest" in education is a sort of shorthand expression for a number of different motives, which focus in the recognition of the necessity of discovering points of genuine and intimate contact between the subject matter of instruction and the vital experience of pupils, an experience that exists and operates independently of attempts to master the subject matter. The etymology of the word "interest," namely, *inter* and *esse*, to *be between*, suggests, if it does not adequately convey, the idea. Interest indicates that no gulf exists between material to be learned, lesson material, and the concrete mind of the pupil—that the mental powers and tendencies find themselves at home in the material of study, that the material awakens congenial responses in the self. So regarded, an interest in a problem, a topic, a subject, is evidence that there is a vital union between the student and his study. Its opposite is the feeling of alienation and repulsion that accompanies the presentation of matter that is foreign to the experience of the student.

Psychologically, interest and attention are closely allied events. They are frequently regarded as the subjective and objective aspects of the same activity. That is to say, the effective assimilation of new material into the course of experience is interest when viewed from the standpoint of the mental affection, the emotion and personal attitude, that accompany it. It is attention when viewed as the active outgoing of mental habits in grasping and mastering the subject matter. Other views regard interest as prior and as the source of attention; or, *vice versa*, conceive interest as the emotional result of a prior act of attention. All views, however, acknowledge the intimate connection of the two; and it is this close connection which is the significant matter for education. Like attention (*q.v.*), interest as a state of mind depends upon the proper balance of the old and the new in experience. Where the material is almost wholly new, there is excess of stimulation; the responsive powers of mind are overwhelmed and confused. Discouragement and aversion result. As the term "aversion" implies, there is a strong tendency for the mind to turn away and devote itself to some more congenial and rewarding topic. Even if this tendency is partly overcome, it means divided, and consequently wasted, energy as compared with the unified, whole-hearted activity where interest is naturally and directly sustained. On the other hand, the thoroughly familiar denotes the mastered, the habitual. It sets off tendencies that work automatically and mechanically. If there is also a new factor about which habits may play, these habitual tendencies will furnish the background for intense and concentrated interest. But if there is no stimulation beyond that evoking the established habits, the result will be ennui, monotony, routine. The effect is that of walking in a treadmill where nothing new is achieved. Put in other words, a certain degree of difficulty, a certain amount of obstacle to be overcome, enough to set the problem of a readjustment of habit, is necessary for sustained interest. If the self is to put itself whole-heartedly into what it is doing, its powers must be thoroughly awakened, and this is impossible without a challenging difficulty.

The fact just stated throws light upon the relation between desire (as standing for interest) and effort, and helps place the relation of the doctrine of interest to that of discipline. As long as children "live in the present," they are absorbed in their immediate concerns. All their powers are directed at and, so to speak, discharged upon the immediately present stimulus. There are no *ends*, that is to say, no conceived results to be reached, after an intervening time, through the controlled adaptation of conditions as means—or the end lies in such a near future that but little thought has to be given to the management of intermediate conditions.

This state of *immediate* interest characterizes the "play activities." When more remote ends are entertained as objects to be reached by the consistent and sustained maintenance of a series of acts that, of themselves, lack immediate interest, (but that are of interest because of their importance for the remoter end in view), we have *mediate* interest. Being dependent on an idea, mediate interest involves an intellectual interest in a way in which the emotional heightening accompanying direct absorption does not. The interest in a more or less prolonged series of acts is dependent upon the persistence of an *idea*—the thought of an end and the thought of the bearing of the immediately present upon the attainment of this end. The control of the activity, and the source of interest, reside in what is *conceived*, what is physically absent, not in perception or what is physically present.

The remoteness of the end in time means of course increase in the number of difficulties to be dealt with; there is a series of difficulties to be dealt with one after another. Consequently the seriousness, the depth of the interest of the self in its objective—its aim—is continually being tested and retested. If the interest is slight and passing, the emergence of a difficulty in an unexpected form or in an unusually strenuous way will distract the mind from its pursuit, and lead to taking up something which has an immediate, non-intellectual value. On the other hand, if the self is deeply concerned with, thoroughly committed to, its object, each successive obstacle will deepen the sense of the importance of the object and increase the *effort* expended in behalf of its realization. In many cases, perhaps the majority of cases, there will be an oscillation: a tendency to surrender the end in behalf of some more immediately interesting object, and a tendency to cling to the end, to emphasize its importance, in order to enlist further effort in its behalf. Under these conditions, while physical effort will go to the means for reaching the end, moral and intellectual effort will be directed to sustaining the idea of the end in such force as to give it motive power.

We have here all the elements of a seeming conflict of interest and effort, with immediate attractiveness, immediate agreeableness on the side of interest, while serious and important values are all on the side of effort. Hence the situation has been frequently completely misinterpreted in theories of education, with respect to both its intellectual and its moral implications. That is, interest has been regarded as an inherently unworthy and objectionable factor, operating only as a temptation away from the objectively important; it has been identified with the attractive and swerving power of the immediately pleasurable over against what thought—or reason—shows to be *really* worth while. This implies that the objectively valuable end is totally lacking in inherent interest, so that sheer effort of the will has to be relied upon as the sole motive for keeping the self in its right course—for keeping it struggling against the seductions of "interest."

The previous analysis should reveal what is at fault in this interpretation. What sustains effort is not sheer appeal to will power, but interest in the end—the interest that is indirect and intelligent, as distinguished from that which is immediate, purely personal, emotional, and sensuous. The genuine educational need is, therefore, not to eliminate interest, but to foster the *indirect* interest, the interest attaching to the end in view, to make it more powerful than the immediate interests which would, if they became motive forces, take the self away from its end, and reduce action from the plane of thought to that of sense. The import of immediate interest is quite different before and after reflection and the conceiving of remote ends have entered in. When thought is not playing an important part, or when the situation is such that there is no need that it should play a considerable role, immediate interest is simply an indication of hearty, wholesome outgoing activity of the self, a sign of its ability to identify itself with its surroundings, to express itself therein and to find itself reflected by the environment. It remains a fundamental trait of all aesthetic and artistic manifestations. Moreover, in the degree in which the interest in the end is seriously sustained and worked out, it tends to transfer itself to interest in the means of reaching the end. A new type of immediate interest is thus developed, one which is as direct, as hearty and spontaneous, as the earlier personal and sensuous interest, but one which depends upon the intervention of thought. When an individual becomes intensely and sincerely interested in an end which reflection holds up, the sense of separation between means and end tends to disappear. The means become saturated with a sense of the value of the end; and the end is so identified with the means of achieving it that it ceases to seem remote and far away; every one of the present means represents, embodies it. This mutual interpenetration of means and end is constantly exhibited in scientific pursuits as well as in endeavors to achieve wealth and political distinction. But there is often a period between the original absence of the end dependent upon reason and the final unification of interest in intellectual end and existent means, when the thought of an end pulls one way while the immediately present conditions pull in another. In this intervening state, there is temporarily a real conflict between thought, standing for continuity of purpose, and reason, immediate interest, standing for the agreeable, the pleasurable, the direct urgency of desire. But, as already indicated, the effective way of dealing with this critical juncture is not to attempt the hopeless task of crushing out all interest by sheer effort in behalf of something totally lacking in interest; it is to reenforce by all possible means the interest in the end, so that its interest may fuse with that of means for its attainment.

We are now in a position to perceive the true and false signification of discipline in connection with interest. A disciplined mind is one that can hold to a train of thought in spite of the attractions and distractions of irrelevant considerations; it means power to attend to the conceived, and to relate the perceived (and what the imagination incidentally presents) to the conceived. A disciplinary process in education is one which tends to bring about the state of mental control. True discipline, in short, is distinctly a matter of intellectual attitude and method: the power to keep thinking in dominant control of the situation when the situation needs reflective survey and estimation. Since this clearly involves the overcoming of obstacles and the holding of mind to what is directly more or less disagreeable, the false notion of discipline arises by ignoring the function of intelligence as the source of concentration, order, and regular sequence, thereby identifying discipline with sheer effort directed to the disagreeable. Hence disciplining methods are supposed to be effective whenever a person is forced to occupy himself with whatever is uninteresting and naturally repellent. Difficulties are multiplied for the mere sake of having difficulties; tasks are assigned as tasks to discipline *will*, the power of attention to the repellent. The error is in isolating will or the power of attentive application from thought as the function of sustaining remote ends and of bringing them into close connection with means, or existent conditions.

This fallacious conception of discipline which relates it to effort to the exclusion of habits of thought is strengthened by an opposite error. One school of educators, noting the waste that comes from trying to work against interest, substitutes appeal to momentary emotional agreeableness, for both appeal to will and to the interest of the remoter end. Like the so-called disciplinary school, it fails to denote that thought, that ideas of ends or purposes, holds the key to the situation. By interest it means various devices that tend to conceal the real end from view, that lessen the need of serious thinking, and that place the control of action in the direct stimulation of present conditions. Interest thus comes to mean a sort of sugar-coating over of difficulties. Since this method inevitably relaxes discipline in its proper sense—that is, the power to utilize thinking as an effective method of guidance of action—its failure to develop continuity of application and serious industry evokes a reactionary appeal to the method of securing "discipline" by the assignment of obnoxious tasks. Then as this method fails to secure motivation and genuine regard for the materials of instruction, it in turn calls out recourse to the method of emotional stimulation. The only way out of this vicious circle is the recognition of the importance of the intellectual factor, the idea of a more or less distant end, and the necessity of reenforcing interest in it as the controlling factor.

We have noticed above that indirect interest involves an intellectual interest. At the outset, this intellectual interest, while genuine and indispensable, is secondary to the interest in achieving an end or purpose—to a practical interest in the broad sense of "practical." The transfer of interest from ends to means is, however, one of the commonest phenomena of experience, having its traditional illustration, on its undesirable side, in the miser's transfer of interest in what money will do to the money itself. But the principle has also its positively valuable side. It shows itself whenever there is developed an interest in thinking for its own sake, an interest in conducting reflection, pursuing inquiries, with no ulterior aim. Different minds differ immensely in their susceptibility to this transferability; but whenever it occurs we have strictly intellectual interests. A certain amount of intellectual interest for its own sake is necessary to a proper degree of detachment, of generosity and impartiality, of comprehensive survey of the field, even in practical matters. Hence it is an end to be cultivated in educational procedure. Some minds are as likely to fall into excess upon this side, however, as others are in the narrowly practical, unintellectual direction. Such minds become academic and scholastic, "abstract" in the bad sense of that term; their knowledge is divorced from influence upon action, theory is separated from practice. Hence ideas remain untested and unfertilized by application, while practice remains hard and narrow because not enlightened and inspired by breadth of intelligence. Owing to various historic circumstances, most schooling has come to favor unduly the fostering of the pale academic type, at the expense of those individuals whose natural and persistent interests are more active and objectively constructive. (See ACTIVITY and CULTURE.)

We have approached the subject of interest from the psychological side. This implies, however, its objective side. The term "interest," or an interest, is constantly used to denote that in which interest is taken. It is used as synonymous with a concern, a value, a dominant direction of thought and action, an occupation that is persistently important. Thus we speak of business, of science, of art, of religion, of politics as interests. This objective use of the term "interest" bears out what was originally said of interest as the point of identification of mind with its object, or subject matter. This identity may be approached and discussed—as above—from the side of the mind; but it may be equally well approached from the side of the subject matter in which the self finds its powers sustained and fulfilled. The fundamental thing, educationally, is that interest has both of these aspects. As a guiding principle or norm in education its influence should be to protect educators from two harmful abstractions: On the one hand, from viewing mind as something which can operate and manifest its nature all by itself in a mental, subjective region. As against this notion (and the many educational practices connected with it) the doctrine of interest holds up to view the need of subject matter, of content, in art, in science, in literature and history, in technical constructive activities, etc., in order that mind may be active and be fulfilled. On the other hand, there is the fallacy which makes the mind equally indifferent to subject matter, which supposes that if it only *will* (if it but will choose to do so), it may apply itself to any subject matter, and that any regard for the inherent choice and spontaneous direction of mind is a concession to a weak and enervating principle. As against this notion, the doctrine of interest is important in maintaining the fact that subject matter is assimilable and capable of having educative influence only so far as it is caught up into and held by certain inherent active tendencies of the self, thereby becoming an interest, a vital concern, a significant occupation of the self.

See EFFORT; FORMAL DISCIPLINE; HERBART.

INTUITION.—A name given to direct, as distinct from mediate or logical knowledge. In the history of thought two types of intuition have been discriminated: sense perception and rational perception. With respect to the former, the chief problem has been whether it is in and of itself a mode of knowledge, or whether it is a mode of judgment, that is, of inferential interpretation. If the former, there is such a thing as knowledge without thinking; in the latter case, the instantaneous character of a perceptual intuition expresses the fact that recurring previous inferences have finally formed an automatically operative habit. The perception is then, in its strict sense, a *re*-cognition, a knowing in terms of prior knowings that involved judging. In this controversy, the party that held that perception was acquired rather than primitive intuitive knowledge is admitted to have been successful. However, as far as the philosophical point at issue was concerned, this conclusion was offset by recourse to sensation as a substitute form of immediate knowledge. The doctrine of rational intuition was first systematically developed by Plato. He felt the need of some way of knowing which should combine the rationality of discursive, or demonstrative, knowledge with the directness and vitality of pure immediacy. So he introduced the conception of a face-to-face perception by pure reason of ultimate absolute essences (see IDEA). This intuition involved a mutual interpenetration of knower and known and an assimilation of the former to the latter. This motif was developed by the Neo-Platonists in their conception of an ecstatic vision transcending all logical categories, and by the mystic school of Christian theologians in the idea of the beatific vision of God.

In the Platonic tradition rational intuition was an envisagement of absolute reality, and implied a quasi-mystic factor. After the collapse of the doctrine of innate ideas (*q.v.*) the rationalistic anti-mystic school introduced the idea of rational intuition of abstract truths, like those of morals and mathematics. This doctrine of an immediate certitude of first and necessary truths became the bulwark of the Scotch school in opposition to the skeptical turn given empiricism by Hume. Kant employed the notion of an intuitive understanding as an ideal of knowledge, unattainable but useful in providing a limiting notion by which both sense perception and reflective judgment could be criticized and their pretensions to yield more than relative knowledge exposed. In contemporary thought Bergson has introduced an interesting variation of the idea of rational intuition. According to him, logical or discursive intelligence has been evolved in the interests of action, and is accordingly quite unadapted to the speculative task of grasping Reality in itself. Intelligence and instinct represent, however, diverging lines of evolution out of a common reality; while a sort of vague penumbra of instinct still surrounds the clear-cut outlines of intellectual knowledge. By retracing that phase of the evolution of reality which has taken the road of instinct, human beings may by an extreme effort of will bring about a fusion of intellectual results with the residual penumbra of instinct they still directly possess, and thereby secure at least a fleeting glimpse of the inner creative impetus of reality itself.

See EMPIRICISM; IDEA; INNATE IDEA; MYSTICISM; NEO-PLATONISM; etc.

ISOLATION.—A term used to express the opposite of correlation (*q.v.*), in instruction, or the method of teaching subjects as separated from one another. It is claimed that only by recognizing arithmetic, geography, history, etc., as independent studies, adequate and complete in themselves, can each subject attain its own due rights and realize its own appropriate end. The logical idea underlying this contention is that the various subjects represent something besides convenient distinctions carved out within a comprehensive unity; it assumes that there are just so many objectively important phases of reality, and that each subject (or group of subjects) stands for just one of these phases. Accordingly by isolation of each subject and then by coordination of the various independent subjects, the subject matter of instruction will be rendered both definite and harmoniously complete.

It may be replied that, philosophically speaking, both isolation and correlation represent stages in growth from the more direct and vital forms of experience to its logical formulation; that is, its organization for purposes of better intellectual control. Experience does not begin with a number of sharply marked off fields, or topics, either requiring to be made more distinct and definite in their separations, or else needing to be bound up together by various correlating devices. It begins with a vague, somewhat confused and fluctuating unity whose parts flow readily into one another, these parts being marked off by various interests and purposes, rather than by objective or logical differences. Growth takes place by a movement toward differentiation, on one hand, and toward interrelation of discriminated parts on the other. Isolation thus represents a goal toward which instruction and learning are moving, not original divisions. The distinctive character of mathematics, as a subject on its own account having its own unique material and special method, follows after a term of study marking the attainment of a logical comprehension. Even then it is undesirable that differentiation should be carried to the point of isolation in its literal sense. For the purposes of all education save that of the specialist it is needful that the interdependence of each study with the other studies—their mutual applications to one another and to life—should be borne in mind. This requirement is met only when correlation and differentiation are used to supplement each other, instead of being treated as rivals.

See CORRELATION.

JUDGMENT.—This term is employed in a larger and more vital sense and in a narrower and more formal one. In its pregnant sense it means the act (or the power) of weighing facts or evidence, in order to reach a conclusion or decision; or (as is usual with words denoting acts) the result, the outcome of the process, the decision reached by the process of reflective inquiry and deliberation. In this sense judgment expresses the very heart of thinking. All thinking is, directly or indirectly, a part of the act of judging, of forming an estimate or valuation after investigation and testing.

The difference in the adequacy of different cases of thinking is due to the care and thoroughness with which the operations of critical summoning and weighing of evidence are performed. The evaluating nature of judgment and its relation to a reasonably reached, intellectually valid, conclusion are suggested by the judicial procedure from which the word "judgment" is derived. There is primarily something at issue, at stake, something which is as yet undetermined, uncertain, but which needs to be decided. Without a crisis of uncertainty of this sort, without a questionable or problematic situation, there would be no judging. Then there follows the calling and hearing of witnesses, presenting all the facts relevant to settling the matter—that is to say, there are the processes of observation, recollection, etc., which bring in the data or evidence upon which a correct decision depends. Then there is the sifting, comparing, classifying, and relating operation by which is determined the respective force, the authority, to be assigned to this fact or that. This weighing or evaluating process involves the use of the general rules or principles bearing upon cases of this sort that have been established in prior experience. Finally the judgment issues in a decision, or declaration that the case is thus and so, within certain limits of probable error. From this sketch it is evident that judging involves in individualized concrete form all the operations of thinking or reflective inquiry, both material and formal: that is, the material operation by which facts are gathered and the formal one by which the facts are weighed and their meaning determined. From the standpoint of logical analysis, existence and meaning are thus the defining traits of every judgment.

The central position occupied by the training of judgment in the scheme of education is obvious. It may be explicitly stated by calling up to view the errors involved in failing to give it a central position. In brief, these consist, on one side, in the amassing of mere information, through observing and memorizing material which is put to no intellectual use; and, on the other, in merely formal exercises in reasoning apart from consideration of subject matter. In contrast with these counterpart errors, judgments involve the gathering of facts, but also the use of reasoning to compare, contrast, place, and interpret the subject matter. Only where these two processes are combined (corresponding to the interrelation of existence and meaning) is there any training which is of value either for the practical deliberations of life or for the theoretical pursuit of science. Conditions that work against the training of judgment are, accordingly, such procedures as the following: The multiplication of isolated sense observations, as in some schemes of object lessons and sense training; the multiplication of logical analyses apart from their bearing on reaching a conclusion; attaching great importance to correct reproduction of things previously learned without employing that material in pursuing some further inquiry; attaching importance to correct results or "answers," quite apart from the mental operations by which the results were reached; exercises where the material and methods are externally dictated, with no opportunity for the employment of judgment in selecting, arranging, and testing; methods in which mechanical skill, automatic rapidity, and accuracy are set above reflective inquiry—as in many so-called "drill" exercises; methods in which opportunity to commit errors is mechanically excluded, or in which, when committed, they are externally corrected without throwing upon the pupil any intellectual responsibility.

In its narrower and more technical sense a judgment is a statement of a relation between two objects, or between two contents of thought, two meanings. This is the meaning which the term "judgment" has gradually assumed in formal logic; from its standpoint the vitally practical meaning of judgment just expounded is sometimes contemptuously looked down upon as merely psychological in character. From the standpoint of judgment proper the actual operation of thinking as performed in life, the formal statement of a relationship *in abstracto*, is one important stage in the development of a controlled judgment. It marks a summing up, a gathering together of the net outcome of prior reflections. Such formulations are indispensable factors in the adequately performed vital judgment. Because the function of formulation is so important, judgment is not unfrequently identified with the statement of relations, or with the *proposition* (*q.v.*).

KNOWLEDGE.—A term of the very widest scope, designating, as will presently appear, a variety of operations and of subject matter that, however, possess at least two elements in common: namely, some connection direct or indirect with intelligence (or reflection) and with certainty, security, assurance, settledness. Like many analogous terms,—conception, judgment, thought, for example,—the term has both an active and a passive sense; it designates both an operation or act, that of knowing, and the result, what is known. Like the term "science," however, the word "knowledge" is itself used mainly in a passive sense to denote the content, the subject matter, which is the outcome of the successful performance of the function of knowing. The verb "to know" and the participle "knowing" retain both senses, designating the act of inquiry, search, finding out, and also the possession of a certain subject matter. The opposite of knowledge is ignorance.

The term "knowledge" covers four distinct connected matters. Of these the two first to be mentioned are the most personal, direct, and practical. They are knowledge in the sense of intelligently acquired skill, and in the sense of acquaintance. We know *how* to walk, talk, skate, etc.; experts know how to weave, dye, work metals, etc. Ability to do things is perhaps the most primary sense of knowledge. The ability is distinguished from instinct only in that it has been intelligently acquired. But even this difference is not consistently maintained, for we speak, popularly, of an instinctive knowledge. The first necessity of a living being is to know how to conduct itself with respect to certain situations; in order to live it must be able to adapt its behavior to the behavior of the things with which its own fortunes are bound up. This necessity includes not only physical needs, but also the fundamentals of social intercourse and the elements at least of some of the social arts. The primary and profound character of this sort of knowledge is seen in the fact that until the rise of philosophy among the Greeks the same word denoted art (technical skill) and knowledge, namely, τέχνη. The well-known recourse of Socrates to the analogies of the arts, his appeal to the procedure of the shoemaker, flute player, carpenter, etc., in his logical discussions was witness to the fact that the control of his material evinced by the artisan in reaching the ends appropriate to his art represented at once the most certain and the most intelligent procedure extant.

Familiarity, acquaintance, are closely connected with knowing how to do, and to a considerable extent they result from the latter and measure its extent. So far as we can adapt ourselves readily and successfully in any situation, we are familiar, acquainted. The rough edges of a strangeness, remoteness, the barriers of understanding nothing, are worn away. In their place there is a sense of intimacy, of inner adjustment. When we know how to behave with respect to a thing, we know what it is like; we are on terms with it; there is mutuality of response. Knowledge in the form of acquaintance is not only the outcome and reward of knowing how, or intelligent skill; but it establishes emotional ties—a capacity for appreciation, or apprehending the thing in terms of its worth, its usefulness for a purpose. Acquaintance, familiarity, normally presuppose a certain amount of friendliness, of agreeableness, as well as a sense of power and ease. But excessive familiarity, too long continued occupation with one subject, "breeds contempt"; it leads to revulsion, a sense of ennui and constraint.

Our third sense of knowledge covers that acquired from others, that attained indirectly by learning from others. Communication by means of language carries us far beyond the limits of personal acquaintance with persons and things, leading us to know *of* or *about* many matters which are within the direct acquaintance of other people. By oral tradition and more especially by written and printed language, this second-hand knowledge comes to include much that is not and that could not be within the direct acquaintance of any living. Such knowledge constitutes information (*q.v.*) and also learning—in the sense of what is learned or is to be learned.

In all the three above-mentioned types of knowledge, intelligence or reflective thought is used, but only secondarily. It is employed as a means of gaining control of things; in enlarging acquaintance with them; in apprehending and understanding things reported by others. It is not, however, used in any sense as a source of knowledge for its own sake. Gradually, however, materials of acquaintance and of information are amassed and systematized not for the sake of increasing familiarity and possession of learning, but for the sake of rational demonstration or of inferential discovery of new knowledge. Men are not contented with the kind of assurance that rests upon personal acquaintance or upon the credit of others; they search for that which opens from rational grounding, from logical sequence and system. Thus a fourth kind of knowledge comes into existence: rational knowledge, science, knowledge *that* so and so is true. Like information, this sort of knowledge is indirect, but it is indirect in the sense of dependence upon logical data and premises, not in the sense of dependence upon the observations and reports of others. From this point of view, knowledge is identical with *science*, and we have no logical right to denominate intelligent skill, matters of acquaintance, of information, *knowledge*, unless they are reduced to general principles and are connected with one another in systematic ways. Otherwise they represent beliefs, opinions, rather than knowledge. This tendency to define knowledge from an exclusively logical point of view has been an important factor in calling out in reaction the philosophy of pragmatism (*q.v.*), which regards this exclusive view of knowledge as the characteristic error of intellectualism (or rationalism, as it is sometimes termed). The purely technical character of knowledge when defined on a purely logical basis, its aloofness from practical considerations, from the affections and aversions (so important a factor in acquaintance) and from the social processes of learning and transmission characteristic of information, are treated as evidence that scientific knowledge, when isolated, is an abstraction. Thus the other types of knowledge are regarded as not only more primitive genetically and psychologically (which would be generally admitted), but also as more final and significant. In fact, knowledge as a system of logical propositions is regarded by it as ultimately of value because of the greater control and the greater richness of content that it supplies to the more direct, active, and social types of knowledge.

Educationally speaking, there can be little doubt that

the order in which the four types of knowledge have been set forth in this article represents the order of their development. The opposition of all modern educational reforms to beginning with so-called "deductive" methods, with systems of definitions, classifications, and laws of explanation, is, in substance, a claim that the logical type of knowledge represents a matured, relatively late, specialized development of more basic bodies of knowing, and is consequently meaningless and educatively harmful when presented in isolation or as a starting point. On the other hand, many of the reformers have, in their reaction against abstractions in education, failed to note the operation of a subordinated factor of reflection and interpretation in even the more primitive modes of knowing, and have thus made the mistake of identifying the "concrete" with the bare physical object, instead of with the centre of an active experience, or interest.

Many questions of instruction are bound up also with the matter of the relation of information or communicated knowledge to personal acquaintance. A flavor of the second-handed, derived, and more or less conventional hangs about information. Its subject matter is not so vitally lived through, so intimately appreciated, as that of familiar acquaintance. Any examination of prevailing modes of instruction will show that the mere bulk of matter communicated in books and lectures tends to swamp the native and active interests operative in intelligent behavior and in the acquaintanceship it brings. Then this matter remains unassimilated, unorganized, not really understood. It stands on a dead level, hostile to the selective arrangements characteristic of thinking; matter for memorizing, rather than for judgment; existing as verbal symbols to be mechanically manipulated, rather than as genuine realities, intelligently appreciated. Yet without this communicated matter, the circle of personal acquaintance is very narrow and superficial, and personal activity hardly gets above the place of routine. The solution is found in realizing that social communication is a very real factor in personal doing and acquaintance. The educational aim is not to multiply information for the sake of information, nor yet to try to exclude it or narrow it down as much as possible. It is to fuse the transmitted matter and the matter of direct behavior and emotional response with as intimate union as possible, so that the former will gain force, vivacity, directness from the latter, while the former is insensibly but continually extended and deepened by the latter. In short, the common error does not consist in attaching great importance to transmitted facts and ideas, but in presenting them in such an isolated way that they are not spontaneously welded with the intense, though narrow, matters of direct concern.

LAW.—Generally speaking, a law is the statement of an order or relation among the elements of an object or situation, this order or relation being a means of understanding, organizing, and controlling other traits of the object or situation in question, and of reducing other situations or objects, apparently unlike, to a form in which the same, or a closely connected, method of treatment is applicable. A law is thus, logically speaking, a statement of a relation or order which is employed as an effective method of procedure in further dealings with phenomena.

The kind of order that is significant and the kind of procedure that is indicated depends, of course, upon the character of the material dealt with. The fundamental distinction of subject matter is that between acts (or functions) and states (or structures). As the primary human concern is the maintenance of life, and especially of group or associated life, the first type of law to emerge into conscious recognition was the rules of order applicable to the activities of human beings in relation to one another,—laws in the *jural* sense, whether political or moral. Now a statement of an order among *acts*, when employed as a determining method with respect to further acts, is obviously a *rule of action*. It presented itself, accordingly, as having authority over phenomena, as in some sense a *command* or *injunction* to act in certain ways. When attention was directed to natural existences, and the effort was made to discover and state a uniform order among them, the inevitable tendency was to conceive of natural law after the analogy of jural law: as a disclosure of a superior authority which "governed" the particulars which were then conceived after the manner of subjects "obeying" law. The course of the authority to govern was referred to God, Nature, Forces, or Reason, according to the tenets of a philosophical school.

In the eighteenth and nineteenth centuries, the advance of science produced the positivistic movement. According to this movement, a law is simply a statement of an order of coexistence or sequence among phenomena (as the elements of a phenomenon). The conceptions of authority, of governing power and obedience, were eliminated, being simply a formulation of uniformity abstracted from phenomena. This conception makes a complete break between jural and scientific law.

This distinction marked a most important advance in science and culture. Stated in this absolute form, it brought with it, however, its own peculiar difficulties. Jural and moral laws were conceived now only as a command, an imperative. Hence they seemed arbitrary, resting in ultimate analysis either upon mere superiority of force, or else upon purely ideal considerations of what should be, what *ought* to be, lacking positive, existential force and efficiency. In the first case, law meant despotism; in the second, an empty abstract conception of what ought to be, as over against what is. On the other hand, scientific and natural law, being conceived as merely a uniformity among things as they exist, was completely divorced from matters of action, save as action was reduced to the type of given physical existences—to the denial, accordingly, of its significant traits *as action.*

Various tendencies have converged to bring forward a third conception of law, which brings the practical and the scientific senses of the term into working relations with each other, eliminating, however, the sense of superior authority and of coercive command. What makes in any given case a statement of an order (whether physical or social) a law is its *use as a method of procedure* in dealing with further cases, with future possibilities. A scientific law is thus not a mere statement of coexistence; it is such a statement employed as a method of procedure in further inquiries, interpretations, and organizations. It is thus in some sense a rule of action, that is, a way of directing or guiding action in the region of investigation. Moreover, the statement of a uniform order is either limited to the particular cases in which it has been already observed, or else in its extension to new cases is hypothetical—a rule of anticipation, prediction, and probable behavior. In addition, through applied science and the arts such uniformities as are observed and abstracted are embodied in methods of controlling and adapting things to human needs, and thus pass into the realm of overt and social action.

From the side of social and moral concerns, a converse movement has taken place. With the development of democracy and freer intercourse, moral and political laws lose alike the form of rigid imperatives and of empty ideals, and tend to be conceived as a conception of an order of action adapted to securing ends of objective value. From both sides, accordingly, the sharp antithesis between a law of natural existence and one of practical endeavor is softened down, so that both intellectual and practical elements are included in the concept of law.

See GENERALIZATION; HYPOTHESIS; also ACTIVITY; PRAGMATISM.

LIBERAL EDUCATION.—The conception of liberal education dates from Aristotle. He distinguished sharply between a liberal education, an end in itself, and a mechanical or professional training, a means for practical ends beyond itself. The chief traits of a liberal education were its association with leisure and its exclusive connection with the faculty of knowing. These two traits were necessarily combined with each other. Slaves, serfs, mechanics, tradesmen, were too much occupied with practical matters to have the leisure requisite for devotion to knowing for its own sake. Only a leisure class was in a situation to devote itself to the cultivation of the mind for the sake of the mind. Even in theoretical matters, however, excessive assiduity evinced an illiberal spirit. The chief material of a liberal education was music (in the Greek sense). The question how far practice was necessary was decided by applying the criterion suggested above. If skill in doing became the chief end, the study was illiberal. Practice for the sake of doing should be relegated to the servile, unfree class of artisans. In a liberal education that amount of practice should be permitted which would promote the understanding and enjoyment of the arts as practiced by others.

The distinction between liberal and servile education was thus based by Aristotle upon the distinction of classes upon which Greek society was founded. Practice and education for practice were essentially illiberal because pursued by persons who were not free themselves or, who if legally free, were so given up to the narrow ends of money making, etc., as to have no interest in the exercise of the knowing faculties for their own sake. This exercise was the appropriate and congenial function for those whose social station relieved them from all menial preoccupations.

The distinction between the free character of knowing and the subservient character of doing which underlay the Aristotelian definition of a liberal education was also associated with several points in his metaphysical and ethical system. Pure knowing, concerned only with the rational relations of immaterial forms, was, according to Aristotle, the highest thing in the universe. It was the final cause of the existence of nature, the supreme end and good. It defined the nature of God as pure activity. It dealt with the reason, the explanation of all else, and was complete in itself—just as a syllogism is self-enclosed, needing no help from outside. In contrast, doing or practice sprang from appetites, which are bodily, not ideal: expressed needs, lack, incompletion, imperfection; and in general was due to man's share in the animal, not the divine, nature. The highest, the freest, or most liberal of all pursuits was a theoretical contemplation and inquiry which were supra-civic.

Aristotle's distinction became basic in all later definitions and classifications of education. It took specific effect in the conception of the seven liberal arts (*q.v.*). His assertion of the supremacy and divinity of the purely theoretical life was employed in the Middle Ages to justify theology as the supreme study, and to place the monastic life above not only secular careers but above that of the parish clergy—the latter being devoted to necessary practices and not to the exclusive cultivation of divine knowledge.

At the time of the revival of learning, however, the domination of theology and allied concerns was taken as a symptom of a professional education, that preparing for the clergy. Liberal education was identified with the humanistic studies, a knowledge of classic antiquity and the Greek and Latin literatures. Although the older classification of the seven liberal arts survived, these arts—such as grammar, rhetoric, logic—were identified, not with "sacred" grammar and rhetoric and with the logic which was a handmaiden of theology, but with that of classic literatures. However, the interest in the content of these literatures tended, while reviving the idea of liberal education, to relegate its conventional divisions to the background.

In the eighteenth century the rise of natural science began to disturb the now orthodox identification of the liberal with the ancient languages. Pure mathematics was unambiguously taken in the fold; the other sciences were left as doubtful claimants. In the nineteenth century the further development of literature and philosophy in the vernacular tongues of Europe gave the living languages a claim for recognition as elements in liberal education. The growth of history and the social disciplines perturbed the content of the idea still further. Liberal education had claimed to be the peculiar representative of man as man, of human interests as such; and history, anthropology, political economy, and sociology seemed to concern themselves with humanity even more directly than did the classic literatures.

As a consequence of such causes, practically all attempt to define a liberal education by some principle of content has been given up, though it is still generally felt that Greek, Latin, and mathematics, at least from algebra through calculus, are peculiarly liberal in character. The attempt is now made to define it from the standpoint of aim, or of a peculiar, if intangible, influence it exercises upon those devoted to it. This end and effect are more easily stated from the negative side than from the positive side. Some would call it scholarship and would say that higher education, as distinctly representing the liberal interest in education, should be given to the promotion of scholarship. Among those representing this idea there is, however, a marked difference of attitude. Some would include research and discovery in the province of scholarship, while others would exclude them as specialized and technical. Many deny the claim of scholarship to represent the cause of liberal education and would substitute a specific refining and ennobling of the mind known as culture. However, the status of various subjects with respect to their power to bestow culture is involved in much uncertainty and polemic discussion. Negatively, the conventional idea of a liberal education is more easily made out. It excludes education designed to prepare one for any special calling, particularly if this calling is closely associated with money making, or if preparation for it involves much manual manipulation and dexterity—such as the laboratory pursuits of a technological education. Latterly, it has been held by professed upholders of the cause of liberal education that it is opposed to education for social service. This notion, however, is mainly an American innovation. Historically, the chief pursuit of the leisure class has been statecraft and diplomacy. One of the leading marks of liberal studies was that it prepared men for managing the state, including the lower classes. In the United States, with the development of democracy, the notion of a special ruling class with a special education fitting it for social control has disappeared. Accordingly education for social service is no longer education for directing the affairs of other people, but for contributing to their happiness and well-being. Such a conception would let in the physician and the engineer. Consequently it is too broad for the purposes of the traditional notion of liberal education.

The fact is that in a society which frankly bases its constitution upon class distinctions, it is comparatively easy to assign a distinct content and a distinct purpose to liberal education. With the growth of social studies, of the democratic ideal, and the increased application of the best scientific intelligence to the conduct of practical affairs, it becomes increasingly difficult to do so. Liberal education becomes a name for the sort of education that every member of the community should have: the education that will liberate his capacities and thereby contribute both to his own happiness and his social usefulness. It has value as a limiting concept to criticize various educational schemes. Thus an education in Latin and Greek may be quite illiberal if pursued by methods which restrict the play of the imagination and the sympathies, and bind down mental appreciations to one limited sphere. The same is obviously the case with education for law, medicine, engineering, or the clergy. In short a liberal education is one that liberalizes. Theoretically any type of education may do this. As matter of fact, all of them fall much short of accomplishing it, some in one respect and some in another. In so far they fall short of being an education in any worthy sense of the word.

See Activity; Culture; Humanism; Liberal Arts.

MANY-SIDED INTEREST.—In the article on Interest (*q.v.*) it is noted that the term "interest" is used in an objective sense to denote the typically important concerns of life—science, politics, religion, art, etc. Herbart defined the aim of education as the development of many-sided interest—that is, of regard for all of these significant human values. The term "interest" obviously designates the active and alert identification of the self with these concerns; the term "many-sided" denotes the need of non-one-sided susceptibility. The notion was the counterpart, from the realistic side, of the current idealistic conception of complete and harmonious development of all the individual's powers or faculties as the aim of education.

MATERIALISM.—The theory that matter is the sole ultimate existence, and that all mental phenomena are in reality effects of matter, so that, if our knowledge of matter were complete, we could deduce from its laws and conditions so-called mental phenomena with the same certainty as phenomena of heat or electricity. The atomic school of antiquity represented by Democritus and Leucippus is generally regarded as the founder of philosophic materialism. These tenets were taken up by the Epicureans and find a classic expression in the *De Rerum Natura* of Lucretius. The atheistic character of this school brought materialism into ill repute, and among the many heresies of the Middle Ages few are frankly materialistic in character. The Epicureans, however, defended the liberty of the will, as they found it necessary to introduce chance and spontaneous variation of direction of motion into matter. Some of the modern materialists have been strong theists, as Joseph Priestley (*q.v.*).

The modern interest in the problem of knowledge and in consciousness (see IDEALISM) has tended to reduce the importance of materialism, if not actually to eliminate it. The objective idealist has claimed that "matter" itself is ultimately but a "category" of thought or spirit in its determination of an objectively knowable world. Subjective idealists have claimed that conscious facts are the only ones directly known, and that "matter" is at most but a dubious inference from mental phenomena. Others have claimed that the principles of the conservation of energy contradict materialism, since the circuit of transformations of energy is complete on the physical side alone. The seeming dependence of mental phenomena upon brain changes is in reality but the concomitance of two independent series—a doctrine that under the name of Parallelism (*q.v.*), has given a turn to the Leibnitzian conception of Preestablished Harmony which has been very popular. Others, like Spencer and Huxley, have held that from one point of view mental phenomena are resolvable into physical; from another, physical into mental. Hence, the conclusion that both series are but symbolic manifestations of some ultimate unknown and unknowable reality. Even those writers, who, like Haeckel, have more openly maintained a materialistic monism, have generally endowed "matter" with some primitive inchoate psychical impulses and feelings and have thus approximated panpsychism or the doctrine that the world and mind are both arrangements of a more basic "mind stuff."

Reference:—

BALDWIN, J. M. *Dictionary of Philosophy and Psychology*, Vol. III, Pt. ii, pp. 620–626.

METAPHYSICS.—The name "metaphysics" as designating philosophy or some one of its branches arose from a misunderstanding of an accidental way of describing certain writings of Aristotle; namely, those coming after the physics. This was shortly taken to mean the things that lie beyond the physical, that are above the natural—a conception which medieval thought identified with the supernatural. This long remained the popular signification, so that Shakespeare, for example, refers to ghosts as metaphysical.

Aristotle himself in the body of his treatise supplied some grounds for identifying his discussions with theology. His formal designation is first philosophy, and this he says has for its object a descriptive definition of being as being, or existence as existence. Each branch of science considers the traits of some set or class of existences; but no science considers the traits that all existences alike possess. Hence they leave room for and indeed require a more general and formal science to take up the matter they leave untouched. So far there is no ground for referring first philosophy, or metaphysics, to anything transcending the subject matter of the sciences. But in the course of his discussions, Aristotle is led to discriminate grades of being and to conclude that only pure actuality, or God, is completely real, or can be said to *Be* without qualification. Hence metaphysics appears as a science of the highest and more real mode of Being.

Throughout the eighteenth and earlier nineteenth centuries "metaphysics" was loosely used to denote inquiries concerned with mind, what would now generally be called psychology; and also to denote any inquiry of an ultimate sort. In the later sense it was generally divided into ontology, or inquiry into Being, and epistemology, or inquiry into the nature and limits of knowing. At present, there is a tendency to revert to the more limited Aristotelian sense, though the term is still widely used as a generic name to cover all sorts of inquiries that do not seem to fall within the scope of any of the positive or mathematical sciences.

Reference:—

BALDWIN, J. M. *Dictionary of Philosophy and Psychology*, Vol. III, Pt. ii, pp. 565–574.

METHOD.—The topic of method represents one of the three typical phases of educational practice, the subject matter of study and the institutional agencies of education being the other two. As in the case of subject matter (see COURSE OF STUDY, THEORY OF), there are important practical matters at issue and also general philosophical considerations. The former is the field of methods (in the plural number), the ways of teaching special subjects in accordance with principles that successful experience has vindicated—often called "Special Methods." The latter centres about the problem of the relation of mental attitude and operation to subject matter. For reasons that will appear in the sequel, this problem passes into that of the relation of the individual self to the objects of the world and social life. Intermediate between the field of specific practices and the one of general theory is the logical question of an underlying uniformity of method in the application of mind to various subjects whether pure mathematics, the natural sciences, or history, literature, and language. This intermediate question usually goes by the name of "general method." The present article is confined to the distinctively philosophic aspect of method, extending the survey, however, to take in those phases of general method that are closely connected.

In a general way method is the obverse and correlative of subject matter. The proper interpretation of the connection and distinction between the two is, however, by no means evident, especially since it has been complicated and to some extent perverted by the pervasive influence of a dualistic philosophy. (See DUALISM.) Mind has been severed from the world; the individual from society and its growth. The two have not only been divorced, but the separation between them has been intensified to the point of complete antithesis. (See HUMANISM AND NATURALISM; and IDEALISM.) All effective knowing and acting involve, moreover, both the mind in the world and individual agency in social conditions and for social aims. Hence, the more the separation is emphasized, the more urgent becomes the question of the possibility of interaction and reciprocal influence. While the distinction of subject matter and method was never sharpened into such extreme opposition as that just indicated, the dualistic antithesis of mind and the world affected men's ideas of these educational subjects. The problem of method was conceived as the problem of the adaptation of an individual mind to a foreign subject matter; as an affair of bringing together two things that naturally and intrinsically have nothing to do with each other. This background influenced the conceptions of discipline, culture, and interest (*qq.v.*). Even where the extreme dualism of mind and the world, self and social institutions, has been professedly surrendered, it is not uncommon to see questions of method of teaching, study, and moral training discussed as if they were essentially matters of adaptation of one thing to another unlike thing. How may the study in question be presented *to* the mind so as to appeal to it? How may the mind be aroused so as to apply itself *to* this topic, naturally alien? Such ways of conceiving, in the concrete, the relations of subject matter and method indicate the intellectual atmosphere in which the discussion of mental operation and application has been bathed.

An analysis of experience shows, however, that experience is not a combination of subject matter and method, or an interaction of two independent factors, one of which supplies content and the other form. The distinction between these two matters is developed within experience itself, and arises for the sake of greater control of the course of experience. As indicated in the article on experience (*q.v.*), experience has a dynamic and a static aspect, one of transition and one of cumulation, of retention. Experience, that is, is always changing, and yet it is not a mere flux. There is always a somewhat that changes, and its transition is not a mere passing away, but is a transformation. Here we have the root of the distinction between content and form, subject matter and method, object and subject. It centres in the distinction of the *what* and the *how* of experience. *What* we experience varies in quality, in value, significance. The transition from one state to another is, therefore, measured by the content it ushers in, while the presence and appreciation of this or that object depends upon the factor of transition. In order to secure the objects that are of positive or greater value and to avoid the objects that are of negative or lesser value, we must control the processes of change by which one content of experience gives way to another and grows into it. Whatever in experience, accordingly, aids in control of its development so as to attain what is desired and exclude what is not wanted, is method, way, form of experience. The objects and subject matters that are influenced by this control constitute the material, the structure of experience.

In the course of an infant's restless activity, light is felt and enjoyed. The light, however, is more or less submerged in the qualities that attend the moving of the head, the arms and hands, and certain intraorganic processes. It is, therefore, a vague and confused object, lacking distinctness. In subsequent experience, it is found by accident (that is, without deliberate effort or conscious intention) that the enjoyment of the light quality—such as it is—coheres with changes of the head, eyes, and position of the body, these qualities not having the value attaching to them that the light quality has. As soon as this connection is apparent, the light acquires the status of an *object*, of material or content; while the qualities of the movements of organs of the body in losing their primary values are reduced to the status of means or agencies for getting the object. Thus occurs the gradual differentiation of object and subject, matter and method. The subject matter does not, however, always present itself as an end to be secured; movement in the desired direction may be impeded by certain contents. These resisting factors then stand out conspicuously as obstacles, hindrances. They also become objects, part of the subject matter of experience, for it depends upon the way they are worked upon whether the desired end is ushered in or not. It should be noted that the distinction between matter and method, material and way of treating it, is not a rigid one. What is subject matter at one time may be a part of method at another, and *vice versa*, according as it functions in a concrete situation. In concrete experience it may happen that the sound quality is the significantly desirable thing and that the light or color quality is of import only as clue or stimulus to the presence of the sound as end. Then the seeing reduces itself to the status of means, agency, method. It falls on the side of the subject, no longer on that of the object.

Two things then characterize the concept of method. Methods with respect to their origin mark the gradual differentiation of certain elements of experience; and, with respect to their function, represent any attitudes and operations that are employed to give the course or sequence of experience a direction that is desirable. Method at bottom is but the way of doing things followed in any given case. Its psychological counterpart is the habits and habitual attitudes that determine the course of experience. It follows that methods are at first formed by a semi-instinctive process of trial, error, and success, and that they operate very largely unconsciously. That is to say, attention is given primarily to the ends and obstacles involved, and the habits respond more or less spontaneously to the idea and perception of these objects.

At this point a serious error is often made in the conception of educational method. Just because these primary ways of doing things which represent method at its primary and deepest level have been formed in relatively accidental fashion and also prior to the period of conscious school instruction; because, moreover, they often mark relatively ineffective and blundering ways of accomplishing ends, there is a tendency to ignore them or to deny that they are methods at all. Method is then conceived as a purely logical matter, in a sense that identifies the logical with a consciously formed and followed enterprise. Such methods are embodied in symbols, and need not be embodied in working attitudes and habits at all. They are formulae for ways in which things consciously ought to be done, not descriptions of the ways in which they *actually* are done. Thus a complete split is introduced between what are called psychological methods (but which might better be termed vital, concrete, or practical methods) and the so-called logical methods—which might better be termed formal and symbolic. The result is that new habits which are largely verbal are grafted on to the older working habits—generally to the detriment of their efficacy; or else, in reaction from the futility of mere formulations of logical abstractions, the spontaneous, habitual attitudes are relied upon, without securing the readjustment and reconstruction needed for higher and more complex ends—for securing a better type of control.

The fundamental question of method in education thus concerns the right cooperation of the unconscious and the reflective factors in the direction of the course of experience. Method, the way of going at a thing, depends at first upon the relation between instinct and desire, on one side, and an end, on the other. The end stands out more or less in consciousness and supplies the basis of conscious guidance. What is educationally important is, therefore, that on one side the proper type of desire be aroused and the proper type of end be conceived on the other. These points are not matters of conscious formulation, but of providing environing conditions that will call out and fix desirable attitudes of response. Only as these attitudes become sufficiently habitual to be effective is there any basis for conscious reflection so as to formulate methods for further conscious employment. When, as is too frequently the case in such subjects as arithmetic and grammar, teachers insist that pupils shall consciously follow certain forms of statement and "analysis" before they have become thoroughly habituated to dealing practically with the situations in which numerical and grammatical values occur, the result is that the formulae come between the pupils and their appreciation of the nature of the situation. They do not respond any longer to the results of the experienced situation, but only to the verbally acquired formulae. The very means that are supposed to render the pupils' operations more intelligent, more logical, result in making them mechanical.

Logical method, in short, as a conscious procedure always implies reflection upon the means which have already been instinctively and hence unconsciously used in reaching ends that make an appeal on their own account. Formulated logical operations are thus the possession of an expert in a subject, one who has already worked through the subject, and who has, therefore, command of the materials to be formulated. They represent the standpoint of a matured, a developed, experience. The commonest school fallacy is that the methods which represent the control of a subject matter gained through long practical experience can be conveyed directly to those who are just beginning to occupy themselves with a topic, so that the procedure of the latter may be made more reasonable and intelligent. Many methods that are condemned as "deductive" are really not deductive at all, but simply represent the attempt to hand over directly to the inexperienced and immature the intellectual technique appropriate to those who have gone through a subject, and who are therefore in a condition to review and systematize the procedures that have proved effective.

The currency of the wrong conception of logical method leads to a reaction almost equally harmful. Considerations of order, sequence, definiteness, of fit adaptation of means to ends, the importance of thoughtful surveys and reviews of ground traversed, together with the need of formulating the practices that have been found helpful, are ignored. Behavior is left on the instinctive or "spontaneous" plane with no care to see that the attitudes that are evoked are those most adequate to their direct end, and also such as to stimulate later reflection. The true difference is not between the merely psychological—the illogical—and the logical but between the unconscious logic of effective adaptation to ends and the conscious logic of formulating the methods that have been successfully employed, so that subsequent procedure may be easier and more fruitful. And this transition, through reflection upon that which has been already accomplished, from the blinder and more instinctive into the more intelligently controlled, should be a constant factor of all growth; it is, indeed, indispensable, if growth is to be truly educative. (See EDUCATION.)

From this conception of method there follow certain considerations applicable to the topic of general method. Strictly speaking, method is thoroughly individual. Each person has his own instinctive way of going at a thing; the attitude and the mode of approach and attack are individual. To ignore this individuality of approach, to try to substitute for it, under the name of "general method," a uniform scheme of procedure, is simply to cripple the only effective agencies of operation, and to overlay them with a mechanical formalism that produces only a routine conventionality of mental quality. Certain features may be found, however, which are involved in the transition from unconscious effort to a more consciously guided process. These features may be abstracted and generalized. While the outcome will not put individuals in possession of a sure key to intellectual efficiency, it will indicate to a teacher the main steps that have to be taken, and suggest the crucial points where conditions of growth have to be carefully maintained and fostered.

The primary factor in general method, so construed, is the existence of a situation which appeals to an individual as his own concern or interest, that is to say, as presenting an end to be achieved, because arousing desire and effort. The second point is that the conditions be such as to stimulate observation and memory in locating the means, the obstacles and resources that must be reckoned with in dealing with the situation. The third point is the formation of a plan of procedure, a theory or hypothesis about the best way of proceeding. The fourth is putting the plan into operation. The fifth and last is the comparison of the result reached with what was intended, and a consequent estimate of the worth of the method followed, a more critical discernment of its weak and its strong points. These five steps may be reduced to three more generic ones. The first and fundamental condition of right method is the existence of some concrete situation involving an end that interests the individual, and that requires active and thoughtful effort in order to be reached. The second is consideration of the nature of the problem, the difficulty or perplexity involved in reaching the end set, so as to form a suggestion or conjecture as to the best way of proceeding to solve the difficulty. The third is the overt effort in which the thought of the plan is applied and thereby tested. Scientific method will be found to involve exactly the same steps, save that a scientific mode of approach implies a large body of prior empirical and tentative procedures which have finally been sifted so as to develop a technique consciously formulated and adapted to the given type of problem.

See SCIENCE.

References:—

DEWEY, JOHN. *Child and Curriculum.* (Chicago, 1902.)
How We Think. (Boston, 1911.)
Studies in Logical Theory. (Chicago, 1903.)
Science as Subject-Matter and as Method. *Science*, N.S., Vol. XXXI, pp. 121–126.

MILLER, I. E. *Psychology of Thinking.* (New York, 1909.)

MONISM.—The name for the philosophical theory which holds that there is but one ultimate substance or reality. The term is quite formal in character, connoting nothing about the nature of the one ultimate being. Thoroughgoing materialism, absolute idealism, panpsychism, pantheism, are alike monistic. The vagueness of the term is enhanced by the fact that the motif of some monistic systems is opposition to dualism, while that of others is opposition to pluralism. Consequently, some contemporary theories are monistic in their denial of dualism (*q.v.*), especially as relates to any final cleavage between mind and matter, and yet are pluralistic in holding that the various forms in which the one ultimate reality occurs do not form an interdependent necessary whole, but are relatively independent of one another, or form real individuals.

MORALITY AND MORAL SENSE.—Morality in its objective meaning is the body of practices, habits, and beliefs which the prevailing enlightened judgment of a period regards as right, and which accordingly it strives to inculcate by all forms of education and tuition, and which, within certain limits, it strives to enforce against individuals who openly transgress. The various theories of morals or ethics arise partly from the efforts to criticize, purify, and systematize current morality in the objective sense, and partly in the effort to discover its ultimate basis and justification.

Moral sense, in its broader usage, denotes the body of judgments current in a community with respect to morality. It is called a "sense" to express its relatively unreasoned character; our more fundamental moral estimates and ideas have become engrained in us by education and habit, and hence are identified with our immediate emotional and practical responses rather than with consciously reasoned out conclusions. In its more technical meaning, "moral sense" denotes one variety of the theory about morality which holds that moral judgments are innate or intuitive, not the results of experience. The term "sense" is used to indicate the notion that the direct perception of right and wrong attaches to particular cases, not to general principles. In the case of its leading historic representatives, Shaftesbury and Hutcheson, it also connoted an assimilation of our moral to our aesthetic perception. Just as a man of good taste responds immediately to the beauty or ugliness of objects, so a man of moral sense appreciates at once the loveliness or baseness of character and acts.

See ETHICS; INNATE IDEAS; INTUITION; MORAL EDUCATION.

NATIVISM.—A term applied to the theories according to which the foundations of all knowledge, or else the essential conditions of some branch of experience, are born in or with the mind or agent. It thus has close associations with the terms *a priori*, innate ideas, and intuition (*q.v.*). In psychology the term has come to be applied particularly to those theories which hold that the extensity of space perceptions is an original, native element in some at least of the sensational qualities, in opposition to those theories which hold spread-outness and depth to be the results of association among qualities themselves lacking spatial quality. The most recent use of the term has been much influenced by modern biological theories of heredity. The old *tabula rasa* conception of sensationalistic empiricism has been made an anachronism by the demonstration of the number and variety of the instinctive non-acquired tendencies. It is only by a figure of speech, however, that these tendencies can be said to be innate in the *mind*—being rather connate with the organism. This conclusion involves quite as complete a reconstruction of the older type of nativism as of the older type of empiricism. The educational importance of the controversy gathers about the question of the relative importance of Nature and Nurture—the relative importance and function of the hereditary tendencies of the organism as compared with the influence of the social and cultural environment. (See HEREDITY.) This question is thoroughly misconceived, however, when treated as a problem of one versus the other. The conditions of the educative growth of an individual are ultimately inherent in the organism, possessing its native tendencies to act and to be susceptible. This fact is all-important in contrast with the belief of a number of eighteenth-century theorists that practice and the influence of economic and political conditions are omnipotent. It is also highly important in showing the necessity of recognizing individual differences of capacity and aptitude. But, on the other hand, the direction given these native powers, the kind of ends for which they become effective, the ways in which they are used depend upon nurture—that is, upon the influence of the social medium consciously and unconsciously exerted.

See ACQUIRED CHARACTERISTICS; GALTON; HEREDITY.

NATURE.—Probably no philosophical conception has had a more general or widespread popular influence than that of nature. Its intellectual career has been facilitated rather than hindered by the variety and ambiguity of senses attached to the term, especially as regards the things to which it has been set in opposition. Recognition of the role of this uncertainty in enhancing the influence of the idea is not necessarily cynical or skeptical in character. The more typical senses of the term are sufficiently near to one another so that they insensibly pass into each other; while all of the more fundamental ideas operative in human history have some vagueness attaching to them, because they stand for deep-lying practical aspirations and for intense emotional attitudes as well as for rational notions which may be accurately defined. The function common to the differing senses of the term nature has been the demand for some standard or norm for the regulation and valuation of human beliefs. It designates whatever is taken to be intrinsic and inevitable in existence and thought, in antithesis to what is external, artificial, and factitious; leaving it to the culture of the time to determine just where the natural, the normal and normative shall be looked for, and just what, in contrast, shall be regarded as secondary and accidental.

The classic conception of nature, as fixed by Aristotle, was an aftergrowth (and to some extent an outgrowth) of the inquiry raised by some of the sophists as to whether religion, morality, and the State exist by nature, or by mutual agreement (convention, tacit or express) or by decree, by enactment of superior authority. This led to an inquiry after the true nature of things, their real essence. Etymologically, φύσις, the Greek word translated "nature," was derived from the verb "to grow," just as the Latin *natura* is from the verb "to be born." Aristotle identified the nature of a thing with the thing in its full or completed growth, which is also the thing in its state of fullest activity or actuality. The nature of an acorn is the oak; the true nature of the human body is the intellectual activity in which the organic processes are most fully realized; the nature of the individual is the state in which alone distinctively human properties (in contrast with those of brutes and gods) come to realization. The distinguishing trait of nature is that the process of realization, involving the four ultimate principles or causes (*q.v.*), takes place from within, in contrast to art (all products of human invention and skill), where the movement is initiated from without. This metaphysical and teleological conception of nature was taken up into patristic and scholastic philosophy. The Stoics retained much of the Aristotelian idea, but conjoined it with the popular sense of nature as the sum total of laws, processes, and events that constitute the world as an organized whole or cosmos,—hence the precept of life in accordance with nature as the supreme moral precept. Through the influence of the Stoics upon jurisprudence, the conceptions of a "state of nature," "natural law," and "natural right" were introduced as affording the norm of eternal justice in distinction from the positive institutions and civil laws which represent the adaptation of this eternal law to temporary and local conditions.

In modern times the conception of nature was first affected by the rise of physical science. It meant the sum total of laws which "govern" natural phenomena. Sir Isaac Newton considered these laws to present the divine legislation for the realm of created things, expressions of a rational will, so that nature might almost be conceived as a divine vice-regent. This meaning was taken up by the Deists and made the basis of a criticism of the miraculous and the supernatural in religion. As the influence of this mode of thinking spread into France, the conception of nature was generalized and made an implement of criticism of everything in the Church and State that appeared to the *philosophes* to be irrational. Since these social institutions were historical products, it is hardly too much to say that the term nature as a eulogistic term was put into opposition to history, and to everything whose existence depended upon historical traditions rather than upon an enlightened reason.

Rousseau agreed with the rationalists in opposition to existing social institutions as artificial and so unnatural, but attacked the philosophers of the enlightenment by including art and science as themselves artificial, sophisticated, and misleading. Nature, according to him, was not to be looked for in conscious reason, but rather in primitive, instinctive, unreasoned impulses and emotions. The natural is the original in the sense both of the primary in time and the creative, the originative. The "return to nature," that concept so influential in educational philosophies if not in school practice, was a return to the primitive untaught sources that condition all teaching. While there was much in Rousseau which would lead his followers to interpret the natural as an idealization of the life of savages into a poetic idyl, there was also much to call attention to the original instincts and principles of growth in children. Through the influence of Rousseau upon Pestalozzi, Froebel, and others, education in accordance with nature came to mean that there were certain intrinsic laws of development or unfolding, physical, mental, and moral, in children, and that these inherent principles of growth should furnish the norms of all educational procedure.

Meantime, the attacks by Rousseau upon civilization in the name of nature called out not merely the interest of Romanticism in picturesque natural beauty untouched by human hands, in folklore, primitive arts and poetry and in peasant life (as more primitive, unsophisticated and unconsciously creative), but also that phase of German philosophy which deliberately set itself to justify culture as being more truly natural than crude nature and than original impulse and instinct. This tendency found expression in all of Goethe's later work, as well as in the philosophers Kant, Fichte, and Hegel, and in Schiller's conception of art as the great civilizing and moralizing agency of humanity. The same movement led to the idea that the nature of man is found in humanity, rather than in the individual; and hence to an idealization of history, since it is in history rather than in the consciously evolved ideas of an individual that humanity is revealed. This movement culminated in Hegel's theory that social and political institutions in their historic manifestation are more truly real than either phenomena of the physical world or the moral efforts of individuals in their individual capacity—that indeed the entire education of the individual consists in effecting in him an assimilation of the spiritual products of humanity in its historic evolution as a progressive realization of spirit. In this way, the criticism of Rousseau's return to nature reached its climax in a wholly antithetical theory.

See CULTURE; HUMANISM AND NATURALISM; ROUSSEAU.

NEO-HUMANISM.—A term sometimes applied to the revival of the Hellenic ideal in German thought in the latter part of the eighteenth century. It differed from the humanism of the fifteenth century in its attachment to Greek rather than Latin culture; in a greater interest in Greek antiquities and art in general as compared simply with literary records, and in appeal to Greek culture as affording an ideal conception of life. Serenity, balance, a recognition of the inevitable limitations of life, the striving for a symmetrical development within these limits, the idea of the central place of a free play of the intellectual powers in securing this proportionate development of all human powers, are some of the traits emphasized and attributed to the Greek view of life. To these must be added the claim of spiritual and intellectual kinship with the Greeks which the Germans put forward. Winckelmann and Goethe are the chief names in this new humanism, the former with his archaeological researches, and the latter in his reaction against romanticism signalized by his *Italian Letters*. In nineteenth-century English thought, Matthew Arnold is a typical representative of the spirit of Neo-humanism in his conception of culture and his appeal for recognition of Hellenism as well as Hebraism.

In the gymnasiums and universities of Germany, Neo-humanism exercised a powerful influence. A new vigor was imparted to the classical studies, but more especially to the study of Greek. No longer content with the merely linguistic, an effort was made to imbibe the Greek spirit by a study of Greek life and literature in all its phases. In Germany this is the period of her most brilliant classical scholars.

See CULTURE; HUMANISM AND NATURALISM; GERMANY, EDUCATION IN; GOETHE; HERDER; WOLF, F. A., etc.

References:—

FRANCKE, K. *History of German Literature*. (New York, 1905.)

PAULSEN, F. *German Education Past and Present.* Tr. by T. Lorenz. (London, 1908.)
Geschichte des gelehrten Unterrichts. (Leipzig, 1896.)
SANDYS, J. E. *History of Classical Scholarship,* Vol. III. (Cambridge, 1908.)
SPRANGER, E. *Wilhelm von Humboldt und die Reform des Bildungswesens.* Contains Bibliography. (Berlin, 1910.)

OBJECT AND SUBJECT.—The older classic use of the terms subject and object was the opposite of that current to-day. According to the Aristotelian logic only substances, things existing as individuals not as qualities or properties of things, could be subjects of propositions and the subject matter of adequate knowledge. Subject and substance were thus practically identified; some trace of this meaning remains in the current use of the term subject matter. Scholastic philosophy, under the influence of Arabian thought, introduced the term "object" to designate things in their "second intention," that is, not as things on their own account, but as objects of thought or mental consideration. A chimera would thus exist objectively but not as a subject; according to the opponents of Platonic realism, universals (man, as distinguished from individual men) also had existence only objectively. Modern philosophy effected a complete reversal of this usage. The tendency began with the introduction of the psychological mode of thinking of Locke and his successors, and was practically completed by Kant. As the function of the self as the centre of thinking, feeling, knowing, was insisted upon, the term subject was more and more used as a synonym for ego, mind, self, and the adjective subjective to denote mental existences. The problem of the relation of subject and object came to mean the problem of relation of mind and the world, especially as they enter into the constitution of knowledge. By the transcendental idealistic school much was made of the fact that the thinking ego is at once subject-object, since the thinking self is capable of presenting itself to itself as object. In self-consciousness, as thus defined, was found the key to the problem of the relation of particular minds or sentient subjects to the world,—a conception that had a great vogue in post-Kantian idealism.

See EPISTEMOLOGY; METHOD; SELF.

OPINION.—A term given to beliefs of a peculiarly personal or individual character, and to beliefs which, though generally current, lack scientific warrant, having their ground in custom rather than in evidence. (The term public opinion is used to denote the beliefs characteristic of a community in so far as these beliefs influence corporate or public action.) One of the objects of education is to produce the habit of mind which discriminates between opinion and grounded conviction, and which prevents opinions being held and asserted dogmatically. Plato among ancient educationalists and Locke among modern have especially insisted upon the harmfulness of confusing opinions and knowledge, and the importance of devising educational methods to safeguard the mind against this danger.

See KNOWLEDGE.

OPTIMISM.—The origin of the conception of optimism throws much light upon its nature. Plato had made the Idea of the Good the central principle of his metaphysics and of his dialectic. He had, however, admitted a passive principle in the constitution of the world sometimes called Matter, sometimes Non-being, sometimes The Other, which was capable of hindering the realization of this Good. Aristotle (*q.v.*) conceived of matter as the potentiality of a process through which ends as complete actualities are realized and thus did away with the Platonic dualism in that form. But in teaching that Nature always acts for the good, or for a final cause, he also admitted a principle of chance in things which was capable of preventing in particular cases the realization of the true end or Good. Aristotle's philosophy might thus be called an optimism upon the whole, tempered by the acknowledgment of unavoidable accidents in details. The Neoplatonists accounted for matter, resistance, and multiplicity by the idea of a series of emanations of which matter was the lowest. Its far remove from The One Good accounted for its appearance of evil. But even this appearance of evil was due to judging from only a partial standpoint; seen in its place in the whole, matter would be apprehended as contributing to its perfection.

St. Augustine (*q.v.*) adapted these conceptions to the

needs of Christian apologetic. The conception of God as Creator compelled him to reject the idea that there is any principle of evil in matter or in the created cosmos at any point. Things that may seem evil to our finite judgment would be seen to enhance the goodness of the whole, could we but perceive from that standpoint. Real evil exists, however, but not cosmologically or metaphysically; it is due to the will of man in disobeying the divine command and substituting his will for the divine will. Even with respect to this, however, St. Augustine was so impressed with the sovereignty of the divine will and power, which must be absolutely good, that even sin was, metaphysically considered, privative rather than a positive reality. Through this influence of the great Father of the Church, optimism became an official part of Christian philosophy.

In the seventeenth century, Leibnitz in his *Théodicée* attempted, in terms of his philosophy of monads and their preestablished harmony, a purely rationalistic proof that this is the best of all possible worlds. Modern optimistic theories, outside of professedly theological circles, really date from Leibnitz. Voltaire, instigated by the destructiveness of the Lisbon earthquake, ridiculed the fashionable Leibnitzian optimism in his poem, *Candide*. However, optimism was in the air in the eighteenth century, being congenial to rationalistic deism and to the beliefs of the social reformers in the indefinite perfectibility of man. (See CONDORCÉ.) Even Rousseau, with his anti-rationalistic tendencies, taught the original goodness of nature and of man, attributing evil to the influence of institutions in destroying equal liberty.

A contemporary of Leibnitz, the Dutch Jew Spinoza, had dealt to the metaphysical basis of optimism the most severe blow that it could have possibly received. He taught that Nature is what it must be by an absolute logical necessity and that considerations of good and evil alike are equally foreign to its nature. They are relative only to man with his desires. Spinoza's teaching had no influence for over a century. Finally the growth of mechanical science and of dislike for the doctrine of final causes in any form in connection with nature prepared the way for a general acceptance of the essentials of Spinoza's view. This change shifted the problem from the question whether the world, or Being, metaphysically considered, is good to the question whether Life, empirically considered, is a good; or in its popular statement whether "Life is worth living." The most marked tendency of recent discussion is the development of the conception of "Meliorism," the idea that at least there is a sufficient basis of goodness in life and its conditions so that by thought and earnest effort we may constantly make better things. This conception attacks optimism on the ground that it encourages a fatalistic contentment with things as they are; what is needed is the frank recognition of evils, not for the sake of accepting them as final, but for the sake of arousing energy to remedy them. The conception of progress practically takes the place of the old notion of the metaphysical Good.

PANTHEISM.—The philosophic or theological theory, according to which God and the Universe are identical. It has both a mystic and a rationalistic form. Spinoza is generally regarded as the typical classic example of a pantheistic philosopher. In the development of modern idealism (*q.v.*) in its absolute form, thought or will or sentiency has often been taken to be the single ultimate reality manifested in both the physical world and the finite centres of consciousness that know and feel this world. These forms of absolute idealism have generally been criticized as pantheistic by their opponents. This claim has been denied by the absolutists on the ground that instead of merging individual selves as unreal in one absolute, they have held that a kingdom of selves is necessary to the reality of the ultimate thought or will. Fichte (*q.v.*), however, was not averse to the epithet ethical pantheism, provided it was understood to stand for the unity of will from which all diversity of individual moral striving took its departure and in which it found its goal.

References:—

Bradley, F. H. *Appearance and Reality.* (London, 1893.)
Fichte, J. G. *Destination of Man.*
Royce, J. *The World and Individual.* (New York, 1901.)
Spinoza, B. *Ethic.*

PEDANTRY.—A term given to the display of knowledge for the sake of its display, especially in the exhibition of knowledge upon unusual topics and subjects irrelevant to current needs and interests and hence lacking application. Probably one indispensable factor in pedantry is that the knowledge exhibited be second hand, or show dependence upon somewhat antiquated authorities, being more or less accompanied by quotations from them. Knowledge that seems vital and important at one epoch may seem a useless affectation at another. At the Renaissance, reformers like Montaigne (*q.v.*) and humorists like Rabelais (*q.v.*) found most scholastic scholarship to be mere pedantry while the successors of the humanists regarded as pedantry the humanists' display of classical allusions and Ciceronian Latinity. Such historic illustrations show that the question underlying pedantry is the readaptation of the learning of the past to contemporary conditions.

See KNOWLEDGE; MONTAIGNE; RENAISSANCE AND EDUCATION.

PERSONALITY.—Personality is closely allied with the conceptions of individuality (*q.v.*) and selfhood. (See SELF.) Taken literally, it means the state or quality of being a person. The concept of person arose in connection with Roman law. To be a person was to be a subject of legal rights and responsibilities; that is, of powers and duties capable of enforcement by civil authority. On this view, a corporation or minor civic group, likely a municipality, was a person; slaves were not persons, while minors were persons only vicariously, or through their authorized representatives. As the external traits of this legal view disappeared, an ethical sense developed out of them; a person is the subject of moral rights and duties. Thus Kant said that the moral law was summed up in the injunctions: Be a Person, and respect others as Persons. A person is an end in and for himself, never a means to anything beyond.

Because of this ethical sense personality is often treated as a "higher" idea than individuality. From another point of view personality is an abstraction compared with individuality. All persons have personality in the same sense; there is nothing distinguishing, nothing concrete about it. Individuality, on the other hand, is always differential; it is something that *specifically* characterizes each self. Individuality expresses what one uniquely *is*; personality expresses what one *has*—a property that one may acquire. In this sense, individuality is deeper than personality. In earlier days children were classed with slaves as intermediate links between things and persons, save that they differed from slaves in the potentiality of personality. This conception of childhood was embodied in methods of discipline, punishment, and instruction, it being assumed that children had no rights of their own. With the development of the democratic idea, rights of personality were extended to children, and methods of education have accordingly undergone considerable reconstruction. No consistent theory upon this point has, however, as yet, been worked out in practice.

PESSIMISM.—In popular usage the disposition to look on the dark side of things; as a systematic philosophy, the theory that existence and life are radically evil, so evil that the only remedy is the negation of the "will to live," the exact antithesis of optimism (*q.v.*) as a philosophy. In considerable part, the motivation of pessimistic systems has resided in the superficial and complacent view of evil as an incident which contributes to the perfection of the whole taken by optimistic systems. Leibnitz's formula that this world is the best of all possible worlds obviously lends itself readily to an extremely pessimistic interpretation. A certain pessimistic tone concerning the world as it *now* exists has also been a marked feature of the most serious and influential religions, such as Buddhism (*q.v.*) and Christianity. In general, nineteenth-century thought reacted in this as in other respects against the characteristic eighteenth-century thought, which had been optimistic. The latter held to the doctrine of natural harmony working inevitably for the increase of perfection and happiness; the former dwelt upon the existence of discord, struggle, and competition. The Darwinian idea of the omnipresence of the struggle for existence accentuated this tendency. While the pessimistic spirit found its most adequate expression in literature, especially poetry, it also found systematic metaphysical embodiment, notably in Schopenhauer and von Hartmann. While systematic pessimism is too contrary to the needs of living beings to secure for itself many consistent adherents, it has made impossible the older type of optimism, and has been a leading factor in bringing about the transformation of optimism into meliorism. The latter holds to the reality of evil as a genuine fact, but emphasizes the possibility, through good will and intelligently directed effort, of a progressive amelioration. It is essentially a doctrine of progress.

See OPTIMISM; SCHOPENHAUER.

PHENOMENALISM.—A name given to two different types of philosophy. According to one theory, what we know is simply the appearances of real things, these appearances consisting of the impressions which they make upon the mind. This view includes within itself many philosophies otherwise diverse from one another. Kantian phenomenalism, for example, is distinguished by the emphasis which it lays upon the synthetic activity of *a priori* powers of the mind in transforming passive impressions into objects concerning which universal judgments are possible. Spencerian phenomenalism emphasizes the fact that the unknowable things-in-themselves have gradually molded the mind, through heredity, in the long-continued evolutionary process, so that the impressions made upon it arrange themselves in modes which somehow parallel the relations of things-in-themselves. The other type of phenomenalism is radical. It holds that there are no things-in-themselves back of the phenomena and causing them, but things are what they are known to be. Shadworth Hodgson in England and Renouvier in France are the best known modern representatives of this kind of phenomenalism. Its influence in developing the radical empiricism of James was considerable.

PHILOSOPHY OF EDUCATION.—*Relation of Philosophy and Education.*—A clear conception of the nature of the philosophy of education in distinction from the science and principles of education is not possible without some antecedent conception of the nature of philosophy itself and its relation to life. Is philosophy capable of being generated and developed without any reference to education? Then a philosophy of education will be simply the application to educational ideas of an outside ready-made standard of judgment, with all its dangers of forcing the facts of education so that they conform to and support the philosophy already formed. In this case, we shall have as many philosophies of education as are required to illustrate diverging philosophic systems. The case will stand quite otherwise if there is an intimate and vital relation between the need for philosophy and the necessity for education. In this case the philosophy of education will simply make explicit the reference to the guiding of life needs and purposes which is operative in philosophy itself. It will not be an external application of philosophy, but its development to the point of adequate manifestation of its own inner purpose and motive. While different philosophies of education will still exist, they will not be so many corollaries of divergent pure philosophies, but will make explicit the different conceptions of the value and aims of actual life held by different persons. It will be seen that different philosophies exist because men have in mind different ideals of life and different educational methods for making these ideals prevail. The chief point of this article is to develop the conception of the internal and vital relation of education and philosophy.

Every seriously minded person may be said to have a philosophy. For he has some sort of a working theory of life. He possesses, in however half-conscious fashion, a standpoint from which weight and importance are attached to the endless flow of detailed happenings and doings. His philosophy is his general scheme and measure of values, his way of estimating the significance that attaches to the various incidents of experience. If pressed to state and justify his working principle, he might reply that while it would not satisfy others, it served its owner and maker. No individual, however, is so eccentric that he invents and builds up his scheme except on the general pattern that is socially transmitted to him. The exigencies and the perplexities of life are recurrent. The same generic problems have faced men over and over; by long-continued cooperative effort men have worked out general ideas regarding the meaning of life, including the connections of men with one another and with the world in which they live. These conceptions are embodied not only in the codes of moral principles which men profess and the religions in which they find support and consolation, but in the basic ideas which have become commonplace through their very generality: such ideas as that things hang together to make a world; that events have causes; that things may be brought into classes; the distinctions of animate and inanimate, personal and physical, and so on throughout the warp and woof of our intellectual fabric. Philosophy aims to set forth a conception of the world, or of reality, and of life which will assign to each of these interests its proper and proportionate place. It aims to set forth the distinctive role of each in a way that will harmonize its demand with that of other ends.

Need of a Philosophy of Education.—Three classes of motives, unconsciously blended with one another, usually operate in making the need for systematic and rational ideas felt, and in deciding the point of view from which the need is dealt with. These motives are the conflict of conservative and progressive tendencies: the conflict of scientific conceptions of the world with beliefs hallowed by tradition and giving sanction to morals and religion; and the conflict of institutional demands with that for a freer and fuller expression of individuality. (1) Some philosophies are marked by a reforming, almost revolutionary, spirit. They criticize the world and life as they exist, and set in opposition to them an ideal world into conformity with which the existent scheme of things ought to be brought. Other philosophies tend rather to justify things as they are, pointing out that if we penetrate to their true nature and essential meaning, each class of things is found to serve a necessary purpose and embody a necessary idea. Plato and Aristotle, Fichte and Hegel, for example, are all of them classified as idealists, but the tendency of Plato and Fichte is to set up an ideal over against the actual; while that of Aristotle and Hegel is to exhibit the rational nature or ideal already embodied in the actual—a difference that clearly corresponds to the ordinary division of men into reformers and conservatives.

(2) Different philosophers interpret their material very differently according to the respective weight they instinctively attribute on the one hand to scientific conceptions of

the world, and on the other to ethical tendencies and aspirations. If one takes his departure from the former, he will explain men's moral and religious beliefs on the basis of the principles furnished by contemporary science, and will deny the validity of all ideas, no matter how influential in life, that do not harmonize with these principles. To others, men's moral aims and efforts are the most significant thing in life and are taken as the key to the nature of reality. The results of science are reinterpreted to bring them into line. During the rapid development of natural science since the seventeenth century, many philosophies have thus made it their chief business to provide a view of reality in which the seemingly divergent claims and standpoints of natural science and morals should be reconciled.

(3) The third moving force concerns the value attached to the principle of free individuality—individuality that confers upon each person a distinctive worth not supplied by any other person and not capable of being summed up or exhausted in any general formula or principle. Some thinkers start by natural preference with the standpoint of law or a general order, or a pervasive and unifying force. Strictly individual traits are then brought into line by reduction (or at least approximation) to the universal. If individuality is not denied as an ultimate reality, it is explained and justified from the standpoint of a comprehensive uniform principle. Such philosophies tend to be deductive in character and to assign greater value to reason, which deals with general conceptions, than to perception, which reveals particulars. Persons with a strong interest in individuality reverse the standard of value and the method of consideration. Specific individuals are taken to be the primary facts; general principles, laws, classes, are derived from comparison of the individuals or are subordinate to them. In method, such philosophies tend to be empirical and inductive, accepting the observations of sense and the particular situations of conduct as the most certain data, and employing rational conceptions only as secondary means of connecting particulars or filling their gaps.

The totality or completeness at which philosophy aims is not quantitative; it is not the greatest possible sum of accurate knowledge. As to this sort of completeness or wholeness, philosophy cannot compete with the special sciences taken in their totality. For all its special facts, philosophy must depend upon these sciences, and so far as organization of the facts into a larger system of knowledge is concerned it must also walk humbly in the path beaten by science. But there is another kind of unity and wholeness with which science is not concerned: unity of attitude and wholeness of outlook. But wholeness means also balance, interaction, and mutual reenforcement of the various values and interests of life: religion, poetry, industry or the business of making a living, politics or the art of living together, morals, science itself. An account of "experience as a whole" is a conception of experience that shows the special contribution which each of these typical interests makes, and the claim for recognition it may legitimately put forth. The only "experience as a whole" that concerns man is an experience whose parts change continuously, but all change into one another as there is occasion, with ease and flexibility, and so as to enrich one another. Its opposite is not our everyday experience with its fluctuations and its endless running out into the new, but one-sided exaggerations of some phase of this everyday experience, or an isolation of its interests so that they restrict one another, and thus impoverish life.

Philosophy of Education, Science of Education, and Principles of Education.—Education is such an important interest of life that in any case we should expect to find a philosophy of education, just as there is a philosophy of art and of religion. We should expect, that is, such a treatment of the subject as would show that the nature of existence renders education an integral and indispensable function of life. We should expect an interpretation and criticism of the materials and methods currently used in education, using this necessary function as the standard of value. Such a treatment is usually presented under the title of "Principles of Education." While no rigid line marks off this discussion from what is termed the "Science of Education," there are differences of aim and spirit that are worth noting, because of the light they shed upon the nature of a philosophy of education. It is possible to start with education as an established fact, with education as it is currently practiced, and to describe and analyze the various factors that enter into it, factors of school organization and administration, of management and discipline, of instruction and the various branches of study. So far as the analysis reveals general principles of individual growth and of social grouping which are operative in the degree that teaching and training are effective, its result rises above the level of recounting and cataloguing relevant phenomena. Hence it deserves the name of a science. This science affords the basis for a critical comparison of the various processes that are currently employed. As teachers are put in intelligent possession of it, their own work becomes less blind and routine; the science, as in other cases, develops a corresponding art which lifts its practitioners from artisans into artists.

Notwithstanding its intellectual and practical value, such an account of education does not cover the whole ground. It works, so to speak, inside of education as a given fact. Another and larger view is possible and desirable, a less professional and a more human view. Education is a concern not merely of school administrators and teachers, of pupils and their parents, but of society. We may have a definite and systematic knowledge of the principles that are at the bottom of the most effective current practice of the day, and may be able to use this knowledge to criticize and correct defective phases of this practice, and yet be thrown back upon mere opinion or mere custom for a judgment as to the value of an educational system as a whole. The general spirit and trend of an established education might be wrong, and yet make possible a scientific account of itself which would be available for rectifying it in details. But the improvement would still be within a scheme which in its main direction and purport was not what it should be.

We have to judge every educational institution and practice from the standpoint of that "whole of experience" which calls it into being and controls its purpose and materials. There exist not merely the principles by which the existing system of education is made effective, but also the principles that animate the entire range of interests of the whole life of the community and that make the existing system what it is. An interpretation and valuation of the educational system in the light of this inclusive social context is the larger and more human view of which we spoke. It utilizes the contributions of science in all its branches to give society an insight into what sort of thing it is undertaking in the training of its members, and it gives society a clearer consciousness of the meaning of the educational office so largely performed by instinct and custom.

Philosophy is the General Theory of Education.—The connection of education and philosophy is, however, even closer and more vital than this sketch of the principles of education, as distinct from the science of education, would indicate. *Philosophy may be defined as the general theory of education*; the theory of which education is the corresponding art or practice. Three interlinked considerations support this statement: (i) Men's interests manifest their dispositions; (ii) these dispositions are formed by education; (iii) there must be a general idea of the value and relations of these interests if there is to be any guidance of the process of forming the dispositions that lie back of the realization of the interests. (i) If at any time the various values of experience are out of harmony with one another, the ultimate cause of the difficulty lies in men's habitual attitudes toward life: the habits of judging and of emotional appreciation that are embodied in their habits of action. Interests, attitudes, dispositions, fundamental habits of mind are mutually convertible terms.

(ii) If we but consent to extend the term education beyond its narrow limitation to schooling, we shall find that we cannot stop short in this extension till we have broadened it to cover all the agencies and influences that shape disposition. Not merely books and pictures, but the machinery of publication and communication by which these are made accessible must be included—and this means the use made of railway and telegraph as well as of the printing press, the library, and the picture gallery. Ordinary daily intercourse, the exchange of ideas and experiences in conversation, and the contacts of business competition and cooperation are most influential in deciding the objects upon which attention is fixed and the way in which attention is given to them.

Every place in which men habitually meet, shop, club, factory, saloon, church, political caucus, is perforce a schoolhouse, even though not so labelled. This intercourse is in turn dependent upon the political organization of society, the relations of classes to one another, the distribution of wealth, the spirit in which family life is conducted, and so on. Public agitations, discussions, propaganda of public meeting and press, political campaigns, legislative deliberations, are in this regard but so many educational agencies. In brief, every condition, arrangement, and institution that forms the emotional and imaginative bent of mind that gives meaning to overt action is educational in character.

(iii) There are but two alternatives. Either these agencies will perform their educational work as an incidental and unregulated by-product, molding men's minds blindly while conscious attention is given to their other more tangible products; or men will have an idea of the results they wish to have attained, will judge existing agencies according as they achieve or come short of these ends, and will use their idea and their estimate as guides in giving the desired direction to the working of these agencies. This brings us, again, to philosophy, which, as we have seen, is the attempt to develop just such an idea. This is what is meant by saying that philosophy is, in its ultimate extent, a general theory of education; or that it is the idea of which a *consciously guided education* is the practical counterpart.

It is, of course, possible to exaggerate the importance of philosophy even when it is conceived in this vital and human sense. Reflection is only one of the forces that move our action, and in the thick of events it gives place to necessities of more urgency. But on the other hand, reflection is the only thing that takes us out of the immediate pressure and hurly-burly of overt action. It is a temporary turning aside from the immediate scene of action in order to note the course of events, to forecast probable and possible issues, to take stock of difficulties and resources, to bring to explicit consciousness evils that may be remedied, to plan a future course of action. Philosophy cannot create values by thinking about them, by defining and classifying and arranging them. But by thinking about them, it may promote discrimination as to what is genuinely desirable, and thereby contribute to subsequent conduct a clearer and more deliberately settled method of procedure in attaining what is desired.

There is always danger that the student of philosophy will become simply a student of philosophic traditions, of something that is conventionally called philosophy but from which philosophic life has departed because the genuine problem in life which called out the formulation has departed from consciousness. When philosophic distinctions are approached from the standpoint of their bearing upon life through the medium of the educational process in which they take effect, the perplexity, the predicament, of life which generates the issue can never be far from recognition.

Relation of the History of Philosophy to Education.— The conception of the intimate connection of philosophy with the fundamental theory of education is borne out by reference to the history of philosophic thought. So far as European history is concerned, philosophy originated at Athens from the direct pressure of educational questions. The earlier philosophy, that of the Greek colonies, was really a chapter in the history of science, dealing with the question how things come to be what they are and how they are made. Then the traveling teachers, known as the Sophists, began to apply its results to the conduct of life, and to use the same methods to discuss moral and social matters. Up to their time, men had attained skill and excellence in the various callings of life and in the business of citizenship through apprenticeship in the customs of the community. The Sophist professed to be able to teach "virtue"; that is, ability in the various functions of life. Some limited their claims to ability to teach the arts of poetry and oratory; others gave instruction in the various industrial arts or in military tactics. Others broadened these pretensions, professing ability to convey power in the management of human affairs, private, domestic, and public. It is impossible to exaggerate the historic significance of these claims. They implied that matters which had always been left to practice, and to practice controlled by the habitudes and ideals of the local community, could be set free from their customary provincial setting and be taught on theoretical grounds, on grounds of intellect.

Naturally these pretensions evoked violent protests from conservatives, who felt that the life of the community was at stake. This conflict of devotion to social customs with a reliance upon abstract knowledge provoked the first great speculative issues. What is the real basis of social organization and of moral responsibilities? Do these rest upon custom, upon enactment by superiors, or upon universal principles of nature?

At first these questions were discussed, as was natural, in a casual and superficial way. But Socrates, Plato, and others disentangled the basic questions involved. What is the nature of the state and of law? What is the true end of life? How shall man know this end? Can virtue or excellence be taught? Is it a matter of practice and habit, or something intellectual—a kind of knowledge? If so, what kind? What is knowledge? What is its standard? If virtue can be learned, how is learning related to knowledge?

These questions might be multiplied almost indefinitely, but it is more profitable to note that they tended to group themselves into three main problems: (*i*) What is the relation of knowledge, of reason, to practice, custom, and the opinions that go with custom? (*ii*) What is the relation of human life, especially of social organization and its virtues and responsibilities, to the nature of the universe, of reality itself? (*iii*) What is the relation of change, and of the particular things that change, to the universal and permanent? In a generation or two these questions were largely cut loose from their original connection with education. Their discussion developed into distinct disciplines, often isolated from reference to practical or social matters: into logic, as a theory of knowledge; into metaphysics, as a definition of the nature of things; into cosmology, or a general account of the constitution of nature. But the fact that the stream of European philosophic thought arose out of the discussion of educational ends and means, remains an eloquent witness to the ulterior motive and purport of philosophic reflection. If philosophy is to be other than an idle and unverifiable speculation, it must be animated by the conviction that its theory of experience is a hypothesis that is realized only as experience is actually shaped in accord with it. And this realization demands that man's dispositions be made such as to desire and strive for that kind of experience. The philosophy of education is not the external application to educational affairs of a conception of reality ready made independently of education; it is just the philosophic conception of a balanced and articulated experience stated so as to be available for shaping intellectual and emotional disposition, so that the existence it describes may become a living fact, not the dream of a philosopher's brain.

Problems of Philosophy and of Education the Same.—Since upon education falls the burden of securing the practical realizing and balancing of the various interests of life, the educator faces, if only in half-conscious, unsystematic form, precisely the same questions that philosophy discusses in the abstract. In the attitude taken to matters of hygiene, physical training, manual training, corporal punishment, etc., there will be expressed, for example, some idea of the connection, or lack of connection, of mind and body, an idea that, made explicit and fitted in with other beliefs, corresponds to some typical philosophical theory of the relation of bodily and mental action. Some practices imply that man is an external compound of body and soul, in themselves two independent forces. Others proceed on the assumption that the body is a temporary shell in which mind is housed, or that the body is a clog upon the development of spirit. Other projects imply that only through the adequate functioning of the bodily organs can there be realized a symmetrical and sound mental life. The various theories held by philosophers as to the relation of knowledge to practice are paralleled in educational procedure. Some assume that contemplative knowledge is an end in itself; others, that knowledge is a mere external prerequisite for successful action, success being measured on the basis of material possessions and power; others that knowledge is an intrinsic condition of a practice that is free and full of meaning. In educational discussion, one or other of these ideas appears in some disguised form in every dispute about cultural *versus* professional or vocational education, and shows itself in most debates concerning the relation of the acquisition of knowledge to the formation of character. The old (almost the first) philosophic question as to the relation of the individual to the established objective order appears in instruction as the question of individual initiative and choice over against the accumulated body of organized knowledge which forms the ready-made subject matter of teaching. The philosophical controversy as to the method of knowledge, with its division of camps into sensationalist and rationalist, has a counterpart in the different methods of learning that are encouraged in schools. The philosophic split between mind and physical nature corresponds to the educational antagonism of humanistic and scientific studies, which also has a genuine, even if indirect, bearing upon the philosophic issue of idealism *versus* realism.

To sum up: Various partial tendencies and interests of life are reflected in native homespun intellectual schemes possessed of strong emotional coloring. These are traditionalized; they float, so to speak, upon the institutions of a society, giving them their sanction and explanation. Philosophies in the formal and technical intellectual sense are generated when these traditional systems are subjected to independent intellectual examination with a view to their rational criticism and supplementation. As the more popular schemes express the standard and the subject matter of the educational procedures of a community, since they naturally aim to shape disposition in the continued acceptance of the customary beliefs and ideals,—so the more conscious philosophies can be tested and objectively embodied only as they are made the working bases of educational processes that develop an experience in harmony with themselves. To convince a small number of the theoretical soundness of the philosophy, while men's lives are still ordered in the mass upon quite another basis, furnishes such a contradiction of the claim of the philosophy to evaluate "experience as a whole" as to place the latter in a ludicrous position.

Character of the New Philosophy of Education.—Every generation and period has its own special problems which decide where the emphasis is thrown. When social conditions and scientific conceptions and methods are both in a state of rapid alteration, the tendency to philosophic reconstruction is especially marked, and the need of working out the newer point of view so that it will throw light upon the spirit and aims of education is especially urgent. The present time is characterized by at least three great movements, of which education must take account in the most radical way if it is to bear any relation to the needs and opportunities of contemporary life—and otherwise intellectual and moral chaos must be the result. These movements are: (*i*) the rapid growth of democratic ideals and institutions; (*ii*) the transformation of industrial life—the economic revolution that began in the later eighteenth century with the application of steam to manufacturing and commerce; (*iii*) the development of *experimental* science, culminating in the idea of evolution and the thoroughgoing modification of older beliefs about the processes and organs of life.

(*i*) The democratic movement radically influences education if only because it inevitably produces the demand for universal education. It is impossible that the type of education adapted to the small class in aristocratic and feudal societies, that alone had an opportunity for an intellectual culture, should be adapted to the needs of a democratic society which demands the development of all. By no possibility could the education of a class become the education of all, for a class education is made what it is by the exclusion of most of the people from the opportunities for which it prepares. A democracy, moreover, signifies a social organization which is maintained, upon the whole, by the voluntary wish of the mass of the people, and which is responsive to changes in their purposes. This implies a much greater dependence upon the intelligence and sympathetic good will of all the members of society than is required in communities where authority and precedent are the mainstays of social arrangements. A distinct type of education is demanded to meet the need for individual freedom and initiative combined with respect for others and an instinct for social unity.

(*ii*) The industrial revolution, with the changes it brought about in modes of association, habits of mind, and increase of commodities, is both cause and effect of the democratic development. From every standpoint it exacts modifications of educational ideas and practices. The importance of labor which it proclaims is a note new in the world's history. The effect of the new inventions in eliminating distance and bringing all mankind within the same circle makes interdependence, which had been preached as an ideal, an operative fact. Since the new industrial régime depends upon the application of science to the control of natural forces, men's best and truest knowledge of nature is put in effective circulation. Men's actions are servile or intelligent according as men do or do not have an appreciation of the ideas which govern their occupations. The extreme specialization and division of labor tend to make men simply small parts of the machines they tend, and only the forethought and oversight of education can avert this menace. The multiplication of material goods makes necessary a higher aesthetic taste to prevent general vulgarization. It also affords new opportunities to the masses which they must be educated to take advantage of. Conversely, the luxury and kind of leisure that had been tolerable or even graceful in past régimes becomes a social menace when the social mechanism makes the responsibilities of production and consumption more and more important.

(*iii*) Philosophers have debated concerning the nature and method of knowledge. It is hardly cynical to say that positiveness of assertion on those points has been in proportion to the lack of any assured method of knowing in actual operation. The whole idea and scope of knowledge-getting in education has reflected the absence of such a method, so that learning has meant, upon the whole, piling up, worshiping, and holding fast to what is handed down from the past with the title of knowledge. But the *actual practice of knowing* has finally reached a point where learning means discovery, not memorizing traditions; where knowledge is actively constructed, not passively absorbed; and where men's beliefs must be openly recognized to be experimental in nature, involving hypothesis and testing through being set at work. Upon the side of subject matter, the ideas of energy, process, growth, and evolutionary change have become supreme at the expense of the older notions of permanent substance, rigid fixity, and uniformity. The basic conceptions which form men's standards of interpretation and valuation have thus undergone radical alteration.

Even this bare sketch should suggest the new forces at work in education, and the need of a theory corresponding to the new attitudes and tendencies of our times, if the present situation is to be approached in a spirit of clear intelligence. We need to know the difference that the democratic ideal makes in our moral aims and methods; we need to come to consciousness of the changed conception of the nature of existence that its spread imports. We must reckon intelligently with the new and gigantic industrial forces that have come into being, securing by education a disposition to subordinate them to general welfare and to equality of opportunity so that they may not plunge us into class hatreds, intellectual deadness, and artistic vulgarity. Unless our science is to become as specialized and isolated a thing as was ever any scholastic scheme whose elaborate futility we ridicule, we must make the experimental attitude the pervasive ideal of all our intellectual undertakings, and learn to think habitually in terms of dynamic processes and genetic evolution. Clearness upon the issues, problems, and aims which our own period has brought to the foreground is a necessity for free and deliberate participation in the tasks that present-day education has to perform. Attaining this clearness, with whatever revision of stock notions it may entail, is the peculiar problem of a contemporary philosophy of education.

For the actual plan of the study of the Philosophy of Education, in the modern curriculum, see EDUCATION, ACADEMIC STUDY OF.

See also ART OF EDUCATION; COURSE OF STUDY, THEORY OF; CULTURE; DEMOCRACY AND EDUCATION; EDUCATION; EXPERIENCE; INDIVIDUALITY; KNOWLEDGE, etc., and the references there given.

References: —

BAGLEY, W. C. *Educative Process.* (New York, 1908.)
BRYANT, S. *Educational Ends.* (London, 1887.)
BUTLER, N. M. *Meaning of Education.* (New York, 1905.)
DEWEY, J. *School and Society.* (Chicago, 1900.)
School and the Child. (London, 1900.)
Child and the Curriculum. (Chicago, 1902.)
Educational Essays. (London, 1910.)
My Pedagogic Creed. (New York, 1897.)
Influence of Darwin on Philosophy. (New York, 1910.)

HARRIS, W. T. *Psychologic Foundations of Education.* (New York, 1908.)
HENDERSON, E. N. *Text-Book in the Principles of Education.* (Chicago, 1911.)
HORNE, H. H. *The Philosophy of Education.* (New York, 1905.) *Idealism in Education.* (New York, 1910.)
MACVANNEL, J. A. *Outline of a Course in the Philosophy of Education.* (New York, 1912.)
O'SHEA, M. V. *Education as Adjustment.* (New York, 1903.)
PARTRIDGE, G. E. *Genetic Philosophy of Education.* (New York, 1912.)
ROSENKRANZ, J. K. F. *Philosophy of Education.* (New York, 1903.)
RUEDIGER, W. C. *Principles of Education.* (New York, 1910.)
SINCLAIR, S. B. *The Possibility of a Science of Education.* (Chicago, 1903.)
VINCENT, G. *Social Mind and Education.* (New York, 1897.)

PLATO.—The educational influence of Plato is so all-pervasive that it is impossible to give an adequate statement of it, even had the subject not been treated under a variety of other topics. In the general article on GREEK EDUCATION it is the ideas and influence of Plato that are expressed for the most part in the discussion on the THEORY OF GREEK EDUCATION. Again, in the article on IDEALISM AND REALISM IN EDUCATION it is chiefly Plato's influence which is discussed. In the article on ETHICS, on LOGIC, on PHILOSOPHY, and especially in PHILOSOPHY OF EDUCATION, it is again Plato's influence which is stressed as fundamental. In the articles on MYSTICISM and NEO-PLATONISM his influence during the late classical and medieval periods is considered. Throughout the entire list of topics relating to the philosophy of education (see ANALYTICAL INDEX in the last volume), Plato's influence is to be noted, especially in such articles as those on KNOWLEDGE, IDEA, LAW, etc. The following article, therefore, is limited to a brief statement of the chief points of Plato's influence on education. The Platonic schools of education, as worked out in an ideal system, are found in their most systematic form in *The Republic*. As stated above, these accord in general with the most advanced educational theory of the Greek people. In a similar way, Plato's most concrete statement of educational practices, as found in *The Laws*, is in general a transcript of contemporary Greek practices. Both are therefore given in substance in the general article on GREEK EDUCATION.

Higher education in Plato's scheme was almost exclusively mathematical, though we know that he encouraged grown men, like his nephew, Speusippus, and Aristotle, to study other branches of science, such as geology, botany, and zoology. That, however, belongs to the history of scientific research rather than to that of education, and it is clear that Plato insisted upon a preliminary training in mathematics for all his students. The whole scheme is really the development of a single thought, which he owed in great measure to the Pythagoreans. The earlier education was directed to the inculcation through time and tune of an instinct for order and harmony. An ordered and harmonious soul is the first requirement of a good citizen; but, besides that, the Greeks felt that the intervals of the octave had their counterpart on a larger scale in the ordering of the heavenly bodies, and that the great universe itself was tuned like a lyre. The aim of education is, therefore, to put the soul in tune with the world and with God. That is why it is mathematical throughout.

It is becoming more and more clear that Plato's *Laws* had a very great influence in the age which immediately succeeded him. Already in his own lifetime the Academy was recognized as a school of politics, and especially of constitutional law. Many cities applied to it for legislators, and in this way the theories of *The Laws* came to be realized in the codes of actual states. This seems to have been the case with the educational principles contained in the work also. It is generally recognized that, by founding the Academy, Plato became the real author of the university system; it is not always noticed that he was also the inventor of the school as we understand it. At Athens in the classical period there were no schools at all, if we mean by a school a public institution with a regular curriculum. Parents sent their sons to one teacher to learn reading and writing, to another to learn music, and so forth; but all these teachers were private tutors, as it were, and quite independent of one another.

In recent times, much attention has been paid to Plato's theory of education, but this has been almost entirely confined to the discussion of the subject in *The Republic*. As has been said, the guiding principles are to be found there, and they are rather assumed than established in *The Laws*. It is from *The Republic* that we learn his view that education is above all a sort of conversion, a turning of the eye of the soul to the light. It is also from *The Republic* that we learn the psychological basis of the system. It is not correct to say, as people usually say, that music is the education of the soul and gymnastics that of the body. Rather these are the education of two different "parts" or elements in the soul, and the excess of either produces an ill-balanced and inharmonious character.

It is also from *The Republic* that we get a fuller knowledge of the higher education in its four main branches of arithmetic, geometry, astronomy, and music, which long survived in the medieval *quadrivium*. But, on the whole, what we chiefly owe to Plato is the idea of an organized school with a definite curriculum, and that is derived from *The Laws*.

Platonic Philosophy of Education.—Plato's treatment of education is a closely interwoven fabric of interpretation of the social and moral conditions of his own day, with principles and problems having a perennial import. His most important contributions to a permanent philosophy of education may be enumerated as follows:—

1. The problem of education is an inherent portion of the philosophic question, and conversely education is treated as the social and moral art through which the theoretical results of philosophy shall be made effective in life. (See PHILOSOPHY OF EDUCATION.) It is no accident that his two chief treatises on the right organization of social life (*The Republic* and *The Laws*) are also chief authorities for his ethics, metaphysics, and educational theory. He retains and continues the Socratic notions that right conduct presupposes true knowledge, and that the theory of true knowledge (logic or dialectic) is of practical or moral importance since it is a necessary instrument in bringing men to a consciousness of ignorance and opinion, with their attending evils, and in providing them with the means of attaining the knowledge that leads to the good. The genuine practice of dialectic as

distinct from the spurious (eristic and sophistic) is thus an integral part of right living. Philosophy is thus no merely theoretical exercise, but defines the method of education, that is, of the conversion of the soul to the good and of the latter's progressive realization. Plato, in avoiding the sharp antithesis of knowledge and practice, also avoids the error, so common in subsequent thought, of making educational theory a mere external annex of philosophy.

2. Plato adds a distinctly new factor to the Socratic conception, in his conviction that knowledge is relative to social organization. That is to say, ignorance and mere opinion are inevitable in the degree in which self-seeking and division infect society, whether these are expressed in despotisms or in anarchic democracies. Such societies involve exclusive "particularity" of knowledge as the counterpart of the division of classes and interests. Instead of affording the universality and permanence which are the patterns upon which true knowledge is modeled, they generate ignorance and casual opinions masquerading as truth. This strict correlation between right knowledge and right social organization involves, as its consequence, the equally strict correlation of educational theory and the theory of politics or sociology—the theory of the organization of the state. So far as the records indicate, Socrates had thought the conversion of the soul to true knowledge might be brought about by personal discipline independently of the action of the social environment.

This interdependence of true knowledge and the right organization of the state is Plato's answer, in anticipation, to the charge brought by Aristotle, and often repeated, that Plato overestimated the importance for right action of a purely theoretical knowledge, and ignored the need of habituation and practice. According to Plato, the attaining of the true theoretical knowledge itself implies and requires a long period of education in a social medium where the individual, acting in accord with principles of unity, balance, and harmony, absorbs into his practical habits the factors which make possible later on an independent theoretical vision. The Platonic social hierarchy, with philosophers at the top as social rulers, follows from his insistence upon social practice as an indispensable prerequisite for genuine knowledge. That Plato is caught in a circle, on the one hand insisting upon true, or philosophic, knowledge as a condition of right social organization and, at other times upon right social organization as an antecedent of philosophic insight, must be freely admitted. Since he had no conception of evolutionary growth, or gradual progress, he could not conceive that the true state should be ushered in otherwise than by a happy conjunction of circumstances; when once hit upon, it must be kept, at all hazards, intact against any further change, even in its minor details.

3. Plato clearly perceives, what later intellectual specialization obscured, that the motive and principle of the organization of the sciences is educational. The various sciences may be literally said, in accord with the Platonic spirit, to be *studies*; their differentiation and coordination is an affair of specifying the subject matter of an adequate education and of designating the proper aim of each branch of knowledge in the educational whole. A purified music and gymnastic (the customary content of Greek education) pave the way for the new studies of nature (astronomy and physics in the form of cosmology); these pass insensibly into mathematics; mathematics into dialectic; dialectic culminates in the apprehension of the final ends, centering in the conception of the Good, whence a reverse, or deductive, movement leads back to the study of politics and ethics. There is, of course, much in the specific content of this account that subsequent philosophy and science have rendered untenable. But the underlying idea that the distribution and correlation of the various sciences is ultimately an educational matter, not an abstract intellectual one, must be regarded as a permanent contribution.

4. Plato states and treats the problem of the place and relations of the individual in society as an educational problem. Society is a complex unity; it involves the active cooperation of a number of diverse functions. Individuals are born with distinctive capacities. From one standpoint the need is that these various individuals' capacities be distinctively harmonized with a coordinated, unified social unity. From another standpoint, the need is that every individual

be trained to intensity and efficiency of action in the particular capacity which distinguishes him by nature. The unity and order of the state suffer when individuals, instead of sticking to the single function for which they are naturally equipped, assume a multitude of activities, thereby encroaching on the sphere of others and introducing conflict into the social whole. Education supplies the means of satisfying the need from whichever side it be regarded. The business of education is to determine the social office for which individuals are fitted by a continuous process of selecting, sifting, and testing, in which the special talents and limitations of each individual are revealed. Practically, there is some truth in the complaint that Plato sacrificed individuality to the supposed requirements of social unity and stability. In theory, however, he held that the discovery of the special capacities of an individual so as to hold him to an occupation that should utilize his powers in the interests of the social whole was the sole method of securing both the true happiness of the individual and the good of the state. The education that discovers and trains the peculiar powers of an individual is at the same time the method by which intrinsic, instead of coerced, harmony is achieved in the state. This conception appears to present a permanent factor in the problem and ideal of education. The limitations in the Platonic treatment are due to the fact that he held the individual variation down to certain fixed limits and types, which corresponded to certain fixed classes in the state. Having the idea of a small number of classes within which variations in individuals fall, he was also led to the notion that the corresponding social classes have to be arranged in an order of inferiority and superiority. Advance since the time of Plato is in the direction of recognizing that individual variations are of the very heart of individuality itself, and that accordingly the development of characteristically individual powers is destructive of the existence of fixed social classes. Variety of social activities conspiring to a cooperative unity of result has thus been substituted for hierarchical subordination of classes as defining the aim of education.

5. The characteristic role, already alluded to, of the aesthetic and the artistic in education represents another

permanent contribution. The aesthetic and artistic provide the connecting link and the solvent factor with respect to the relation of the practical and the theoretical in education —an idea which is at the basis of Schiller's conception of education. On the one hand there is the need of practice, of repeated exercise, of habituation in education. This, by itself, tends to routine, and thus to a limitation of rational insight. But not so, if it is based upon spontaneous, uncoerced tendencies—upon play instincts. In this case, education, even as habituation, or practice, involves the emotional attitudes of the individual and an aesthetic subject matter which, through its inherent content of proportion, harmony, balance, and nobility, effects an insensible transition to rational insight. The treatment of gymnastic as well as of music is directed by this principle; Plato's well-known attack upon poetry and dramatic art is based not upon a depreciation of the educational function of art and aesthetic appreciation, but upon his belief in their supreme educational significance and the consequent need of their supervision and control in the interests of the state.

References:—

BOSANQUET, B. *The Education of the Young in the Republic of Plato.* (Cambridge, 1901.)

NETTLESHIP, R. L. "The Theory of Education in the *Republic* of Plato." In *Hellenica*, edited by Evelyn Abbott. (London, 1880.)

PLAY.—A name given to those activities which are not consciously performed for the sake of any result beyond themselves; activities which are enjoyable in their own execution without reference to ulterior purpose. For a long time the theory of play most generally held was that most thoroughly elaborated by Herbert Spencer; namely, that play represents the overflow of superfluous energy, the base line from which to measure excess being the amount of energy required to maintain the level of health and perform imposed tasks. Since children are relieved of most of the duties connected with getting a living, they naturally have a relatively larger amount of excess energy at disposal. Since the channels of the discharge of the superfluous energies are those of necessary and useful works, it is not surprising that plays largely simulate practical activities. The more prolonged study of the plays of animals and savages impressed Groos with the extent to which plays represent acts that are useful in later life. He formulated the idea that the chief thing about play is that it gives preparatory exercise in later necessary functions. This is usually regarded as a rival theory to that of "surplus energy," but it is evident that the theories are framed from different standpoints and have no point where they touch each other. One theory might be correct as an account of the causal conditions of play, and the other as an account of its value.

As a matter of fact, however, the theory of surplus energy seems to be influenced by a survival of the once general conception that individuals are naturally averse to any kind of activity; that complete quiescence is the natural stage of organic beings; and that some fear of pain or hope of pleasure is required in order to stir individuals to effort which in itself is painful. The fact of the case is that from intra-organic stimuli, the organism is in a constant state of action, activity indeed being the very essence of life. When the myth of natural quiescence is surrendered with its accompanying myth of the need of a special premium in order to arouse an inert agent, it ceases to be necessary to search for any special cause or any special object in order to account for play. The only thing necessary is to state the conditions under which organic activity takes this or that form. So considered, we find various forms, which are of sufficient importance, educationally at least, to justify differentiation; namely, play, amusement, art, work, labor, drudgery.

In any case the starting point is the active processes in which life manifests itself. As stimuli direct this activity one way or another, some of its modes are peculiarly rewarding. The stimulus not only arouses a certain kind of activity, but the responsive activity returns upon the stimulus so as to maintain it and to vary it. These variations supply the stimuli for keeping up more action. The moving spool draws the organic response of the kitten to itself; this response continues to give the spool the kind of movements which continue to excite organic reactions. There is no difference in kind between the spool as a stimulus and a mouse, save that the latter has peculiar stimuli of the sense of smell and, when crunched by the teeth, of taste, that call out special responses. In like fashion, a baby plays with certain stimuli so as to keep up, with certain variations, a certain mode of action. Seeing a thing in a certain way evokes responses that make further seeings enjoyable.

After such processes have been frequently repeated, they are complicated by the fact that an idea of the result of prior activities is superadded. It may be that the idea of this result as a possible outcome will be a sufficient stimulus to keep the activity going after it has ceased to afford adequate stimuli so far as its direct results are concerned. If the idea of the result operates as a stimulus to renew the otherwise flagging activity, and if, in addition, the accomplishing of the result involves a certain selection and arrangement of acts antecedent to it, we get a type of activity sufficiently contrasted to be termed work. But as action involving the idea of an end grows naturally out of a spontaneous activity, so "work" in this psychological sense is inevitably preceded by play and grows insensibly out of it. The chief point of difference is not the agreeableness of one and the disagreeableness of the other, but that in the case of work the idea of an end enforces reflection on the relation of means to end, and stimulates a corresponding readjustment of activities originally spontaneous. Not only is the satisfactoriness of the activity not the main differentia, but, with increasing complexity of powers, prior activities are too simple to afford the necessary stimulation (and hence the desired satisfaction) unless they are expanded by a less immediate and more indirect adjustment of means to ends. At one stage of development, the relation between end and means is so close that if the dominating idea is that of playing "set the table," anything will be turned to account for a table and for dishes. With maturity of perception, the activity is not sufficiently complex to be enjoyed unless things can be devised and employed that are objectively adapted to the end. Action requires a greater amount of intellectual control and of practical check in order to be satisfactory, or worth while. At this point, and not at that of utility *versus* freedom, or of that which is an end for itself *versus* that which is a mere means for something else, lie the differentia between play and work.

Further distinctions are due to social conditions. The stimuli to activity become more social as intelligence develops. The interests and occupations of adults are the points of departure and the directing clues of children's actions. (See IMITATION; and INFANCY.) Certain plays have outcomes and methods that are determined by social conventions; such plays, carried on by rules, are games. But the distinctions of amusement, labor, and drudgery also arise from social conditions.

Labor is a fact of economic origin. Wherever industry is subdivided, as it is beyond the fishing and hunting stage of civilization in greater or less measure, the product of work is not a direct stimulus to the prior process, for this product is not itself enjoyed or consumed, but is exchanged for another object (or for money). This means that the direct end of action is not its adequate stimulus; that something not directly cared for is done for the sake of a more ulterior end. This implies the possibility at least of the direct activity being itself so disagreeable that there is an aversion to it, which is overcome only because of the need for the ultimate object. Under certain conditions of economic life, labor almost inevitably takes on this externally enforced quality, and, as it is intrinsically irksome, becomes drudgery. The notion, referred to earlier in this article, that man is naturally averse to action and hence is moved to it only by fear of evil or love of reward, was taken into psychology from economic theory at a time when industrial life consisted mainly in wage-earning under conditions themselves repulsive. Amusement is differentiated from play by a sort of contrast effect. Children do not normally play for the sake of amusement, any more than for the sake of any end beyond the action itself. They live in their actions, and these actions are called play because of certain qualities they exhibit. But adults (as well as children whose surroundings are socially abnormal) need relief from labor, especially from drudgery. Powers not used at all, or used under enforced and distorted conditions during working hours, need stimulation. The things outside the ordinary routine activity of labor that yield this stimulation constitute amusements. The fact that they are called recreations and are employed for purposes of relief indicates a contrast-effect not normally present in the play of childhood.

It is also desirable to distinguish an attitude of mind as playful. Matthew Arnold, for example, called ability to occupy the imagination fruitfully with a subject, the ability to allow the mind to play freely about the subject, a sign of culture. This attitude of mind is distinguished from inability to enjoy intellectual activity upon a subject except in the interest of some preconceived theory or some practical utility. This capacity to draw satisfaction from the immediate intellectual development of a topic, irrespective of any ulterior motive, represents a genuine outgrowth of the play attitude—a special form which it may take. Unless play takes this intellectual form, the full spirit of scientific inquiry is never realized; much, if not all, of what is termed the love of truth for truth's sake in scientific inquiry represents the attitude of play carried over into enjoyment of the activities of inquiry for its own sake. The putting forth of observation, reflection, testing, is enjoyed on its own account, irrespective of ulterior by-products, just as in early childhood certain strenuous and even hazardous forms of physical effort may be intrinsically satisfactory.

Play and Education.—The account that has been given indicates, in outline, the chief educational problems connected with the topic of play. The original discovery of its importance in education, by Plato, and its rediscovery by Froebel, may be said to constitute the basic principles of the method of instruction. The foundation of all later growth is the activity of the earlier period, which, so far as the consciousness of the individual is concerned, is spontaneous or playful. Hence the necessity that the earlier plays be of such a sort as to grow naturally and helpfully into the later more reflective and productive modes of behavior. This means that play should pass insensibly into work (though not necessarily into labor), and that earlier play and work alike be of the kinds which afford exercise in the occupations that are socially useful. For a genuine initiation into them through play means not only that the individual has acquired, under conditions of least resistance and greatest economy, the skill required for efficiency judged from the social standpoint, but that he has done so through the engaging of his own imagination and emotions. In other words, the natural transition of play into work is the means and the only means of reconciling the development of social efficiency with that of individual fullness of life.

Other educational problems arise from the economic conditions under which industry is carried on at present, with its extreme specialization of labor and its control by reference to a medium of exchange instead of by commodities valued on their own account. It is a part of the business of education to fortify and enrich the imagination so that the mechanical phases of industry shall not leave an unformed mind at the mercy of sense, appetite, and trivial fancy. It is a part of its business to come into sufficiently close contact with the conditions of industry so that those who go from school into industry shall be trained to understand the whole of which their work is a small fraction, and thus to see a meaning in their work which they could not otherwise perceive. Moreover, it is necessary that the plays and games of the school should be so directed as to instil a love for and capacity in wholesome forms of recreation and amusement. Perhaps there is no more neglected aspect of social education at the present time than just here. Because amusement is contrasted with serious things we have forgotten that the function of recreation, of the spending of the hours of leisure, is one of the most serious questions, intellectually and morally, of life, and that any educational system is defective which does not make systematic provision for this as well as for the hours of work.

See ACTIVITY; ARTS IN EDUCATION; COURSE OF STUDY, THEORY OF; FROEBEL; GAMES; INSTINCTS; KINDERGARTEN.

References:—

APPLETON, L. E. *Comparative Study of the Play Activities of Adult Savages and Civilized Children: An Investigation of the Scientific Basis of Education.* (Chicago, 1910.)

COLOZZA, G. A. *Psychologie und Pädagogik des Kinderspiels.* Tr. from Italian by Christian Ufer. (Altenburg, 1900.)

GEORGENS, J. D. *Das Spiel und die Spiele der Jugend.* (Leipzig, 1884.)

GROOS, K. *Play of Animals.* Tr. by E. L. Baldwin. (New York, 1898.)

Play of Man. Tr. by E. L. Baldwin. (New York, 1901.)
HALL, G. S. *Adolescence*. (New York, 1908.)
Aspects of Child Life and Education. (Boston, 1907.)
Youth, its Education, Regimen, and Hygiene. (New York, 1906.)
HENDERSON, E. N. *Principles of Education*. (New York, 1911.)
JOHNSON, G. E. *Education by Plays and Games*. (Boston, 1907.)
MCDOUGALL, W. *Social Psychology*. (London, 1910.)
MILDEBRANDT, P. *Das Spielzeug im Leben des Kindes*. (Berlin, 1904.)
MUTHESIUS, K. Die Spiele der Menschen. *Pädagogisches Magazin*, pp. 137. (Langensalza, 1899.)
SPENCER, H. *Principles of Psychology*. (New York, 1896.)
STRACHAN, J. *What Is Play? Its Bearing upon Education and Training; A Physiological Inquiry*. (Edinburgh, 1877.)

PLURALISM.—The opposite of monism (*q.v.*); the theory according to which there are a number of independent ultimate principles of reality or real beings. It includes systems as diverse as the atomism of Democritus, the monadism of Leibnitz and Herbart, and the radical empiricism of William James (*qq.v.*).

POSITIVISM.—A philosophic term derived from the French term *positif*, whose connotation is quite different from that of the corresponding English adjectives. In its most general sense positivism means a philosophic theory which does not recognize any facts or principles save those known and verified by the methods of the mathematical and physical sciences. A strict positivistic philosophy thus confines its assertions to the relations of coexistence and sequence that are ascertained to exist among natural events, and is agnostic as to any realities, whether conceived as substances or forces, which lie behind or beyond these natural events and their spatial and temporal relations. Positivism is used more specifically to denote the philosophy of Auguste Comte (*q.v.*), who combined a philosophy of history and society, and a social and religious ideal with a scientific agnosticism.

According to his view of history, mankind passes through three stages of intellectual development, these stages controlling the accompanying phases of life. The first is the theological, in which events are explained on an animistic basis in the broad sense of that term. Events are explained by reference to personal volitions and emotions of non-human beings. In the second, or metaphysical, stage forces are substituted for these personal beings, monotheism being the transition point. The metaphysical stage culminates in the idea of Nature as the ultimate and unifying force. Then comes the positivistic stage, when men content themselves with trying to ascertain accurately the facts and events of the space and time world as that shows itself to sense perception. The intellectual development is paralleled by a social-religious development. The theological stage, although most inadequate intellectually, was highly favorable to social organization because of the emphasis it put upon powers akin to those of man. The metaphysical stage, with its emphasis upon impersonal abstract forces, was unfavorable to the nurture of intimate social relations. The association of individualism in the eighteenth century with the conception of Nature as the ultimate norm represented the logical outcome of the metaphysical stage. The problem of the present or scientific era is to combine the religious and social spirit of the theological age with the objective, impersonal, intellectual attitude ushered in by the metaphysical stage. The method of effecting this combination constitutes the constructive portion of Comte's Positivism.

Since we can know only the spatial and temporal associations of phenomena, we must surrender all hopes of any objective or ontological synthesis. Some kind of synthesis, however, is necessary in order to give mankind that unity of outlook, belief, and aim which is requisite for its own unified organization, and is necessary to supply the motive force of social devotion which religion supplied in the past. The solution is to make a "subjective synthesis," an organization of scientific knowledge from the standpoint of its bearing upon social life and in the interest of the unification of that life. This amounts practically to substituting "Humanity" for Divine Beings and for Natural Forces as the ultimate standard of value and centre of reference, recognizing, however, that Humanity is not an ontological reality, but an ideal, whose existence is capable of becoming more and more of a fact in the course of human history. To make Humanity an object of religious devotion and to construct a religion of humanity, modeled on the whole upon medieval Catholicism, were more or less logical consequences of this conception.

While Comte succeeded in organizing a church, with branches still maintained in France and England, to represent his ideas and inaugurate his new religious scheme, his chief influence has been in general conceptions which have deeply affected the thinking of those who would not term themselves Comtians or even Positivists. That natural science does not itself tend to the promotion of social organization and welfare; that scientific specialization by itself is likely to be disintegrative; that modern life is sorely in need of a method such as was supplied by the religions of the past for bringing knowledge into connection with practice and conduct; that the ultimate purpose of science must be prediction of the future and social control,—are ideas that Comte developed with great power and that have become deeply engrained in contemporary culture.

See COMTE, AUGUSTE.

References:—

BALDWIN, J. M. *Dictionary of Philosophy*, Vol. III, Pt. ii, pp. 634–638.

CAIRD, E. *Social Philosophy of Comte.* (Glasgow, 1893.)

PRAGMATISM.—The conception (though not the word) pragmatism was first proposed by the American mathematician and logician, C. S. Peirce, in an article published in 1878 in the *Popular Science Monthly*, upon "How to Make Our Ideas Clear." The gist of the notion is that the *meaning* of any idea or conception lies in the consequences that flow from an existence having the meaning in question, so that the way to get a clear conception is to consider the differences that would be made if the idea were true or valid. In conversation Mr. Peirce used the term "pragmatism" to designate this view of the nature of conceptual meanings. Some twenty years afterwards William James proposed the use of this idea as test of the meaning and worth of specifically philosophic conceptions. He argued that the point of any philosophic doctrine or issue lies in the particular differences that would follow if the idea in question were true, and that if no differences can be made out, the doctrine or issue is wholly verbal. This theory is strictly a method for determining the meaning of concepts; it is not a theory of their truth nor of their relation to existence. Pragmatism in this narrower sense, Mr. Peirce has since wished to call Pragmaticism, to differentiate it from a later extension which Mr. James and others gave the doctrine.

In his *Psychology* and his *Will to Believe*, James had pointed out the influence of interest, choice, and emotional factors upon our beliefs and had made a plea for the recognition of the validity of these factors under certain circumstances. Schiller of Oxford devoted himself to a reform of logic in the direction of greater concreteness and usefulness through recognition of the part played in thinking by emotional and volitional factors, and generalized the underlying idea into the theory that all knowledge is purposive or teleological. This view James adopted as part of the pragmatic conception. Since interest, choice, and effort are involved in knowledge, knowledge is essentially experimental and in constant process of making. Since, by common consent, truth is the goal in which knowledge proper terminates, it follows that truth is not something antecedent to our intelligent activities, but something following upon them and produced by them. Since truth involves the relation of *objects* to thought, this making of truth logically implies a making of reality. So, by a natural extension, pragmatism was widened from a theory of the purposive character of knowledge and a theory of truth as the successful working out of knowledge, to the theory that reality itself is plastic and is in course of construction through the cognitive efforts of man. This aspect of pragmatism, Schiller called Humanism.

In his *Psychology*, James had suggested, and to some extent used, the idea that intelligence, or man's knowing power, evolved as an instrument of adaptive response to stimuli, lying between sensory stimuli and motor response. Dewey and others took up this suggestion, and developed on the psychological side the idea that thinking or reflective attention is the counterpart and complement of habit. Habit expresses the mode of response to old and well-established stimuli; thinking to stimuli where novelty and a doubtful or precarious factor are marked features. This conception was also more or less systematically applied to a reconstruction of traditional logical theory. Logic was treated as a systematized account of the procedures of thinking in adapting beings living in a social environment to the control of novel and uncertain features of existence, these features being treated as possessed of objective character. On the moral side, the notion was extended to the theory that standards and ideals are not fixed and *a priori*, but are in a constant process of hypothetical construction and of testing through application to the control of particular situations. This general logical and ethical view, known specifically as instrumentalism, was also adopted by James as a part of pragmatism in its wider sense.

It is generally admitted that pragmatism, while still in a formative state, has exercised an influence as a philosophic ferment out of proportion to the number who have definitively accepted it. It falls in line with the growing influence of the theory of evolution, asserting that reality itself is inherently and not merely accidentally and externally in process of continuous transition and transformation, and it connects the theory of knowledge and of logic with this basic fact. It connects with historic spiritual philosophies in its emphasis upon life, and upon biological and dynamic conceptions as more fundamental than purely physical and mathematical ideas. While claiming to be strictly empirical in method, it gives to thought and thought relations (universals) a primary and constructive function which sensational empiricism denied them, and thus claims to have included and explained the factor that historic rationalisms have stood for. In somewhat similar fashion, it claims to mediate between realistic and idealistic theories of knowledge. It holds to reality, prior to cognitive operations and not constructed by these operations, to which knowing, in order to be successful, must adapt itself. In so far, it is realistic in tendency, and pragmatism is usually recognized to have been an influential factor in calling out the reaction against the Kantian and Neo-Kantian idealisms dominant upon its first appearance. But it does not hold that the adaptation of intelligence to existence is a matter of literal conformity or sheer reproduction by way of copying, but rather that it is an adaptation in the interest of a further evolution of life in complexity and richness of meaning. Hence it claims to recognize and include the verifiable facts as to the role of thought in the world which have given rise to the idealistic exaggeration. Although the issue as to the future of pragmatism is still pending, the present writer may be pardoned for calling attention to its advantages as a working hypothesis in educational theory. In its conception of knowledge as a present living process (not a collection of static results) and its conception of knowledge as having a concrete purpose to fulfill in situations of practical experience (not something existing complete in itself in a purely theoretical region) it adopts and tries to justify the position which any one must of necessity assume in his endeavor to develop intelligence and make knowledge a vital factor in character and conduct.

See also EXPERIENCE; EMPIRICISM; INDUCTION AND DEDUCTION; KNOWLEDGE; LOGIC; etc.; also EDUCATION, and the references there given.

References:—

BAWDEN, H. H. *The Principles of Pragmatism; a Philosophical Interpretation of Experience.* (Boston, 1910.)

BERTHELOT, R. *Un Romantisme utilitaire; Étude sur le Mouvement pragmatiste.* Vol. I, *Le Pragmatisme chez Nietzsche et chez Poincaré.* (Paris, 1911.)

CARUS, P. *Truth on Trial,* etc. (Chicago, 1911.)

DEWEY, J. *How We Think.* (Boston, 1911.)

Influence of Darwin on Philosophy and other Essays. (New York, 1910.)

Studies in Logical Theory. (Chicago, 1903.)

"Does Reality Possess Practical Character?" In *Essays Philosophical and Psychological in Honor of William James.* (New York, 1908.)

HUIZINGA, A. VAN C. P. *The American Philosophy of Pragmatism Critically Considered in Relation to Present-Day Theology.* (Boston, 1911.)

JACOBY, G. *Der Pragmatismus; neue Bahnen in der Wissenschaftslehre des Auslands; eine Würdigung.* (Leipzig, 1909.)

JAMES, W. *Pragmatism.* (New York, 1909.)

Principles of Psychology. (New York, 1890.)

Pluralistic Universe. (New York, 1909.)

The Meaning of Truth. (New York, 1909.)
Will to Believe. (New York, 1897.)
MOORE, A. W. *Pragmatism and Its Critics.* (Chicago, 1910.)
SCHILLER, F. C. S. *Humanism; Philosophical Essays.* (London, 1903.)
SCHINZ, A. *Anti-pragmatisme; Examen des droits respectifs de l'aristocratie intellectuelle et de la démocratie sociale.* (Paris, 1909.)
See also the files of the leading philosophical journals, *e.g. Journal of Philosophy, Psychology and Scientific Methods; Mind; Philosophical Review*; also the *Psychological Review Index.*

PROBLEM.—Every conscious situation involving reflection presents a distinction between certain given conditions and something to be done with them; the possibility of a change. This contrast and connection of the given and the possible confers a certain problematic, uncertain aspect upon those situations that evoke thought. There is an element, which may be slight or which may be intense, of perplexity, of difficulty, of confusion. The need of clearing up confusion, of straightening out an ambiguity, of overcoming an obstacle, of covering the gap between things as they are and as they may be when transformed, is, in germ, a problem. It does not follow, however, that this problematic aspect must be consciously recognized as a problem; it may operate without its being formulated so as to direct the course of thinking and endeavor. (See METHOD.)

The primary position of problems with reference to stimulating and guiding thought—the problem fixing the beginning of reflective inquiry and a solution its end—accounts for the prominent place occupied by the asking of questions and setting of problems in educational practice. There are, however, two common and allied errors regarding the nature of the problem. When it is overlooked that the problematic factor may be implicit in the situation, rather than existing as a separate factor, the necessity of a natural inclusive situation of experience will be ignored; it will be assumed that the mere asking of a question in words, or the setting of a task, constitutes a problem. But in reality, all that the question as formulated in language can do is to *suggest* some difficulty arising within the pupil's own experience. It cannot create the problem, nor can it even serve to remind the pupil of a genuine problem unless especial pains are taken to use it simply as a stimulus to focus some problem occurring quite independently. This suggests the second error: supposing that what is a genuine problem for one person, such as the teacher, is necessarily a problem or the same problem for another. As matter of fact, the conditions in experience, the context, determine whether a matter is or is not a problem and what sort of a problem it is.

PROCESS.—With the development of dynamic conceptions of the world, mind, and society, it became necessary to express the idea of a succession of changes in which, in spite of changes, an identity of character is maintained, especially if the series of changes manifests a characteristic unity of result. Process is the term in most general use to designate this idea. In recent educational literature, we find, for example, such phrases as "educative process," "learning process," and "teaching process." In each case there is a complex series of changes tending toward a single, effective result.

See ACTIVITY; FUNCTION.

PROGRESS.—The conception of progress may perhaps be best defined through comparison with such terms as development, evolution, growth (*q.v.*). Like them it involves the idea of a series of changes which have a cumulative direction, in which the earlier members do not merely surrender their place to the later but have a certain continuity with them, so that all taken together form the history of one character or subject. The idea of progress differs in explicitly connoting change toward a more desirable state of affairs, something higher, better, more perfect. It also suggests, if it does not explicitly affirm, that conscious intention and effort play some part in bringing about the improved condition. Ancient Greek philosophy was familiar with the conception of evolution as applied both to organic life and to the world in general. It lacked, however, the idea of progress. Changes were conceived either as forming an endless cyclical round of passage away from and return to the same state of affairs; or as evidence of a certain falling away from true, or eternal, being, with possibly some attempt to return to the more perfect state from which a lapse had occurred. But this improvement was not progress but recovery of a prior state. Medieval thought was too dominated by the conception of the fall of man, of a recovery or redemption effected through supernatural agencies and involving an ultimate violent destruction of all things, to entertain the conception of progress.

A great part of the permanent significance of Francis Bacon is the clearness and force with which he asserted both the need and the possibility of progress, to be brought about through a scientific knowledge of natural conditions and taking effect in inventions directed toward ameliorating the lot of man. The result was a radical change in the conception of the meaning of wants and of the power of knowledge. Wants in the static philosophy had always been treated as evidence of deficiency and imperfection, mere absence of true being. Now they were increasingly treated as the dynamic, motive forces of progress—a point of view which found a classic expression first in the social philosophy of Adam Smith and then of the utilitarian school. The object of knowledge was no longer taken to be the final cause (*q.v.*), a static perfection, but productive or efficient causes, a knowledge of which would enable prevision of and adaptation to future conditions and, in many cases, deliberate control of the means of reaching ends. The mechanical point of view of modern science is thus partly the offspring, partly the source, of the growing importance of the notion of progress. The philosophy of the eighteenth-century enlightenment was animated throughout by conceptions of the prospect of the indefinite prefectibility of man. Conditions that had previously been regarded as inevitable accompaniments of the human lot, political despotism, subjection of masses to intellectual authority, sickness and poverty, were regarded as due to man's ignorance and lack of freedom, and as sure to pass away with the growth of science, and with economic and political freedom. While one result was an outbreak of utopias and millennial schemes of all kinds, anarchistic, communistic and socialistic, nevertheless we owe to this movement of the eighteenth century our present almost religious faith in the need of progress and in the possibility of making it the ruling principle of human affairs. The reflex effect of the idea of continual amelioration upon education has been very great. The materials and methods required in a progressive society differ profoundly from those appropriate to a stationary society. Since progress is not automatic but requires trained intelligence and forceful character, progressive societies depend for their very existence upon educational resources. Moreover, the conditions that are favorable to progress are also favorable to the release of energy from the restrictions of customs and convention; and only through education can the forces thus set free be safeguarded against undirected and destructive manifestation.

PROPOSITION.—According to one school, a proposition is the linguistic form in which the logical function of judgment is embodied. According to another school, it is the logical form in which the psychological function of judging acquires an objective logical status. In either case, a proposition is regarded as occupying the position of the primary complete unit of knowledge, lying between the term or concept, on one hand, and reasoning or consecutive discourse, on the other. A proposition is the assertion of a relation, positive or negative, between objects, it making no difference as to the logical character of the proposition whether these objects are physical, mental, or mathematical elements, or complex social and historical events. In the traditional Aristotelian scheme, every proposition consists of a subject, that about which something is asserted, and a predicate which affirms or denies something of the subject. Modern logicians generally agree that the subject-predicate form is not essential to a proposition, marking a peculiarity of the Aryan group of languages rather than a fundamental logical property. In all existential propositions, however, as distinct from those which assert simply a universal connection of elements without reference to whether the elements connected are themselves taken to exist, it may be said that there must always be a logical subject, namely, the existence denoted by the relation asserted in the proposition. This subject, however, need not be either the psychological or the grammatical subject, and need not even appear in the proposition as a linguistic form. Predication is then the entire qualification which is referred to the existence in question. Aside from the distinction of affirmative and negative propositions, the most important distinctions are the universal and the particular, the former being hypothetical, asserting a relation between conditions irrespective of the existence at any time or place of the conditions so related, and the latter asserting one or more things to which the relation applies.

For educational purposes, the interest attaching to the topic of propositions has to do with the importance for thought and knowledge of explicit statement and formulation. All thinking involves abstraction, but this abstraction evaporates into vagueness and ambiguity unless fixed and held before the mind by means of a term (*q.v.*) so that it may be referred to some situation, that is to say, made concrete through application. It is the function of a proposition thus to fix and apply ideas otherwise vague and fluctuating. While the importance of propositions or formal statements has been often wrongly understood, through failing to see the need of an empirical situation out of which a meaning or idea emerges and to which it is applied, it is none the less true that the stating, the holding and defining, function is absolutely indispensable to any adequate acquisition of knowledge. While the particular form of words in which the act of holding and stating is expressed may be more or less arbitrary, the function of reviewing, summarizing, and holding together is indispensable, even to the earliest and crudest operations of knowing.

RATIONALISM.—In its technical philosophic usage, this term stands for a theory regarding the origin of knowledge opposed to empiricism. It holds that the source and final test of knowledge and truth are not found in experience, which is identified with sense-perceptions or the impressions which things make on the mind, but in certain rational principles, or ultimate concepts. These are variously viewed in different rationalistic systems. Some take them to be innate in the mind; others as pure intuitive principles immediately discerned by the mind, while the Kantians regard them as transcendental categories which are aroused into action by the stimulation of sense, and which then operate to synthesize what would otherwise be a chaotic manifold into orderly objects and connected groups of objects. Kant thought he had reconciled empiricism and rationalism. He conceded to the former that all knowledge originates with and from experience, and that in no case can knowledge transcend the limits of experience, or phenomena in space and time. On the other hand, rational *a priori* principles, certain general functions of logical or conceptual thought, are necessary in order that there may be any such thing as objective experience, so that a rationalistic factor was also introduced. In the nineteenth century, Herbert Spencer attempted a conciliation of empiricism and rationalism on quite a different basis. He held that space and time, causation and certain moral beliefs, are *a priori* for the individual, but that these rational intuitions can be shown, on grounds of evolutionary science, to be the consolidated accumulated results of racial experience.

In its more popular usage, rationalism stands for reliance upon reason as distinct from faith. This meaning of the term goes back to certain tendencies to rationalize Christian theology found in medieval philosophy; but the special vogue of the conception dates from the controversy between the deistic upholders of natural religion in the eighteenth century and their orthodox opponents who upheld the claims of supernaturally revealed religion, including miracles. In this particular sense of the term rationalism, empiricism itself was rationalistic, at least in its more current forms. On the other hand, there are a few types of empiricism which admit, on grounds of experience, a mystical factor, and such empiricisms are allied with doctrines of faith as an instrumentality of knowledge. Contemporary discussion evinces tendencies to use the term rationalism in a third sense, namely, to denote theories which conceive experience to be purely intellectual or cognitive in character, and which reduce emotions and volitions to combinations of cognitive elements or processes. Intellectualism, as distinct from voluntarism, would seem, however, to be a better term for this meaning.

SCIENTIFIC METHOD.—*Science and Education.*—The term science in the sense of knowledge (*scientia*) was long used to include the entire subject matter of study. (See KNOWLEDGE.) During the last two or three centuries the term has been commonly restricted to one of two senses: first as a general method of organization or investigation applicable to the phenomena of almost any field; second, as a term to include the various aspects of the study of natural phenomena; that is, natural science. The first aspect of the term is discussed under the captions EXPERIMENTATION, HYPOTHESES, INDUCTION AND DEDUCTION, LOGIC, etc. (*qq.v.*). Even in the second aspect of the term, the sciences form too large a part of modern education to be discussed adequately in one article. The historical development, the present place of the sciences in education, their scope and method are therefore presented in this work under the following captions: ANTHROPOLOGY; ASTRONOMY; BOTANY; GEOGRAPHY; GEOLOGY; HYGIENE; NATURE STUDY; PHYSIOLOGY; PHYSICS; SANITARY SCIENCE; ZOOLOGY, etc. The applied aspects of these subjects are treated in the articles dealing with the various aspects of professional and technical education; for these see AGRICULTURAL EDUCATION; INDUSTRIAL EDUCATION; MEDICAL EDUCATION; PHARMACEUTICAL EDUCATION; PHYSICAL EDUCATION; SANITARY SCIENCE, EDUCATION IN.

Philosophical Concept of Science and Scientific Method. —Science is usually defined as systematized knowledge. The definition, while correct as far as it goes, is incomplete. Everyday knowledge, the knowledge held in solution in "common sense," is systematized. It is not a casual heap of disconnected scraps. The bonds of union and the principles of arrangement in such knowledge are mainly practical and social. The knowledge is ordered, but it is not ordered from the standpoint of and for the sake of knowledge. Not, then, the presence of systematization characterizes science, but the presence of a peculiar principle and method of systematizing. Science is knowledge systematized from the standpoint of and for the sake of knowledge, as distinct from the standpoint of practice and social intercourse. Specifically this means that the subject matter of knowledge is (*a*) selected, (*b*) formulated, and (*c*) arranged with special reference to the exhibition of the relations of intellectual dependence which its various parts sustain to one another. A typesetter will specify and arrange his knowledge of letters with reference to their effective use in his calling. The letters will be arranged (systematized) in his case with the same reference to convenience of use. A scientific treatment considers them as vowels and consonants, and subdivides vowels and consonants with a view to exhibiting principles of unity and of graded diversification among them.

Further analysis shows that the arrangement which brings to light relation of intellectual interdependence is one which is concerned with the subject matter from the standpoint of premiss and conclusion in inference. That is to say that a scientific systematization of subject matter means the subject matter is organized so as to promote the easy passage of thought from any portion to any other through logical inference. The material is selected and disposed so that one part is a logical conclusion from other parts, while in turn it serves as a premiss from which, in combination with other parts, still further conclusions may be drawn. Moreover this premiss-conclusion relation is two-sided. On the one hand, it is concerned with proof or testing. Certain considerations in the subject matter may be resorted to in order to guarantee or justify certain other propositions. On the other hand, it has to do with facilitating the inferring of new conclusions, or the promoting of discovery. In any given science we attempt to state our knowledge in such form that it will answer both of these requirements: so that we may test any given proposition by noting whether and how it follows from other propositions taken as established, and also may utilize given propositions to arrive at others not previously known. The processes of obtaining data (or evidence), of definition (or fixation of meaning), of generalization (or reduction to principles), and of classification (or graded grouping) characteristic of any science, are the means taken to satisfy these requirements.

The conception of science derived from emphasizing the method which yields systematization, instead of resting in the mere fact of the accomplished system, has important educational consequences. What is taught as science is often nothing more than a peculiar or technical body of information (*q.v.*). Externally speaking, it is science. That is, at some time it was actually reached by processes of reflective inquiry conforming to the general canons just mentioned. Moreover, it is labeled science in the educational scheme. But in so far as the pupil is unaware of the processes of reflective thought which give the information its characteristic scientific status, it has no real right to the title of science, and in so far as he does not himself go through these processes and thereby take an active part in performing the specific logical processes that transform the body of facts and laws into a science, there is no genuine study of *science*. There is merely the acquisition of a certain bulk of externally communicated information, information which is, indeed, distinctive in its technical terminology, but which for that very reason is more remote from any actual thinking on his own part than acquired information of a more familiar sort.

It may be seriously questioned whether these considerations do not throw light upon the failure of much science teaching to realize the expectations of those who have been especially urgent in securing the introduction of science into the curriculum. When science is taught as so much ready-made subject matter, instead of as a subject matter in process of making, by means of the mastery and use of certain methods of inquiry and reflection, there is no more reason to expect results of intellectual enlightenment or practical utility than in the case of memorizing a collection of nonscientific material. While the introduction of laboratory equipment and the use of experiment and observation furnishes, of course, one indispensable factor in the teaching of science as method, it does not of itself meet the entire need. It is possible for students to gain facility in the manipulation of materials and apparatus without gaining an insight into the significance of what is done from the standpoint of its role in genuine thinking, or the making of valid knowledge. As long as the ideal of the acquisition of information persists as the dominant ideal, so long the salient value of science for educational purposes, the mastery of the most effective methods of thinking and their translation into personal attitudes and habits will be obscured or ignored.

When science is approached from the standpoint of method, it is obvious that no absolutely new operations are involved in it. It does not depart from the factors employed in the reflective examination of any topic (see PROBLEM; HYPOTHESIS; EXPERIMENT; also METHOD and INDUCTION) so far as introducing new operations is concerned, but only by supplying the conditions of increased control and care under which to carry on these operations. If scientific methods departed essentially from the methods of reflection and deliberation employed in the daily affairs of life, education in them would be of comparatively little avail outside of the specialized pursuit of a science. But since they present a purification and intensification of the usual methods through making precise and adequate the conditions that enter into their use, proper teaching of scientific method affords the most effective of all agencies for correcting, extending, and confirming the habits of reflection indispensable to a cultivated and useful life. This proper teaching, in addition to the emphasis upon intellectual method already considered, demands that the growth of scientific problems out of the situations of everyday life be taken into account, instead of plunging at once into the technical scientific material without a modulated transition, and that pains be taken to insure application of scientific results to the interpretation of everyday situations.

SELF.—The conception of self reminds one of St. Augustine's saying about time: Everybody knows what it is, but no one can tell. Its connotation is not easy to give satisfactorily, but there is little difficulty in picking out the objects which it denotes. We do not regard sticks and stones as selves; most persons would deny that plants had self-hood, and would ascribe it only doubtfully to animals with the exception, probably, of dogs, horses, and such other animals as have a close relation to man. Three elements seem to be involved in self-hood. The first is capacity for feeling, especially feeling pleasure and pain. The second is the capacity to think of these experiences, to objectify them, as it is usually said. Merely to suffer pains and enjoy pleasures as they come and go, without recollecting them, connecting them with objects as their causes and without making the objects ends of anticipation, desire, and aversion, would hardly mark off a self.

The self involves the duration of a centre of pains and pleasures through a succession of experiences so that the passing experiences, in spite of their diversity and transitoriness, get referred to one another. These statements do not mean that there is any capacity for feeling pleasures and pains by themselves in isolation from all other qualities, but simply that the traits of objects in virtue of which they affect the well-being of a living creature for good or evil become a centralizing and focusing point, with respect to which objects are remembered and anticipated. Thus there is effected a mutual cross reference which is basic to the existence of self-hood. This integration of experiences with one another, effected on the basis of the painful or pleasurable quality of the experiences, constitutes thought in its germinal and basic form. The third and culminating element is the social. While the two elements already mentioned would secure a certain massing and inchoate unification of experiences, they would not constitute self-hood. A contrast is required. When living beings live together under conditions where they have to consult, in directing their experiences and forming their ends, the welfare of others, each is compelled to distinguish others from himself, and, by a correlative process, his own being and aims from those of others. Without the consciousness of *alter*, there can be no consciousness of *ego*; and the more distinct the consciousness of others, the more definite the thought of one's ego. The older notion that one begins with a clear notion of his own self-hood and then proceeds by a process of inferential projection, guided by analogy, to attribute self-hood to others, goes contrary to the facts. The child is treated by others as an end in himself; that is, as a being whose feelings, thoughts, and aims are to be respected and as one who is like his fellows in the claims made upon him, and he accordingly learns to think of himself in the same way. He *becomes* a self, as he becomes an integrated yet distinct member of an association whose constituent elements have rights and duties with respect to one another. The point comes out clearly in the distinction between two types of selfishness: spontaneous and reflective. Ordinary selfishness does not mean that an individual is consciously thinking of himself and of his own advantage and deliberately preferring his own welfare to that of others. It means rather that he is unconsciously engrossed in certain objects and a certain course of conduct without thinking of its relation either to himself or to others. As others, however, find this course obnoxious to their own welfare, they manifest disapproval and attribute conscious intention. In this way, they tend to make the person relate his action to a conscious centre. As a result, deliberate or reflective selfishness and unselfishness become possible.

While, then, self-hood has a natural psychological basis, it is, in its realization, a social and a moral fact. This social and moral quality constitutes its importance from the educational point of view. In tribal societies, the well-being that constitutes the central point of reference in determining and judging conduct is to a large extent that of the group *en masse*, as over against other groups. Self-hood seems to belong to the tribe or clan, rather than to its members. There is correspondingly little sense of distinctive personality or subjectivity. The individual belongs, quite literally, to his group. With the rise of distinctions of superior and inferior, of chieftainship and kingship, a few, the rulers, think of themselves as having a special position, special ends, and a welfare which is to be specially, even uniquely, consulted. They achieve, in brief, a sense of self-hood. In the Greek city-state, each free citizen was treated, in his capacity of free citizen, as an individual, but self-hood was denied to slaves, serfs, and women, and, except in a latent sense, to children. Even with reference to free individuals, self-hood was not emphasized so much as the duty of subordination to the community interest. Early and medieval Christianity gave a powerful impetus to the sense of individuality, through the introduction of the notion of an eternal well-being or misery, depending upon the relation taken to God through the Church. The social organization remained such a fundamental factor in determining this relationship, however, that the conception of subjectivity still remained undeveloped. Instead of the idea of the self there appeared that of a "soul" which was possessed by all as an individual entity. In Protestantism, the individual became overt; the Church consisted of individuals who had, through direct relationship to God, found salvation, instead of its being the instrumentality by means of which the individual attained salvation. The growth of the principle of subjectivity was also emphasized by political conditions. The conception of the State underwent a change analogous to that of the Church. Instead of being, as in classic thought, prior to the individual, it was made by the free choice and voluntary compact of individuals. The formula of Kant, that every individual is to be treated morally as an end in himself, never as a means to others, is perhaps the first explicit and sweeping statement of the modern principle of the universality of self-hood.

This growth of the democratic spirit has modified the conception of childhood. The tendency is to conceive of children as already members of a social whole, in virtue of which they possess rights, instead of having rights merely potentially, in virtue of a future social membership. This conception corresponds to the extraordinarily rapid growth of interest in the education of the young characteristic of the last century. Education is conceived as a public duty which is owed to the young. The conception has also modified, almost transformed, in fact, the discipline of the young, and has affected, though less completely, the methods of teaching. The growing displacement of harsh and punitive discipline by milder methods and by greater regard for personal intelligence, and the disposition to use methods that throw more intellectual responsibility upon the pupil and less, comparatively, upon teacher and text, are practical expressions of the extension of the principle of self-hood of children. It is obvious that the revolution—for it is hardly less than that—brings new dangers and difficulties with its gains. When children are treated in external ways as full-fledged selves, while their power of reflection and the habit of judging from a social point of view are not cultivated, the result is a mere relaxation of external control, without the development of control from within through the formation of a genuine self-hood.

A marked characteristic of the modern conception of the self, as developed by psychologists, is the latitude given to diversity, in contrast with the rigid unity of the older notion. This extends not merely to recognition of specific and ineradicable differences of structure and function in different selves, but also to the coexistence of different and ununified tendencies, almost minor selves, in the same person. Because of the dependence of the self upon modes of social treatment, a person who enters into different sets of associations tends to develop selves that are only loosely connected with one another. A child is one person in family life, and another with his fellows upon the street, just as an adult may have one self in business and another at home or in the church. Unity of self is not an original datum, but an achievement. The responsibility of the school in coordinating into an orderly whole the diversity of social tendencies which, in the complexity of contemporary life, tend to dissipate and distract self-hood, is constantly increasing. Another aspect of the variety of the self is seen in James's distinction of a bodily, a social, and a spiritual self. The influence of reference to well-being may make itself felt in different and only loosely connected fields. Pleasures and pains referred directly to the body tend to build up the thought of the bodily self. The social self (using the term social in a narrower sense than it has been used before in this article) depends upon the thought of the self that is attributed to others—the thought of one's self as reflected in popularity, reputation, esteem by others, etc. (See SELF-CONSCIOUSNESS.) The spiritual self refers to the unification of experiences with reference to some ideal self-hood to which one aspires, or to one's thought of one's self as reflected, not in current esteem, but in the mind of some ideal judge that one imagines to have perfect insight and to pass upon one's character.

See CHARACTER; INDIVIDUALITY; PERSONALITY.

References:—

ANGELL, J. R. *Psychology.* (New York, 1906.)

BALDWIN, J. M. *Mental Development in the Child and the Race.* (New York, 1895.)

COOLEY, C. H. *Human Nature and the Social Order.* (New York, 1910.)

JAMES, W. *Principles of Psychology*, Ch. X. (New York, 1890.)

SELF-CONSCIOUSNESS.—The popular and the philosophic meaning of this term (the latter being derived from the German idealistic philosophy) have nothing in common.

In idiomatic usage, self-consciousness indicates that attention is given to the thought of one's self which one assumes to be held by others, so that this thought intervenes between the person and effective attention to the object in hand. One is thinking about himself and about others' attitude to himself when he should be thinking about some work or subject matter. Thus the term contains a shade of disparagement. Self-consciousness takes two forms according as it accompanies a pleasurable or a painful idea of self. The first shows itself in showing off, "performing," to attract the notice of others, etc. But to some people the idea that the attention of others is upon them is painful, instead of tickling their vanity; and their self-consciousness manifests itself in shyness, constraint, embarrassment and confusion, when doing things in the presence of others, unless they "forget" themselves. While vanity and timidity are natural biological traits, their transformation into the two types of self-consciousness mentioned is the product of the social environment, being the reflex effect of the way in which others treat a child, especially in "noticing" him.

There are two considerations intermediate between this popular meaning and the philosophic one noted below. One of these involves a bad or at least doubtful meaning, while the other expresses an important factor in an intelligent life. Both are moral in nature. The first is introspective curiosity concerning the goodness of one's motives, the disposition to think about one's self from the moral point of view. Since this may easily lead to a morbid interest in one's self which is none the less egotistic because concerned with one's goodness or holiness, and because such a morbid interest tends to be paralyzing to frank and generous overt action, self-consciousness in this sense gets the doubtful meaning referred to. The good meaning is associated with the Socratic "Know thyself" as the basis of morals. This does not imply a purely "inner" or introspective knowledge of self, but rather a knowledge of one's proper end, of what one is good for, of the duties and responsibilities through which one enters into such relations to the world and to others as are required to realize one's self.

The recent technical philosophic meaning of self-consciousness comes ultimately from the Kantian philosophy.

Kant, in developing his doctrine that knowledge is impossible without the operation of certain functions of thought, was led to insist upon the unity of thought, which accompanied the activity of all the thought functions. Without this reference to a logical unity, the cognitive correlate of the unity of the objective world would be lacking. Kant referred to this ultimate unity as the transcendental ego, and as the "I think" which must accompany all knowing experiences—that is, all ideas of objects as objects. He insisted, however, upon its merely formal and logical character. He insisted that it was not to be identified with mind, the self, soul, spirit, in any concrete sense. His successors, especially Fichte and Hegel, regarded this restriction as itself illogical and identified self-consciousness with the principle of ultimate unity differentiating, while relating, the objective and the subjective world, physical and mental phenomena. According to the modern Hegelians (Caird, Henry Jones, etc.) self-consciousness is the highest and most complete (or "concrete") of all categories, overcoming the one-sidedness of all purely physical and psychological principles of explanation, by penetrating to a spiritual unity expressed in both. In many writers, like the last named, self-consciousness tends to become a glib term by reference to which all difficulties are disposed of.

SENSATIONALISM.—A theory of knowledge in accordance with which knowledge is obtained through sensations, and in ultimate analysis consists simply of the qualities and elements revealed in sense perception. Sensationalism has been a natural offspring of empiricism (*q.v.*) in most of the forms in which empiricism has been held. Many of the most influential of empiricists were not themselves sensationalists, however: witness Francis Bacon and John Locke. Some of their successors have given their theories a sensationalistic turn, however, and their rationalistic opponents have seized upon this interpretation as proof that empiricism finds its *reductio ad absurdum* in sensationalism. The most coherent and complete sensational theories were formulated in the later part of the eighteenth century and the early nineteenth century, by Condillac and Helvétius in France and James Mill in England.

The strong and the weak points of the educational counterpart of sensationalism are the same as those of the strictly philosophic conception. The insistence upon sense training, and the substitution of perception of objects for memorizing verbal formulae has been of great help in getting instruction away from empty generalities, which, although labeled rational and logical, were either meaningless to the pupil or else were accepted by him on external authority. Sense training for its own sake, however, as an end-all and be-all becomes a formal gymnastic, or else ends in the accumulation of meaningless particulars.

STIMULUS AND RESPONSE.—These are conceptions introduced by the biological method of thinking. They correspond to the conceptions of cause and effect in physical matters and supplement the defects of that conception, in its traditional formulation, when applied to the phenomena of living beings. The older conception of cause and effect was that of a sequence of occurrences in which the consequent bears no relation of relevancy or adaptation to the antecedent. In the changes characteristic of living organisms the later event has a tendency to continue or to alter the earlier in a specific direction, so that the whole process is cumulative toward a given result—in general the sustaining of life. In this cumulative sequence, as distinct from the mere series of shifting alterations of non-living things, the earlier event functions as stimulus, the later as response. The two terms are thus strictly correlative, that which determines the character of a stimulus being the response which it evokes, while the response comes as an answer, so to speak, to the need of readaptation expressed by the stimulus.

Applied to the events of mental life, the conception of stimulus-response means that sensations are not the units or elements of knowledge, but are rather the occasions for adaptive adjustments to the environment. Movements, instead of being intruders from the physical region into the psychical or a sort of inexplicable physical annex to a psychical antecedent, are the resulting adaptive changes. The central brain processes corresponding to thought are explained upon the basis of this conception as the preparation for a new type of response, new, that is, in distinction from habitual responses which act through the medium of the cord and lower ganglia. As stimuli become more complicated, and as some of them, like those of eye and ear, have reference to conditions distant in space and hence indicate possible experiences remote in time, the immediate stimuli check one another's tendency to call out an immediate response, and a state of tension or suspense of overt action is brought about. Response is delayed until a new stimulus, representing more adequately the complexity of special stimuli, is elaborated. Upon this basis, thinking is always relative to action, namely, to the transformation of habitual activities into a mode of conduct adapted to a complex situation having novel features and remote implications.

See ADAPTATION; CONTROL; FUNCTION; PRAGMATISM.

References: —

DEWEY, J. Reflex Arc Concept, *Psychol. Rev.*, Vol. III., pp. 357–370.

MILLER, I. E. *Psychology of Thinking.* (New York, 1909.)

SUBJECT.—A term used to express the reality, or conception, to which the predicate of judgment refers. Following the grammatical analogy, the logical theory of judgment was first built up on a subject-predicate basis. From the first, however, there was an attempt to penetrate below the mere linguistic distinction and find some ultimate traits corresponding to it. Upon the whole, two methods have been pursued. According to one, the ultimate object of knowledge is always an individual, an individual being defined as that capable of existence on its own account. These individuals have adjectival qualities and relations, which, when stated, form the predicate. The essential trait of the predicate as distinct from the subject is thus that it cannot exist alone but is always attached to a real individual. The above view is, in effect, the Aristotelian, which was embodied in the scholastic logic. It identified "subject" and "substance." There were difficulties about the genuine reality of individual physical things as exhibited to sense perception; and even in Aristotle there is another strain according to which not the individual, but the form or universal, as manifested in the particular, is the true object of knowledge. Exaggerated emphasis upon the individuality of the subject was the logical basis of scholastic Nominalism, as like emphasis upon the universal nature of the object of knowledge was the source of "Realism." In general, the way out was at least suggested by Aristotle. Individuals were regarded as forming a graded series of hierarchical classes, from sensible physical things through human souls, higher spiritual essences up to divine spirit,—a class with a unique member. These classes were regarded as objectively real. Thus they were at once universal as regards the particulars included within them, and individual in virtue of the objective unity of the class. When particulars were known, it was really this inclusive generic unity which was known, as, for example, we know a table by recognizing the class character of table it manifests.

The other way of interpreting the subject-predicate distinction is that of modern idealism. The subject is the ultimate reality known; the predicate is an ideal meaning referred to this reality as its qualification. Absolute reality and true knowledge alike imply the synthetic unity of world and mind, thing and meaning, object and self. Thus there is, therefore, a hierarchical system of judgments, according to the degree of the qualification of reality by ideal meanings, going from superficial sense perception up to self-consciousness (*q.v.*) as the highest reality and truth, in which reality as subject and ideal meaning as predicate completely interpenetrate each other. Thus the goal of judgment is reached; knowledge and being become one.

Upon the whole the modern tendency of logic is to substitute a general relational theory of judgment for the subject-predicate theory. The influence of mathematics has been of chief importance in this regard, for there seems to be no sense in distinguishing subject and predicate in a proposition expressing an equation or other mathematical function. All the terms seem to be on the same level, and judgment seems to consist simply of the statement of the relation that connects them. This theory is now being developed as the logical basis of Neo-realism. Relations and terms (or things, elements, existences, and subsistences or essences) both exist equally in objective nature, and are independent of and "external" to each other. Knowledge itself is simply one of the external relations into which things may enter without being affected thereby. This movement is still too new to exhibit the method by which it expects to avoid the difficulties that have beset every system of atomistic pluralism from the metaphysics of the Megaric school to that of Herbart.

Those who deny that the subject-predicate relation is the proper form of judgment or knowledge treat it as either a purely linguistic or a merely psychological matter. As psychological, the subject stands for the term that happens to come first to mind, or for that which is best known and best established in a particular individual's mental history. The predicate expresses the term that happens to suggest itself later in time, or else that which is new to the individual and still in process of learning and assimilation. The distinction, in other words, is wholly relative to the individual's growth in knowledge, having nothing to do with the realities known.

In regard to the subject-predicate distinction, like many others, pragmatism (*q.v.*) attempts to mediate between the idealistic and the realistic theories. It starts with the principle termed merely psychological by Neo-realism, namely, that the subject stands for the old and established in knowledge, the predicate for the new and still growing. It interprets the logical distinctions of individual and general, existential and ideal, which have been embodied in the classic theories of judgment from this standpoint. But it holds that the growth of knowledge is not merely psychological, but real. There is a genuine reconstruction of the old through its qualification by the new. This conception of judgment is assimilated to the biological process of readaptation in growth, knowing being accordingly treated as this process of organic readaptation brought to intentional control.

For SUBJECT in another of its meanings see SELF.

SYLLOGISM.—According to Aristotle every real object of knowledge is a "concretion" of form and matter, or a realization of the potentialities of energy. Form and energy (or actuality) in this scheme correspond to the universal of knowledge, while matter and potentiality correspond to particulars. This is to say that the true and valid object of knowledge is the embodiment of a universal in particulars. In Aristotelian logical theory this idea was expressed in definition as giving the real nature of any subject, definition stating the genus (universal, productive energy), and its specific differences (particulars, potentialities). These conceptions are the basis of the theory of the syllogism as the adequate and demonstrative method of perfect knowing. For the syllogism is in its essence a statement, at once analytic and synthetic, of the connection of a universal with particulars. Its model form is the statement of the universal as the major premise—Man is mortal; the statement of a particular as falling under rule of this universal—Socrates is a man; while the conclusion closes the system by making the explicit application of the generic rule to the specific case—Socrates is mortal. Three "figures" of the syllogism were discriminated, depending upon the relation of the subject and predicate to each other in the matter of drawing the conclusion; and the cases of each figure were enumerated, depending upon whether propositions were affirmative or negative and upon the way of uniting universal and particular propositions. Rules were thus laid down for all kinds of correct and incorrect reasoning, according as reasoning did or did not correspond to the models thus set forth. Since the first figure (illustrated in the syllogism regarding mortality and Socrates) was taken as the standard of the connection of universal and particular, rules were also given for the reduction of the second and third figures to the first.

Aristotle's own interest in the entire field of the sciences, and his vital sense of the real connection in nature of universals and particulars, prevented his conception of syllogistic reasoning from degenerating into merely formal argumentation. In the Middle Ages there was little or no interest in natural phenomena, and there was great interest in moral and religious conceptions based upon authority and expressed in dogmas. The major premises were thus taken bodily from revelation and the doctrines of church fathers and councils, and the syllogism became the instrument of the rational systematization of church doctrine. In the earlier period of Scholasticism (*q.v.*) the interest was constructive. After the work of systematizing theology had been performed, later Scholasticism tended to degenerate into more or less verbal disquisitions and into subtle refinements of argumentation. There was little care for subject matter and a great deal for the appearance of rigid syllogistic form. The reaction of the Renaissance and Reformation against Scholasticism tended to bring the syllogism into disrepute, and the innovators almost without exception condemned it as giving the pretended form of knowledge without its substance. The increasing interest in the particular, represented within Scholasticism itself in the nominalistic movement, and corresponding to the rising individualism of the age, fostered this disregard of the syllogism. The most severe blow to it, however, was given by the rise of physical science with its demand for accurate observation and its transfer of interest to discovery of the new rather than demonstration of the old. After a while, a compromise was worked out, according to which the syllogistic logic was accepted for deductive reasoning, while the new logic formulated the inductive method of reasoning. When it was realized that mathematics, the typical deductive science, did not depend upon syllogistic reasoning, it was necessary to give up this compromise. The best opinion at present holds that the syllogism is not so much a mode of reasoning as a way of exhibiting the result of a particular reasoning so as to facilitate the discovery of any fallacy in its course. As a way of expounding and testing the results of prior reasonings, the syllogism is likely to remain a powerful adjunct of thought.

SYSTEM.—When an end of considerable importance has to be accomplished by an arrangement of means and agencies of various unlike kinds, the whole is called a system. The conception closely resembles that of organization, but system excludes the notion of external arrangement and control to a greater extent than does organization. It also emphasizes to a greater degree the idea of function performed or use rendered, while organization is a more structural conception. The notion of self-maintaining order within a complex adaptation of means to an end is an idea of great value. In educational theory the importance of logical systems was recognized before that of any other kind, to such an extent that there was a tendency to neglect all other modes of systematization. Logical systems involve definitions to fix the basic concepts and a principle of classification worked out in graded fashion. The result is that a very large number of facts and ideas are arranged as a series of premises and conclusions, going by orderly steps from the general to the particular. A logical system represents the purely intellectual ideal, and serves as a norm in all scientific effort. The methods of abstraction, generalization, and classification involved in such a deductive arrangement are not, however, suited to the earlier stages of the apprehension of any subject, for they imply that the mind has already made a preliminary acquaintance with the material, and has reached a point where it has a need for its logical ordering. So-called inductive methods of education have, accordingly, reacted against the notion of logical systematization. In some cases, there was no constructive substitute, and the result was confusion and distraction. Herbart contributed the idea of psychological systems: the coherence of analogous bodies of ideas that select and assimilate, without conscious abstraction and choice, congenial material. Educational thought since Herbart's time has removed the somewhat mechanical and external scheme for creating these psychological systems, found in Herbartianism, by developing the ideas of spontaneous tendencies and social influences as natural foci for the systematizing of experiences.

TERM.—The element of logical or reflective knowledge as stated in a proposition: equivalent, in one logical terminology, to the meaning or concept; in another, to the verbal form in which the logical meaning is expressed. The chief distinctions among terms were formulated by Aristotle and by the Scholastics who wrought out the terminology of formal logic. Some of the more important distinctions are positive, negative, and privative; singular, universal, and particular, and denotative and connotative. The denotative function of a term is the reference it makes to existences. Directly or indirectly, a logical meaning intends to apply to, to refer to, concrete existence. Terms that particularly perform this office point to, designate, denote. The connotation of a term, on the other hand, is the attributes or meanings which it implies. Division and classification are correlative to denotation; definition and generalization to connotation. Closely related distinctions are the use of terms in extension and in intension. The extension of a term is the species covered by the scope of the term, as the different kinds of vessels for navigation included within the scope of the term "ship"; its intension is the assemblage of properties necessary to define the meaning of "ship."

More important perhaps, for educational purposes, than these formal distinctions is that between popular and technical terms, which are the pedagogical equivalent for concrete and abstract terms. By seeing things used, by participating in their use, by engaging in conversation, every one gathers, from the broader context of use, a certain number of meanings. These constitute the popular (or, as they are sometimes called, psychological) terms of thought. In science, these meanings are wrought over, elements are excluded and added, with reference to the meaning of a term as one element in a logical system. This process gives technical terms. It is a long road from the popular meanings of triangle, water, metal, to the respective mathematical, physical, and chemical meanings. A large part of a wise skill in instruction consists in the proper gradation or modulation of transitions of this nature.

See SYSTEM.

THEISM.—The intellectual formulation of the belief in a single, conscious, spiritual, ultimate reality, God, the creator and redeemer of the world. It is opposed generically to atheism and polytheism and specifically to pantheism and deism: To the former, by its insistence upon the distinctive and independent personality of God; to the latter, by its greater emphasis upon the active presence of God in the world and especially in human affairs. Historically, theism has been associated with Christianity and deism with "natural religion," involving a denial of revelation, and of the intervention of the supernatural in the natural. Deism has denied miracles while theism has admitted their possibility. In some of its later forms, theism tends to approach, however, the earlier deism.

THEORY AND PRACTICE.—The term theory is used to denote any intellectual principle; that is, any conception which is employed to explain and organize a body of facts. Its sense varies from the subjective to the objective; that is, from the notion of an unproved idea to a law. So far as its usage is distinguished from that of the term hypothesis (*q.v.*), theory is reserved to designate the more ultimate and inclusive principles of explanation, as the Newtonian theory of gravitation, the Darwinian theory of evolution. The educational importance of the conception, so far as it does not fall within the function of hypothesis in thinking, centres about the problem of the relation of theory and practice.

As noted elsewhere (see LIBERAL EDUCATION), Aristotle distinguished between theoretical and practical knowledge, to the advantage of the former. It alone is universal, demonstrative, and complete or self-enclosed, which is as much as to say that it alone is knowledge in the full sense of the term. Practical knowledge is a *pis aller* in default of the possibility of something better, having to do with what is contingent and particular, varying with accidental circumstances. This conception affected the whole concept of liberal education, and furnished the intellectual basis for the discrediting of vocational and professional training. Its modern counterpart is the identification of the practical with utility, meaning by utility something which serves personal advantage or at most an external and mechanical type of social need. The separation of theory and practice clearly affects the meaning of both. Theory is not only isolated from application to life, but practice is separated from the intellectual and all that that term connotes. Since it is impossible to rate very highly that which is taken to be antithetical to intelligence, the "practical" thus reduces itself to what is connected with making money or securing the material commodities of existence. With such a background, the only ground that could be urged for "practical" studies was the bare fact that, being practical, they were indispensable, together with a disparagement of theory as futile, idle, and unverifiable.

The change in educational philosophy which is occurring at present is due to causes which render doubtful the basic idea of the divorce of theory and practice,—causes which give theory, properly understood, a practical value and practice an intellectual function and content. These causes are, first, the growth of a practice, or art of knowing, involving the use of experimentation; secondly, the development of industry on the basis of science; and, thirdly, the evolutionary conception of intelligence as an agency of purposive adaptation of the environment to the expansion of life. Under the conditions in which Aristotle wrote and the older cultural tradition obtained, knowledge was a matter of personal excellence, depending upon an insight which was native, a divine gift. There was, in pure science, no art of knowing having its specific equipment and technique. With the incoming of modern methods of natural science, the situation has radically changed. While, of course, superior natural endowments will always count, knowledge has ceased to depend exclusively upon intellectual genius. In fact, the working of natural gifts severed from the common possession of appliances and technique is looked upon with suspicion, as an attempt to evolve knowledge out of inner consciousness. Knowing in its best form, science, has become an organized art pursued by those professionally trained to carry it on. When knowing has itself become a form of practice, it appears absurd to try to keep sharp lines of demarcation between theory and practice, since its effect would be to identify theory with those intellectual exercises that by their nature fall short of knowledge. The line is further obliterated because the practice of the art of knowing in the natural sciences involves the actual manipulation of physical materials and appliances in experimentation in order to bring about changes in natural phenomena. Progress in knowledge began systematically when those occupied with inquiry borrowed the tools and methods of those engaged in the practical arts. Even Greek mechanics remained a branch of geometry, not available for the investigation and explanation of natural events, because of the Greek contempt for manual work and machinery. The new science of nature arose when the conceptions of energy, space, time, motion, and matter of necessity employed in the industrial arts were taken over into the theory of physics and chemistry.

The influence of the industrial revolution is the obverse

of the change just mentioned. When theoretical science borrowed freely from the practical arts, its results were naturally available for the promotion of the latter. When practice was a routine matter, a blind following of traditions worked out by rule of thumb, it was natural to place it in antithesis to reason. But when invention of machinery for the effective utilization of natural forces followed in the footsteps of scientific discovery (when, indeed, the need for some invention became a chief motive in setting scientific problems and stimulating scientific inquiry), it was henceforth impossible to maintain the idea of practice as something resting on custom, to the exclusion of thought. The third cause, the influence of evolutionary biology, has hardly been felt outside of philosophic circles, while the first two causes have more or less consciously affected every one's thinking; but it implies a profound change in the whole conception of the nature of thought and reason. According to it, the organs of mind—the sense structures and the brain—have been evolved in the process of the development of living organisms as part of the evolution of life itself in complexity and scope. Thought cannot, therefore, be put in opposition to action but appears as the chief instrumentality in the emancipation and enrichment of action. The antithesis is no longer between theory and practice but between idle and unverifiable thinking and thinking to a purpose, between blind and enlightened practice.

See Activity; Culture; Experience; Pragmatism.

TRADITION.—Tradition denotes both a process and thing. As a noun, it designates a doctrine which is currently accepted in a community and which is handed on from generation to generation, being accepted on the authority of its past currency rather than because of any independent examination and verification. This use is often extended to cover any legend or story which is continuously handed down in a community, irrespective of the amount of belief attaching to it. As a process, tradition has a wider meaning, being used to cover the entire operation of transmission by which a society maintains the continuity of its intellectual and moral life. As a fact, tradition has of course always been operative. As a conception, its influence dates from the reaction against the rationalism of the eighteenth century. Rationalism, especially in France, had maintained, either overtly or implicitly, the desirability of making a *tabula rasa* of all beliefs derived simply from the past and accepted from custom and social authority. It upheld the ideal of a new construction of doctrines and institutions based upon conscious rational processes. As against this conception, the "traditionalists" asserted the necessity of utilizing the corporate and logically unproved beliefs of the past, and emphasized the educative value of institutions in continuously shaping all men's ideas and aspirations. The principle of social tradition was advanced from different points of view and in different interests by thinkers otherwise as unlike as Edmund Burke, De Maistre, and Hegel, and was accepted, in a modified form, by radicals of the school of John Stuart Mill. In contemporary discussion, it has been absorbed in the larger topic of social influences.

See Heredity, Social; Imitation.

TRANSCENDENTALISM.—Taken generically, transcendentalism is a name for the philosophies that are antithetical to empiricism (*q.v.*), that is, for theories that appeal to a principle or a reality that transcends or goes beyond experience. The term received its current technical use from Kant. He made a distinction between the transcendental and the transcendent. The former signifies those *a priori* principles which are necessary to the existence of a cognitive experience, that is to an experience that can go beyond the assumed subjectivity of sensations and give them a reference to objects. To prove the necessity and the legitimacy of the transcendental in this sense is one of the chief purposes of Kant's critical philosophy. The transcendent, on the other hand, is illegitimate, signifying *a priori* principles that do not enter into the constitution of any possible experience. The Ideas of God, the Universe (as a real completed objective whole) and a spiritual soul substance constituting the Self are the leading transcendent conceptions. As Kant's successors attempted to break down this opposition, the philosophies of Fichte, Schelling, and Hegel are often called transcendentalism. In American thought, Emerson, Alcott, and the group of writers loosely associated with them are known as the New England Transcendentalists. In spirit, they were not so much opposed to empiricism in its technical sense as to intellectual Philistinism and to conventionalism expressed in social, moral, and religious beliefs.

TRUTH.—Truth is originally a social and moral concept, having to do with honesty and sincerity in communication. It is transferred to the corresponding intellectual virtue, veracity of thinking. But certain difficulties connected with the question of rightness of thinking carried the matter over into the metaphysical and epistemological region. In order to achieve valid belief or knowledge, thought must correspond to objects, to "Reality." Truth from this standpoint covers the entire problem of the relation of Mind and Existence, Thought and Reality. There are three typical theories regarding the nature of this relation: the Realistic, the Idealistic, and the Pragmatic. The first, the common-sense view, takes correspondence to be an ultimate and unanalyzable quality, given in the very nature of the knowing relation. Our beliefs, judgments, propositions, etc., are true if they agree with the objects to which they refer. More specifically, judgments are true if the relation of terms or meanings which they express corresponds with the relation between objective elements or things. This conception was first definitely formulated by Aristotle. The conception appears adequate and final. But analysis shows that it merely restates the fundamental demand of knowledge that the results of thought agree or correspond with the things thought about: it states the problem as if it were a solution. Technically, the difficulty is manifested in the assertion that correspondence is ultimate and unanalyzable. How then is error possible, aside from wilful lying? Or, how do we know, in a given case, that the relation among our conceptions agrees with the relation among things? If we can compare a conception directly with a thing, error is wholly unnecessary; if we cannot, we are confined to the relation among our ideas and there is no way of ascertaining its agreement with that of things. The dualistic assumption underlying the common-sense notion is its undoing. Hence the idealistic theory that truth is complete coherence or consistency among our ideas. Reality is conceived as a system of thought or meanings which is total and absolute. Our thinking is a reproduction of this absolute thought, or a partial participation in it. Incompleteness of thought always, when carried to its explicit realization, reveals itself as logical inconsistency, that is, contradiction, while the degree of consistency attained evidences the degree of embodiment in our finite thinking of objective truth or reality. This theory is derived from Plato, according to whom ultimate Being, Truth, and Reason are identical. While the Scholastic logic was based upon Aristotle, it also retained the gist of the Platonic conception in its identification of final Being and Truth with God.

The pragmatic conception reverts to the notion of correspondence, and attempts to analyze it. It interprets it as adaptation of thought to controlling things in the direction of a unified, satisfactory experience, not as bare conformity. Our beliefs and judgments are true in the degree in which they "work." Working means capacity to adapt themselves, through their expression in action, to things, this adaptation not being a passive accommodation but a use of things to get the end for the sake of which thinking exists. The essential points of this theory are the teleological character of all thinking (or that thinking exists for a specific purpose, not simply to reproduce or conform to what is already in complete existence), and the identification of truth with a tested verification of thought, this testing being experimental. Since, upon any theory, our only way of telling whether a given conception is true or not is to find out whether it is capable of experimental verification, pragmatism claims it is simpler to identify truth with the verified conception. The theory results from a union of the biological conception of thinking as purposive adaptation, and the experimental use of hypotheses in natural science.

See Hypothesis; Method; Pragmatism.

References:—

Dewey, J. *Studies in Logical Theory.* (Chicago, 1903.)
James, W. *Pragmatism.* (New York, 1907.)
Meaning of Truth. (New York, 1909.)

JOACHIM, H. H. *Nature of Truth.* (Oxford, 1906.)
RUSSELL, BERTRAND. *Philosophical Essays.* (London, 1910.)
SCHILLER, F. C. S. *Studies in Humanism.* (London, 1907.)

UNIVERSAL.—The logical opposite of the particular: variously conceived at different times and by different schools as an objective ontological archetypal Being in imitation of which and by partial participation in which particular things exist; as a class or genus of individuals, having objective existence and supplying the norm which limits the variations of particulars and gives them knowable character; as a law which while found only in particulars governs them; as a mental concept abstracted from individuals which alone exist; as a mere word a common noun which is applied to a multitude of things in spite of their particular differences. Much of the logical discussion of Scholasticism turned about the nature and meaning of universals, and differences upon this point were the cause of the formation of the rival schools of Realism, Nominalism, and Conceptualism (*qq.v.*).

See LAW; PRINCIPLE.

UTILITARIANISM.—The doctrine that the standard of judging the rightness of an act lies in the consequences of that act with respect to its effect upon the pleasure and pain of those affected by it. As a moral theory it is opposed to theories which, like the Kantian, hold that morality is a matter of motive not of results, and to intuitionalism which holds that rightness is directly perceived by a moral faculty, not reflectively calculated. Historically, utilitarianism is a development from hedonism, which holds that the end of desire and the highest good of man is pleasure. In fact, utilitarianism has allied itself, till recently, with the hedonistic psychology of desire and pleasure. It differed from hedonism in the fact that its primary concern was with the standard of estimating rightness and wrongness rather than with the end of action, and especially in its insistence that the pleasure and pain of all affected by an act, not simply the personal well-being of its doer, are to be taken into account. John Locke is commonly regarded as the founder of utilitarianism, though the word was not used till the latter part of the eighteenth century, nor was the theory consistently worked out by him. Through emphasis upon future rewards and punishments, a kind of theological utilitarianism was developed and widely accepted among the English divines of the eighteenth century. David Hume put the emphasis squarely upon social well-being. Jeremy Bentham was the first to work out the theory in a comprehensive form. He was essentially a reformer of legislation, administration, and penal methods. His interest was not so much in the standard of private morality as in discovering and elaborating a principle that might be employed to judge the rightness or wrongness of public acts. The formulae of the greatest good of the greatest number, and every one to count, in its calculation, for one and only one, are attributed to him. Through the influence of Bentham utilitarianism became the philosophical creed of democratic radicals. It was a register in the sphere of ethical theory of the growth of democratic aspirations. James Mill had a psychological interest which Bentham lacked and effected an alliance of the new ethical theory with sensationalistic and analytic psychology. The English economists following in the school of Adam Smith took an active part in the spread of the new doctrine, while the ethical writers generally pointed to the free play of economic forces as one of the chief agencies in uniting personal interest and general happiness. During the nineteenth century the reaction against individualism clearly showed that the weak point of utilitarianism was its association with hedonistic and sensationalistic psychology. John Stuart Mill modified the doctrine by introducing the idea of differences in the quality of pleasures which were more important than considerations of their quantity. Herbert Spencer made a further modification by linking it with the theory of evolution. According to him, rightness should be deductively arrived at by a consideration of the tendency of the consequences of an act upon the furthering of the life process of evolution. We cannot say at present that the rightness or wrongness of an act is equivalent to its pleasure or pain giving quality. At the end of the evolutionary process the individual will be completely adjusted to his environment, natural and social, and then the utilitarian ethics will be absolute in their validity, not relative as at present. Looking over the history of utilitarianism, it is evident that it has met the social and political needs of the times more adequately than any of its rivals, but that it has been badly handicapped by its adoption of a false psychology of motive, desire, pleasure, and pain. When the hedonistic factor, which came in by an historic accident rather than by intrinsic necessity, is dropped out, utilitarianism tends to merge in a broader doctrine of morals, according to which social well-being, taking into account all of its complexity, is the objective standard of morality.

References:—

ALBEE, E. *History of English Utilitarianism.* (London, 1902.)

BENTHAM, J. *Principles of Morals and Legislation.* (Oxford, 1879.)

DEWEY AND TUFTS. *Ethics.* (New York, 1909.)

HALÉVY, E. *La Jeunesse de Bentham.* (Paris, 1901.)

LOCKE, J. *Essay Concerning Human Understanding.* (Oxford, 1894.)

MILL, J. S. *Utilitarianism.* (London, 1863.)

SIDGWICK, H. *Method of Ethics.* (London, 1890.)

SPENCER, H. *Principles of Ethics.* (London, 1892–1893.)

STEPHEN, L. *The English Utilitarians.* (London, 1900.)

VALIDITY.—The soundness or strength of a principle or truth (*q.v.*). It applies alike to moral and to logical conceptions. It is closely associated with the processes of demonstration and proof (*q.v.*), but approaches more nearly the notion of value (*q.v.*). Aesthetic ideas would be spoken of, for example, as valid or invalid, although not, strictly speaking, subject to demonstration, while moral principles are demonstrated in other than logical ways.

VALUES, EDUCATIONAL.—The notion of educational values was introduced in connection with consideration of the end or aim of education. The values most commonly enumerated are culture, discipline, information (or knowledge), and utility (*qq.v.*). It is a fact worth noting that even those writers who proclaim that character is the ultimate end of education have not provided a place for character as a distinct educational value. While various theorists proclaimed that one value or another was *the* end of education, it could not be denied that each of the terms represented an indispensable value. Attempts were made to distribute and systematize the studies of the curriculum by showing that each represents predominantly a certain value—*e.g.* arithmetic, in some of its phases utility, in others discipline; geography, information; literature, culture; etc. Such a procedure obviously ignores, and implicitly denies, the unity of the educative process, making of education a mechanical patchwork of isolated elements.

It is necessary to make at least a preliminary distinction between values which are such in themselves and values which are instrumental. The first includes those goods which are, in the pregnant idiom of common speech, invaluable. We here confront the seeming paradox that on the one hand there is no value save that of being good for something, of being of force, strength, validity, in the achievement of something. But on the other hand, unless we are to be lost in an endless circle, this "something" which confers value on its means must be valuable on its own account, not as an instrument of attaining something beyond itself. Attempts to state this ultimate "value" almost always run over into ethical discussions, especially into the controversy between the perfectionists and the hedonists. The former, influenced by Kant, draw a line between worth, which is ultimate and self-enclosed, and values, which are relative and secondary. Character, according to the Kantians, alone possesses worth. According to the hedonists, pleasures are the ultimate values which constitute and measure the value of all else. The root of the difficulty appears to lie in the attempt to set up an abstraction. Value is in reality an abstract noun denoting not just one undefinable thing but the entire complex of valuable things. The conception of valuable things throws us back upon the attitude of individuals in choosing and pursuing. Things are valuable when they are valued; that is, when they are esteemed and chosen; they are not chosen because of some external trait of value contained in them. Want, effort, and choice are more fundamental concepts than value. Hence the significance of the term "invaluable." Strictly speaking, it denotes the negation of value, not in the sense of lacking value but in the sense of representing that which, in the given situation, is outside the sphere of valuation. It is not compared at all with other ends, but is that which effectively controls the comparing and weighing of consciously considered ends. In other words, we value, or evaluate, objects only when in doubt and in the process of choosing. Value is a category of reflective comparison, or choice, not one of things in themselves. All values are instrumental, for the ultimate of any situation is invaluable.

Applying this to the matter of educational values, it appears that discipline, knowledge, character, and so forth, are phases of the educational process which the specific needs of various situations bring to consciousness from time to time. The ultimate end is simply life itself, an increase of its own vitality, and an enriching of its meaning. This is invaluable, and so undefined except with respect to the need which shows itself in life at a given time. Discipline becomes a value from the need of methodic power in the guidance of life; knowledge, because of the need of insight and judgment; utility, because of the need of control of the conditions of the environment, and so on. When separated from the needs specifically indicated by situations, these "values" all have an exasperating way of slipping into one another. Knowledge for example is made an end, or "value," in itself, only when taken to signify not just objective information but also the attitude of good judgment in its use, and the refining and broadening of outlook that this information, when assimilated into personal habits, brings with it. So taken, it includes both discipline and culture. Similarly discipline means a sort of formal gymnastics unless we consider the ends for which the power gained is employed. If any one of these values has the superiority over the others, it is undoubtedly culture, for the simple reason that the term culture most readily suggests the entire process of the effective growth of life itself, not some one specific and isolated thing. But culture in this full sense is not what has conventionally figured as culture in discussions of educational values, for that has usually meant something which is specifiable in opposition to other specific ends. In brief, the whole question of values in education depends upon the nature of education (*q.v.*) itself. The attempt to settle, once for all, apart from specific situations and the differing needs of individuals, the question of values and to lay down their order of precedence, goes with the notion that there is some external or objective end beyond itself to which the educative process is a mere means. Recognize that the educative process is in the last analysis identical with the process of life, and that life is not life save in growth, and education itself becomes an invaluable or ultimate. As life in its specific manifestation exhibits now this, now that, need, a special aim is required to meet this need, and this or that special means becomes a value. But it is as hopeless to consider educational values by themselves in the abstract, as it would be to determine the inherent value of beefsteaks, diamonds, books, or statuary apart from the specific situations in which they are to function in the lives of specific individuals.

Reports of Dewey's Addresses

REASONING IN EARLY CHILDHOOD[1]

When I seriously began to give my mind to the subject that was selected for me, I found nothing very special to say about the reasoning of early childhood. There is not any reasoning of early childhood which is different from the reasoning of later childhood, adolescence, or adults. There is reasoning in little children just as there may be in a grown up man or woman, but there is not reasoning of early childhood if you mean by that "of," something which as reasoning can be marked off definitely from reasoning somewhere else.

I have come to believe that reasoning itself, the capacity or ability to reason (or that bundle of minor abilities of which reasoning consists), is not capable of being improved with growing years, or, at least, its improvement is not sufficiently marked to be worth mentioning. Professor James in his *Psychology* speaks in this way about organic memory—"the power to retain." Later investigations have led to some modification of his statement, but it is generally admitted that the power to improve radical or fundamental memory is slight. Unfortunately, however, the converse statement is not true. Retrogression is entirely possible, with both memory and reasoning. There is something for educators to do even if they cannot fundamentally improve the power of reasoning; their task is to furnish conditions so that this power can be kept together without a falling off of its pristine capacity. This is not a merely negative task although it is here stated in negative terms. The problem is to prevent

1. Stenographic report of paper presented before the Department of Kindergarten Education, Teachers College Alumni Conference, February 21, 1913.

[Stenographic report of a paper read before the Department of Kindergarten Education, Teachers College Alumni Conference, 21 February 1913. First published in *Teachers College Record* 15 (1914): 9–15.]

the falling off or going backward, but accomplishing this prevention requires a great deal of positive activity in keeping the ability up to concert pitch.

Since the power of reasoning in little children does not differ fundamentally from that of adults, if we want to understand it in children we must study it in ourselves. There are of course differences in the concrete thoughts of children and adults, and these are differences in subject matter. These reduce to two heads, covering a variety of detail:

(1) There are different objects to think about, and different purposes for which to think, because children and grown-ups have different kinds of acts to perform—different lines of occupation, in short. The adult has obviously more complicated activities to carry on; he has concerns that continue over longer stretches of time so that more details enter in, and results are postponed. Hence he must be continually looking far ahead. The *process* of thinking is essentially the same for little children; but there is such a difference in the materials with which the thinking is done, and the ends or objects for the sake of which it is carried on, that the impression is easily created that the thinking itself is of a radically different order.

(2) There is another difference between children and adults. The objects and ends of adults, because long continued, have a definitely established character, have a more specialized organization. The absence of a high degree of specialization in vocation and in particular duties among children, gives opportunity for a freer and more flexible play, a greater open-mindedness and greater susceptibility to new ideas than the average adult succeeds in retaining.

The process of thinking has been often explained. There are just three elements or constant conditions. (1) The end to be reached. (2) The selection of the means by which to arrive at it. (3) The possibility of new discoveries in working toward the end.

(1) If there is an end ahead to be reached there must be a forward movement, a certain span of time between the person and the object to be attained. It is significant that all of the words like "attaining" and "achieving" have the idea of

a forward movement, and imply a certain distance between ourselves and something a little way ahead of us in time.

(2) For the sake of the something ahead that we want to attain there must be a selecting and arranging of various means and materials which will enable us to reach that end. These words "selecting" and "arranging" have a mechanical sound. If we had a box of cut-up pieces of wood and all we had to do was to pick out some of these and put them together, the operation would be mechanical; but in thinking, this selecting and arranging are done for the sake of reaching an end—something ahead of us, something which we have not but are trying to get. Hence they cannot be of such a mechanical character as the words indicate. In other words, this selecting and arranging always involve something of *experiment*, relative to an element of uncertainty, and (what is more important) to the need and possibility of discovery.

(3) The selecting and arranging of means and materials, if there is an end ahead, is by the very nature of the case a tentative process, as much a process of experiment and discovery as the operations of a scientific man in his laboratory. It might appear to any one who entered a chemist's laboratory that he selected a pinch of this and a pinch of that and mixed them together much as a cook in the kitchen selects salt, and milk, and flour and beats them together. The latter may be a routine act, but where there is thinking, or intellectual experimenting, there is something new, something really distinct in the end to be reached, different from any prior experience. Unless there is something in some degree novel in the purpose or end, then there is no thinking, only a performance of a routine act, following a formula which has been given so that there shall be no possibility of doing the wrong thing. Only when the end to be reached is something ahead instead of something behind, something still to be done instead of something which has been accomplished, do the selections and arrangements have intellectual quality. They represent an experiment of the mind and of the imagination. The zest and joy of discovery cling to them.

The ends which a young child has are different from

those of the grown-up and the materials, means and habits which he is able to fall back upon are different, but the process—one involving these three factors—*is exactly the same.*

There is a difference in the psychological context which needs to be mentioned because it is so important practically. Just because the child's ends are not so complex and not so remote in the future, the tendency to put every idea in immediate action is stronger with the child. His dramatic instinct or his play impulse is markedly more active, more urgent and intense. This creates the appearance of a great difference in the quality of the thinking itself, but it is a difference in the psychological landscape, as it were, rather than a difference in the actual process of thinking itself. The child's end is not far ahead and so the immediately physical and motor character of the selecting and arranging comes out more markedly. The physical elements and the tendency to adapt them to immediate use are present in grown people, but are disguised and translated by substitutes. Adults use words and other symbols as the media for selection and arrangement, but words are not dramatic enough for the thinking of the child in a great many situations. He wants to reach his end with his whole body instead of doing it with the muscles of the throat and tongue alone. Adults carry on a constant physical activity of a suppressed kind; to get a remote and far-reaching end, they employ minute and invisible kinds of expression. A child wants to bring into play in an active and overt way his hands and arms and legs.

While native rational power can hardly be improved to any great extent, if at all, it can easily be allowed to decrease. A child can be surrounded with conditions which cause the power to be dissipated and rendered ineffective. If a child is bright, the power can be drafted off in all kinds of futile and irrelevant ways which result in mind-wandering, inability to control the attention or centre the mind on a topic around which the selecting and arranging of materials are to be carried on.

This dissipation may take place in three ways. (1) Plain frittering away of time. It is called frittering away of time or wasting time, but this is merely another phrase for fooling away intellectual energy. This comes from not having any purpose in view. "Amusing" in the worst sense of amusing, means that there is no *recreative* element, but only dissipation of energy. It is not enough to *catch* a child's attention; it must be *used*, and this implies an end. The mind should be carried on to something new. A lesson may be beautifully planned and given, but if the child does not get intellectually something he did not have before, he is frittering away his time. He may be wasting his mental capacity when he is doing things which seem to the teacher to be very important. Merely to manipulate materials may have no meaning to the child. The *teacher* may be getting some intellectual exercise, may be arriving somewhere or thinking, but unless there is an end in the child's own experience, then *for him* it is a case of frittering. To manipulate purely symbolic material of some sublime mathematical or spiritual truth, unless the child has some equivalent counterpart, is thus a case of frittering away energy. (2) Another thing which makes for retrogression is the amount of purely dictated work that the individual has to do. The measure of thinking in a child or adult is not in the repetition of the past, but in seeking for a future, not in following the old, but in reaching out for the new. Dictated work alone eliminates the attitude of searching, of reaching out, experimenting. Undoubtedly the best way to train animals, horses and dogs, to do their stunts is to assign a specific thing to be done, dictate it and give a reward when that particular thing is accomplished—and something else when it is not done. Children are animals too. It may be that physical habits are most readily formed by a process which is largely dictation; but it must be borne in mind that in the latter case, while the physical habit will have intellectual meaning to us, to the child it will be senseless, and hence his mental capacity may be reduced.

(3) The third thing which has a detrimental effect upon the child is presenting ready-made, finished formulae upon the basis of which he is to act. Since there should be reaching out for something new, the process of selecting and arranging materials should be more or less experimental and tentative, a process of trying this or that to see how it will work, then retaining the things that carry toward the end

and dropping the other things. This process requires some spontaneity and leeway; and too definite and finished formulae are hostile to this freedom of personal experimentation. Conscientious teachers are prone perhaps to fail *here* more than at any other point. They want to forestall all failures. They want to dig the little plant up by the roots to see that the roots are growing and growing in the right direction. It is quite safe to say that no two grown persons get the same result by the same method unless the situation is an exceedingly simple one. Sometime after you have had a complicated question on your mind, if you will ask yourself just how you reached a result, and go back and try to recall every step you took and misstep also, and then compare it with any formula that can be devised, you will see the difference between the consciously formulated method and the method unconsciously but vitally used. What is called thinking is very largely a series of intuitions. Something comes into the head—it sprouts. It does not come by any formula which was there before. We say "I think," but "I" do not, *it* thinks. There is something which is deeper than our *conscious* rule.

The orderly method is good but it comes as a *result* (often comparatively late). What might seem to a grown up person to be disorder might seem to a child's mind, order, in the way he selects and arranges things. The mere fact that a certain order of thinking does not fall into the teacher's schedule of thinking means that a child is one person and the teacher another. Yet we imagine that there is just one right way to think and if another person does not get results in the same way that we do, we conclude that there is something wrong.

Perhaps the most difficult thing to get is intellectual sympathy and intellectual insight that will enable one to provide the conditions for another person's thinking and yet allow that other person to do his thinking in his own way and not according to some scheme which we have prepared in advance. This applies quite as much to the teaching of the elementary school subjects, such as arithmetic and grammar, as to the reflections of the adult discoverer. At present we often think that a child has no right to solve a problem or do a sum at all unless he goes through a certain form.

There is one point which has not been touched—the question of the materials appropriate for the thinking of young children. This matter cannot be easily anticipated or cleared up in advance of actual contact with actual children. But we may ask what ends occupy the attention of most children. They will be found to fall under two heads—(1) The very small child has as his chief end the adjusting of one of his physical organs to another. He has to learn what the lower animals have to start with. He has to work out by practical experimentation how to make his hand and eye work together, his ear and eyes work together, how to manage and manipulate physical materials by means of his own organs. Intellectual thinking accompanies this process of experimenting with physical activities so as to reach certain results. There is the question of an end to be reached, and this is cleared up by managing, manipulating, coordinating the operations of the senses and muscles. Here we have one of the great reasons, on the physiological side, for the success of the kindergarten movement. In various ways (whatever reasons may have been given for the process) it has secured a large opportunity for direct muscular adjusting, and for manipulation of various kinds of objects. If the young child has an end which he wants to reach and has sufficient freedom in choice and arrangement of materials *to work out for himself the end he is after*, there is sure to be a genuine keeping going of the thinking process.

(2) The other great problem for a little child is to get along with other people. He has the definite occupation of adjusting his conduct, in a real give and take of intercourse to that of others. He needs to make other people realities to himself, while he gets the power to make himself real to them. There is an adjustment of behavior which includes a good deal more than that of outward or muscular acts. The questions arising from the groupings of persons are the most perplexing problems of life even for grown up people; but for the children, the problem is especially acute owing to their dependence upon others and their inability to make their way physically and industrially.

Material selected then from situations of physical control and social adaptation (especially from the two in connection with one another) is most appropriate for the work of the teacher in maintaining the mental acuteness, flexibility, and open-mindedness, the dominant interest in the new and in reaching ahead that are at once such marked traits of the life of childhood and such essential factors of thinking.

LECTURES TO THE FEDERATION FOR CHILD STUDY

The Federation for Child Study is an organization of women connected with the Society for Ethical Culture of New York City. It works in chapters. Several of these groups of women are meeting weekly to study, under a leader, different books relating to childhood. Papers are read and discussed by the members.

Occasionally a special course of lectures is given by a distinguished lecturer.

This year this active body of women have secured Dr. John Dewey to give lectures upon "Some Leading Ideas in Modern Education."

1. On Rousseau, Pestalozzi, Froebel and Montessori

In the first lecture Dr. Dewey showed that the great importance of Rousseau in educational theory is due to his emphasis upon the principle of growth according to nature. Rousseau does not distinguish, however, says Dr. Dewey, between growth as setting the *end* to be reached and supplying a method for reaching the true educational end. We find, he says, some things in Rousseau vital and operative today, and also others that are false and misleading.

Rousseau never instituted a school nor any particular technique to carry out his ideas.

Rousseau confuses, as we do today, two unrelated ideas of nature: one meaning of native unlearned capacities and an order of development; the other meaning opposition to social life and to culture. Both of these confusions persist to this day.

[Reported by Jenny B. Merrill and published in *Kindergarten-Primary Magazine* 26 (1914): 186, 215, 251, 255–56.]

Pestalozzi and Froebel, while accepting the theory of natural development, did lay out definite methods of procedure to put these ideas into execution. They founded schools.

In all three, false and true, good and bad have been mingled.

The elementary school of today is largely Pestalozzian in character. What commonly goes as pedagogy in the popular mind is largely Pestalozzian, so that it becomes a vital matter to discriminate in his teachings the sources of power from weakness.

Pestalozzi taught that education has its model in Nature. We must develop in Nature's order. He accentuates the idea that Nature is a revelation of the divine. He is preeminently reverent and religious.

This is true also of Froebel and of Montessori.

Pestalozzi shared with Rousseau the theory of innate powers which unfold in an intrinsic order; we educate for good or ill according as we facilitate this order; if we interfere, we weaken the natural sources of power.

One great difference between Rousseau and Pestalozzi is that Pestalozzi believed in and looked for political regeneration by means of education. Rousseau did not. He, Rousseau, believed a social and political revolution must come before education could be put on the right basis. So Rousseau took the child out of society, educated him apart from the social whole in isolation under a tutor.

Pestalozzi's deepest motives were philanthropic. He should be Saint Pestalozzi equally with Saint Francis! He believed social life with our fellow beings essential to education and to the improvement of society in the end.

He believed that Nature educates for social life and by means of social life. First and foremost he believed in the educational power of the *family circle*. Another one of Pestalozzi's best contributions is that intellectual development comes through social activities.

Education requires a natural, social environment which to Pestalozzi was the *family* circle, or something which approximates it in the school.

This home atmosphere creates a direct feeling for *reality*. It is an immediate, close environment, and enforces particular immediate relations adapted to future situations. Nature's road leads to reality.

This is vital. It is not an idea which lends itself to mechanizing.

Pestalozzi gathered twenty vagabonds and made a household of them. They worked in the fields in summer and spun and wove in the winter. Meanwhile they learned to read, to write, and recite the catechism.

We talk about "education by doing" but select the *remote*. We do not put the children in social relations and get their judgments in these social groups. The child loses the sense and feeling of reality.

2. *On Social Motives in School Life*

Dr. Dewey's lecture was a comprehensive review of the relations of education to social life, and to national life. He said that this whole movement of education to build up national life was first conceived by Germany.

Frederick the Great and his advisers were the first statesmen to realize the value of the school as a political instrument. Their object was to build up the German nation over against competitors.

France after 1870 took the same view of education in relation to the state and set to work to nationalize its schools.

England attained its national unity much earlier, but only in our day has England nationalized her schools.

"Industrialism" is the product of these national tendencies. Germany again first saw the possibilities in her schools as a national asset in industrialism, and set to work to educate her citizens in industries as a good economic project.

In the United States we do not realize the struggle of nation against nation as they do in Europe.

In our country the movement in education that corresponds to "nationalism" in Europe, is more social in its character. It did its work so thoroughly by the thirties and forties of the Nineteenth Century that we are apt to overlook the comparative recency of the movement.

Our movement was more broadly human and was started in many cities under philanthropic societies.

There were all kinds of humanistic schemes introducing sentiment on a wide scale. The idea had taken deep root that most evils spring from ignorance. If minds were only enlightened, humanity would leap forward. Horace Mann was the great representative of this movement in our country. Our early presidents, as Jefferson and Madison, fully believed that the stability of democratic government is bound up with a certain amount of knowledge. It was not a question of the United States over against other nations, as it was in Europe. Education was essential in a republic.

This period in the United States was not only one of great philanthropic interest, but also it was a great missionary period in the churches. The churches established schools, feeling it to be their business to supply better education industrially, intellectually and morally.

There was great motive power from philanthropy and the activity of the churches. Almost every public school started as a more or less philanthropic or charity school.

Gradually these schools were taken over by the municipality.

Dr. Dewey seemed to be taking us up on a mountain top to give us a broad, historic survey of the past century in order to help us see more clearly the social motives that were so prominent in building up our schools, but were for a time lost sight of. He is himself the great apostle of modern school social interests. His *School and Society* is our great educational classic. No teacher can afford to have it absent from his book-shelf.

Dr. Dewey proceeded to show in his lecture that in our early history, great stress was laid upon the individual.

There were so many natural resources, prosperity was stimulating, and the individual could go out and carve his own future. There was much land awaiting his coming. Individual ambition was greatly stimulated.

Individuals were to be aroused to the idea that all could succeed for themselves. This was true up to the Civil War. Our people were not conscious, as were the Germans, of the great need of training to national ends.

More recently there has been a gathering of tendencies to formulate a distinct philosophy of social principles in education. There is a tendency to test the various parts of educational machinery on the basis of its contribution to social efficiency.

3. *On Pestalozzi*

Pestalozzi and his followers, strange to say, have forced upon elementary education almost as great an incubus as they have relieved.

This principle of proceeding from the simple to the complex led him to analyze and arrange graded series in language lessons, in form, in drawing, which are unnatural, unnecessary and unchildlike, as for example, ab, eb, ib, ob, ub, ba, be, bi, bo, bu.

In drawing he used various combinations of straight and curved lines. In music and arithmetic similar reductions to the elements supposed by him to be simple. This is what Pestalozzi called "psychologizing education"—that is reducing all subjects to elements. It was poor psychology for the child. It was imposing upon the child the adult point of view, which is not simple, but difficult for the young mind.

It is natural teaching when the child deals with much more complex things, as in home life. The child gradually analyzes things into parts by finding their uses. In reality Pestalozzi did put things to social uses, for his children worked in the home and in the field. This was good.

Pestalozzi recognized the value of first impressions, that imperfection in the bud means imperfection in the fruit.

Montessori is undoubtedly a follower of Pestalozzi, although she has been original in working out her own problems. She, too, analyzes too much, attempts to present simple elements of form which the child may get just as well and better from the ordinary objects in the home. She shows the same religious devotion. She, too, appreciates the social side.

Because social relations are the deepest, we find it better to have objects connected with social life rather than any specific didactic materials.

Next month we will consider Froebel's materials and his relation to Pestalozzi.

4. Comparison of Herbart and Froebel

Dr. Dewey thinks that Froebel was more formal in his later writings than in his earlier, and that the modern, progressive kindergartner is finding inspiration in his earlier work. He thinks that many forms of his gifts are for children from seven to ten years of age.

The modern kindergartner is studying child nature, is experimenting and endeavoring to emancipate the earlier Froebel.

Dr. Dewey's chief objection to prevalent kindergarten ideas is that they educate through artificial symbols rather than through social life. There is a spirit of complacency as if full truth had been achieved.

Kindergartners generally do not study children and experiment enough.

Herbart was the first to question the doctrine of formal discipline. He believed in systematizing subject matter. He accepted existing studies and endeavored to reform the method of presenting them.

He followed Pestalozzi for earlier years.

He considered what to select and how to arrange so as to gain moral effect.

He gave too much value to cultural subjects. He lacked imagination. He did not think of education as a re-living but as a re-constructing of the past for the present to get a better future.

Herbart valued conduct above all else. Subject-matter must function in life. It must appeal to interest. Froebel and Herbart both believed in a technical system of education.

Froebel felt emotionally the development from within. He was romantic and yet highly formal. He believed in a peculiar type of subject-matter manipulated in a peculiar way. He felt the importance of industry and work. The human being should be trained for work through and by work. ("God works.")

Children should be busy in their play and free in their work.

Development equals active creating and is new at each stage.

The philosophy of his time influenced Froebel. This philosophy taught "the law of parallelism," identity back of everything and a parallel in the psychic world. It idolized symbols.

Dr. Dewey thinks the first part of *Education of Man* is fine if not taken too literally, but does not approve the latter part.

Those who listened to Dr. Dewey were deeply grateful for his broad outlook. They realized a master mind was scanning the history of education and relating its lessons. They realized the great importance of studying the history of education, and yet not yielding up to one or all of the great educational thinkers the privilege of continued experiment and investigation.

Dr. Dewey's *How We Think* is being read widely by teachers. He tells us so simply and so clearly how we think, that we exclaim, "Yes, that is just how we do it. Why has it taken so long to tell it in such a simple way?" Is it not because it takes the greatest thinker to go to the root of thinking?

In this course of lectures, Dr. Dewey has spoken in such a simple conversational style that it has been hard to realize what an immense field he has covered. The writer of these reports took copious notes, and it was not until going over these that she fully realized how much ground Dr. Dewey had covered and how impossible it is in a short column to do justice to the lectures.

In one of these lectures Dr. Dewey said with his quaint humor, "Most of our thinking is post-mortem. Ideas rarely precede action, especially in social matters. Movements usually grow out of emergencies rather than out of any theory." He further said that this is certainly true of our recent interest in vocational work in the schools. There is a certain vagueness in these ideas of "social efficiency" and the value of statistics.

Dr. Dewey told a story to help illustrate this point, of

a certain village blacksmith who was a man of natural shrewdness, so that his shop became a sort of forum for discussing matters of local interests. Possibly the business of shoeing horses may have suffered somewhat. Are we to take the broad or the narrow view? If efficiency experts had been sent to gather statistics—how many horses shoed, etc.—could they have also found records of the good accomplished by exchange of opinions and discussions among the men?

"Are we aiming," Dr. Dewey asked, "at social conformity or social transformation? Should the educational authorities take it for granted that the present social status is accepted finally and educate for it? or, should they take the more imaginative, more ideal and recognize the possibility of changes in the future?" We must not forget that persons are effective agents in bringing about transformations in social matters. Unless we intelligently consider, are we not likely so to educate as to fit persons into narrow niches?

This leads to a two-fold evil. First, it tends to perpetuating class distinctions which our democratic ideals strive against. It is a movement away from democracy. Second, it educates on the basis of a static society, whereas the forces of science and invention bring about changes in industry and society, and even in political institutions themselves. The narrower point of view in education would not pay even in dollars and cents. For example, there is no longer a building made as in the past. Steel construction has altered everything; so the use of cement and concrete is coming to make new possibilities in building.

Thus one merely trained for a specific line of industry may find his specific knowledge useless by the time he is a man. So with steam, electrical and gas engines. No one can foresee what changes the future has in store.

Then to take the narrow and the static view in educating industrially is not to be permanently efficient. We must recognize society as a rapidly-changing society. No education is competent that does not turn out pupils able to meet changes. It may seem, at first sight, more practical to take the narrow view, the lines of least resistance. It is easier to stir up an interest in trade schools, in vocational schools, in continuation schools than to attend to a more general reorganization of the school curriculum, but the latter is what is needed. Such a reorganization should aim to make all individuals more capable to take care of themselves because of general equipment.

It is possible to prevent waste in the beginning of education, although it seems the most difficult principle to work upon.

We know that large numbers of children leave our schools between twelve and fourteen years of age. The fundamental problem is pre-vocation before twelve.

It has already been proved that boys and girls do not leave school wholly because of necessity to earn a living. Many urge their parents to let them work. It has also been proved that this early work of children is not profitable. They get into "blind alleys," and there is no way out to better pay as they grow older.

A most tragic story was recently related in a popular magazine. A factory inspector asked a large number of boys whether they would like to go back to school. They were working in factories that were not very good types, and hours were much longer than school hours, and yet the majority were better satisfied with factory than they had been in the school!

Changes must come in our schools. To sum up the whole question, we must decide whether we are going to use industry for education or let industry use education for its own purposes.

We have an educational inheritance adapted to the leisure classes. We have patched it up, but never seriously transformed it.

At the close of this lecture several questions were asked Dr. Dewey. One of the questions led Dr. Dewey to explain that children were required to skim over too much ground. Close, intensive study of one point is rare. Children do not need to memorize so much information, but they do need to learn how to get knowledge when they need it. We all need to get rid of the conception that we go to school to get information. We go to acquire certain habits, as physical control, management of materials, how to gather information when we need it to help us go on.

We must avoid too early specialization. We need prevocational training if it is not made too technical. Several cities are now doing good work along such lines. Dr. Dewey seemed to think almost any experiment would have to be pretty poor, not to improve upon many present courses in the seventh and eighth school years!

PROFESSOR DEWEY'S REPORT ON THE FAIRHOPE EXPERIMENT IN ORGANIC EDUCATION

When Marietta L. Johnson came out of the South a year or so ago and won a hearing among northern teachers for the educational experiment which she had been carrying on for six years at Fairhope, Ala., she alone could speak of her work from first-hand knowledge. Even when the Fairhope League was organized in the hope of putting her work on a permanent basis, Mrs. Johnson's word for what she had actually accomplished had to be taken on faith. People listened, believed and were glad, for from a region where illiteracy lies heaviest and the needs of childhood are most marked there had apparently come a gleam of promise.

The first rounded presentation of her work was published in *The Survey* last December, but even then, save for one or two hasty visits of educators traveling in that region, who could report nothing more definite than favorable impressions, no educational authority from the North had gone to Fairhope to see for himself.

This situation no longer exists. Prof. John Dewey of Columbia University, invited by the Fairhope League to visit Mrs. Johnson's school, has returned "without any doubt as to the school having made good." Professor Dewey's fourteen-year-old son accompanied him.

At the end of their first day Professor Dewey's son reported that all the children he talked to were "crazy about the school" and before the visit ended he begged to be left in Fairhope himself.

In his report to the league Professor Dewey says that before going he had expected that it would be necessary to make allowances because of obstacles against which the school had worked,—the inherent difficulties of any new step as well as the lack of means to secure properly trained

[First published in *Survey* 32 (1914): 199.]

teachers. "But while there were, of course, many details susceptible of improvement," he goes on, "I did not find it necessary to make nearly as many allowances as I had anticipated." To quote further:

"In my judgment the school has demonstrated that it is possible for children to lead the same natural lives in school that they lead in homes of the right sort outside of school; to progress bodily, mentally, and morally in school without factitious pressure, rewards, examinations, grades, or promotions: while they acquire sufficient control of the conventional tools of learning and of the study of books—reading, writing, and figuring—to be able to use them independently.

"The demonstration is all the more striking because of the odds against which Mrs. Johnson has labored and because of the simplicity of the means by which the results have been attained. Anybody who went to Fairhope expecting a revelation of wonderful new methods and devices would come away much disappointed. There are no tricks of the trade, no patent devices, no unique nor even peculiar appliances, no methods in one sense of that term.

"If the expression be not misunderstood, I would say that what impressed me most on the side of educational procedure was negative; namely, the absence of all special devices calculated to make up for the lack of the various forms of pressure usually brought to bear upon children. What has been done is simply to provide the conditions for wholesome, natural growth in small enough groups for the teacher (as a leader rather than as an instructor) to become acquainted with the weaknesses and powers of each child individually, and then to adapt the work to the individual needs.

"As a demonstration that normal growth and education are really identical, the school is more impressive than if it had had more external appliances and more skilled teachers at its command. In the latter case, the question might have been raised as to how far the desirable results were to be charged to the account of teachers and equipment and methods of instruction better than are found in the ordinary school. This does not mean, of course, that Mrs. Johnson's own personality has not counted for a very great deal—the existing school would have been impossible without such a personality, but at the same time what she has done has been to give her time, energy, devotion, and intelligence to seeing to it that the children had the opportunities of growth undistorted by external pressure."

Freedom in the school, declares Professor Dewey, is treated as a mental and moral matter, not as a matter of whim or caprice. He goes on:

"The school was not only orderly in the intellectual and moral sense—the only standard that ought really to be applied—but displayed a decent external order of the usual kind—save for the greater freedom of physical posture and movement and conversation. Both in Mrs. Johnson's own classes and in the manual training, taught by Mr. Johnson, children were busy, active and interested in their work, and there was no fooling at all."

Professor Dewey urges that Fairhope be kept as the experiment station and that its method be made to "spread and permeate the rural schools of the county and then of adjacent counties." The very simplicity of rural life in the South, he says, makes its education more plastic to radical changes.

As a further means of propagating the ideas and practices of the school he urges the training of local young men and women to carry on similar work in the vicinity, and the preparation of teachers from the North to undertake the work in the North. Mrs. Johnson, says Professor Dewey, should be relieved from constant financial worry. A guarantee fund covering a span of years, he declares, would give her opportunity for supervision; for greater attention to the assisting teachers; for her training work, as well as for trips north to make her work known and to give assistance and supervision to like attempts there.

THE PSYCHOLOGY OF SOCIAL BEHAVIOR

I

The first lecture, on "The Biological Basis of Behavior and Impulsive Activity," was given Monday evening, February 16th. After an introduction by President Richmond, Professor Dewey launched out at once into his discussion.

Bacon taught that men must study and control nature, —that knowledge is power. We have recovered somewhat from the first flush of expectation aroused by the great triumphs of his method, for while we have been successful in acquiring knowledge and power in the realm of inanimate nature, the other great problems—the moral and social ones —are still out of our control. We must increase our human knowledge, for our present science of human nature is, according to Professor Dewey, as pitifully inadequate as was the exact science of Bacon's day.

We can, therefore, have only a program at present, a possible method of approach, rather than a solution. The present lectures are chiefly a contribution to method.

The first necessity in any method is a knowledge of our elements, in this case a knowledge of man's original capacities. Without such knowledge we shall never be able to judge the various Utopias proposed from time to time. Utopias, according to Professor Dewey, are like perpetual motion machines. We shall always have them with us, but they spring essentially from a lack of knowledge of the elements of the problem.

No serious attempts at the solution of the problem of man's original capacities were made until after the middle of the last century, after Darwin. The first attempts were

[First published as a summary of Dewey's lectures in *Union Alumni Monthly* 3 (1914): 309–26.]

wrong in form. They were attempts to discover the innate ideas, whereas the beginnings of mind are undoubtedly simpler. The method was also wrong, consisting, as it did, in the introspection of mature minds.

Darwin studied children somewhat, but it was James who first saw the specific facts and their significance. He recognized that instincts and impulses are the original elements, and that they are more numerous in man than in the animals; so numerous, in fact, that they commonly inhibit one another. James noted, also, that modifications of instincts are the normal thing both in animals and in man.

Professor Dewey then proceeded to discuss these elementary statements. Instincts and impulses are so numerous that we react instinctively practically to every state and change in our environment. Selective attention is what is the acquired state. For there is no single power of attention, but a very large number of different attentions: ordinary attention is a collection of these, a summing up of a number of them, each definite though of much diversity. Most mental acts and reactions are similarly complex, and the analysis of even the simplest is extremely difficult and baffling. Thus spelling seems a simple act. Yet all investigations hitherto undertaken have failed to reach satisfactory explanations as to the causes of poor spelling. Spelling is a very complex act. Professor Dewey discussed seeing in a similar way, showing that it was an immensely complicated matter.

The many factors entering into these and other similar acts make many combinations and permutations possible. Hence the great modifiability of human reactions, and what we call educability. Failure to recognize this has had its bad effects on theories of motives. Nothing is more common than drawing up lists of human motives. The idea that man is actuated by a few simple motives—or by one, e.g., self-interest, or pleasure—was characterized by Professor Dewey as pure fiction. Such false explanation has given our social sciences a wrong twist at the very start. Even when the number of supposed motives has been quite large the result has been unfortunate. As a matter of fact, few acts have a single motive or even a single group of motives: in a sense a man's whole character is the motive power of every act he performs.

Moreover, motives are most often really habits, formed under social and other influences. Classification tends to take cause for effect in these cases and to hold that motives cause social phenomena, when most probably they are effects of social states. Professor Dewey illustrated this by comparing the savage mind with the civilized mind, holding that the differences here are not innate, but are the result of the difference in social states. He then stated the general subject of his lectures as the modification of social and mental facts by one another.

When any question of social reform arises, there are found to be two groups in the community, (1) those who think any desirable change practical, and (2) those who think human motive so fixed that any great change is impossible. Hence a great need of a social science and a method that will give us the facts, so that in each case we may know whether man is modifiable in the proposed way, for there is great social waste in propagating and carrying out schemes of social betterment that cannot succeed, just as it is important to be able to meet those who "merely from lack of imagination" fail to recognize the great modifiability of human nature.

As instances of modifiability, Professor Dewey noted some of the many forms of fear that arise, not naturally, but through social teachings, e.g., fear of punishment, of poverty, of losing caste, of hell, of the Lord, etc. Similarly, pugnacity, a primitive instinct of our nature, has been drafted off into many useful and other channels. In all such matters we must get at the facts more completely than we have done.

He discussed similarly a number of famous theories: Mallock's, that great political leaders must have great pecuniary rewards; the theory that there is an instinctive aversion to work; the theory of equality in the state as opposed to oligarchy. All were used to emphasize the need of a more elaborate collection of facts and a more scientific method in handling them.

II

The second lecture, on the "Formation of Mind by Social Occupations and Beliefs," was delivered Tuesday evening, February 17th.

Infants cry instinctively and without thought of any results. If, however, certain results occur—certain behavior on the part of parents or others—the instinct may become modified by these accidental consequences. It may become a "learned" impulse, that is, an impulse plus an intention. The child may mean to do it to secure certain results. The culture we get from others is all of this type. No training can be entirely foreign to instinct. Nurture must be built upon nature, and the two cannot be separated.

Neither can individual and social fields be separated. Professor Dewey discussed the theory that "generosity is originally social, while acquisitiveness is not." In some communities acquisitiveness is a social virtue, and generosity is a vice. Both may be social; or neither may be: both really need social control.

Gregariousness, again, is a fundamental instinct and must be reckoned with: nevertheless it is not the same as sociableness. Mere crowding is no sign of the social. Men may be gregarious and lonely. Education is needed to bring out social values. There is also an instinct of privacy. Too much gregariousness is too much to stand. This instinct also may be turned to account and have social value, as in science and art, and in thought in general.

Fear seems anti-social or non-social, yet it, too, has social values of many sorts, such as fear of punishment or of disapproval.

In seeking to clear up the relation of man to society we must first discover man's original traits. Attempts in this direction are very old. Thus Plato studied the traits of civilized communities, and from these sought the traits of individuals. Athenians were artistic; Spartans pugnacious, and so on. But can original traits be discovered in this way? Is not adult psychology largely a social product? Professor Dewey held that it is largely the environment that makes men have certain traits rather than others. We should thus be caught in a vicious circle, except for the fact that human beings are not born adults. We can study the child.

Babies are not without traits, else they could not learn. Man learns much because his nature is very rich. So rich is it, indeed, that at first it cumbers him to the point of helplessness. His instincts are loose and ravelling ends, and need help if they are to be carried to completion. Children brought up alone, like Kipling's Mowgli, said Professor Dewey, would be "idiots." Traditional psychology was profoundly wrong when it used to treat of the mind as solitary —as if it developed by itself in interaction with its environment.

Professor Dewey then gave a list of the impulses that are most useful in social development: 1. The watching and following up instinct,—seen even in very young children, who will follow a light with their eyes; 2. The brooding, hovering reactions, the affectionate regard for things as well as persons; (Lower animals do not sympathize with or brood over things.) 3. Timidity, caution—the foundation of judgment; 4. Pugnacity, tearing things apart—connected with logical analysis; 5. The play instinct—which Professor Dewey thinks is strongly developed in scientists, hunters of facts and truths; 6. The sense of symmetry and harmony—which he connected with logic and the sense of fairness.

Professor Dewey then laid considerable stress on the fact that children do not have two worlds, one of things and one of persons. Both elements are always entering in, and things always have social significance. This is also true of adults. We do not merely know; we also take an attitude toward things known, and this attitude is the attitude of our community, though we gain it without conscious learning. This is what makes it possible for man to advance rapidly from generation to generation, as the general tone of society changes. Our science is due to our tone toward the whole world; savage science is due to the savage tone toward it. This "tone" corresponds to the "traditional ideas" emphasized by Boas.

III

The third lecture, on "Mind and Language," was given Monday evening, February 23rd.

It is a remarkable thing that our thinking and our language are so closely bound up together, though language is so clearly a social product, and was not invented for thinking, but for social communication and intercourse. Nevertheless, the connection is inevitable. All men think in language of some sort. As Plato says, we talk to ourselves in thinking.

To show how this comes about, Professor Dewey examined the social conditions under which language originates. Children are controlled, taught, encouraged and discouraged, and their instinctive activities thus come to their notice and acquire meanings. This is the first awakening of the intelligence. Similarly things get meanings through experiment and use, and stand for definite relations. Later the child learns manners, and rudeness and politeness, with their social meanings, come to be recognized. These last are conventional and may include bodily expressions. Thus, among certain savages noisy eating is a courteous way of showing enjoyment at meals, and loud wailing is a sign of grief. Such acts are a kind of language. The instinctive sounds and cries have come to have meanings for others, and as they develop become real language. Speech is a kind of manners.

On the other hand, coöperation, as in hunting, is impossible without signals, and the voice was soon discovered to be the means of giving them most conveniently and economically. Gestures, however, play a very large part in savage inter-communication. Professor Dewey noted, also, that written language was originally pictorial gesture, and that it was developed and simplified to form writing.

In the course of time the number of signs, each with its meaning, increased and accumulated, until every social group brought to its members a large store of ideas thus preserved—chiefly in sounds or words. Thus we have the cumulative effect of civilization through language; and thus the range of intelligence of an individual comes to be closely dependent upon the language he uses. Professor Dewey called attention to the striking cases of Laura Bridgman and Helen Keller, whose minds were awakened by the acquirement of language.

The meanings of words are dependent upon social use. Names are keys of actions and rules and powers, not signs of ideas and information. The latter view Professor Dewey characterized as a "cold-storage" idea of language—a bookish library theory. The essential rule of language is that it is a symbol of action and that it makes common action possible. He discussed the reproach that "men are governed by phrases," and concluded that men must be so governed unless they are to be animals. The question is, "What phrases?"

Professor Dewey then discussed the matter of magic in names. Naming a thing takes the named object out of the general and puts it into the particular, establishes a relation of knowledge and intimacy and power. By an extension of this feeling, savages come to connect magic with name-giving. Personal names must be kept secret. The savage feels better able to resist and defy those who cannot order him under his true name, and he comes to fear those who might do so. Similarly, the names of the dead must not be spoken, for fear of recalling or angering them. The use of good names for evil things, to avoid causing their arousal, was noted as occurring "even among the Greeks." Of a similar nature are all spells and charms, and even the solemnity and impressiveness of the careful formalities found in documents and rituals. The chosen words carry with them a sense of power and fulfillment.

Somewhat similarly, even in our day and civilization, certain words tend to have a spell-like power over men's minds. Professor Dewey mentioned evolution, socialism, vibrations, infinity, forever, and, in philosophy, substance, essence, etc., as words of this class, having a power quite out of proportion to any contents they may have.

He mentioned, also, the seriousness attached to name-giving,—baptismal ceremonies, and the various elaborate rites among savages.

Names are also titles. To give a name dignifies the object and brings it up out of the common mass. Hence ultimately the general idea of office and rank.

In short, language raises what it touches from the physical condition to the realm of ideas, and of spirit, and on one side this leads directly to science, law, commerce, literature, and the like, which are not like magic, but are high modes of human intercourse.

IV

The fourth lecture, on "Emotionality and Rationality in Social Behavior," was given on Tuesday evening, March 24th.

Professor Dewey in this lecture changed from general considerations to the discussion of the individual mental life, and in this field he found the simplest distinction for purposes of classification to be that between the emotional and the rational. He then discussed these two phases of mental life, and especially the influence of the emotional over the rational.

Emotions are aroused in us by what affects us deeply, getting under our acquired habits, and calling forth our primal and unlearned attitudes of mind,—loves and hates, hopes and fears, elations and depressions. Politics and religion are subjects of this sort, and because of the violent reactions they arouse are regularly taboo in clubs and other general organizations.

Emotion is a state of suspense and instability. Anger, fear, hope and love cease to be themselves when completed. While they last, however, the whole body is literally affected. When we are elated or afraid we are pleased or scared all over. This "all-overness" is the essential trait of emotionalized activity.

Rationalized activity, on the other hand, runs only in selected channels. It is limited and distributed in its effect on the body. In a case of illness the physician illustrates rationalized activity; a relative of the patient may illustrate the emotionalized state. The relative meets the situation as an emotional whole; the physician analyzes and reacts to the details. Savages and children lack the habit of analysis.

Professor Dewey then proposed these definitions: Rationalized reaction is differentiated reaction; emotionalized reaction responds to a situation as a mass.

The two forms are not entirely exclusive of one another. Man without emotions is intellectually dead. Rationalized mental life either uses special emotions (such as curiosity), or else certain emotions have become steady. The true opposite of emotionalized action is routine action, which is split up like the rationalized, but which lacks emotion. Savages have a great aversion to routine. If necessary they add song and dance to their labors in order to add the emotional element. External pressure and the hope of reward take the place of this in civilized life,—with results that are not altogether good. The emotional side is likely to leak out in vices.

Emotion is by nature monopolizing, engrossing and attractive. It uses superlatives and is dogmatic. It makes the mind inaccessible to certain ideas, incapable of realizing those that are contrary or that are inconsistent with the emotions. Rationally, we ought to break up the mass and confine the emotion to the object properly arousing it. Professor Dewey gave many interesting and amusing illustrations at this point.

When emotions are felt in common by a number of persons, or by a group, movements, schools, and even a "spirit of the age" may be the result.

In any mind, however, the emotions control the details of thought. Any great sustained work in science or thought requires a controlling and sustained emotion. Analogies like that which Newton drew from the apple rest on feeling, and such emotional flashes may be very important. Logical processes must follow and develop the idea, but it is the emotional attitude that naturally anticipates, foreruns and invents proof and support.

Idealization is another form of surrender and commitment to a situation. Partisanship, hero-worship and patriotism are forms of idealization. In this sense we are all artists; we all idealize.

The acme of emotional idealism is the mystical religious experience, which is a condensed and distilled essence of what is found in all emotional states. On this head, Professor Dewey quoted largely Mr. James's *Varieties of Religious Experience*, calling attention to the detailed resemblance to other emotional experiences.

V

The fifth lecture, on "Crises and Behavior," was given on Thursday evening, March 5th.

Human conduct in order to be effective must be orderly and organized. Man first orders his bodily acts, then certain sequences of acts, and finally arrives at a plan of life.

Any such plan of life will be frequently invaded or threatened. The future is uncertain, and no plan can foresee the details. Physical facts also are sure to invade in unexpected ways. All this will be especially true among savages. Such invasions, or threats of them, are called crises.

With civilization these crises are minimized. Our life is steady and confident compared with that of savages. Not only do we know much more of nature and her laws, but our course of conduct is much more flexible and readjustable. We desire discoveries and changes; the savages do not. Even the Greeks did not. Politically we have arrangements to make new laws; the Greeks and Romans had no law-making bodies. Savage life is controlled by complicated chains of unchangeable customs. They are very far from having the freedom that certain poets and philosophers have supposed.

Savages, therefore, live with risks at a maximum, and with a rigid set of customs as their only method of conduct; the result is a series of crises, frequent and intense. The savage is, therefore, very emotional. He is always meeting new difficulties and always reacting to them in customary and undifferentiated ways. These customary acts and rites, however, tend to discharge and relieve the emotions, and to create confidence and illusions of success. Hence comes the illusion of their having magic power.

Success and failure thus come to be the great ideas. Good fortune, bad fortune, and the like, are deeper in savages than any thoughts of morals, truth, or reasonableness. Man is primarily interested in his own fate. Man's natural attitude toward things is not to ask what they are, but what they will do to him. This is the state of mind in animism.

A catalogue of the crises of savage life, said Professor Dewey, would exactly parallel the list of their rites.

In the individual life lie the crises of birth, puberty, marriage and death; and all these have their rites. In nature we have the recurrent crises of the seasons, especially of spring and autumn; and no savage people is without rites for sowing seed, and for joyous celebration of the harvest. Moreover, these, as recurrent and calculable, become formal and more inspiring in nature. Then there are the accidents of life, occasional illness, mental aberrations, etc., in the individual life, or pestilence, famine, war, victories, etc., in the group life, or perhaps danger from animals or from earthquakes, volcanic eruptions, flood or fire, or threats from shooting stars or comets, or, indeed, from anything irregular or extraordinary. All these situations have their customary acts and rites.

Professor Dewey then discussed the ideas that savages associate with their crises. The Algonquin Indians have generalized the cause of the crisis feeling under the name manitou. It is a mysterious, solemn power which may be compared in a sense with an electric charge. It may be found anywhere and in anything. It is found in brave warriors, sacred objects, sacred persons. Any animal hard to track or kill has it, e.g., the rabbit or the wildcat.

Manitou on the whole makes for health, but among nations where existence is harder and fear more prominent the power is more evil. Thus in Polynesia and Melanesia witchcraft and evil spells are the commonest association.

Other nations have not gone so far as to generalize, and we find merely a system of taboos, or commands absolutely forbidding certain things.

Discussing taboos, Professor Dewey said that many of them have arisen simply from the dislike of any change in habit or custom. Thus taboos on certain foods arose from the tribes not eating them in earlier history. Taboos on certain relations of men and women had their origin in certain divisions of labor. In a similar way are to be explained some of the details of religious rites, such as the retention of bronze or stone implements after civilization had advanced beyond them.

"Beginnings" always have religious significance, as being a break with previous established things. "Success" and "prosperity" are regularly thought of as inherently perilous. (The Greeks believed that the gods were "envious." Moderns believe in the "evil-eye," and some of us "knock wood.") Strangers are dangerous, and savages have rites to mitigate the danger from them.

Death is, however, the great crisis. Savages, like children, find it unnatural and unreal, except in cases of death by violence, in battle or by accident. Hence all other deaths and sicknesses are commonly supposed to be caused by witchcraft. Various taboos and rites are connected with death. On one hand there is the burying of the possessions of the dead, caused originally by an aversion toward anything that had touched the dead body; on the other hand there is the series of rites connected with ancestor worship.

VI

In the sixth lecture, given Friday evening, March 6th, Professor Dewey continued his subject, taking up the "Rationalistic Control of Crises."

Emotions are attitudes that pass naturally into action when restraint has been removed. The lost equilibrium must somehow be reëstablished. Industry, art and science are the ordinary forms taken for such action.

The earliest form of activity is that with tools, that is, the useful arts. These express a rationalistic control of things by methods of proved value. Such acts are effective, but not very interesting, mechanical rather than human. The situation arising from them is that of "toil." Now men are human beings (a fact often overlooked, said Professor Dewey), and are not interested in the uninteresting. They can be kept at toil only by stern necessity. It is not at all wonderful that savages follow only the interesting; the wonder is that civilized men are so rational.

Among savages, however, the lines are not clearly

drawn. Their implements are rarely purely useful, and there enters in an admixture of ceremonial and the finer arts. The crafts that make useful things make them also beautiful. If savage products are ugly, they are so from excess of ornament; their ugliness is not like the bareness of our ugliness. Professor Dewey quoted authority as to the singular beauty of the products of prehistoric man as well as those of savages. Two conditions conduced to this state of things: (1) Useful articles were not made for market and trade, and (2) industrial economic activities were connected with religion. Work and religious rites went on together, and no distinctions were made. Thus one Mexican savage dances while others hoe, weed, plant, etc., and his part is no less serious and exhausting than theirs.

Many crises are periodical and recurrent, and in such cases the rituals are more formal. Dancing grows to be a serious occupation, and its pantomime and singing come to reflect industrial occupations, useful arts, and the operations of nature. Professor Dewey gave illustrations from Australian savages, the Egyptians, and the Greeks and Romans. Such primitive pantomime, he said, is at once emotional, imaginative and practical, and as civilization develops may grow in directions implied by any one of its sides. Thus, among the Romans the religious activities came to be confined to special elected officials. Religion thus became prosaic and routine and businesslike, and life escaped the yoke of religious custom and was free to develop along practical lines. Athens, on the other hand, developed the imaginative and ideal sides of religion. As belief in magic grew less the rites were performed for their emotional value, and the performance was finally given for the onlookers. The result was a detachment and an ideal quality. Thus dancing, rhythm, song and plots were worked into artistic form.

The development of science has been slow and indirect. Man does not think for the sake of thinking, but reacts practically to situations as they arise. Thinking occurs through crises when the stimulus is of the right sort, but the natural man hates uncertainty, and in such cases rushes to a conclusion. This habit hinders progress in thought, but produces legends, myths, etc., and, when the power of religion has subsided, brings forth philosophic systems.

But the process of finding solutions is pleasant. It is a sort of game or hunt, and has been enjoyed more and more with time, so that at present scientists utilize and cultivate doubt for the mere pleasure of the hunt.

The great change to true science was brought about chiefly through an alliance between the useful arts and the abstract philosophies and sciences. In the 16th century intellectual men began to use tools, and not merely their brains. The astronomers took up the lens which heretofore had been made and used only for spectacles. That was a typical case, often repeated. Contempt for the craftsman had first to cease in order that this might happen.

Our age, finally, is a new development in history. The violence of crises is much diminished, though the number of them is still great. They come, however, now rather as individual shocks than as communal. Our communities are specialized and broken up, and do not react to them as wholes. Hence the increased importance of the individual in modern life.

VII

The seventh lecture, on the "Development of Private Judgment and Initiative," was given on Thursday evening, March 12th.

The nature of the Self is not to be defined. We know what it is to be a Self, but all definitions are meagre in comparison with the vivid fact. In its social relations, the Self is always the center of action and suffering. Certain traits in it are dominant and inevitable; others are transient. The first belong to the Self. Some of the traits are original, others acquired, but they are characteristic and consistent.

No two of us are the same Self. This is not accidental, but essential. Two peas in a pod are alike, but are not Selves, —that is the virtue of things,—but with human beings it is not so. We are not members of a class: each of us is unique. Historically the knowledge of this has been a growth. Custom has no use for individuals, and in simple states men are treated merely as members of a class.

Natural differences, however, do not of themselves constitute personality. They must be fused and developed. This is done in social life, which modifies them also. Thus an industrial society will not develop or be congenial to poets. The best developed personalities will in every case be of the type of the surrounding community. Each class also will develop its type. Thus it is a quality of the rich to be supercilious; and of the poor to be kind. Societies get the type they like and encourage and pay for. This law is as inevitable, said Professor Dewey, as that cacti should grow in deserts.

On the other hand, men have aggressive as well as accommodating tendencies. Men measure their strength by the resistance they can overcome: rejection may be a spur to effort. Many men like to get ahead by making themselves feared by others. Being a criminal may tempt certain persons. Children pretty regularly try out those in authority,—see how far they can go.

For most of us there are some persons with whom we agree; others whom we avoid; others whom we beat down. This is at first experiment. We learn thus what we are, and when it behooves us to be subservient, evasive, or aggressive. Self is thus something wrought out of original tendencies in the course of social intercourse.

A wholly consistent self is a practical impossibility. There are different groups to be responded to, and we tend to be different in each group. The child learns that what will go with other children will not be possible with grown-ups. And men similarly. Conscious hypocrisy, said Professor Dewey, is one of the rarest things in the world. Consistency is equally rare. Unity of personality is a moral ideal rather than a fact.

The periods of life also have their selves. The past self of our childhood and our mature present self may hardly have a speaking acquaintance with one another. Professor Dewey then went into a discussion of the characteristics of youth. Some have held that youth is radical and idealizing; others that it is conservative and conforming. It may well be both. With respect to things current in everyday life, youth is painfully conscious of deviations from conformity. In wider fields beyond, they show imaginative preferences, are radical, reforming, idealizing. They are a good influence in society in spite of the smiles of their elders. "Fools rush in where angels fear to tread," said Professor Dewey, "but that is why the world on the whole is more indebted to its fools than to its angels."

A discussion of heroism came next. Admiration is the natural response to exhibitions of power. Even the conquered admire. Being a "good loser" is founded in man's nature. Admiration is a sort of elation from feeling that we are participating in the success. A child idealizes his parents because they are the strong persons in a group in which he has a share. So in life, conspicuous ability in a group or nation attaches naturally to someone who stands out conspicuously; or, if there is no one, we hunt for or invent one. Thus the village with its professional ball-player or prize fighter feels with a glow of satisfaction and pride that its merits are at last beginning to be recognized. This sense of vicarious success is found in all men.

Approval is not merely sentimental, but often means active support. Power thus becomes not merely referred to, but conferred on men. This is often the case in politics, war and religion. Nothing succeeds like success, and, on the other hand, men lose power by the mere fact of a defeat.

Selfhood is representative of others. The I implies the thou, he, she, you and they. As in a good play each character shows what he is by responding to and calling out certain acts in others; so in life. No man can be a character if alone. He must get a response, else we do not know that we are selves.

Egotism and selfishness are hard to define in the abstract, though we know them in real life, and object to them. But we object also to self-less persons. One must assert himself, but when assertion passes certain limits it becomes a bad trait. Much selfishness is simply a lack of sense of self. The man simply follows certain impulses and tastes. Genuine thought of self includes thought of others and of one's social relations, as citizen, professional man, etc. Self-consciousness, in a good sense, is to know what one is and is good for socially.

The progress of civilization may be measured by the degree in which it produces individuality.

VIII

The last lecture of the course, on the "Significance of the Rise of Social Sciences," was given Friday evening, March 13th.

Social problems are interesting more persons today than at any other time previous to the eighteenth century. Indeed, the social problem itself is a modern way of looking at things, and it is coming to cover a wide range. Church unity, for instance, is being discussed not as a religious, but as a sociological question. "What will be the gain to the community?" is the form it now tends to take. In other centuries the question concerned religion itself and the creeds. This is an extreme case, but illustrates how far the social significance of acts and proposals is thought to extend. The number of problems that are considered as strictly social, on the other hand, is very large. Professor Dewey mentioned some of them: War, Liquor, Labor, Women and Child Labor, Labor Insurance, Reform of Courts, Prison Reform, Suffrage, Eugenics, City Hygiene, City Housing, City Planning, Marriage and Divorce, Tuberculosis, etc. In the past these would have been classified otherwise,—as political, novel, scientific, religious, etc. They are no longer isolated problems, but parts of the general question of the right ordering of human intercourse. This is a distinguishing trait of modern thought.

In the face of these numerous problems, sociological thought and action is in urgent need of becoming more scientific,—in the sense of having definite points of view, and definite instruments for attacking questions. We need more light, more adequate records and methods of inquiry.

Putting that matter aside for the moment, Professor Dewey continued by discussing one psychological feature common to all the social problems of our day.

Human affairs in the past were controlled and carried on by direct contact and response between individuals. This has ceased to be so. Society is much larger than it was, and we are, to a very large extent, influenced by persons we have never seen.

Plato was of the opinion that the state could not safely exceed the number of those who could recognize one another. Aristotle thought that the territory of the state should not be larger than could be taken in with the eye; the citizens not more than could hear a speaker. Their own states they thought too large to be true states. In ancient times, and, indeed, up to the eighteenth century, government was chiefly local. Local communities were almost undisturbed, except in times of war or for taxation.

Modern states are much bigger, but are also much more affected by influences from outside. Prosperity, routine of work and life, etc., are no longer local merely, but are fixed and determined from some perhaps distant source. Even the country village is caught in the general movement. The villagers read the newspapers and magazines, follow the fashions, make experiments of a thousand sorts; they are visited by friends, and they themselves use the trolleys, the telephones, and the rural post. They keep up with the times. Strictly local customs and traditions have well nigh disappeared. The doings of Europe are nearer than the next county was before the 18th century, and this not merely for news, but practically through the markets and through immigrants.

All this is so new that old thoughts and habits are at a loss to suit themselves to the change. The wonder is that the demoralization has not been greater. The downfall of Rome was due to migration, and it took a thousand years to recover from this disorganization. Yet we to-day are taking movements of populations with strange ideas, customs, etc., that are much larger. We have stood it, but not without shock. Old ideas and customs have met strange, contemptuous ones, and there has been a breakdown of class lines.

We cannot understand certain modern pathological phases of our life—increase of divorce, criminality, vagabondage and unemployment, relaxation of discipline, deterioration of manners, etc.—without reference to the breakdown of local traditions and customs, the lack of local social pressure, and the increase of outside and foreign influences.

In speaking of foreign influences, Professor Dewey noted that race prejudice in some of its present forms is a new thing. The "Yellow Peril" is a form that is strictly modern, and made possible only by immigration.

Continuing, he said that the older theory of representative government had broken down. It was believed that every man would be more active for his own private interests than any other, however wise, could be for him; therefore, all should vote and justice would be done. This may not have failed entirely; politics has been humanized; but the conception of each man alert and vigorous for his own interests is now grotesque. Men act in parties, and usually do not even know one man in fifty that they vote for. Professor Dewey gave a humorously true account of a New Yorker facing a huge ballot containing hundreds of names, few of which he had ever heard before, and none of which he really knew anything about. The growth in size and complexity in the modern state has changed the form of governmental problems. The old town-meeting has become impossible. Proposals like the short ballot, the initiative, etc., are attempts to get back to closer touch. Certainly we must get into touch or fall into indifference. It is one of our problems.

Many economic problems have the same source. The modern workman knows little of the source of his work, the use of it, the demand for it, or the social value of it. Men are doing work toward which they feel no interest or even an aversion. The average efficiency of workmen, said Professor Dewey, is calculated as 40 per cent—eloquent testimony that the man is not interested. It is bad for men to live so. This is a very serious phase of the labor problem.

Our civilization is not like a "melting pot," but rather like a conflict. And in order to meet the situation we must have social sciences comparable to the natural sciences. Under the old state there was no need of science, but at present the possibility of wise action depends upon being able to know the facts and draw intelligent inferences from experiments. We must meet the situation and not be overwhelmed by it. The twentieth century must create the social sciences, as the last century created the natural ones, said Professor Dewey, ending as he began.

PROFESSOR FOR SUFFRAGE

Summer Students at Columbia Hear Dr. Dewey's Arguments.

Prof. John Dewey talked to the Summer students of Columbia about woman suffrage and education yesterday afternoon. He was scheduled to speak on suffrage only, and so many people came to hear him that many could not get inside the doors. Women teachers would be better educators and boys particularly would be better educated by women if the women were enfranchised, Prof. Dewey said.

"Women are shut out of the most important social function," he said. "To have education what it should be we should have the educators educated. Education is life and experience. You can't have a real democracy where there is caste and cliques or sets. Women are shut out from the culmination and seal for full citizenship, the outward and visible sign of the inward and spiritual grace which is liberty."

[First published in *New York Times*, 9 August 1912, p. 3.]

Appendixes

Appendix 1

THE PROBLEM OF TRUTH IN THE LIGHT OF RECENT DISCUSSION[1]

by Josiah Royce

The question: What is Truth? is a typical philosophical problem. But it has been by no means at all times equally prominent throughout the history of philosophy. The ages in which it has come to the front have been those wherein, as at present, a keenly critical spirit has been predominant. At such times metaphysical interests are more or less subordinated, for a while, to the problems about method, to logical researches, or to the investigations which constitute a Theory of Knowledge.

Such periods, as we know, have recurred more than once since scholastic philosophy declined. And such a period was that which Kant dominated. But the sort of inquiry into the nature of truth which Kant's doctrine initiated quickly led, at the close of the eighteenth century, to a renewed passion for metaphysical construction. The problem regarding the nature of truth still occupied a very notable place in the doctrine of Fichte. It constituted one of the principal concerns, also, of Hegel's so much neglected and ill-understood *Phänomenologie des Geistes*. And yet both in the minds of the contemporaries of Fichte and of Hegel, and still more in those of their later disciples and opponents, the problem of truth went again into the background when compared with the metaphysical, the ethical, and the theological interests which constructive idealism and its opponents, in those days, came to represent. Hence wherever one looks, in the history of philosophical opinion between 1830 and 1870, one sees how the problem of truth, although never wholly

1. An address delivered before the International Congress of Philosophy at Heidelberg, in September, 1908.

[First published in *William James, and Other Essays* (New York: Macmillan Co., 1911). For Dewey's reply, see this volume, pp. 64–78.]

neglected, still remained, for some decades, out of the focus of philosophical interest.

But the scene rapidly changed about and after the year 1870. Both the new psychology and the new logic, which then began to flourish, seemed, erelong, almost equally to emphasize the importance of a reconsideration of the problem as to the nature of truth. These doctrines did this, especially because the question whether logic was henceforth to be viewed as a part of psychology became once more prominent, so soon as the psychological researches then undertaken had attracted the strong interest of the philosophical public. And meanwhile the revived interest in Kant, growing, as it did, side by side with the new psychology, called for a reinterpretation of the problems of the critical philosophy. The reawakening of Idealism, in England and in America, called attention, in its own way, to the same problem. The modern philosophical movement in France,—a movement which was, from the outset, almost equally made up of a devotion to the new psychology and of an interest in the philosophy of the sciences, has coöperated in insisting upon the need of a revision of the theory of truth. And to complete the story of the latest philosophy, recent tendencies in ethics, emphasizing as they have done the problems of individualism, and demanding a far-reaching reconsideration of the whole nature of moral truth, have added the weight of their own, often passionate, interest to the requirements which are here in question.

The total result is that we are just now in the storm and stress of a reëxamination of the whole problem of truth. About this problem the philosophical interest of to-day centers. Consequently, whether you discuss the philosophy of Nietzsche or of mathematics,—whether the *Umwertung aller Werte* or the "class of all classes,"—whether Mr. Russell's "Contradiction" or the *Uebermensch* is in question,—or whether none of these things attract you at all, so that your inquiries relate to psychology, or to evolution, or to the concepts of the historical sciences, or to whatever other region of philosophy you please,—always the same general issue has sooner or later to be faced. You are involved in some phase of the problem about the nature of truth.

So much, then, as a bare indication of the historical process which has led us into our present position. I propose, in the present address, to offer an interpretation of some of the lessons that, as I think, we may learn from the recent discussions of the problem whose place in all our minds I have thus indicated.

I

It seems natural to begin such a discussion by a classification of the main motives which are represented by the principal recent theories regarding the nature of truth. In enumerating these motives I need not dwell, in this company, upon those historical inferences and traditions whose presence in recent thought is most easily and universally recognized. That Empiricism,—due to the whole history of the English school, modified in its later expressions by the Positivism of a former generation, and by the types of Naturalism which have resulted from the recent progress of the special sciences,—that, I say, such empiricism has affected our modern discussion of the nature of truth,—this we all recognize. I need not insist upon this fact. Moreover, the place which Kant occupies in the history of the theory of truth,—that again is something which it is needless here to emphasize. And that the teaching of Fichte and of Hegel, as well as still other idealistic traditions, are also variously represented by present phases of opinion regarding our problem, we shall not now have to rehearse. I presuppose, then, these historical commonplaces. It is not, however, in terms of these that I shall now try to classify the motives to which the latest theories of truth are due.

These recent motives, viewed apart from those unquestionably real influences of the older traditions of the history of philosophy are, to my mind, three in number:

First, there is the motive especially suggested to us modern men by the study of the history of institutions, by our whole interest in what are called evolutionary processes, and by a large part of our recent psychological investigation. This is the motive which leads many of us to describe human life altogether as a more or less progressive adjustment to a natural environment. This motive incites us, therefore, to judge all human products and all human activities as instruments for the preservation and enrichment of man's natural existence. Of late this motive, whose modern forms are extremely familiar, has directly affected the theory of truth. The result appears in a part, although not in the whole, of what the doctrines known as Instrumentalism, Humanism, and Pragmatism have been of late so vigorously teaching, in England, in America, in Italy, in France, and, in still other forms, in Germany.

From the point of view which this motive suggests, human opinions, judgments, ideas, are part of the effort of a live creature to adapt himself to his natural world. Ideas and beliefs are, in a word, organic functions. And truth, in so far as we men can recognize truth at all, is a certain value belonging to such ideas. But this value itself is simply like the value which any natural organic function possesses. Ideas and opinions are instruments whose use lies in the fact that, if they are the right ones, they preserve life and render life stable. Their existence is due to the same natural causes that are represented in our whole organic evolution. Accordingly, assertions or ideas are true in proportion as they accomplish this their biological and psychological function. The value of truth is itself a biological and psychological value. The true ideas are the ones which adapt us for life as human beings. Truth, therefore, grows with our growth, changes with our needs, and is to be estimated in accordance with our success. The result is that all truth is as relative as it is instrumental, as human as it is useful.

The motive which recent Instrumentalism or Pragmatism expresses, in so far as it takes this view of the nature of truth, is of course in one sense an ancient motive. Every cultivated nation, upon beginning to think, recognizes in some measure such a motive. The Greeks knew this motive, and deliberately connected both the pursuit and the estimate of truth with the art of life in ways whose problematic aspects the Sophists already illustrated. Socrates and his followers, and later the Stoics as well as the Epicureans, also considered, in their various ways, this instrumental aspect of the nature of truth. And even in the Hindoo Upanishads one can find instances of such humanistic motives influencing the inquiry into the problem of truth. But it is true that the historical science of the nineteenth century, beginning, as it did, with its elaborate study of the history of institutions, and culminating in the general doctrines regarding evolution, has given to this motive an importance and a conscious definiteness such as makes its recent embodiment in Pragmatism a very modern and, in many ways, a novel doctrine about the nature of truth.

II

But closely bound up with this first motive in our recent thinking there is a second motive, which in several ways very strongly contrasts with the first. Yet in many minds these two motives are so interwoven that the writers in question are unaware which motive they are following when they utter their views about the nature of truth. No doubt one may indeed recognize the contrast between these motives, and may, nevertheless, urge good reasons for following in some measure both of them, each in its own way. Yet whoever blindly confuses them is inevitably led into hopeless contradictions. As a fact, a large number of our recent pragmatists have never learned consciously to distinguish them. Yet they are indeed easy to distinguish, however hard it may be to see how to bring them into a just synthesis.

This second motive is the same as that which, in ethics, is responsible for so many sorts of recent Individualism. It is the motive which in the practical realm Nietzsche glorified. It is the longing to be self-possessed and inwardly free, the determination to submit to no merely external authority. I need not pause to dwell upon the fact that, in its application to the theory of truth, precisely as in its well-known applications to ethics, this motive is Protean. Every one of us is, I suppose, more or less under its influence.

Sometimes, this motive appears mainly as a skeptical motive. Then it criticizes, destructively, traditional truth and thereupon leaves us empty of all assurances. But sometimes it assumes the shape of a sovereign sort of rationalism, whereby the thinking subject, first rebelling against outer authority, creates his own laws, but then insists that all others shall obey these laws. In other cases, however, it takes the form of a purely subjective idealism, confident of its own but claiming no authority. Or again, with still different results, it consciously unites its ethical with its theoretical interests, calls itself "Personal Idealism," and regards as its main purpose, not only the freeing of the individual from all spiritual bondage, theoretical and practical, but also the winning for him of an inner harmony of life. In general, in its highest as in some of its less successful embodiments, when it considers the sort of truth that we ought most to pursue, this motive dwells, as Professor Eucken has so effectively taught it to dwell, upon the importance of a *Lebensanschauung* as against the rigidity and the pretended finality of a mere *Weltanschauung*.

But meanwhile, upon occasion, this same motive embodies itself in various tendencies of the sort known as Irrationalism. In this last case, it points out to us how the intelligence, after all, is but a single and a very narrow function of our nature, which must not be allowed to supersede or even too much to dominate the rest of our complex and essentially obscure, if fascinating, life. Perhaps, on the very highest levels of life, as it hereupon suggests to us: *Gefühl ist alles*. If not, then at all events, we have the alternative formula: *Im Anfang war die Tat*. Or, once again, the solving word of the theory of truth is Voluntarism. Truth is won by willing, by creative activities. The doer, or perhaps the deed, not only finds, but *is*, the truth. Truth is not to be copied, but to be created. It is living truth. And life is action.

I have thus attempted to indicate, by well-known phrases, the nature of this second motive,—one whose presence in our recent theories of truth I believe that you will all recognize. Despite the Protean character and (as you will all at once see) the mutually conflicting characters of its expressions, you will observe, I think, its deeper unity, and also its importance as an influence in our age. With us at present it acts as a sort of ferment, and also as an endless source of new enterprises. It awakens us to resist the most various kinds of doctrinal authority,—scientific, clerical, academic, popular. It inspires countless forms of Modernism, both within and without the boundaries of the various confessions of Christendom. As an effective motive, one finds it upon the lowest as also upon the highest levels of our intellectual and moral life. In some sense, as I have said, we all share it. It is the most characteristic and the most problematic of the motives of the modern world. Anarchism often appeals to it; yet the most saintly form of devotion, the most serious efforts for the good of mankind, and our sternest and loftiest spiritual leaders, agree in employing it, and in regarding it as in some sense sacred.

Our age shares this motive with the age of the French Revolution, of the older Idealistic movement, and of the Romantic School. All the more unfortunate, as I think, is the fact that many who glory in the originality of their own recent opinions about the nature of truth, know so little of the earlier history of this motive, read so seldom the lesson of the past, and are thus so ill-prepared to appreciate both the spiritual dignity and the pathetic paradox of this tendency to make the whole problem of truth identical with the problem of the rights and the freedom of the individual.

III

I turn herewith to the third of the motives that I have to enumerate. In its most general form it is a very ancient and familiar motive. It is, indeed, very different from both of the foregoing. Superficially regarded, it seems, at first sight, less an expression of interests that appear ethical. At heart, however, it is quite as deep a motive as either of the others, and it is in fact a profoundly ethical motive as well as a genuinely intellectual one. One may say that, in a sense and to some degree, it pervades the whole modern scientific movement, is present wherever two or three are gathered together for a serious exchange of scientific opinions, and is, in most cases, the one motive that, in scientific assemblies, is more or less consciously in mind whenever somebody present chances to refer to the love of truth, or to the scientific conscience of his hearers.

I have called this third on our list of motives an ancient

motive. It is so. Yet in modern times it has assumed very novel forms, and has led to scientific and, in the end, to philosophical enterprises which, until recently, nobody would have thought possible.

It would be unwise at this point to attempt to define this motive in abstract terms. I must first exemplify it. When I say that it is the motive to which the very existence of the exact sciences is due, and when I add the remark that our scientific common sense knows this motive as the fondness for dispassionately weighing evidence, and often simply names it the love of objectivity, I raise more questions in your minds regarding the nature of this motive than at this point I can answer. If, however, anybody suggests, say from the side of some form of recent pragmatism, that I must be referring to the nowadays so deeply discredited motives of a pure "Intellectualism," I repudiate at once the suggestion. The motive to which I refer is intensely practical. Men have lived and died for it, and have found it inestimably precious. I know of no motive purer or sweeter in human life. Meanwhile, it indeed chances to be the motive which has partially embodied itself in Pure Mathematics. And neither the tribe of Nietzsche nor the kindred of the instrumentalists have been able justly to define it.

What I am just now interested to point out is that this motive has entered, in very novel ways, into the formulation of certain modern theories of truth. And when I speak of its most novel forms of expression, the historical process to which I refer is the development of the modern critical study of the foundations of mathematics.

To philosophical students in general the existence of metageometrical researches, which began at the outset of the nineteenth century, has now been made fairly familiar. But the non-Euclidean geometry is but a small fragment of that investigation of the foundations of mathematical truth which went on so rapidly during the nineteenth century. Among the most important of the achievements of the century in this direction were the new definitions of continuity and the irrational numbers, the modern exact theory of limits, and the still infant theory of Assemblages. Most important of all, to my mind, were certain discoveries in the field of Logic of which I shall later say a word. I mention these matters here as examples of the influence of a motive whose highly technical applications may make it seem to one at a distance hopelessly intellectualistic, but whose relation to the theory of truth is close, just because, as I think, its relation to truly ethical motives is also extremely intimate.

The motive in question showed itself at the outset of the nineteenth century, and later in the form of an increased conscientiousness regarding what should be henceforth accepted as a rigid proof in the exact sciences. The Greek geometers long ago invented the conception of rigid methods of proof and brought their own methods, in certain cases, very near to perfection. But the methods that they used proved to be inapplicable to many of the problems of modern mathematics. The result was that, in the seventeenth and eighteenth centuries, the mathematical sciences rapidly took possession of new realms of truth, but in doing so sacrificed much of the old classic rigidity. Nevertheless, regarded as the instrumentalists now desire us to regard truth, the mathematical methods of the eighteenth century were indeed incomparably more successful in adjusting the work of the physical sciences to the demands of experience than the methods of the Greek geometers had ever been. If instrumentalism had been the whole story of man's interest in truth, the later developments would have been impossible. Nevertheless the modern scientific conscience somehow became increasingly dissatisfied with its new mathematical possessions. It regarded them as imperfectly won. It undertook to question, in a thousand ways, its own methods and its own presuppositions. It learned to reject altogether methods of proof which, for a time, had satisfied the greatest constructive geniuses of earlier modern mathematics. The result has been the development of profoundly novel methods, both of research and of instruction in the exact sciences. These methods have in many ways brought to a still higher perfection the Greek ideal of rigid proof. Yet the same methods have shown themselves to be no mere expressions of a pedantic intellectualism. They have meant clearness, self-possession, and a raising of the scientific conscience to higher levels. Meanwhile, they proved potent both in conquering new realms and in discovering the wonderful connections that we now find linking together types of exact truth which at first sight appeared to be hopelessly diverse.

In close union with the development of these new methods in the exact sciences, and, as I may say, in equally close union with this new scientific conscience, there has gradually come into being a reformed Logic,—a logic still very imperfectly expounded in even the best modern textbooks, and as yet hardly grasped, in its unity, by any one investigator,—but a logic which is rapidly progressing, which is full of beauty, and which is destined, I believe, profoundly to influence, in the near future, our whole philosophy of truth. This new logic appears to offer to us an endless realm for detailed researches. As a set of investigations it is as progressive as any instrumentalist can desire. The best names for it, I think, are the names employed by several different thinkers who have contributed to its growth. Our American logician, Mr. Charles Peirce, named it, years ago, the Logic of Relatives. Mr. Russell has called it the Logic, or the Calculus, of Relations. Mr. Kempe has proposed to entitle it the Theory of Mathematical Form. One might also call it a new and general theory of the Categories. Seen from a distance, as I just said, it appears to be a collection of highly technical special researches, interesting only to a few. But when one comes into closer contact with any one of its serious researches, one sees that its main motive is such as to interest every truthful and reflective inquirer who really grasps that motive, while the conception of truth which it forces upon our attention is a conception which neither of the other motives just characterized can be said adequately to express.

In so far as the new logic has up to this time given shape to philosophical theories of truth, it in part appears to tend towards what the pragmatists nowadays denounce as Intellectualism. As a fact Mr. Bertrand Russell, the brilliant and productive leader of this movement in England, and his philosophical friend Mr. George Moore, seem to regard their own researches as founded upon a sort of new Realism, which views truth as a realm wholly independent of the constructive activities by which we ourselves find or pursue truth. But the fact that Mr. Charles Peirce, one of the most inventive of the creators of the new logic, is also viewed by the Pragmatists as the founder of their own method, shows how the relation of the new logic to the theory of truth is something that still needs to be made clear. As a fact, I believe that the outcome of the new logic will be a new synthesis of Voluntarism and Absolutism.

What I just now emphasize is, that this modern revision of the concepts of the exact sciences, and this creation of a new logic, are in any case due to a motive which is at once theoretical and ethical. It is a motive which has defined standards of rigidity in proof such as were, until recently, unknown. In this sense it has meant a deepening and quickening of the scientific conscience. It has also seemed, in so far, to involve a rejection of that love of expediency in thinking which is now a favorite watchword of pragmatists and instrumentalists. And when viewed from this side the new logic obviously tends to emphasize some form of absolutism, to reject relativism in thinking, to make sterner requirements upon our love of truth than can be expressed in terms of instrumentalism or of individualism. And yet the motive which lies beneath this whole movement has been, I insist, no barren intellectualism. The novelty of the constructions to which this motive has led,—the break with tradition which the new geometry (for instance) has involved,—such things have even attracted, from a distance, the attention of some of the least exactly trained of the pragmatist thinkers, and have aroused their hasty and uncomprehending sympathy. "This non-Euclidean geometry," they have said, "these novel postulates, these '*freie Schöpfungen des menschlichen Geistes*' (as Dedekind, himself one of the great creative minds of the new logical movement, has called the numbers),—well, surely these must be instances in favor of *our* theory of truth. Thus, as we should have predicted, novelties appear in what was supposed to be an absolutely fixed region. Thus (as Professor James words the matter), human thought 'boils over,' and ancient truths alter, grow, or decay." Yet when modern pragmatists and relationists use such expressions, they fail to comprehend the fact that the new discoveries in these logical and mathematical fields simply exemplify a *more* rigid concept of truth than ever, before the new movement began, had been defined in the minds of the mathematicians themselves. The non-Euclidean geometry, strange to say, is not a discovery that we are any freer than we were before to think as we like regarding the system of geometrical truth. It is one part only of what Hilbert has called the "logical analysis" of our concept of space. When we take this analysis as a whole, it involves a deeper insight than Euclid could possibly possess into the unchangeable necessities which bind together the system of logical relationships that the space of our experience merely exemplifies. Nothing could be more fixed than are these necessities. As for the numbers, which Dedekind called *"freie Schöpfungen,"* —well, his own masterpiece of logical theory is a discovery and a rigid demonstration of a very remarkable and thoroughly objective truth about the fundamental relations in terms of which we all of us do our thinking. His proof that all of the endless wealth of the properties of the ordinal numbers follows from a certain synthesis of two of the simplest of our logical conceptions, neither one of which, when taken alone, seems to have anything to do with the conception of order or of number,—this proof, I say, is a direct contribution to a systematic theory of the categories, and, as such, is, to the logical inquirer, a dramatically surprising discovery of a realm of objective truth, which nobody is free to construct or to abandon at his pleasure. If this be relativism, it is the relativism of an eternal system of relations. If this be freedom, it is the divine freedom of a self-determined, but, for that very reason, absolutely necessary fashion of thought and of activity.

Well,—to sum up,—this third motive in modern inquiry has already led us to the discovery of what are, for us, novel truths regarding the fundamental relations upon which all of our thought and all of our activity rest. These newly discovered truths possess an absoluteness which simply sets at naught the empty trivialities of current relativism. Such truth has, in fact, the same sort of relation to the biologically "instrumental" value of our thinking processes as the Theory of Numbers (that "divine science," as Gauss called it) has to the account books of the shopkeeper.

And yet, as I must insist, the motive that has led us to

this type of absolutism is no pure intellectualism. And the truth in question is as much a truth about our modes of activity as the purest voluntarism could desire it to be. In brief, there is, I believe, an absolute voluntarism, a theory of the way in which activities must go on if they go on at all. And, as I believe, just such a theory is that which in future is to solve for us the problem of the nature of truth.

I have illustrated our third motive at length. Shall I now try to name it? Well, I should say that it is at bottom the same motive that lay at the basis of Kant's Critical Philosophy; but it is this motive altered by the influence of the modern spirit. It is the motive which leads us to seek for clear and exact self-consciousness regarding the principles both of our belief and of our conduct. This motive leads us to be content only in case we can indeed find principles of knowledge and of action,—principles, not mere transient expediences, and not mere caprices. On the other hand, this motive bids us decline to accept mere authority regarding our principles. It requires of us freedom along with insight, exactness side by side with assurance, and self-criticism as well as search for the ultimate.

IV

In thus sketching for you these three motives, I have been obliged to suggest my estimate of their significance. But this estimate has so far been wholly fragmentary. Let me next indicate the sense in which I believe that each of these three motives tends, in a very important sense, to throw light upon the genuine theory of truth.

I begin here with the first of the three motives,—namely, with the motive embodied in recent instrumentalism. Instrumentalism views truth as simply the value belonging to certain ideas in so far as these ideas are biological functions of our organisms, and psychological functions whereby we direct our choices and attain our successes.

Wide and manifold are the inductive evidences which the partisans of such theories of truth adduce in support of their theory. There is the evidence of introspection and of the modern psychological theory of the understanding. Opinions, beliefs, ideas,—what are they all but accompaniments of the motor processes whereby, as a fact, our organisms are adjusted to their environment? To discover the truth of an idea, what is that for any one of us but to observe our success in our adjustment to our situation? Knowledge is power. Common sense long ago noted this fact. Empiricism has also since taught us that we deal only with objects of experience. The new instrumentalism adds to the old empiricism simply the remark that we possess truth in so far as we learn how to control these objects of experience. And to this more direct evidence for the instrumental theory of truth is added the evidence derived from the whole work of the modern sciences. In what sense are scientific hypotheses and theories found to be true? Only in this sense, says the instrumentalist, —only in this sense, that through these hypotheses we acquire constantly new sorts of control over the course of our experience. If we turn from scientific to moral truth, we find a similar result. The moral ideas of any social order are practical plans and practical demands in terms of which this social order endeavors, by controlling the activities of its members, to win general peace and prosperity. The truth of moral ideas lies solely in this their empirical value in adjusting individual activities to social demands, and in thus winning general success for all concerned.

Such are mere hints of the evidences that can be massed to illustrate the view that the truth of ideas is actually tested, and is to be tested, by their experienced workings, by their usefulness in enabling man to control his empirically given situation. If this be the case, then truth is always relative to the men concerned, to their experience, and to their situations. Truth grows, changes, and refuses to be tested by absolute standards. It *happens* to ideas, in so far as they *work*. It belongs to them when one views them as instruments to an end. The result of all this is a relativistic, an evolutionary, theory of truth. For such a view logic is a part of psychology,—a series of comments upon certain common characteristics of usefully working ideas and opinions. Ethical theory is a branch of evolutionary sociology. And in general, if you want to test the truth of ideas and opinions, you must look forward to their workings, not backward to the principles from which they might be supposed to follow, nor yet upwards to any absolute standards which may be supposed to guide them, and least of all to any realm of fixed facts that they are supposed to be required, willy nilly, to copy. Truth is no barren repetition of a dead reality, but belongs, as a quality, to the successful deeds by which we produce for ourselves the empirical realities that we want.

Such is the sort of evidence which my friends, Professor James and Professor Dewey, and their numerous followers, in recent discussion, have advanced in favor of this instrumental, practical, and evolutionary theory of truth. Such are the considerations which, in other forms, Mach has illustrated by means of his history and analyses of the work of modern science.

Our present comment upon this theory must be given in a word. It contains indeed a report of the truth about our actual human life, and about the sense in which we all seek and test and strive for truth, precisely in so far as truth-seeking is indeed a part of our present organic activities. But the sense in which this theory is thus indeed a true account of a vast range of the phenomena of human life is not reducible to the sense which the theory itself ascribes to the term "truth."

For suppose I say, reporting the facts of the history of science: "Newton's theory of gravitation proved to be true, and its truth lay in this: The definition and the original testing of the theory consisted in a series of the organic and psychological functions of the live creature Newton. His theories were for him true in so far as, after hard work, to be sure, and long waiting, they enabled him to control and to predict certain of his own experiences of the facts of nature. The same theories are still true for us because they have successfully guided, and still guide, certain observations and experiences of the men of to-day." This statement reduces the truth of Newton's theory to the type of truth which instrumentalism demands. But in what sense is my account of this matter itself a true account of the facts of human life? Newton is dead. As mortal man he succeeds no longer. His ideas, as psychological functions, died with him. His earthly experiences ceased when death shut his eyes. Wherein consists to-day, then, the historical truth that Newton ever existed at all, or that the countless other men whom his theories are said to have guided ever lived, or experienced, or succeeded? And if I speak of the men of to-day, in what sense is the statement true that they now live, or have experience, or use Newton's theory, or succeed with it as an instrument? No doubt all these historical and socially significant statements of mine are indeed substantially true. But does their truth consist in my success in using the ideal instruments that I use when I utter these assertions? Evidently I mean, by calling these my own assertions true, much more than I can interpret in terms of my experience of their success in guiding my act.

In brief, the truth that historical events ever happened at all; the truth that there ever was a past time, or that there ever will be a future time; the truth that anybody ever succeeds, except in so far as I myself, just now, in the use of these my present instruments for the transient control of my passing experience chance to succeed; the truth that there is any extended course of human experience at all, or any permanence, or any long-lasting success,—well, all such truths, they are indeed true, but their truth cannot possibly consist in the instrumental value which any man ever experiences as belonging to any of his own personal ideas or acts. Nor can this truth consist in anything that even a thousand or a million men can separately experience, each as the success of his own ideal instruments. For no one man experiences the success of any man but himself, or of any instruments but his own; and the truth, say, of Newton's theory consists, by hypothesis, in the perfectly objective fact that generations of men have really succeeded in guiding their experience by this theory. But that this is the fact no man, as an individual man, ever has experienced or will experience under human conditions.

When an instrumentalist, then, gives to us his account of the empirical truth that men obtain through using their ideas as instruments to guide and to control their own experience, his account of human organic and psychological functions may be,—yes, is,—as far as it goes, true. But if it is true at all, then it is true as an account of the characters actually common to the experience of a vast number of men. It is true, if at all, as a report of the objective constitution of a certain totality of facts which we call human experience. It is, then, true in a sense which no man can ever test by the empirical success of his own ideas as his means of controlling his own experiences. Therefore the truth which we must ascribe to instrumentalism, if we regard it as a true doctrine at all, is precisely a truth, not in so far as instrumentalism is itself an instrument for helping on this man's or that man's way of controlling his experience. If instrumentalism is true, it is true as a report of facts about the general course of history, of evolution, and of human experience,—facts which transcend every individual man's experience, verifications, and successes. To make its truth consist in the mere sum of the various individual successes is equally vain, unless indeed that sum is a fact. But no individual man ever experiences that fact.

Instrumentalism, consequently, expresses no motive which by itself alone is adequate to constitute any theory of truth. And yet, as I have pointed out, I doubt not that instrumentalism gives such a substantially true account of man's natural functions as a truth seeker. Only the sense in which instrumentalism is a true account of human life is opposed to the adequacy of its own definition of truth. The first of our three motives is, therefore, useful only if we can bring it into synthesis with other motives. In fact it is useless to talk of the success of the human spirit in its efforts to win control over experience, unless there is indeed a human spirit which is more than any man's transient consciousness of his own efforts, and unless there is an unity of experience, an unity objective, real, and supratemporal in its significance.

V

Our result so far is that man indeed uses his ideas as means of controlling his experience, and that truth involves such control, but that truth cannot be defined solely in terms of our personal experience of our own success in obtaining this control.

Hereupon the second of the motives which we have found influencing the recent theories of truth comes to our aid. If instrumentalism needs a supplement, where are we, the individual thinkers, to look for that supplement, except in those inner personal grounds which incline each of us to make his own best interpretation of life precisely as he can, in accordance with his own will to succeed, and in accordance with his individual needs?

To be sure, as one may still insist, we are always dealing with live human experience, and with its endless constraints and limitations. And when we accept or reject opinions, we do so because, at the time, these opinions seem to us to promise a future empirical "working," a successful "control" over experience,—in brief, a success such as appeals to live human beings. Instrumentalism in so far correctly defines the nature which truth possesses in so far as we ever actually verify truth. And of course we always believe as we do because we are subject to the constraint of our present experience. But since we are social beings, and beings with countless and varied intelligent needs, we constantly define and accept as valid very numerous ideas and opinions whose truth we do not hope personally to verify. Our act in accepting such unverified truths is (as Professor James states the case) essentially similar to the act of the banker in accepting credit values instead of cash. A note or other evidence of value is good if it *can* be turned into cash at some agreed time, or under specified conditions. Just so, an idea is true, not merely at the moment when it enables somebody to control his own experience. It is true if, under definable conditions which, as a fact, you or I may never verify, it *would* enable some human being whose purposes agree with ours to control his own experience. If we personally do not verify a given idea, we can still accept it then upon its credit value. We can accept it precisely as paper, which cannot now be cashed, is accepted by one who regards that paper as, for a given purpose, or to a given extent, equivalent to cash. A bond, issued by a government, may promise payment after fifty years. The banker may to-day accept such a bond as good, and may pay cash for it, although he feels sure that he personally will never live to see the principal repaid by the borrower.

Now, as Professor James would say, it is in this sense that our ideas about past time, and about the content of other men's minds, and about the vast physical world, "with all its stars and milky ways," are accepted as true. Such ideas have for us credit values. We accept these ideas as true because we need to trade on credits. Borrowed truth is as valuable in the spiritual realm as borrowed money is in the commercial realm. To believe a now unverified truth is simply to say: "I accept that idea, upon credit, as equivalent to the cash payments in terms of live experience which, as I assert, I could get in case I had the opportunity."

And so much it is indeed easy to make out about countless assertions which we all accept. They are assertions about experience, but not about our present experience. They are made under various constraints of convention, habit, desire, and private conviction, but they are opinions whose truth is for us dependent upon our personal assent and acquiescence.

Herewith, however, we face what is, for more than one modern theory of truth, a very critical question. Apparently it is one thing to say: "I accept this opinion upon credit," and quite another thing to say: "The truth of this opinion consists, solely and essentially, in the fact that it is credited by me." In seeming, at least, it is one thing to assert: "We trade upon credit; we deal in credits," and quite another thing to say: "There is no value behind this bond or behind this bit of irredeemable paper currency, except its credit value." But perhaps a modern theory of truth may decline to accept such a difference as ultimate. Perhaps this theory may say: The truth *is* the credit. As a fact, a vast number of our human opinions—those, for instance, which relate to the past, or to the contents of other men's minds—appear, within the range of our personal experience, as credits whose value we, who believe the opinions, cannot hope ever to convert into the cash of experience. The banker who holds the bond not maturing within his own lifetime can, after all, if the bond is good, sell it to-day for cash. And that truth which he can personally and empirically test whenever he wants to test, is enough to warrant his act in accepting the credit. But I, who am confident of the truths of history, or of geology, or of physics, and who believe in the minds of other men,—I accept as valid countless opinions that are for me, in my private capacity and from an empirical point of view, nothing but irredeemable currency. In vain do I say: "I *could* convert these ideas into the cash of experience *if* I were some other man, or *if* I were living centuries ago instead of to-day." For the question simply recurs: In what sense are these propositions about my own possible experience true when I do not test their truth,—yes, true although I, personally, *cannot* test their truth? These credits, irredeemable in terms of the cash of my experience, —wherein consists their true credit value?

Here one apparently stands at the parting of the ways. One can answer this question by saying: "The truth of these assertions (or their falsity, if they are false) belongs to them whether I credit them or no, whether I verify them or not. Their truth or their falsity is their own character and is independent of my credit and my verification." But to say this appears to be, after all, just the intellectualism which so many of our modern pragmatists condemn. There remains, however, one other way. One can say: "The truth of the unverified assertions *consists simply in the fact that*, for our own private and individual ends, *they are credited*. Credit is relative to the creditor. If he finds that, on the whole, it meets his purpose to credit, he credits. And there is no truth, apart from present verifications, except this truth of credit." In other words, that is true for me which I find myself accepting as my way of reacting to my situation.

This, I say, is a theory of truth which can be attempted. Consider what a magnificent freedom such a theory gives to all of us. Credit is relative to the creditor. To be sure, if ever the day of reckoning should come, one would be subject, at the moment of verification, to the constraints of experience. At such times, one would either get the cash or would not get it. But after all very few of our ideas about this great and wonderful world of ours ever are submitted to any such sharp tests. History and the minds of other men,—well, our personal opinions about these remain credits that no individual amongst us can ever test for himself. As your world is mainly made up of such things, your view of your world remains, then, subject to your own needs. It ought to be thus subject. There is no absolute truth. There is only the truth that you need. Enter into the possession of your spiritual right. Borrow Nietzsche's phraseology. Call the truth of ordinary intellectualism mere *Sklavenwahrheit.* It pretends to be absolute; but only the slaves believe in it. "Henceforth," so some Zarathustra of a new theory of truth may say, "I teach you *Herrenwahrheit.*" Credit what you choose to credit. Truth is made for man, not man for truth. Let your life "boil over" into new truth as much as you find such effervescence convenient. When, apart from the constraints of present verification, and apart from mere convention, I say: "This opinion of mine is true," I mean simply: "To my mind, lord over its own needs, this assertion now appears expedient." Whenever my expediency changes, my truth will change.

But does anybody to-day hold just *this* theory of truth? I hesitate to make accusations which some of my nearest and dearest friends may repudiate as personally injurious. But this I can say: I find a great many recent theorists about truth talking in just this spirit so long as they feel free to glorify their spiritual liberty, to amuse their readers with clever assaults upon absolutism, and to arouse sympathy by insistence upon the human and the democratic attractiveness of the novel views of truth that they have to advance. Such individualism, such capriciousness, is in the air. Our modern theorists of truth frequently speak in this way. When their expressions of such views are criticized, they usually modify and perhaps withdraw them. What, as individuals, such teachers really mean, I have no right to say. Nobody but themselves can say; and some of them seem to say whatever they please. But this I know: Whoever identifies the truth of an assertion with his own individual interest in making that assertion may be left to bite the dust of his own confusion in his own way and time. The outcome of such essential waywardness is not something that you need try to determine through controversy. It is self-determined. For in case I say to you: "The sole ground for my assertions is this, that I please to make them,"—well, at once I am defining exactly the attitude which we all alike regard as the attitude of one who chooses *not* to tell the truth. And if, hereupon, I found a theory of truth upon generalizing such an assertion,—well, I am defining as truth-telling precisely that well-known practical attitude which is the contradictory of the truth-telling attitude. The contrast is not one between intellectualism and pragmatism. It is the contrast between two well-known attitudes of will,—the will that is loyal to truth as an universal ideal, and the will that is concerned with its own passing caprices. If I talk of truth, I refer to what the truth-loving sort of will seeks. If hereupon I define the true as that which the individual personally views as expedient in opinion or in assertion, I contradict myself, and may be left to my own confutation. For the position in which I put myself, by this individualistic theory of truth, is closely analogous to the position in which Epimenides the Cretan, the hero of the fallacy of the liar, was placed by his own so famous thesis.

VI

And yet, despite all this, the modern assault upon mere intellectualism is well founded. The truth of our assertions is indeed definable only by taking account of the meaning of our own individual attitudes of will, and the truth, whatever else it is, is at least instrumental in helping us towards the goal of all human volition. The only question is whether the will really means to aim at doing something that has a final and eternal meaning.

Herewith I suggest a theory of truth which we can understand only in case we follow the expressions of the third of the three modern motives to which I have referred. I have said that the new logic and the new methods of reasoning in the exact sciences are just now bringing us to a novel comprehension of our relation to absolute truth. I must attempt a very brief indication as to how this is indeed the case.

I have myself long since maintained that there is indeed a logic of the will, just as truly as there is a logic of the intellect. Personally, I go further still. I assert: all logic is the logic of the will. There is no pure intellect. Thought is a mode of action, a mode of action distinguished from other modes mainly by its internal clearness of self-consciousness, by its relatively free control of its own procedure, and by the universality, the impersonal fairness and obviousness of its aims and of its motives. An idea in the consciousness of a thinker is simply a present consciousness of some expression of purpose,—a plan of action. A judgment is an act of a reflective and self-conscious character, an act whereby one accepts or rejects an idea as a sufficient expression of the very purpose that is each time in question. Our whole objective world is meanwhile defined for each of us in terms of our ideas. General assertions about the meaning of our ideas are reflective acts whereby we acknowledge and accept certain ruling principles of action. And in respect of all these aspects of doctrine I find myself at one with recent voluntarism, whether the latter takes the form of instrumentalism, or insists upon some more individualistic theory of truth. But for my part, in spite, or in fact because of this my voluntarism, I cannot rest in any mere relativism. Individualism is right in saying, "I will to credit this or that opinion." But individualism is wrong in supposing that I can ever be content with my own will in as far as it is merely an individual will. The will to my mind is to all of us nothing but a thirst for complete and conscious self-possession, for fullness of life. And in terms of this its central motive, the will defines the truth that it endlessly seeks as a truth that possesses completeness, totality, self-possession, and therefore absoluteness. The fact that, in our human experience, we never meet with any truths such as completely satisfy our longing for insight, this fact we therefore inevitably interpret, not as any defect in the truth, but as a defect in our present state of knowledge, a limitation due to our present type of individuality. Hence we acknowledge a truth which transcends our individual life. Our concepts of the objectively real world, our ethical ideals of conduct, our estimates of what constitutes the genuine worth of life, —all these constructions of ours are therefore determined by the purpose to conform our selves to absolute standards. We will the eternal. We define the eternal. And this we do whenever we talk of what we call genuine facts or actualities, or of the historical content of human experience, or of the physical world that our sciences investigate. If we try to escape this inner necessity of our whole voluntary and self-conscious life, we simply contradict ourselves. We can define the truth even of relativism only by asserting that relativism is after all absolutely true. We can admit our ignorance of truth only by acknowledging the absoluteness of that truth of which we are ignorant. And all this is no caprice of ours. All this results from a certain necessary nature of our will which we can test as often as we please by means of the experiment of trying to get rid of the postulate of an absolute truth. We shall find that, however often we try this experiment, the denial that there is any absolute truth simply leads to its own denial, and reinstates what it denies.

The reference that I a little while since made to our assertions regarding the past, and regarding the minds of other men, has already suggested to us how stubbornly we all assert certain truths which, for every one of us, transcend empirical verification, but which we none the less regard as absolutely true. If I say: "There never was a past," I contradict myself, since I assume the past even in asserting that a past never was. As a fact our whole interpretation of our experience is determined, in a sense akin to that which Kant defined, by certain modes of our own activity, whose significance is transcendental, even while their whole application is empirical. These modes of our activity make all our empirical sciences logically possible. Meanwhile it need not surprise us to find that Kant's method of defining these modes of our activity was not adequate, and that a new logic is giving us, in this field, new light. The true nature of these necessary modes of our activity becomes most readily observable to us in case we rightly analyze the methods and concepts, not of our own empirical, but rather of our mathematical sciences. For in these sciences our will finds its freest expression. And yet for that very reason in these sciences the absoluteness of the truth which the will defines is most obvious. The new logic to which I refer is especially a study of the logic of mathematics.

VII

That there are absolutely true propositions, the existence of the science of pure mathematics proves. It is indeed the case that, as Russell insists, the propositions of pure mathematics are (at least in general) hypothetical propositions. But the hypothetical character of the propositions of pure mathematics does not make the truth that a certain mathematically interesting consequent follows from a certain antecedent, in any way less than absolutely true. The assertion, "*a* implies *b*," where *a* and *b* are propositions, may be an absolutely true assertion; and, as a fact, the hypothetical assertions of pure mathematics possess this absolutely true character. Now it is precisely the nature and ground of this absoluteness of purely mathematical truth upon which recent research seems to me to have thrown a novel light. And the light which has appeared in this region seems to me to be destined to reflect itself anew upon all regions and types of truth, so that empirical and contingent, and historical and psychological and ethical truth, different as such other types of truth may be from mathematical truth, will nevertheless be better understood, in future, in the light of the newer researches into the logic of pure mathematics. I can only indicate, in the most general way, the considerations which I here have in mind.

At the basis of every mathematical theory,—as, for instance, at the basis of pure geometry, or pure number theory, —one finds a set of fundamental concepts, the so-called "indefinables" of the theory in question, and a set of fundamental "propositions," the so-called "axioms" of this theory. Modern study of the logic of pure mathematics has set in a decidedly novel light the question: What is the rational source, and what is the logical basis of these primal concepts and of these primal propositions of mathematical theory? I have no time here to deal with the complications of the recent discussion of this question. But so much I can at once point out: there are certain concepts and certain propositions which possess the character of constituting the doctrine which may be called, in the modern sense, Pure Logic. Some of these concepts and propositions were long ago noted by Aristotle. But the Aristotelian logic actually took account of only a portion of the concepts of pure logic, and was able to give, of these concepts, only a very insufficient analysis. There is a similar inadequacy about the much later analysis of the presuppositions of logic which Kant attempted. The theory of the categories is in fact undergoing, at present, a very important process of reconstruction. And this process is possible just because we have at present discovered wholly new means of analyzing the concepts and propositions in question. I refer (as I may in passing state) to the means supplied by modern Symbolic Logic.

Well, the concepts of pure logic, when once defined, constitute an inexhaustible source for the constructions and theories of pure mathematics. A set of concepts and of propositions such as can be made the basis of a mathematical theory is a set possessing a genuine and unquestionable significance if, and only if, these concepts and these propositions can be brought into a certain definite relation with the concepts and propositions of pure logic. This relation may be expressed by saying that if the conditions of general logical theory are such as to imply the valid possibility of the mathematical definitions and constructions in question, then—but only then—are the corresponding mathematical theories at once absolutely valid and significant. In brief, pure mathematics consists of constructions and theories based wholly upon the conceptions and propositions of pure logic.

The question as to the absoluteness of mathematical truth hereupon reduces itself to the question as to the absoluteness of the truths of pure logic.

Wherein, however, consists this truth of pure logic? I answer, at once, in my own way. Pure logic is the theory of the mere form of thinking. But what is thinking? Thinking, I repeat, is simply our activity of willing precisely in so far as we are clearly conscious of what we do and why we do it. And thinking is found by us to possess an absolute form precisely in so far as we find that there are certain aspects of our activity which sustain themselves even in and through the very effort to inhibit them. One who says: "I do not admit that for me there is any difference between saying yes and saying no,"—says "no," and distinguishes negation from affirmation, even in the very act of denying this distinction. Well, affirmation and negation are such self-sustaining forms of our will activity and of our thought activity. And such self-sustaining forms of activity determine absolute truths. For instance, it is an absolute truth that there is a determinate difference between the assertion and the denial of a given proposition, and between the doing and the not doing of a given deed. Such absolute truths may appear trivial enough. Modern logical theory is for the first time making clear to us how endlessly wealthy in consequences such seemingly trivial assertions are.

The absoluteness of the truths of pure logic is shown through the fact that you can test these logical truths in this reflective way. They are truths such that to deny them is simply to reassert them under a new form. I fully agree, for my own part, that absolute truths are known to us only in such cases as those which can be tested in this way. I contend only that recent logical analysis has given to us a wholly new insight as to the fruitfulness of such truths.

VIII

An ancient example of a use of that way of testing the absoluteness of truth which is here in question is furnished by a famous proof which Euclid gave of the theorem, according to which there exists no last prime number in the ordinal sequence of the whole numbers. Euclid, namely, proved this theorem by what I suppose to be one device whereby individual instances of absolute truths are accessible to us men. He proved the theorem by showing that the denial of the theorem implies the truth of the theorem. That is, if I suppose that there is a last prime number, I even thereby provide myself with the means of constructing a prime number, which comes later in the series of whole numbers than the supposed "last" prime, and which certainly exists just as truly as the whole numbers themselves exist. Here, then, is one classic instance of an absolute truth.

To be sure Euclid's theorem about the prime numbers is a hypothetical proposition. It depends upon certain concepts and propositions about the whole numbers. But the equally absolute truth that the whole numbers themselves form an endless series, with no last term, has been subjected, in recent times, to wholly new forms of reëxamination by Dedekind, by Frege, and by Russell. The various methods used by these different writers involve substantially the same sort of consideration as that which Euclid already applied to the prime numbers. There are certain truths which you cannot deny without denying the truth of the first principles of pure logic. But to deny these latter principles is to reassert them under some other and equivalent form. Such is the common principle at the basis of the recent reëxamination of the concept of the whole numbers. Dedekind, in showing that the existence of the dense ordinal series of the rational numbers implies the existence of the Dedekind *Schnitte* of this series, discovered still another absolute, although of course hypothetical, truth which itself implies the truth of the whole theory of the so-called real numbers. Now all such discoveries are indeed revelations of absolute truth in precisely this sense, that at the basis of all the concepts and propositions about number there are concepts and propositions belonging to pure logic; while if you deny these propositions of pure logic, you imply, by this very denial, the reassertion of what you deny. To discover this fact, to see that the denial of a given proposition implies the reassertion of that proposition, is not, as Kant supposed, something that you can accomplish, if at all, then only by a process of mere "analysis." On the contrary, Euclid's proof as to the prime numbers, and the modern exact proofs of the fundamental theorems of mathematics, involve, in general, a very difficult synthetic process,—a construction which is by no means at first easy to follow. And the same highly synthetic constructions run through the whole of modern logic.

Now once again what does one discover when he finds

out such absolute truths? I do not believe, as Russell believes, that one in such cases discovers truths which are simply and wholly independent of our constructive processes. On the contrary, what one discovers is distinctly what I must call a voluntaristic truth,—a truth about the creative will that thinks the *truth*. One discovers, namely, that our constructive processes, viewed just as activities, possess a certain absolute nature and conform to their own self-determined but, for that very reason, absolute laws. One finds out in such cases what one must still, with absolute necessity, do under the presupposition that one is no longer bound by the constraints of ordinary experience, but is free, as one is in pure mathematics free, to construct whatever one can construct. The more, in such cases, one deals with what indeed appear to be, in one aspect, "*freie Schöpfungen des menschlichen Geistes*," the more one discovers that their laws, which are the fundamental and immanent laws of the will itself, are absolute. For one finds what it is that one must construct even if one denies that, in the ideal world of free construction which one is seeking to define, that construction has a place. In brief, all such researches illustrate the fact that while the truth which we acknowledge is indeed relative to the will which acknowledges that truth, still what one may call the pure form of willing is an absolute form, a form which sustains itself in the very effort to violate its own laws. We thus find out absolute truth, but it is absolute truth about the nature of the creative will in terms of which we conceive all truths.

Now it is perfectly true that such absolute truth is not accessible to us in the empirical world, in so far as we deal with individual phenomena. But it is also true that we all of us conceive the unity of the world of experience—the meaning, the sense, the connection of its facts—in terms of those categories which express precisely this very form of our creative activity. Hence, although every empirical truth is relative, all relative truth is inevitably defined by us as subject to conditions which themselves are absolute. This, which Kant long ago maintained, gets a very new meaning in the light of recent logic,—a far deeper meaning, I think, than Kant could conceive.

In any case, the new logic, and the new mathematics, are making us acquainted with absolute truth, and are giving to our knowledge of this truth a clearness never before accessible to human thinking. And yet the new logic is doing all this in a way that to my mind is in no wise a justification of the intellectualism which the modern instrumentalists condemn. For what we hereby learn is that all truth is indeed relative to the expression of our will, but that the will inevitably determines for itself forms of activity which are objectively valid and absolute, just because to attempt to inhibit these forms is once more to act, and is to act in accordance with them. These forms are the categories both of our thought and of our action. We recognize them equally whether we consider, as in ethics, the nature of reasonable conduct, or, as in logic, the forms of conceptual construction, or, as in mathematics, the ideal types of objects that we can define by constructing, as freely as possible, in conformity with these forms. When we turn back to the world of experience, we inevitably conceive the objects of experience in terms of our categories. Hence the unity and the transindividual character which rightly we assign to the objects of experience. What we know about these objects is always relative to our human needs and activities. But all of this relative knowledge is—however provisionally—defined in terms of absolute principles. And that is why the scientific spirit and the scientific conscience are indeed the expression of motives, which you can never reduce to mere instrumentalism, and can never express in terms of any individualism. And that is why, wherever two or three are gathered together in any serious moral or scientific enterprise, they believe in a truth which is far more than the mere working of any man's ephemeral assertions.

In sum, an absolute truth is one whose denial implies the reassertion of that same truth. To us men, such truths are accessible only in the realm of our knowledge of the forms that predetermine all of our concrete activities. Such knowledge we can obtain regarding the categories of pure logic and also regarding the constructions of pure mathematics. In dealing, on the other hand, with the concrete objects of experience, we are what the instrumentalists suppose us to be, namely, seekers for a successful control over this experience. And as the voluntarists also correctly emphasize, in all our empirical constructions, scientific and practical, we express our own individual wills and seek such success as we can get. But there remains the fact that in all these constructions we are expressing a will which, as logic and pure mathematics teach us, has an universal absolute nature,—the same in all of us. And it is for the sake of winning some adequate expression of this our absolute nature, that we are constantly striving in our empirical world for a success which we never can obtain at any instant, and can never adequately define in any merely relative terms. The result appears in our ethical search for absolute standards, and in our metaphysical thirst for an absolute interpretation of the universe,—a thirst as unquenchable as the over-individual will that expresses itself through all our individual activities is itself world-wide, active, and in its essence absolute.

In recognizing that all truth is relative to the will, the three motives of the modern theories of truth are at one. To my mind they, therefore, need not remain opposed motives. Let us observe their deeper harmony, and bring them into synthesis. And then what I have called the trivialities of mere instrumentalism will appear as what they are,—fragmentary hints, and transient expressions, of that will whose life is universal, whose form is absolute, and whose laws are at once those of logic, of ethics, of the unity of experience, and of whatever gives sense to life.

Tennyson, in a well-known passage of his "In Memoriam," cries:

> Oh living Will that shalt endure
> When all that seems shall suffer shock,
> Rise in the spiritual rock,
> Flow through our deeds and make them pure.

That cry of the poet was an expression of moral and religious sentiment and aspiration; but he might have said essentially the same thing if he had chosen the form of praying: Make our deeds logical. Give our thoughts sense and unity. Give our Instrumentalism some serious unity of eternal purpose. Make our Pragmatism more than the mere passing froth of waves that break upon the beach of triviality. In any case, the poet's cry is an expression of that Absolute Pragmatism, of that Voluntarism, which recognizes all truth as the essentially eternal creation of the Will. What the poet utters is that form of Idealism which seems to me to be indicated as the common outcome of all the three motives that underlie the modern theory of truth.

Appendix 2

REALISM AND THE EGO-CENTRIC PREDICAMENT

by Evander Bradley McGilvary

Mr. Perry's article on "The Ego-Centric Predicament"[1] has been frequently referred to in such a way as to indicate that many regard it as pointing out a plight which realists inevitably share with idealists.[2] To quote from Mr. Dewey: "To my mind, Professor Perry rendered philosophic discussion a real service when he coined the phrase 'ego-centric predicament.' The phrase designated something which, whether or no it be real in itself, is very real in current discussion, and designating it rendered it more accessible to examination. In terming the alleged uniform complicity of a knower a predicament, it is intended, I take it, to suggest, among other things, that we have here a difficulty with which all schools of thought alike must reckon; and that consequently it is a difficulty that can not be used as an argument in behalf of one school and against another. If the relation be ubiquitous, it affects alike every view, every theory, every object experienced; it is no respecter of persons, no respecter of doctrines. Since it can not make any difference to any particular object, to any particular logical assertion, or to any particular theory, it does not support an idealistic as against a realistic theory. Being a universal common denominator to all theories, it cancels out of all of them alike. It leaves the issue one of *subject-matter*, to be decided on the basis of that subject-matter, not on the basis of an unescapable attendant consideration that the subject-

1. *Journal of Philos.*, Vol. VII, pp. 5 ff. The references to Mr. Perry, except as otherwise stated, are to this article.
2. Mr. Bush's "The Problem of the 'Ego-centric Predicament,'" *Journal of Philos.*, Vol. VIII, pp. 438–439; and Mr. Dewey's "Brief Studies in Realism," II, *ibid.*, Vol. VIII, pp. 546 ff., [*Middle Works* 6: 111–22] are two of the more important papers in which this bearing of the problem is enforced. The subsequent references to Mr. Dewey will be to the article just mentioned.

[First published in *Philosophical Review* 21 (1912): 351–56. For Dewey's reply, see this volume, pp. 79–84.]

matter must be known in order to be discussed. In short, the moral is quite literally, 'Forget it,' 'Cut it out'" (pp. 547–8).

Mr. Dewey's interpretation of Mr. Perry's paper is on all points but one the interpretation that I put on it; but this one point is so important that I should like to set it before the readers of Mr. Dewey's paper.[3] I do not understand Mr. Perry, in terming the alleged complicity of a knower a predicament, to suggest that we have here a difficulty with which all schools of thought alike must reckon. On the contrary, he seems to suggest that we have here a difficulty only for idealism, and for idealism only "in so far as that theory is established by an appeal to the ego-centric predicament" (p. 5). In short the position of the paper is not that the predicament is an unavoidable one, but that it is unavoidable only if a certain method be pursued. "My contention," says Mr. Perry, "is that it [*i.e.*, ego-centricity] proves nothing; or rather that it proves only the impossibility *of using a certain method* to solve the problem [of discovering the precise nature of the modification of a thing in its becoming known]. In other words, it is not an argument, but a *methodological* predicament" (p. 8, my italics). It is a predicament which goes with and only with one of the methods used by idealism to prove the truth of idealism. And Mr. Perry's moral is quite literally, "Forget *that method*," "Cut that method out."

It should be very clear that Mr. Perry's argument has one bearing on philosophical issues if my interpretation be true; and that, if Mr. Dewey's interpretation be true, it has another and a totally different bearing. On Mr. Dewey's interpretation the "ego-centric predicament" is one from which the epistemological realist can not extricate himself, and the best he can do is to ignore it. According to my

3. This interpretation is not presented primarily as an exposition of Mr. Perry's position, but rather as a statement of a meaning which his words may bear. If Mr. Perry did not intend them to be taken in this sense the purpose of my present discussion is not defeated; for the problem is whether a realist is *necessarily* involved in the ego-centric predicament when he recognizes the presence of consciousness in every experience. I present my interpretation therefore as one which I must place upon Mr. Perry's words if I am to accept the conclusions of his paper as sound.

interpretation, it is a predicament which any one can avoid by refusing to use the method of which it is the necessary result. According to one interpretation the ego-centric predicament makes the position of the realist analogous to that of the "foodist" in Mr. Dewey's striking illustration (pp. 549–550). According to the other interpretation, it makes the position of the writer of the paper exactly the same as that of Mr. Dewey when the latter says "that there is no terminus to such a discussion" (p. 550) as that between the "foodist" and the "eaterist." According to one interpretation realist and idealist alike depart from a "*common* premise" accepted by both alike (p. 549). According to the other, the realist is using an *argumentum ad hominem*; the idealist's premise is not accepted by the realist, but is denied.

There is just one fact that seems to militate against my interpretation, but that fact appears again and again in the paper, making my interpretation appear not only mistaken, but obstinately mistaken. The fact to which I refer is that Mr. Perry considers the circumstance he calls the ego-centric predicament an indisputable fact (p. 5). Is this not accepting the idealist's premise? I think not, but I must show why I so think.

Mr. Perry accepts "the fact that $R^c(E)$ can not be eliminated from one's field of study, because 'I study,' 'I eliminate,' 'I think,' 'I observe,' 'I investigate,' etc., are all cases of $R^c(E)$. In short $R^c(E)$ is peculiarly ubiquitous. There can be no question concerning the fact. . . . But we are left in doubt as to what the fact proves . . ." (p. 7). But what is $R^c(E)$? The reply that first suggests itself to the reader is that R^c means "any form of consciousness that relates to an object" (p. 6). If this reply furnishes the only key to the understanding of what Mr. Perry accepts, then Mr. Dewey is justified in regarding him as an "epistemological" realist, *i.e.*, one who contents himself with the trivial assertion: "To be a mind is to be a knower; to be a knower is to be a knower-of-objects. Without objects to be known, mind, the knower, is and means nothing" (p. 550).

But a more careful examination of the paper should make one pause here. Does Mr. Perry commit himself to the view that R^c means "any form of consciousness that relates to object"? It is well to bear in mind the context in which this meaning is given to R^c. "What I mean by *ontological idealism*," says Mr. Perry, "is best expressed by the proposition: Everything (T) is defined by the complex, I know T. *For the purposes of this proposition*, the 'I' is in no need of any definition beyond what it contains from its being the initial term in this complex. In order to make it plain that the term is generalized, I shall substitute *ego*, or E, for the pronoun. The term T is primarily distinguished from other terms only in that it has unlimited denotation; it refers to anything and everything. It is desirable that the operation or relation 'know' should be freed from its narrower intellectualistic meaning; and it will, therefore, prove convenient to use the expression R^c, to mean any form of consciousness that relates to an object" (pp. 5–6). The words I have italicized, "For the purposes of this proposition," seem to indicate that when Mr. Perry defined the meaning of R^c to be "any form of consciousness that relates to an object," he was giving this meaning as the one which this symbol must be taken to bear in the proposition which expresses the *idealistic* doctrine that every object is defined by its relation to the subject or *ego*. As Mr. Perry is known not to be an idealist, it would seem that, when later he says he accepts the fact that $R^c(E)$ is ubiquitous, this accepted fact should be regarded as accepted in a way not inconsistent with his realistic views, unless such an interpretation of what he says is made impossible by other things he says. For surely it is one thing to accept a fact; it is another thing to accept a particular interpretation of a symbol which is used to express this fact. It is hardly fair to identify the two acceptances.

Now I can not but feel that the words with which the article concludes should be taken into account, when we try to decide what Mr. Perry accepted when he accepted the fact $R^c(E)$ as ubiquitous: "But we may still have recourse to that analysis of all the elements of the complex, of T, E, and R^c, which would be required in any case before our conclusions could assume any high degree of exactness. Having discovered just what an ego is, just what a thing is, and just what it means for an ego to know a thing, we may hope to define more precisely what transpires when a thing is known by an ego. And until these more elementary matters have been disposed of we shall do well to postpone an epistemological problem that is not only highly complicated but of crucial importance for the whole system of philosophical knowledge" (p. 14). I may remark by the way that this does not read like a warning served in a controversy by one side on the other "not to depart from their *common* premise" (Dewey, p. 549). It has rather the appearance of a warning served by the author on the reader that R^c may upon analysis not prove to be what the predicamented idealist thinks it is, namely, a "form of consciousness that relates to objects." The mention of the three problems, "just what an ego is, just what a thing is, and just what it means for an ego to know a thing"—problems which are here represented as requiring investigation by the method of analysis—points back to the second paragraph of the article, from which I quoted a moment ago: "What I mean by *ontological idealism*," etc. It is made quite apparent, to me at least, that the "I" or E, which for the purpose of the idealistic proposition "is in no need of any definition," in Mr. Perry's opinion does require further analysis. Likewise it is made quite apparent that the idealistic interpretation of R^c, as "any form of consciousness in relation to an object," is unsatisfactory to Mr. Perry, else further analysis of R^c would not have been called for. This very demand for further "analysis of all the elements of the complex, of T, E, and R^c" seems to prove that when Mr. Perry accepted the *fact* $R^c(E)$ he did not accept a premise common to idealism. The idealist converts this fact, accepted by both realist and himself, into a premise for his idealistic conclusion by giving a certain interpretation to this fact. It is only the fact as thus interpreted that can serve as such a premise, and it can so serve only when a further premise is used, namely, that *this particular* relation R^c, thus interpreted, must be "taken to define, exclusively and exhaustively, *all* the connections" between the terms thus related (Dewey, p. 550). This latter premise is one that Mr. Perry expressly repudiates. Let us recall his own words. Some six months after the publication of "The Ego-Centric Predicament," Mr. Perry contributed to "The

Program and First Platform of Six Realists."[1] In this Program he says: "The same entity possesses both immanence, by virtue of its membership in one class, and also transcendence, by virtue of the fact that it may belong also to indefinitely many other classes. In other words, immanence and transcendence are compatible and not contradictory predicates. In its historical application, this implies the falsity of the subjectivistic argument from the ego-centric predicament, *i.e.*, the argument that because entities are content of consciousness, they can not also transcend consciousness; it also implies that, so far as based on such subjectivistic premises, the idealistic theory of a transcendent subjectivity is gratuitous."

This means that when T stands in the complex $TR^c(E)$ it has "immanence"; but when this same T stands in some other complex TR^nT', it has "transcendence" with respect to the former complex. This may be illustrated by the fact that a man may have immanence in a family, by virtue of his membership in the family, and also transcendence *of that family*, by virtue of the fact that he belongs to various other organizations, such as the Republican Party, a country club, and the Society for Psychical Research. Transcendence of family by the possession of connections that are not family connections does not involve forfeiture of family connections. Nor are these other connections,—accessory and adventitious so far as his family connections are concerned,—to be "defined, exclusively and exhaustively," by his family status. In the same way the fact that T belongs to a consciousness complex does not preclude it from belonging to other complexes, and the status it has in these other complexes is not to be defined, exhaustively and exclusively, by reference to the consciousness complex to which it also belongs. "An entity possesses some relations independently of one another." For this reason "the subjectivistic argument from the ego-centric predicament" is declared by Mr. Perry to be invalid; that argument assumes that "because entities are content of consciousness they can not also transcend consciousness." In face of such a statement by Mr. Perry,

1. *Journal of Philos.*, Vol. VII, pp. 393 ff. [*Middle Works* 6, Appendix 2.] The passages which I quote are on p. 398.

it is somewhat amusing that Mr. Dewey, whose position has been so frequently misconstrued just because it has been interpreted subjectivistically, should suggest that Mr. Perry's doctrine is a conclusion from a subjectivistic premise held in common with the idealist. It is quite true that Mr. Dewey does not say explicitly that he is referring to Mr. Perry, but the reader who finds that Mr. Dewey's second "Study" begins with a reference to Mr. Perry's "ego-centric predicament" is likely to remain under the impression that it is Mr. Perry and realists of his ilk that Mr. Dewey has in mind when he likens "realists" to "foodists."

In this paper I purposely avoid further discussion of the bearing of the "ubiquity" of consciousness upon realism. I do this because I suspect that the realists who so far have developed views that are in agreement will find themselves differing from each other very considerably on this point. These differences will have to be threshed out among themselves, with the help of criticism from others. But this criticism from others will not help them if it is based on a misunderstanding of what they agree upon, and on a mistaken supposition that they are in the same predicament with the idealist who appeals to ego-centricity.

Appendix 3

PROFESSOR DEWEY'S "AWARENESS"

by Evander Bradley McGilvary

It is a shame to be asking Professor Dewey to take up so much time in answering what are regarded as irrelevant questions. But he has been so good in the past that I am going to take the liberty of putting two more questions. I shall put them entirely in Mr. Dewey's own words, so far as I can; and I shall request Mr. Dewey to forget, so far as this is possible, that in my former queries I seem to him to have confused his position with my own. The two questions I wish to lay before him concern the passage on the basis of which my previous unfortunate questions were raised. That passage I shall requote here so that all the data pertinent to my present inquiries may be seen at a glance: "Of course on the theory I am interested in expounding the so-called action of 'consciousness' means simply the organic releases in the way of behavior which are the conditions of awareness, and which also modify its content."[1] In this sentence it seems to be asserted that organic releases in the way of behavior are the conditions of awareness.

There are two other passages, in the essay from which the above quotation is made, which must be cited before I can put my questions. "Awareness means *attention*, and attention means a crisis of some sort in an existent situation; a forking of the roads of some material, a tendency to go this way and that" (p. 73). "A mistake is literally a mishandling; a doubt is a temporary suspense and vacillation of reactions; an ambiguity is the tension of alternative, but incompatible mode of responsive treatment; an inquiry is a tentative and retrievable (because intra-organic) mode of activity entered upon prior to launching upon a knowledge which is public, ineluctable—without anchors to windward

1. "James Memorial Volume," page 69. [*Middle Works* 4: 125–42.]

[First published in *Journal of Philosophy, Psychology and Scientific Methods* 9 (1912): 301–2. For Dewey's reply, see this volume, pp. 79–84.]

—*because* it has taken physical effect through overt action" (pp. 69–70). A comparison of these two statements has led me, perhaps mistakenly, to think that for Mr. Dewey doubt, ambiguity, and inquiry are all cases of awareness. But these cases of awareness, if indeed they be such, are all said to be characterized by what seem to me to be not organic releases, but organic inhibitions.

My two questions, now, are these: (1) Where in these cases of awareness, if they be such, are "the organic releases in the way of behavior which are the conditions of awareness"? (2) Even if it should prove to be the case that what I have called organic inhibitions are included by Mr. Dewey within the more generic term "organic releases," why are these "organic releases" called "the conditions of awareness" rather than the awareness itself? In other words, if awareness be literally these suspenses and tensions and intra-organic modes of activity, can these suspenses and tensions and intra-organic modes of activity be properly called also the *conditions* of awareness?

There are of course several other questions that I am keeping intra-organic and therefore retrievable—two anchors weighed from the windward, I have found, are enough at a time. But if the above two questions are answered, I hope that I may get from these answers a clew to the answers of the others.

Appendix 4

PROFESSOR DEWEY'S "BRIEF STUDIES IN REALISM"

by Evander Bradley McGilvary

In the interesting "Studies in Realism," which Mr. Dewey has recently published,[1] he has done two things. In addition to presenting more fully than he had done before his own view of the nature of perception, he has criticized the doctrine of perception held by "epistemological" and "presentative" realists. It is this criticism of realism that I wish to examine in this paper.

The cardinal error Mr. Dewey finds in this realism is perhaps best summed up in these words: "Until the epistemological realists have seriously considered the main propositions of the pragmatic realists, viz., that knowing is something that happens to things in the natural course of their career, not the sudden introduction of a 'unique' and non-natural type of relation—that to a mind or consciousness—they are hardly in a position to discuss the second and derived pragmatic proposition that, in this natural continuity, things in becoming known undergo a specific and detectable qualitative change" (p. 554). The realists criticized are guilty, then, of believing that knowing is a sudden introduction of a "unique" and non-natural relation.

There are three adjectives in this charge, but I presume that only one of them has any dyslogistic significance. The suddenness of the introduction of any relation can hardly be objected to by any empiricist who sticks to his last. Nor can the recognition of the uniqueness of any relation be reasonably considered by Mr. Dewey as an anti-empirical procedure. He has himself recognized at least one unique relation and has given an excellent statement of what a unique relation is: "Here, if you please, is a unique relation

1. This JOURNAL, Vol. VIII., pages 393 ff. and pages 546 ff. [*Middle Works* 6: 103–22.]

[First published in *Journal of Philosophy, Psychology and Scientific Methods* 9 (1912): 344–49. For Dewey's reply, see this volume, pp. 79–84.]

of self and things, but it is unique, not in being wholly incomparable to all natural relations among events, but in the sense of being distinctive, or just the relation that it is" (p. 552). This sentence shows that the adjective that really is meant to count in Mr. Dewey's indictment is the adjective "non-natural."

Now why should the consciousness relation, which "epistemological" and "presentative" realists recognize, be considered non-natural? The answer seems to be that for them this relation is a relation *"to a mind."* A very cursory glance over the pages of Mr. Dewey's articles will show that the realists he is criticizing, whether "presentative" or "epistemological," are constantly represented as holding that the thing known in perception is in relation "to a knower" or "to consciousness." Every criticism he passes against these realists presupposes for its validity that these realists are committed to the doctrine that there is a non-natural "mind" or "consciousness" or "knower," and that anything in order to get known must get into a non-natural relation to this non-natural term. It is possible that these criticisms could be stated in other forms which should leave out of account this presupposition, so thorough-going in the form in which Mr. Dewey has stated them, but what the criticisms would then be would largely be a matter of conjecture. As the criticisms now stand they have direct pertinence only to some type of non-naturalistic realism which is based on the recognition of "mind" as an indispensable "knower" in every perception.

Relation to a mind or consciousness or knower! This is a thesis which some years ago was quite generally supported, and among realists even now Messrs. Bertrand Russell and G. E. Moore still maintain this thesis. But most of the American thinkers, whom the American Philosophical Association's "Committee on Definitions" would class as "epistemologically monistic realists," have been as outspoken against this thesis as Mr. Dewey himself. For instance, Mr. Woodbridge and the contributors to the "First Program and Platform of Six Realists" have made it fundamental to their respective realisms that consciousness is a relation *between* things and not a term of a relation or a relation of things to mind.

Now Mr. Dewey has, in the commendable way so characteristic of him, made his criticisms as impersonal as possible. With two or three exceptions he has named no names; but he has made it, nevertheless, quite obvious that the "epistemological" and "presentative" realists he has in mind are those whose views are similar to Mr. Perry's. His reference to Mr. Perry's phrase, "ego-centric predicament,"[2] near the beginning of his second paper, seems to be a clear indication of his meaning, so far as "epistemological" realism is concerned. As regards "presentative" realism his position is made unmistakable. "Many realists . . . have treated the cases of seen light, doubled imagery, as perception in a way that ascribes to perception an inherent cognitive status. They have treated the perceptions as *cases of knowledge*, instead of as simply natural events having, in themselves (apart from a *use* that may be made of them), no more knowledge status or worth than, say, a shower or a fever. What I intend to show is that if 'perceptions' are regarded as cases of knowledge, the gate is opened to the idealistic interpretation. The physical explanation holds of them as long as they are regarded simply as natural events—a doctrine I shall call naïve realism; it does not hold of them considered as cases of knowledge—the view I call presentative realism" (p. 395). All epistemologically monistic realism, thus, is explicitly brought within the scope of his criticism.

Now how does Mr. Dewey show that when perceptions are regarded as cases of knowledge the gate is opened to the idealistic interpretation? After stating his own "naïve" realistic position he says: "But suppose that the realist accepts the traditionary psychology according to which every event in the way of a perception is also a case of knowing something. Is the way out now so simple? In the case of the doubled fingers or the seen light, the thing known in perception contrasts with the physical source and cause of the knowledge. There *is* a numerical duplicity. Moreover, the thing known in perception is *in relation to a knower*, while the physical cause is not as such *in relation to a knower*. Is not the most plausible account of the difference between

2. Of the bearing of which on the realistic position I have written elsewhere, *Philosophical Review*, Vol. XXI., pages 351 ff.

the physical cause of the perceptive knowledge and what the latter presents precisely this latter difference—namely, *presentation to a knower*? If perception is a case of knowing, it must be a case of knowing the star; but since the 'real' star is not known in the perception, the knowledge relation must somehow have changed the 'object' into a 'content.' *Thus* when the realist conceives the perceptual occurrence as a case of knowledge *or of presentation to a mind or knower*, he lets the nose of the idealist camel into the tent. He has not great cause for surprise when the camel comes in—and devours the tent" (pp. 395–6; most of the italics mine).

It is as clear as anything can be that here the gate is opened to the idealistic interpretation by the introduction of the phrases and clauses I have italicized. Once deny that a case of knowledge is a presentation of the thing known to a "mind" or "knower," and the proof that an idealistic interpretation is involved in the treatment of perceptions as cases of knowledge loses all cogency. But this is just the denial that is made by many realists who still regard perceptions as cases of knowledge. These realists, however, in so regarding perceptions are "presentative" realists according to Mr. Dewey's definition. In other words, Mr. Dewey's proof of the essentially idealistic character of "presentative" realism requires two premises. One is that perceptions are cases of knowledge, and the other is that perceptive knowledge is presentation to a "knower." Without the latter premise the proof halts, and Mr. Dewey must do without this premise if he is to represent the position of these realists correctly. Mr. Dewey's proof then leaves untouched the question whether these realists have given ground for the idealists' neglect of the physical explanation given by realists of such cases as doubled imagery (p. 395).

Now everything that is further urged in these two articles against "presentative" and "epistemological" realism assumes that all the advocates of this realism believe perception to be a presentation of objects "to a mind." Hence the whole argument is void as against these realists who, while being "presentative" and "epistemological," deny the existence of a "mind" to which objects are presented. It is quite possible, as I have already suggested, that some of the reasons urged against this type of realism can be restated so as to bear against it, but it is evident that in the form in which they have been stated by Mr. Dewey they are beside the mark, if the mark is this type of realism.[3]

But there is one specification of the charge against "presentative" realism which it is possible here to examine without regard to the fact that it is implicated in the general misunderstanding already alluded to. Mr. Dewey says that if "presentative" realism be true the physical conditions which cause perception ought to be perceived along with other objects. "In the case of the seen light, reference to the velocity of light is quite adequate to account for its occurrence in its time and space difference from the star. But viewed as a case of what is known (on the supposition that perception is a case of knowledge), reference to it only increases the contrast between the real object and the object known in perception. For, being just as much a part of the object that causes the perception as is the star itself, it (the velocity of light) *ought* to be part of what is known in the perception, while it is not. Since the velocity of light is a constituent element in the star, it should be known in the perception; since it is not so known, reference to it only increases the discrepancy between the object of the perception —the seen light—and the real, astronomical star. The same is true of any physical conditions that might be referred to: *The very things that, from the standpoint of perception as a natural event, are conditions that account for its happening are, from the standpoint of perception as a case of knowledge, part of the object that ought to be known but is not*" (pp. 396–7).

3. The fact that such an acute thinker as Mr. Dewey can criticize an adverse view without realizing that he is thoroughly misapprehending it should make him more sympathetic with the failure of the critics of instrumentalism in understanding its presuppositions. It may also be suggested that perhaps one reason for Mr. Dewey's misunderstanding questions asked of him by a realist, questions that concern his view of consciousness, is that Mr. Dewey misunderstands the questioner's view of consciousness and is thus led to impute to the questioner an imputation to Mr. Dewey of a view which the latter has first erroneously imputed to the questioner. (See Mr. Dewey's "Reply," this JOURNAL, Vol. IX., pages 19 ff.) [*Middle Works* 4: 143–45.]

The simplest way to answer this criticism is to challenge the statement. Why *ought* anything to be perceived that is not perceived? Either we have an empiricist theory of perception or we have an apriorist theory. Apriorism can, from its own presuppositions, lay down the law as to what ought to be. The genuine empiricist may also be concerned with what ought to be, but, in matters theoretical, what ought to be is for him only what he is led by experience to expect. If these expectations are not realized, he does not decline to accept what comes instead; he merely tries next time not to cherish such vain expectations. Now our past experience does not justify us in saying that whenever anything is perceived the physical conditions which give rise to our perception of it are all perceived. If then we persist in saying that nevertheless they *ought* to be perceived, this "ought" is evidently not an "ought" of empirically warranted expectation, but an "ought" of *a priori* legislation. It is a bit of sheer dogmatism, of licentious intellectualism; and the use of such an "ought" by an avowed opponent of dogmatism and intellectualism for the purpose of demolishing an empirical realism comes as a startling surprise, not unrelieved by a touch of humor.

"Presentative" realists who regard consciousness as a selective relation among things, a relation unique in the sense of being the distinctive relation it is and comparable to other natural relations,[4] have in this conception of consciousness a means of explaining why the physical conditions of perception as a case of knowledge are not themselves perceived. This explanation consists in showing that what has to be explained is an instance of a general characteristic of selective relations. This characteristic is exemplified when the chisel of the sculptor, though it is the physical condition of the marble's assuming a similitude to the model, does not itself enter into the relation of similarity with statue and model. Suppose, for another instance, that my room-mate at college invites me to spend

4. "Experience and its Inner Duplicity," this JOURNAL, Vol. VI., page 232: "In answering this question I beg the reader not to allow the term 'togetherness' as I have employed it to prejudice him. Like every general term, it emphasizes common features and slurs over peculiar features."

the holidays at his home and that there I meet his sister whom I subsequently marry. When I thus enter into the matrimonial relation with the girl of my choice, must she and I include her brother in the family constituted by our marriage, because forsooth he was the condition of our coming to know and love and wed each other? Must we likewise marry the clergyman who officiated at the ceremony, and also marry the marriage-license which authorized it, because they too are the conditions of the marriage? What a monstrously redundant polygamy such an "ought" requires every bride and groom to commit! It seems the most "natural" thing in the world that new relations should arise and sometimes arise suddenly, and yet that the conditions, physical and otherwise, which brought about these relationships should not be included in the specific relational complexes produced by them. Why should we deny to the consciousness relation a similar privilege of obtaining among just the terms its conditions see fit to assign to it, without intruding ourselves upon it with the arbitrary demand that it should be more catholic in its terms than it naturally is?

Appendix 5

WORK AND CITIZENSHIP: THE WISCONSIN EXPERIMENT IN INDUSTRIAL EDUCATION by H. E. Miles[1]

Providence seems to be waiting with innumerable suffering children on one side and an abundance of willing and competent teachers on the other—waiting only for the old-fashioned school teacher to open the door of his prejudice and inexperience to let the social and industrial forces that have built up this country share in a common-sense direction and control of our chaotic educational situation. Such a control has been accomplished to the satisfaction of the educators and people of Wisconsin. When will the rest of the country wake up and act? The way is clear and simple.

A Perfect School in a Month

In any progressive, up-to-date community a substantially perfect industrial school for children of fourteen to sixteen years of age can be started in from four to twelve weeks. What is more, it can secure superior teachers who will incidentally exert a reflex influence upon our present out-of-touch, out-of-date school workers to the untold betterment of the present common schools.

There is nothing of speculation in this statement. It is a statement of simple fact demonstrated in most, if not all, the places where it has been tried. Such a school was started at Racine, Wis., a year ago on about forty-eight hours' notice from the state authorities, and on four weeks of preparation by the local authorities. Twenty-five such schools were started in other places in Wisconsin last September. In Sheboygan, for instance, a bright, prosperous industrial com-

1. President, Wisconsin State Board of Industrial Education; Chairman, Committee on Industrial Education, National Association of Manufacturers.

[First published in *Survey* 29 (1913): 682–85. For Dewey's reply, see this volume, p. 104.]

munity of 40,000 people, the class in woodworking is taught by a splendid German of middle age with heart as young as the children's. He was an apprentice in Germany, then a journeyman, and then, in this country, journeyman, foreman and employer, successively. No seventy dollar a month common-school teacher has a tithe of that man's experience and ability as an instructor.

At the end of six weeks there were 350 children, fourteen to sixteen years old, from the industries in this school, with 100 more on the waiting list, and an estimated still 150 more to come in when the authorities fully enforce the law as they must.

Teachers in Abundance

Industrial education must begin with the millions of industrially inclined children fourteen years of age. The buildings are ready in our present school plants, adequate with little or no extension, and there are so many more teachers than are needed as to make this question negligible. I have given the experience of Sheboygan and Superior, industrial towns without college or other so-called superior sources of supply. Racine is the same sort of town; she started with a teacher of woodworking, professionally trained. He soon left for a higher salary. In the emergency the foreman of the pattern room in one of the big factories took his place and was found to be one of the best teachers on the force. He discovered, too, that the professionally trained teacher had made no allowance in his pattern work for the shrinkage in the metal, and had been making patterns that would not "draw" out of the sand.

Says the superintendent at West Allis: "We are especially fortunate here in getting men teachers from the shops who have had college training. In the West Allis shops we find college men from the best technical schools of the country who are serving as apprentices. Our nearness to Milwaukee enables us to get women, too." Says Mr. McIver of Oshkosh: "We have no difficulty in getting teachers for our carpentry, etc., or for the girls' work in sewing, etc. I find that men who have had actual shop experience in commercial work, together with some school training, are the most desirable."

The charge that there is lack of teachers can only be made by those who are quite uninformed, more especially by teachers and public educators themselves. This is because they turn their backs upon the real source of supply and look to normal schools and to teachers of their own sort for instructors in vocational education. Germany and other countries that have successful vocational training do not admit such instructors. They require that vocational instructors shall have spent a considerable period, usually three years, in actual employment in the industries.

If those who are responsible for this new phase of education in this country will look to the industries for men to teach the vocations, as they would look to the law for men to teach law or to dentists for teachers of dentistry, and theologians for theology, they will find more efficient teachers than they need.

Wisconsin's Demonstration

By the Wisconsin law the local industrial schools are in the control of a committee consisting of two employers, two employes and the city superintendent. This union of the social forces most interested becomes a new social leaven and is directly responsible for splendid results. It cannot be said which is happiest and most devoted to the work, the employes, the parents, the employers, the school teachers or the pupils.

The following word comes from the city superintendent of Superior:

> My experience with the work thus far in Superior has been exceedingly encouraging. The quality of young men who are seeking help in the industrial school leads me to believe that many young men will be far more serviceable to their community, and will be helped much personally by the opportunities they have in the industrial school.
>
> Our day continuation school is not only interesting boys and girls who never were much interested in the regular day schools,

but it relieves the regular day schools of problems which were a constant source of annoyance, and problems which they could not personally solve, and leaving them free to expend their energies on others who are being benefited by their efforts. There is hearty co-operation on the part of everybody concerned, and at present every permit pupil in the city that comes under the law is attending the continuation school regularly.

The influence of this sort of work, the effects of the wonders to be accomplished by approaching the mind through the motor activities, the creative desires and everyday interests of the young people will almost revolutionize the practice of the common school teachers, as they themselves now declare.

Where Shall the Control Be?

Be it known in particular that the views here expressed concerning the necessity of separate and practical boards of control are not primarily the business man's views, though he is wholly devoted to them. They are primarily the views of the most enlightened of our educators, the Wisconsin law being written and advanced by her foremost educators, and accepted devotedly, intelligently and determinedly by all her people upon the initiative and suggestion of these educators.

Back of these educators and their findings lies the experience of all the foremost industrial nations of the world, who, by sore experience, found a teachers' control in the end impossible and unendurable; and the joint control humanly perfect.

The teachers who wish to keep in their own hands this control are either selfish at the great expense of the child life of the nation or are uninformed. Sherwin Cody of Chicago, secretary of the permanent committee on commercial studies of the National Education Association, says of the proposed law in Illinois that at bottom this is the question, "Will the educators accept 49 per cent of the control, and give the business men 51 per cent, or will they insist on having 51 per cent or nothing?"

If any state or community expects to play with this question by leaving attendance at vocational schools optional, its effort is too inconsiderable for attention. Vocational education is not a boon, nor a privilege. On the part of the child it is a birthright; upon the state it is an essential, inescapable obligation. We are trying now to live "half slave and half free," half educated and half uneducated. The difficulties in so doing are everywhere apparent.

Surely no student of our social life can believe that the working people and the captains of industry will yield a point that vitally affects millions of our people, except as they be assured in advance that the schools will take the life of the day as it is, and fit the children thereto. In this matter of assurance is the crux of the question, and that assurance comes through the appointment of special state and local boards, consisting substantially, as in Wisconsin, of equal numbers of employers, employes and educators.

You cannot "fool all the people" for long, nor often. As a leader in the National Society for the Promotion of Industrial Education says: "We educators have fooled the public twice, once with mechanical drawing, and then with manual training, making both remote, unrelated, of very little practical value. Shall we try to fool the people a third time? If we do there'll be worlds of school teachers looking for jobs."

In Illinois, Indiana and some other states the school teachers insist on keeping the control. In so doing they would only fulfill the prediction of C. A. Prosser, substantially this: "It seems, in some quarters, that we shall begin wrong, and cut and fit as Germany did for fifteen years before we get right."

Connecticut and a Single Board

It has been said that insistence upon separate boards of control befogs the real issue, which is only a matter of the quality of instruction to be given, and that, for instance, Connecticut is doing well with a single board of control. It might similarly be said that it makes no difference what sort of a board of directors a corporation has, if only its executive officers are right. What assurance is there that the executive officers will be right, unless the directors are such as know how to choose the executive officers, and require right procedure from them? The present Connecticut board consists of four manufacturers, two lawyers and one educator. We might well be satisfied with so practical a board. It is like giving to the friends of vocational education their own sort of board, and then abolishing the other board, the old-time board as it exists in some of the states, and giving to the vocational board all the schools of the state.

Connecticut, however, is doing little more than experimental work in vocational education, spending what might be called a large sum of money in two cities only, Bridgeport and New Britain. When she gives vocational education to every child that needs it, to newsboys, cash girls and all, she will find that it is all that a specially selected state board, assisted by special boards in each locality, can do to institute and develop fully the new system. She will find it worth while to profit by the experience of five European nations, infinitely ahead of us in this respect.

Indiana has a state board of professional educators. In negotiations for legislation for vocational schools this board absolutely refused to admit to its membership any laymen. Then it conceded two, and at last three or four out of eleven, and also "advisory" committees in the localities.

Illinois and about two-thirds of all the states have no state boards, but, instead, state superintendents elected by the people—"the essential quality in the superintendent being that he is a 'vote getter.' " The state superintendent in Illinois is a professional autocrat, desirous, apparently, of perpetuating himself. He has proposed and advocated only bills so perpetuating himself and his powers. The last bill I have seen having his support provides for a state board of education of which the state superintendent shall be chairman, and which would "give him advice and suggestion." How is that for a substitute for the real thing?

Cultural Values

It is here that the school teachers' propaganda is weakest. Culture is what you *do not* get in our common schools. It is what the children in Wisconsin's industrial schools get all the time, and through every pore: love of work, industry, concentration, accuracy, appreciation of ordered processes, fellowship in service, instant and constant appreciation of cause and effect—all these and other things added to courses in hygiene, citizenship, rights and obligations, etc.

Culture is the training of the mind and body. Too long has it been made a matter of the closet and failed of real development in the great body of our people.

The immigrant population hunger for this schooling. The first man I saw in the evening class was from a German University, and better looking than those of us who were inspecting the school. Whatever may be said of immigration, this must be granted—if we receive the immigrant, get, as I believe, great value in his service, and give him the franchise, we must educate him in the principles that underlie our institutions and in our language. In some places restriction is temporarily put upon the number of immigrants; otherwise, the schools would be overwhelmed.

A False Perspective

We judge a tree by its fruit. And all too often by the fruit that comes to market. We don't look under the tree at the windfalls, the corrupted and lost.

Those who see the splendid school buildings, good looking teachers, vast expense, and the few children who graduate and judge by this are pretty content.

See the truth. Note that half of all the fruit of our tree of public education is windfall in the sixth grade, and only one-twentieth ripens from the elementary school, and one-thirtieth from the high, and you get an entirely new conception. The waste, waste, waste! We simply don't educate, and can't be complacent with either those who would perpetuate the present control, or methods.

The Cost

The yearly expense is less than half that of the ordinary elementary school per pupil, running from $7 to possibly

$20, rarely, perhaps $30. There are today about 5,000 children in the continuation day industrial schools, and as many adults in the evening and day schools.

The difference between murder and neglect is only one of degree. Other cities can let their children suffer another twelve months, when they must yield to the Wisconsin demonstration. Can they not be moved to quicker action? Each twelve months is of vital consequence to 10,000,000 children, or more, and yet our school teachers prate and few dare to stand for the truth and complete justice and for action that is fully intelligent.

Appendix 6

EDITOR'S INTRODUCTION TO *INTEREST AND EFFORT IN EDUCATION* by Henry Suzzallo

It is a pleasant privilege to present the following monograph to the profession and the public, for there is no discussion which is more fundamental to the interpretation and reform of current teaching than this statement of the functions of interest and effort in education. Its active acceptance by teachers would bring about a complete transformation of classroom methods. Its appreciation by the patrons of the schools would greatly modify current criticism of the various programs of educational reform. The worth of this presentation is well summarized in the statement that, if teachers and parents could know intimately only one treatise on educational procedure, it is greatly to be doubted that any other could be found which would, within small compass, so effectively direct them to the points of view, the attitudes of mind, and the methods of work which are essential to good teaching.

By good teaching we here mean that provision of school experience wherein the child is whole-heartedly active in acquiring the ideas and skill needed to deal with the problems of his expanding life. That our present instruction falls far short of this standard must be obvious to all who are not blinded by their professional adherence to narrow scholastic measures of efficiency, or by their loyal appreciation of the great contributions already made by schools in spite of their defects. Somehow our teaching has not attracted children to the school and its work. Too many children leave school as soon as the law allows. Too many pupils, still within the compulsory attendance age, are retarded one, two, or more grades. Too many of the able and willing of mind are only half-engrossed with their school tasks. And of those who

[Published as the editor's introduction to *Interest and Effort in Education* (Boston: Houghton Mifflin Co., 1913), v–x. For Dewey's book, see this volume, pp. 153–97.]

emerge from the schools, duly certified, too many are skillful merely in an outer show of information and manners which gives no surety that the major part of their inner impulses are capable of rational and easy self-direction. For a long time we have tolerated these conditions in the belief that economic pressure drives the poor out of school, and that the stupidity or perversity of children accounts for their retardation and their half-heartedness. But recent investigations have made us skeptical of these easy defenses. The pressure of poverty does not seem to be so great an influence on the elimination of pupils as that attitude of child and parent which doubts the worth of further schooling. And we find that many children, whom we have considered backward or perverse, are merely bored by the unappealing tasks and formalities of school life. The major difficulty with our schools is that they have not adequately enlisted the interests and energies of children in school work. Good teaching, the teaching of the future, will make school life vital to youth. In so doing it will not lose sight of the demands and needs of an adult society; it will serve them better in that it will have a fuller coöperation of the children.

A single illustration will suffice to show how completely we may fall short of realizing public purposes in education if we fail to center our attention on the fundamental function and nature of the learning process.

At the present hour we are very deeply concerned with the universal education of youth. To this end we have established a compulsory school attendance age, forbidden child labor, and provided administrative machinery for executing these legal guarantees of the rights of children. Yet, a guarantee of school attendance will never of itself fulfill the purposes of state education. The parent and the attendance officer, reinforced by the police power of the state, can guarantee only one thing,—the physical presence of the child at school. It is left to the teacher to insure his *mental attendance* by a sound appeal to his active interests. A child's character, knowledge, and skill are not reconstructed by sitting in a room where events happen. Events must *happen to him*, in a way to bring a full and interested response. It is altogether possible for the child to be present physically, yet absent mentally. He may be indifferent to school life, or his mind may be focused on something remote from the classroom. In either case he is not attending; he does not react to what occurs. The teacher has not created an experience for him; she has not changed the child at all. Yet society has guaranteed him freedom from industrial exploitation and provided a school system for one purpose,—that he should be changed from an immature child with meager knowledge and power into a responsible citizen competent to deal forcefully with the intricacies of modern life.

Our whole policy of compulsory education rises or falls with our ability to make school life an interesting and absorbing experience to the child. In one sense there is no such thing as compulsory education. We can have compulsory physical attendance at school; but education comes only through willing attention to and participation in school activities. It follows that the teacher must select these activities with reference to the child's interests, powers, and capacities. In no other way can she guarantee that the child will be present. The evil of the elimination of pupils cannot be solved simply by raising the compulsory school age; or that of retardation by promoting a given percentage of pupils regardless of standards of grading; or that of half-hearted work by increasing the emphasis upon authority, uniformity, coercion, drill, and examination. The final solution is to be found in a better quality of teaching, one which will absorb children because it gives purpose and spirit to learning.

Appendix 7

OUTLINE OF *INTEREST AND EFFORT IN EDUCATION*

I. Unified Versus Divided Activity

1. The educational lawsuit of interest *versus* effort
2. The case against the current theory of effort
3. The case against the current theory of interest
4. Each is strong in its attacks upon the opposite theory
5. Both fail to recognize the identity of facts and actions with the self
6. Both are intellectually and morally harmful
7. The child's demand for realization of his own impulses cannot be suppressed
8. Emphasizing outward habits of action leaves the child's inner nature to its caprices
9. Making things interesting substitutes the pleasure of excitation for that of activity
10. The result is division of energies
    (*a*) In disagreeable effort it is simultaneous
    (*b*) In adventitious interest it is successive
11. When properly conceived, interest and effort are vitally related

II. Interest As Direct and Indirect

1. A brief descriptive account of interest
2. The active or propulsive phase
3. The objective phase
4. The emotional phase
5. Interest is primarily a form of self-expressive activity

[Published as the editor's outline in *Interest and Effort in Education* (Boston: Houghton Mifflin Co., 1913), pp. 97–102. For Dewey's complete work, see this volume, pp. 153–97.]

6. Direct or immediated interest
7. Indirect, transferred or mediated interest
8. Two thoroughgoing errors
    (*a*) Selecting subject-matter regardless of interest
    (*b*) Making method a device for dressing up unrelated materials
9. The criterion for judging cases of transferred interest
    (*a*) Are means and ends intrinsically connected?
    (*b*) Two illustrative cases
10. Means and end are stages of a single developing activity
    (*a*) Three illustrations
11. Failure follows the appeal to adventitious or substituted interests
12. The true relation of subject-matter and the child's activities
13. Consequences of this view for pleasure and happiness
14. There is no rigid line between direct and indirect interests
15. Indirect interests are symptomatic of the expansion of simple activities into more complex ones
16. Indirect values become direct
17. Interest is legitimate only when it fosters development
18. Genuine interest indicates personal identification with a course of action

III. Effort, Thinking, and Motivation

1. The demand for effort is a demand for continuity in the face of difficulties
2. It has no significance apart from an end to be reached
3. Persistent but obstructed activity creates conflicting tendencies; dislike and longing

4. The emotion of effort or stress is a warning to reflect
   (*a*) On the worth of the end
   (*b*) On the provision of new means
5. The experience of difficulty may have a double effect
   (*a*) To weaken the impetus in a forward direction
   (*b*) To increase consciousness of the end
6. A conscious aim inspirits and guides in two ways
   (*a*) It makes the individual more conscious of his purpose
   (*b*) It turns his energy from thoughtless struggle to reflective judgment
7. The difference between educative and uneducative tasks
8. The criteria to be borne in mind:
   (*a*) Is it so easy that it fails to stimulate thought?
   (*b*) Is it so difficult that it discourages activity?
9. Some specific consequences of violating these criteria
10. Good teaching must stimulate initiative
11. Difficulties and effort occur normally with increased depth and scope of thinking
12. Motive is a name for end in its active or dynamic capacity
13. Personal motivation cannot be thought of apart from an object or end in view
14. The problem is not to find a motive, but materials and conditions for the exercise of activities
15. The use and function of subject-matter is to promote the growth of personal powers

IV. Types of Educative Interest

1. Genuine interest is always marked by the absorption of powers in an occupation or pursuit

2. Activity includes all the expressions that involve growth of power
   - (*a*) It specially includes: Power to realize the meaning of what is done
   - (*b*) It excludes action under external constraint, random reaction, and habitual action
3. True educative interests or activities vary indefinitely
4. Physical activity
   - (*a*) In so far as physical activity has to be learned it is intellectual in value
   - (*b*) The importance of school occupations which involves the exercise of senses and movements
   - (*c*) Sense organs are simply the pathways of stimuli to motor responses
   - (*d*) Growth of knowledge occurs in adapting sense-stimulus and motor response
   - (*e*) The great value of a wide range of play games, and occupations
5. Constructive activity
   - (*a*) The use of tools and appliances makes possible development through complicated activities of long duration
   - (*b*) The use of intervening tools distinguishes games and work from play
   - (*c*) Work is distinguished from play only by the presence of an intellectual quality
   - (*d*) Children need both work and play
6. Intellectual activity
   - (*a*) The intellectual phases previously subordinate, develop and become dominant
   - (*b*) Interest in the theoretical becomes direct
7. Social activity
   - (*a*) The child early identifies his concerns with those of others
   - (*b*) His social interest also suffuses his interest in things
   - (*c*) Impersonal material should be presented in the rôle it actually plays in life

(*d*) There is a close connection between social and moral interests
(*e*) Interest itself is not selfish; its character depends upon its objects

Appendix 8

L'ÉDUCATION AU POINT DE VUE SOCIAL

I

On parle beaucoup de "la société." En fait ce mot couvre des conceptions très diverses. Il existe *des* sociétés, non *une* société, sauf dans un sens purement abstrait ou idéal. Pour étudier l'éducation au point de vue social, notre première démarche sera donc de définir exactement notre conception de ce terme de *société*, sinon nous risquerions fort de nous tromper, ou pis encore, de tromper les autres. En ce qui me concerne, comme on le comprendra, je me place tout naturellement au point de vue de la vie sociale qui m'est la plus familière, celle des États-Unis. Mais, de nos jours, les problèmes de tous pays civilisés sont sur beaucoup de points identiques. Les forces en jeu sont les mêmes, ils poursuivent les mêmes fins. Dans la famille des états modernes, l'analyse de l'éducation au point de vue de l'un de ses membres a bien des chances de s'appliquer en quelque mesure à tous les autres. Partout nous retrouvons les mêmes aspirations démocratiques, partout le même intérêt, toujours croissant, pour l'expansion industrielle, la même prédominance de la science dans les préoccupations humaines. Or ces facteurs sont précisément ceux dont l'influence me paraît devoir être décisive dans les conceptions nouvelles de l'éducation aux États-Unis.

Je n'entends point, par là, cependant, confondre, en matière d'éducation, les deux points de vue social et national. Sans doute ils ne peuvent guère se séparer complètement l'un de l'autre. Le point de vue national contient nécessairement quelque chose du point de vue social; il s'en rapproche aisément plus que de l'idéal abstrait d'une éducation in-

[First published in *L'Année pédagogique* 3 (1913): 32–48. For the re-translation of Dewey's article into English, see this volume, pp. 113–27.]

dividuelle. Pour ne pas être purement formel, l'idéal social doit se modeler sur les contours d'un groupement existant, tel qu'un État. Cependant les points de vue national et social diffèrent entièrement par leurs caractères principaux. Quelques lignes d'histoire éclaireront leur rôle respectif dans l'éducation américaine. Elles nous enseigneront, par la même occasion, comment, pendant longtemps, l'idéal national et l'idéal individualiste ont pu marcher de front aux États-Unis, sous le drapeau de ce dernier.

Au début du XIXe siècle, presque tous les hommes d'État américains admettaient qu'un gouvernement publicain ne peut se maintenir que par la culture intellectuelle des citoyens. Tout gouvernement représentatif était voué à la ruine, si les membres de l'État qui choisissent les législateurs (et parmi lesquels ces derniers sont choisis) n'étaient pas suffisamment instruits. On éprouvait une véritable répulsion pour toute centralisation. "Le meilleur gouvernement était celui qui gouverne le moins." L'idée d'une armée permanente, toute mesure, en un mot, tendant à renforcer le pouvoir matériel de l'autorité étaient mal vus de la nation. Pour la masse des citoyens, l'idéal résidait dans l'obéissance volontaire à la loi volontairement acceptée, obéissance spontanée et non imposée par l'autorité. Puis, l'expérience montra l'utopie de cet idéal et la nécessité de prendre pour fondement l'éducation. On attendit tout de la culture. On crut naïvement à la toute-puissance du savoir pour gouverner l'action, à l'infaillibilité de l'école pour procurer le savoir. De la sorte, les points de vue social et national furent inconsciemment identifiés. On vit dans l'éducation une nécessité patriotique, le salut de la république. On attendait d'elle la suppression du crime, de la misère, l'épanouissement d'une génération de citoyens loyaux et autonomes. Grâce à l'isolement à la fois géographique et politique du pays, ce patriotisme ne dégénéra pas en un nationalisme étroit. Au contraire, on arriva, non sans quelque naïveté, semble-t-il, à identifier la cause républicaine en général et la mission de donner asile aux opprimés de tous pays. Si l'on consulte les documents de cette époque on n'y découvre nulle part le désir conscient de recourir à l'éducation pour fortifier les États-Unis contre d'autres pays. Son seul but, était d'assurer l'existence de la république en formant des citoyens intelligents et vertueux.

En tout cela, l'éducation présente un caractère nettement social; mais ce caractère se manifesta simplement dans l'organisation scolaire. Elle avait pour fin de procurer à chacun le moyen de s'instruire, de rendre, dans ce but, l'école accessible à tous, d'établir une filière régulière de l'école primaire jusqu'à l'université. On ne concevait pas que le but démocratique poursuivi impliquât des programmes ou un type spéciaux d'instruction. En fait pour autant qu'on pût parler d'une doctrine pédagogique précise au début du XIXe siècle, celle qui dominait était celle du développement harmonieux des facultés de l'individu (l'idéal de Pestalozzi). De la sorte, l'éducation scolaire était ce que nous appellerions aujourd'hui individualiste. L'époque de la colonisation avait besoin d'hommes d'initiative, capables de faire leur chemin, de créer leur carrière, de dompter la nature. Dans un pays neuf, dont les ressources naturelles n'étaient pas encore exploitées, dont le sol n'était même pas colonisé, on pouvait estimer que l'individu serait utile au pays par les moyens mêmes qui assureraient son succès personnel.

Dans son esquisse auto-biographique, l'ex-Président Roosevelt remarque qu'au temps de sa jeunesse, l'idée dominante de l'éducation était de "faire son chemin dans le monde." Chacun devait réussir s'il s'attelait à sa tâche avec intelligence. On parlait beaucoup de *self-help*, de succès, et très peu de devoirs publics ou sociaux. Cette époque toucha à sa fin. Le sol était habité, ses ressources exploitées, une grande inégalité s'établit dans la répartition de la fortune. Dès lors, non seulement l'idée que chacun peut faire fortune devenait absurde, mais des privilèges apparaissaient; ils avaient l'appui de la loi, de l'administration civile et des tribunaux. Les divisions de classes, les luttes sociales dont on avait cru le pays immunisé, devinrent particulièrement âpres. Dès cette époque, qu'on peut placer dans les deux dernières décades du siècle dernier, une nouvelle philosophie pédagogique vit le jour; on chercha une théorie qui fût démocratique au sens social du mot et non nationaliste ou individualiste.

Cette esquisse historique, si incomplète soit-elle, facilitera la compréhension des remarques qui vont suivre. Par abréviation, j'appellerai *point de vue social de l'éducation* ce point de vue spécial qui se fonde sur la critique des doctrines et des pratiques traditionnelles, ces dernières représentant les vestiges de condition qui, non seulement appartiennent au passé, mais sont en opposition avec la conception démocratique. Cette lutte contre les buts et le contenu de l'éducation traditionnelle, vise plus que l'individualisme politique et économique dont je viens de parler. Elle s'attaque aussi bien aux méthodes d'enseignement, à la discipline de l'éducation qu'à son contenu et en particulier à la notion générale de *culture*, ce produit d'une éducation spéciale, destinée à des classes spéciales: la classe cultivée et la classe dirigeante.

II

Tous les réformateurs de l'éducation, depuis le XVIe siècle jusqu'à nos jours, ont critiqué certaines traditions pédagogiques et, en particulier, le verbalisme exagéré, pur symbole du savoir. Mais c'est une entreprise bien plus vaste, de s'attaquer à l'idée même qui préside au culte du langage, à l'idée que le savoir est un bien en soi (ce qu'il devrait être, assurément) et le bien suprême; que l'éducation des facultés mentales, en permettant d'acquérir le savoir et d'en jouir, est la fin dernière de toute instruction supérieure. Cet idéal, formulé par Aristote, a depuis lors toujours régné sous une forme ou l'autre. Il a rencontré un double appui, d'une part dans les théories de l'éducation, de l'autre dans les systèmes métaphysiques qui ont cru voir dans la raison la seule réalité de l'univers, réalité se suffisant à elle-même, s'expliquant par elle-même, c'est-à-dire au fond, la Divinité, tandis que l'exercice de cette raison, dans la joie de connaître, leur paraissait le seul bien digne de l'homme. Sans doute, cette idée n'a pas toujours été conçue sous une forme aussi explicite ou dans un sens aussi libre et aussi noble qu'au temps des Grecs; c'est même le contraire qui s'est produit. Ce qui a persisté, c'est l'idée que la culture consiste à posséder un grand nombre de connaissances, qu'elle repose par conséquent sur l'acquisition du savoir, conçu tantôt comme un ensemble d'informations, tantôt comme une discipline de certaines facultés, les facultés cognitives.

Une nouvelle tâche s'imposa cependant: l'éducation des masses; on comprit qu'il fallait viser plus à l'utilité qu'à la culture. Mais, en fait, les conceptions dominantes persistèrent et se transmirent telles quelles aux nouvelles écoles. On se borna, au fond, pour faire face aux conditions nouvelles à réduire l'instruction soit dans son étendue, soit dans sa difficulté; mais on continua à considérér le savoir comme une entité, ayant en elle-même ses origines et ses limites. La seule différence était que, pour l'éducation des masses (qui, par nature, doit être strictement élémentaire) on choisissait de préférence des enseignements d'un caractère pratique. On ne peut dire évidemment que le point de vue social, en pédagogie, part de la critique des conceptions traditionnelles du savoir; ce serait courir au-devant d'un malentendu. On peut sans doute estimer médiocrement l'instruction et mépriser l'intelligence; c'est là du reste une attitude peu conforme aux intérêts d'une société vraiment démocratique. Mais cette attitude est bien différente de celle du point de vue social, lorsqu'il critique simplement une certaine notion de la nature de l'instruction, de son origine, de son but, de sa portée, telle que la conçoivent divers systèmes pédagogiques. La conception aristotélicienne de la connaissance pure, nous présente quelque chose qui naît de la raison, faculté purement *cognitive*, *théorique*, quelque chose d'infiniment supérieur à la simple connaissance, adaptation créée par les besoins de la vie. Celle-ci est au service d'un but, celle-là existe pour elle-même. Sitôt qu'on renonce à cette conception, on peut encore estimer hautement le savoir mais, pour être conséquent, on doit lui chercher un autre but, le placer dans un contexte différent. Ce nouveau point de vue modifiera, du tout au tout, soit nos méthodes d'acquisition du savoir, soit nos jugements sur la valeur des différentes branches d'instruction.

Ainsi, d'après les traditions des classes aisées, l'instruction qui a le plus de valeur est celle qui s'éloigne le plus de toute application utilitaire lors même que cette application consiste à servir l'État. Seule l'instruction pure est vraiment libérale; toute autre, même celle qui nous rend utiles à notre concitoyen, est tenue pour servile, vulgaire, "mécanique." L'idée d'une "raison" isolée, se suffisant à elle-même, tel est, le point de départ de ces divisions traditionnelles en arts libéraux et arts mécaniques, avec les distinctions correspondantes entre une culture qui est un bien par elle-même et une culture subordonnée à un but, entre la connaissance pure et la connaissance appliquée ou professionnelle. Certes, on reconnaîtra toujours à l'instruction sa valeur inestimable, mais, si on envisage au point de vue social son rôle pédagogique, on devra le chercher dans ce qu'il y a de plus essentiel au bien-être de la société, dans les domaines intellectuels dont la valeur pratique est la plus directe, dont l'utilité pour la vie sociale est la plus immédiate.

J'ai signalé plus haut comment le culte rendu par l'éducation traditionnelle aux symboles verbaux repose sur une foi profonde dans la valeur de l'instruction. On comprend le rapport qui existe entre cette notion purement théorique de l'instruction et l'idée courante qui place la littérature au faîte de l'éducation. Quel objet conviendrait à l'esprit pur, sinon celui qui se présente au plus haut degré comme purement mental. En vertu de son caractère idéal et immatériel, l'esprit ne peut exercer sa propre activité que sur un objet immatériel. La matière ne possède pas sa fin en elle-même, elle ne vaut que par sa subordination à une fin plus élevée qu'elle. L'esprit se trouve donc infecté à son contact aussitôt qu'il s'abaisse jusqu'à elle. L'esprit, la raison pure, ne prennent jamais directement connaissance du monde physique. Ils l'entrevoient seulement par l'intermédiaire des sens, qui sont eux-mêmes matériels. Le monde physique ne saurait donc être un objet digne de la science suprême. L'idée, la pensée, la vérité pure, telles sont les vraies manifestations de l'esprit et sa véritable nourriture. De là, la primauté du langage dans l'éducation, puisque le langage enregistre et conserve les idées et les vérités en tant qu'idées et vérités et indépendamment du monde physique.

Sans doute on n'a pas été jusqu'à proclamer que les mots constituent un sujet d'étude plus élevé que les objets matériels. Mais, ce qui est certain c'est que, lorsque cette opinion a surgi pour d'autres causes, la conception de la connaissance pure est venue la justifier et la sanctionner.

Tout homme qui voit dans l'étude du langage et de la littérature quelque chose de plus noble, de plus idéal, de plus conforme à une culture libérale que dans celle des sciences, est, consciemment ou non, profondément influencé par cette foi dans la quasi divinité de l'esprit pur. S'il en était autrement, sa conviction ne pourrait se fonder que sur un autre dogme, celui en vertu duquel la valeur de la littérature réside dans les services qu'elle rend, dans l'étendue et la richesse de sa sphère d'application. Cette proposition peut se discuter: en tout cas, on le remarquera, elle substitue déjà visiblement le critère de l'utilité sociale au critère de la valeur en soi de la connaissance pure.

Ainsi que je l'ai dit, l'idée d'une origine sociale et d'une fonction sociale de la connaissance entraîne une conception nouvelle des meilleurs moyens d'acquérir l'instruction. Il en dérive aussi une appréciation nouvelle de ses éléments principaux. L'idée d'une liaison intrinsèque entre la connaissance et la raison, faculté cognitive pure, avait favorisé l'emploi de la méthode dialectique. Les vérités universelles, les premiers principes, les concepts, les idées, tout cela était supposé inné dans l'esprit et les relations logiques par lesquelles les vérités sont coordonnées devaient l'être aussi. Les définitions devinrent des fétiches, les divisions logiques et les classifications furent les temples où on les adorait. Les sens sont physiques; ils se rapportent aux besoins de l'homme, ils fournissent le stimulant nécessaire à l'action. La connaissance qu'ils nous transmettent était donc considérée comme d'un ordre inférieur, comme une concession à l'utilité, concession nécessaire, puisque l'esprit est lié à un corps, mais qu'il fallait limiter à un minimum. L'expérimentation, elle aussi, d'après cette théorie était un mode d'accès aux vérités d'ordre inférieur. Elle comprend une action extérieure: l'usage des muscles, des appareils mécaniques, la manipulation de choses matérielles; comment la comparer à la logique pure qui déduit, par des moyens internes, les conséquences de certaines vérités premières? Chose étrange: alors que, dans la recherche de la vérité scientifique, les méthodes d'observation et d'expérimentation ont complètement supplanté la méthode dialectique, celle-ci règne encore dans les écoles! Le règne de cette méthode contribue à rehausser encore l'estime où l'on tient certaines formes de l'expression littéraire. La production littéraire, en effet, ne se préoccupe guère de l'observation et de l'expérimentation, mais des idées, de leur rapport logique. La morale, la politique, la philosophie, l'histoire même, en devenant des branches de la littérature ont employé ses méthodes d'interprétation et d'exposition.

III

J'ai dû, à mon regret, introduire dès le début dans cette définition philosophique de la connaissance, un point de vue, non seulement un peu abstrait et spéculatif, mais encore douteux et contesté. C'était le meilleur moyen d'établir clairement cette thèse: que le point de vue social dans l'éducation implique, non une adaptation superficielle du système existant, mais un changement radical de base et de but: une révolution.

Dans ce point de vue social, la conception de l'origine, de la méthode et du rôle de la connaissance, de l'éducation de l'intelligence, s'éloigne autant de celle qui prévaut dans les écoles traditionnelles, que la logique baconienne se séparait de la scholastique du XIVᵉ siècle. Ce point de vue social, en effet, aspire à introduire dans l'éducation les nouvelles méthodes d'investigation qui, en dehors des écoles, ont révolutionné les procédés de la science, qui ont entraîné à leur suite une révolution politique et industrielle. Il tend à montrer quel rôle joue, dans notre vie, la connaissance, qui naît de la vie pratique, qui sert à la perfectionner et à l'enrichir.

Ces vues peuvent paraître ambitieuses. Avant de les critiquer, il faut bien en saisir l'étendue; à défaut, on objecterait, comme on l'a fait trop souvent, que le mouvement social, en éducation, consiste à dédaigner la science et à la subordonner simplement aux besoins pratiques, à opposer l'utilité à la culture pour sacrifier celle-ci à celle-là. Qu'on examine soigneusement la conception sociale de l'éducation; on découvrira que le conflit entre la science et l'action, entre la culture et l'utilité, n'est qu'une conséquence du dualisme actuel. Or la réorganisation sociale de l'éducation tend précisément à supprimer ce dualisme, non à perpétuer l'un de ses termes aux dépens de l'autre. La base du conflit réside elle-même déjà dans un dualisme social: la distinction entre les classes aisées et les classes laborieuses. La conception sociale doit donc se proposer un double but; d'une part, il faut que l'action, le travail, cessent d'être considérés comme choses serviles, mécaniques, qu'ils deviennent libéraux et s'éclairent au contact de la science et de l'histoire; d'autre part, l'instruction ne doit plus constituer le signe distinctif d'une classe, on ne doit plus voir en elle un objet d'agrément, un stimulant intellectuel, mais bien une nécessité de toute action sociale libre et progressive.

Quelques mots sur certains enseignements typiques me permettront de préciser mieux cette conception trop vague et trop spéculative des fins sociales de l'éducation. J'ai beaucoup parlé de la science; j'ai pu paraître la placer fort au-dessus de la littérature; cependant j'estime que la littérature et le langage peuvent fort bien être étudiés à un point de vue social. Certainement même, la vogue actuelle des études littéraires tient à ce fait que, quelque idée que l'on se fasse de leur fonction, elles se rattachent aux intérêts sociaux et servent à les éclairer. D'autre part, les sciences naturelles, elles aussi ont été parfois enseignées dans un esprit abstrait et rationaliste; on les a dissociées de leurs attaches humaines, de leur origine et de leur rôle; on a enseigné la science comme si elle constituait un ensemble de faits et de vérités exprimant une action réciproque entre l'esprit pur, hors du temps et de l'espace, et un monde strictement objectif, dans lequel personne ne vit si ce n'est accidentellement, sans aucun lien avec les aspirations et l'activité sociales.

Le point de vue social de l'instruction, au contraire, accentue l'élément humain qui a toujours résidé au fond des études linguistiques. Il rattache l'enseignement de la science à ses origines historiques, aux besoins, à l'activité de l'homme. Pour lui, la science est, parmi les préoccupations humaines, celle qui vise à la conquête du milieu, et, par là, à une vie plus libre, plus sûre, plus riche. C'est seulement le jour où elle cessera de se présenter comme un chaos de faits particuliers, disséminés dans l'univers pour le service de besoins purement théoriques de l'homme, que la science deviendra vivante et bienfaisante pour tous, et non plus seulement pour quelques spécialistes. Spencer avait de la science une haute opinion. Il lui réservait la première place dans l'éducation. Cette doctrine reposait, en somme, sur la vieille conception rationaliste de la connaissance. Il nous fallait connaître l'univers pour l'utiliser à notre profit. Mais Spencer omettait de se demander comment cet objet d'étude, qui ne s'adresse, par définition, qu'à nos facultés purement intellectuelles, pouvait retenir l'attention de la masse des élèves, dont les intérêts sont surtout pratiques. Il semblerait avoir admis que tous les enfants normaux étaient des pédants en herbe. Nos idées, notre connaissance des faits ne sauraient influer sur notre conduite, si elles n'agissent de concert avec nos mouvements affectifs. Spencer, sans doute, l'a reconnu en maintes occasions; et, pourtant, il semble ne s'être jamais demandé par quel moyen la science, enseignée comme objet de pure compréhension intellectuelle, pourrait bien pénétrer dans les rouages de l'action, devenir partie intégrante de nos activités pratiques.

Le point de vue social se fonde sur ce fait très différent, que la science est, déjà par elle-même, un élément prédominant de l'activité sociale. Que nous enseigne avant tout l'histoire, depuis cent cinquante ans, sinon le spectacle d'une évolution sociale provoquée elle-même par une révolution industrielle? Au cours de cette révolution, nous voyons l'activité humaine constamment liée à la connaissance des forces physiques et de leur transformation. Rien n'est plus simple, sans doute, que de présenter les procédés de l'industrie de notre époque comme les résultats de l'application de la science; au point de vue de l'investigation scientifique, cela est exact. Cela ne l'est plus pour la communauté, et, surtout, pour l'enfant, pour la jeunesse des écoles. Ce serait en effet renverser l'ordre actuel des choses que de leur proposer de commencer par la science pour arriver à ses applications. Pour eux, dans toute recherche, la science se montre suspendue dans le phénomène social. Ce n'est pas elle qui se présente à eux, abstraite et isolée, attendant son application aux actes des hommes, ce sont ces actes des hommes qui s'offrent à leur étude, tout imprégnés des faits et des principes de la science. Jour après jour, ils contemplent le fonctionnement de la vapeur, de l'électricité, ils emploient le téléphone et le télégraphe. Tout cet ensemble d'objets familiers constitue l'œuvre de l'homme, qui, elle, n'a pu être réalisée que grâce aux lois et aux faits de la science. Le problème de l'éducation ne réside donc pas dans l'acquisition d'une science pure et isolée pour en rechercher ensuite l'application à notre vie de chaque jour; il consiste à extraire cette science des œuvres de l'homme dans lesquelles elle exerce déjà son action.

Le reproche de bas utilitarisme qu'on adresse couramment à ces vues, est sans fondement. D'abord, en effet, il néglige cette circonstance que la jeunesse scolaire, exempte du souci de gagner sa vie, envisage les faits dans un esprit tout différent de celui de l'adulte pour lequel l'industrie est le gagne-pain. Pour l'enfant, dans la machine à vapeur, dans la locomotive, le moteur électrique, le téléphone, la faucheuse etc., l'instrument économique, l'outil qui rapporte figurent à l'arrière-plan. Ce qu'il y voit, ce sont les faits qui répondent à ses instincts d'activité, à sa curiosité, à son besoin de comprendre. Suivant toute vraisemblance, si dès l'enfance on s'appliquait à cultiver cet intérêt intellectuel, pour le porter sur le mécanisme pratique de la vie sociale, l'intérêt étroit et utilitaire qui envahit actuellement la vie de l'adulte se transformerait graduellement en une attitude plus conforme à la raison. Tandis que, en séparant le point de vue de la culture et celui de la pratique, loin de fonder l'éducation de l'avenir sur un principe qui lui soit intrinsèque, on lui impose, bien malencontreusement, tout le poids de méthodes surannées.

Une seconde erreur de ce reproche d'utilitarisme consiste à ne pas voir comment la conception sociale de l'éducation aborde les faits de la vie industrielle dans leur sens social le plus large. Non seulement il n'y est aucunement question d'isoler les activités économiques de leur contexte social, mais au contraire, l'idée maîtresse en est d'étudier les procédés de la mécanique, de l'industrie et du commerce pour les envisager spécialement dans leurs causes et leurs effets, au triple point de vue intellectuel, social et politique. Toute recherche, toute application qui implique un contenu scientifique, enferme aussi l'expression naturelle du mécanisme des formes sociales. En conséquence, l'éducation trouvera profit à recourir à ces recherches, à ces applications, pour mettre en relief la portée humaine de toute activité.

Si nous essayons de définir la culture, nous arriverons

à la concevoir comme le pouvoir, disons l'habitude acquise, de notre imagination, de contempler dans des choses qui, prises isolément, se présentent comme purement techniques ou professionnelles, une portée plus vaste, s'étendant à toutes les choses de la vie, à toutes les entreprises de l'humanité. Aussi longtemps que les sciences seront opposées aux humanités, elles ne pourront, certes, aspirer à la position à laquelle elles ont droit. C'est seulement lorsqu'on aura constaté leur caractère humain qu'on en fera des instruments universels. Comme simple objet d'étude, elles peuvent sans inconvénient être séparées de l'histoire de leur genèse; celle-ci n'a rien à voir avec leur vérité actuelle. Mais dans la poursuite des fins pédagogiques, ce qui vaut est d'un ordre différent; ce sont les conditions sociales qui ont fixé l'attention de l'homme sur certains problèmes, suggéré certaines hypothèses, orienté certaines investigations; ce sont les circonstances qui ont suscité le progrès dans tous les domaines; c'est l'influence de ces découvertes sur la santé de l'homme, sur son confort, sur la production et la distribution des richesses etc.; ce sont, enfin, les transformations politiques engendrées par toutes ces causes. Voilà ce qui importe. Or, tout cela enveloppe le fait scientifique pur d'une sorte de revêtement humaniste, et c'est là ce qui donne leur seule valeur aux études linguistiques et littéraires, ce qui les rend objets de culture.

L'examen des études historiques n'est pas moins convaincant. Nous y voyons en général prédominer deux éléments principaux: d'abord la tendance nationaliste, qui recourt à l'histoire pour préparer des citoyens à l'État, non à un État idéal, théorique, mais à l'État concret tel qu'il existe actuellement; puis, une conception sur laquelle s'appuie vaguement cette tendance, la conception intellectualiste, l'idée que l'accumulation du savoir possède par elle-même une valeur de culture capable d'instruire et d'éclairer. La distinction entre le but nationaliste et le but social, est très tranchée: le premier voit dans l'État, tel qu'il existe au moment donné, la mesure de toutes les valeurs pédagogiques. Or, cet État dans sa situation actuelle, est entouré d'autres États qui ont leurs intérêts propres, et ces intérêts divers sont le plus souvent opposés, sinon hostiles. Enfin cet État présente toujours le spectacle de la domination de quelques familles, de certaines classes dans la conduite des affaires. De la sorte, le but nationaliste de l'éducation, tout en favorisant le développement du patriotisme, qui est certainement, par lui-même, une valeur sociale, tend à accentuer certaines divergences, certains caractères spécifiques qui séparent chaque État des autres. En s'attachant aux luttes historiques, en célébrant les victoires et les défaites, il cultive un antagonisme latent, toujours prêt à s'éveiller et à s'enflammer. Plus ou moins consciemment, l'enseignement historique sert à chanter les louanges du régime existant. La nation est identifiée avec la méthode du gouvernement en vigueur. Exalter celle-là, c'est idéaliser celui-ci. L'historicisme tend toujours au conservatisme, quand il ne dégénère pas jusqu'à entretenir simplement l'automatisme réactionnaire.

Tout autre est l'attitude de l'enseignement de l'histoire, lorsqu'il s'inspire du point de vue social. Ce qui le préoccupe dans les souvenirs du passé, ce ne sont pas des événements plus ou moins intéressants, ce ne sont pas les lois qu'il en peut abstraire pour le présent, ni même les exemples qui nous stimulent à agir comme nos pères ont agi. Dans un sens, il est vrai, en s'adressant à l'histoire, il lui demande des leçons. Mais ce ne sont pas des leçons au sens courant du terme, modèles d'action ou motifs de conduite. Ce sont, en dernière analyse, des leçons de méthode. Elles nous montrent comment le passé explique le présent, avec ses œuvres, ses tendances, avec ses imperfections et ses chances de succès. L'état social dans lequel nous vivons est trop rapproché et trop complexe pour que nous puissions le saisir. Il nous incite à réagir plus qu'à réfléchir. Pour le contempler en penseur, il nous faudrait une attitude de spectateur; un certain recul est nécessaire. L'étude de l'histoire seule peut nous le procurer. Elle nous décrit un mécanisme social plus simple que celui, infiniment complexe, qui nous entoure; le premier explique le second. En isolant, dans leur forme primitive, certains facteurs, elle les révèle à nos yeux, alors qu'ils nous auraient échappé. Elle les développe dans une ligne tout autre que celle suivant laquelle les circonstances immediates les auraient fait apparaître.

L'histoire me semble être ainsi comme une sociologie

concrète, exerçant l'élève à l'étude pratique du mécanisme social dans sa structure et dans son fonctionnement. En nous enseignant des situations sociales relativement simples, elle nous exerce à mieux comprendre un présent plus complexe. Si le passé n'était que le passé, l'éducation pourrait dire à l'histoire: "Laissez les morts enterrer leurs morts." Seuls, quelques spécialistes s'en plaindraient. Mais que de faits, dans le passé qui ne lui appartiennent pas en propre! Que de faits, dont la qualité de "passés" est d'intérêt nul, tandis que leur immense portée réside dans les observations qu'ils nous fournissent sur le mécanisme de l'action humaine et sur son fonctionnement dans les conditions les plus diverses!

Les enseignements de l'histoire, on le voit, ne sont pas directement pratiques. Ils ne procèdent ni de l'idéal, ni de l'empire tyrannique . . . ou sanctifié . . . de l'habitude. Ils sont intellectuels. Ils nous amènent à comprendre le présent par une préparation spéciale de nos habitudes mentales, des instruments de notre pensée. Or, si nous ne pouvons espérer atteindre à la compréhension parfaite des choses, il est pour le moins incontestable que tout progrès dans cette voie est un véritable gain. L'acte de demain en devient plus intelligent. C'est indirectement une force nouvelle. Une compréhension plus juste des faits sociaux fait partie, déjà en elle-même, du mécanisme social de l'avenir.

Le changement le plus important introduit dans l'éducation par la conception sociale réside probablement dans les exercices connus sous le nom de "travaux manuels" et, à un niveau différent, d' "éducation industrielle." Comme leur nom l'indique, on a cherché, avant tout, dans les travaux manuels, un moyen d'exercer la main et, parfois, de faire appel aux instincts moteurs de l'enfant. On attendait d'eux, aussi une préparation pour les carrières qui réclament une certaine dextérité de la main. Mais au point de vue social, cette pratique des travaux manuels doit être considérée comme une véritable profession en miniature, analogue aux métiers de l'adulte qui sont à la base de la vie sociale. Comme ces métiers, elle forme un centre autour duquel gravitent toutes nos notions; elle soulève des problèmes qui obligent à réfléchir et à résoudre. Comme eux aussi, elle peut, habilement dirigée, provoquer chez l'enfant des efforts, des tâtonnements utiles, de précieuses expériences de coopération sociale. Ce qui distingue ce travail social en miniature de l'enfant de celui de la vie adulte, c'est que le premier s'accomplit en dehors de toute considération de lucre et par suite en pleine liberté d'esprit. Il rappelle en cela le jeu, dans son sens le plus large, intimement lié au fonctionnement des instincts de l'enfant, aux idées qu'évoquent ceux-ci et non aux idées du but utile et de la valeur d'échange de l'objet produit.

Outre l'habileté acquise, outre les enseignements qui se dégagent d'une pratique intelligente du jardinage, du tissage, du travail du bois ou des métaux, de la cuisine etc., les habitudes formées au contact d'un travail productif exercé sur une base large et libérale, ne peuvent manquer d'imprimer au travail de l'élève un caractère hautement humain. On peut retirer, j'estime, une éducation sociale véritable de tout métier, de toute occupation quelconque d'une portée sociale, pourvu qu'ils réclament et développent un effort intellectuel chez ceux qui le pratiquent, et qu'ils présentent une utilité économique pour la société. Autrefois, en matière d'éducation professionnelle, on estimait que les hommes devaient être élevés pour devenir fermiers, ingénieurs, architectes, charpentiers etc. Aujourd'hui la conception est autre: chacun doit se consacrer à un travail qui, directement ou indirectement, contribue à enrichir les intérêts de la communauté, qui élargisse la vie de la collectivité. S'il importe au point de vue social qu'un individu spécialement doué puisse devenir astronome, peintre, etc., il faut aussi que ceux qui en possèdent le don naturel soient préparés à devenir de bons fermiers, de bons mécaniciens, de bons charpentiers etc. Du moment où les hommes doivent être capables par leur travail d'être utiles aux autres, ils doivent être préparés à le faire intelligemment, tout à la fois avec l'habileté technique nécessaire, et avec l'intelligence plus large qui perçoit les relations existant entre les choses et notamment entre l'acte individuel et les intérêts collectifs. Aussitôt que l'on cesse d'opposer l'une à l'autre la connaissance pure et l'activité pure, le problème de l'éducation professionnelle se transforme. Son but n'est plus de préparer l'homme en vue du régime industriel établi, mais de faire appel à l'industrie, aux travaux professionnels, comme à une forme pédagogique. Par ce moyen, on relèvera le niveau intellectuel de l'activité pratique et c'est le régime industriel établi qui, en dernier ressort, s'en trouvera transformé.

J'espère avoir démontré, par cette simple esquisse, que l'idéal social de l'éducation, tel que je le conçois, n'est pas simplement un moyen d'amender le type actuel d'éducation, en lui apportant de-ci, de-là, quelques améliorations. C'est plutôt un appel à la reconstruction radicale des principes pédagogiques, fondée sur une conception nouvelle. Tant que la science, loin d'imprégner librement la vie pratique de chacun et de chaque jour, était la propriété de quelques-uns, tant que la profession du savant prenait rang au-dessus de toutes les autres, l'éducation académique et livresque répondit aux besoins courants. Elle était belle et précieuse par ses promesses, sinon par ses résultats. On comprend qu'elle fût glorifiée aux dépens des autres et que l'éducation lui fût presque exclusivement consacrée. Du reste, la tradition et l'apprentissage se chargeaient suffisamment de conduire aux autres professions, qui forment les assises de l'édifice social. Mais aujourd'hui la situation est différente. La science est devenue expérimentale; les procédés industriels ne consistent plus en de simples tours de mains, transmis de génération en génération; ils recourent aux méthodes de la science. Le dualisme des temps passés n'est plus possible. Le salut des sociétés démocratiques est au prix de la disparition d'une oligarchie, la plus exclusive de toutes, la plus dangereuse aussi, qui prétendait monopoliser au profit de quelques privilégiés, les bienfaits de l'intelligence et les meilleures méthodes, tandis que les travaux pratiques, exigeant un moindre effort de l'esprit et moins d'initiative, demeuraient le lot du grand nombre. Ces distinctions disparaîtront définitivement le jour où, sous l'influence de l'éducation, la science et l'activité pratique se trouveront unies pour toujours l'une à l'autre. C'est là le principe, la loi, qui domine toute la conception sociale du but de l'éducation et qui en dérive directement.

TEXTUAL APPARATUS

INDEX

TEXTUAL COMMENTARY

The published articles that appear in this volume resulted in many cases directly from John Dewey's public and professional activities during 1912–14. A number of other such activities during the same period were also reflected in papers apparently never published and not extant; references to this second group of works offer interesting insights into his thinking and writing at the time.

Among the addresses that have been lost are six weekly lectures in January and February 1913 to the Colony Club in New York City on modern philosophy, and, in the spring of 1913, lectures on "The Training of Thinking in Children" to the Teachers College Alumnae. Also that spring, Dewey read a paper on "Social Education" to the Association of Women High School Teachers; the following winter, 1914, he gave a course of five weekly lectures under the auspices of the Federation for Child Study.

Two other lost works—one apparently written out and the other probably only planned—provide illuminating biographical footnotes for these years. The piece never written was to have been Dewey's first presentation to the Aristotelian Society of Great Britain. On 19 December 1913, he accepted the Society's invitation to prepare a paper for one of the following year's general sessions. The letter of invitation was among records destroyed or lost between 1939 and 1945,[1] and we therefore cannot know what topics were suggested to Dewey. In his response, however, he wrote,

> Just which topic I write upon I shall be glad to decide a little later. The topic interesting me most just at present is . . . The Significance of Logical Natures or Essences. Perhaps it could be conveniently put under [topic] three as an inquiry conducted from

1. Alec Kassman, Honorary Secretary and Editor of the Aristotelian Society, to Jo Ann Boydston, 10 May 1969.

the pragmatic standpoint. But if the decision can be left till later correspondence I shall be glad.

As the Society's 1914 *Proceedings* indicate,[2] and as the Honorary Secretary and Editor wrote me in 1969,

> It is quite certain that Dewey did not contribute a paper to the Proceedings for the Session 1914/1915 or indeed for any other Session. . . . I can only conclude that among the unforgiven sins of Kaiser Bill must be included the fact that he deprived us of a contribution from one of the most eminent philosophers of his day.[3]

Finally, among the unpublished and lost papers for this period is the one that provided the occasion for the first meeting between Dewey and Bertrand Russell. Dewey accepted the invitation of T. S. Eliot, then a student at Harvard and president of the Harvard Philosophic Club, to address the Club in 1914; he chose as his topic "What Are Minds?" and read the paper on 20 March. On 22 March, Bertrand Russell wrote to Lady Ottoline Morrell,

> Dewey (the third pragmatist with James and Schiller) has been here. I met him at lunch yesterday and then had a walk with him. To my surprise I liked him very much. He has a large slow-moving mind, very empirical and candid, with something of the impassivity and impartiality of a natural force. He and Perry and I had a long argument about "I"—Dewey saw a point I was making but Perry didn't—[4]

Of all the persons he met in this country, Russell wrote Lady Ottoline a few days later, "Dewey pleased me most."[5] The two had further contact that spring when Russell went to Columbia University to attend a meeting of the New York Philosophical Club and to read his address "The Relation of Sense-Data to Physics."[6] Late the night of the meeting, he wrote to Lady Ottoline,

> At four I lectured and from five to 11.45 I was engaged in a discussion with a philosophical club on a paper of mine previously

2. *Proceedings 1914* (London: Williams and Norgate, 1914), abstract of minutes, pp. 425–26.
3. Kassman to Boydston, 10 May 1969.
4. Ottoline Morrell Papers, #1008, 22.3.14, Humanities Research Center, University of Texas at Austin.
5. Morrell Papers, #1010, 26.3.14.
6. Papers of the New York Philosophical Club, Special Collections, Butler Library, Columbia University.

distributed. . . . It roused great opposition, as I knew it would. The most effective criticism was from Dewey, who again impressed me very greatly, both as a philosopher and as a lovable man.[7]

With the characteristic modesty and diffidence that made Russell see him as "lovable," Dewey sent his colleague F. J. E. Woodbridge, editor of the *Journal of Philosophy, Psychology and Scientific Methods*, the manuscript for the first published paper in this volume, providing him in advance with two reasons he might use if he wanted to reject the material. In August, Dewey wrote,

> I have finished my first (& likely my last) screed on Bergson. It is deucedly long, probably too long for the Journal, but I tho't I'd give you the first chance at it. Maybe as Bergson is coming here it would be better not to publish in a Columbia journal any way.[8]

The paper, "Perception and Organic Action," appeared in November in *Journal of Philosophy, Psychology and Scientific Methods* 9 (1912): 645–68.

That same month, Dewey addressed the New York Philosophical Club on "What Are States of Mind?" Following the Club's usual practice, copies of the paper were distributed to the members in advance of the meeting on 21 November 1912. One of those members deposited his copy with the Club's papers in Butler Library of Columbia University. It is published here for the first time.

Teachers from throughout New York City gathered on 28 February 1913 in Milbank Chapel at Teachers College to organize a Teachers League of New York, which subsequently became the New York Teachers Union, an affiliate of the American Federation of Teachers. Dewey, ever committed to active participation in social and political causes, joined in organizing the League and addressed the meeting. His address, "Professional Spirit among Teachers," which appears in the present volume, was first published in *American Teacher* 2 (1913): 114–16.

The years spanned by writings in this volume also saw the genesis of a significant piece of work not published until

7. Morrell Papers, #1022, 24.4.14.
8. Dewey to Woodbridge, 26 August 1912, Special Collections, Butler Library, Columbia University.

1917: Dewey's "The Need for a Recovery of Philosophy," which appeared in *Creative Intelligence: Essays in the Pragmatic Attitude* (New York: Henry Holt and Co., 1917; *The Middle Works of John Dewey, 1899–1924,* Volume 10). *Creative Intelligence* was the subject of much discussion, planning, and correspondence that began in August 1913 between Dewey and Horace Kallen.

Dewey's deep involvement in the contemporaneous debates about which direction vocational education should take—whether it should be part of the regular school program or be conducted in separate vocational schools—is illustrated by the appearance in the present volume of four articles on that topic. The first of these was his address to the Seventh Annual Meeting of the National Society for the Promotion of Industrial Education at Grand Rapids in October 1913, "Should Michigan Have Vocational Education under 'Unit' or 'Dual' Control?" which was published in the Society's *Bulletin 18* the same year.

Two organizations of which Dewey had been president met together in New Haven in December 1913 to hear his address to the joint session of the American Philosophical Association and the American Psychological Association. That address was "Psychological Doctrine and Philosophical Teaching," which was published the following year in *Journal of Philosophy, Psychology and Scientific Methods* 11 (1914): 505–11.

In the winter and spring of 1914, Dewey gave a series of eight weekly lectures, the "Ichabod Spencer Lectures in Psychology," at Union College in Schenectady, New York. His own typescript or notes are not extant; a detailed, apparently verbatim report of the lectures does exist and is the basis for the article's text that appears in this volume. A headnote to the report of the lectures, to which he gave the title "The Psychology of Social Behavior," says the material is "soon to appear in book form," a projection that was, however, never realized.

Four other items that, like those already discussed, were published only once before their inclusion in the present volume also deserve special comment. One is the brief undated statement on Max Eastman's *Enjoyment of Poetry* (New

York: Charles Scribner's Sons, 1913) found in the Eastman Papers.[9] Since no previous publication has been located, we can assume that the statement was written for a dust-jacket advertisement or similar promotion at the request of the publisher.

The second is Dewey's article, "In Response to Professor McGilvary," which has a somewhat complicated background. The first step in the discussion between Dewey and McGilvary in public print was the appearance of Dewey's essay, "Does Reality Possess Practical Character?" in *Essays, Philosophical and Psychological, in Honor of William James* (New York: Longmans, Green, and Co., 1908), to which McGilvary replied with "Professor Dewey's 'Action of Consciousness,'" in *Journal of Philosophy, Psychology and Scientific Methods* 8 (1911): 458–60. Dewey responded in turn with "A Reply to Professor McGilvary's Questions," *Journal of Philosophy, Psychology and Scientific Methods* 9 (1912): 19–21. These three essays, which constitute, in effect, the first stage of the controversy, are all in *Middle Works* 4. McGilvary subsequently continued the discussion with three more articles: "Realism and the Ego-centric Predicament," *Philosophical Review* 21 (1912); "Professor Dewey's 'Awareness,'" *Journal of Philosophy, Psychology and Scientific Methods* 9 (1912); and "Professor Dewey's 'Brief Studies in Realism,'" *Journal of Philosophy, Psychology and Scientific Methods* 9 (1912). Dewey's "Brief Studies in Realism," about which McGilvary writes, appear in *Middle Works* 6; the McGilvary articles are Appendixes 2, 3, and 4 in this volume. Also in this volume is Dewey's culminating essay answering the three McGilvary articles, "In Response to Professor McGilvary," first published in *Journal of Philosophy, Psychology and Scientific Methods* 9 (1912): 544–48.

The third item to be noted briefly is Dewey's review of F. C. S. Schiller's *Formal Logic*, entitled "A Trenchant Attack on Logic," which appeared in the *Independent* 73 (1912): 203–5. Schiller had sent Dewey a copy of his book and apparently had expressed a desire to have it reviewed for the *Journal of Philosophy, Psychology and Scientific Methods* by

9. Max Eastman Papers, Lilly Library, Indiana University, Bloomington.

a trained, sympathetic logician—in this case, Dewey—who wrote back on 5 March 1912 to say that,

> Mr. Slosson has just asked me to review it for the Independent, which I shall do. Accordingly it would be better for me not to write the review for the Journal of Philosophy. I have spoken to Dr. Bush who has the reviews in charge about getting it in the hands of a reasonably sympathetic person.[10]

The last item in this group of four is "Education from a Social Perspective," which appears here re-translated from the French. The French translation of the article, "L'Éducation au point de vue social," first appeared in *L'Année pédagogique* 3 (1913): 32–48; that translation is Appendix 8 in this volume. The hypothesis that Dewey did not write the article in French is supported by two parallel instances in the Dewey canon. First, in Dewey's presentation to the Société française de philosophie on 7 November 1930 (on the occasion of his receiving an honorary doctorate from the University of Paris), "Trois facteurs en matière de morale," a note specifies that Dewey read his paper in English and that it was translated into French by Charles Cestre for publication in the *Bulletin de la société française de philosophie* 30 (1930): 118–27.[11]

The other instance is Dewey's article "Le développement du pragmatisme américain," *Revue de métaphysique et de morale* 29 (1922): 411–30. The French translator is not known; however, the paper was re-translated by Herbert W. Schneider and published in *Studies in the History of Ideas*, Vol. 2 (New York: Columbia University Press, 1925), Supplement, 353–77. Schneider wrote to me in 1963 that Dewey saw and approved his translation, which had been made when the original English manuscript could not be located.[12] Except for "Education from a Social Perspective," which appeared only in French, the eight articles just discussed appeared in a single printing before the present edition; that first printing serves as copy-text here.

10. Dewey to Schiller, 5 March 1912, Department of Special Collections, University of California at Los Angeles.
11. Re-translated by Jo Ann Boydston, "Three Independent Factors in Morals," *Educational Theory* 16 (1966): 197–209.
12. Schneider to Boydston, 21 October 1963.

Of the twenty-one articles and reviews, seventy encyclopedia articles, and five reports on Dewey's addresses that appeared in twenty-one separate sources between 1912 and 1914, few were reprinted and only two were revised by Dewey.[13]

"A Policy of Industrial Education" was Dewey's first publication in the newly founded *New Republic* 1 (1914): 11–12, and serves as copy-text; it subsequently appeared in *Manual Training* 16 (1915): 393–97, "with permission of the Republic Publishing Company," with some re-styling of accidentals but no substantive changes. Similarly, the 1912 and 1913 *Cyclopedia of Education* volumes 3–5, in which Dewey's seventy contributions appeared, were reprinted from the same plates in May 1914 without change.

Interest and Effort in Education, which builds on Dewey's widely distributed 1896 monograph, "Interest in Relation to Training of the Will,"[14] was—for a book subsequently so well known—curiously ignored by reviewers at the time of its original publication.[15] This small volume was undoubtedly reprinted a number of times as almost 24,000 copies were sold during the thirty years it was in print, 1913–43. In the publishing records made available by Houghton Mifflin, however, no information about the number of printings or dates of printings appears. Three copies of the book (Dewey Center a, b, and c) collated on the Hinman Machine against the copyright deposit copy (A351909) were found to be invariant. The deposit copy has served as copy-text for the present volume.

Neither of the two items revised by Dewey offers a problem of copy-text. "Nature and Reason in Law" was first published in *International Journal of Ethics* 25 (1914): 25–32; that printing serves as copy-text for this edition. The article

13. The editorial principles and procedures used in preparing volumes of the *Middle Works* are discussed fully by Fredson Bowers in *The Middle Works* (Carbondale: Southern Illinois University Press, 1976), 1: 347–60.
14. *The Early Works of John Dewey, 1882–1898*, ed. Jo Ann Boydston (Carbondale: Southern Illinois University Press, 1972), 5: 111–50; discussed in the Note on the Texts, 5: cxxxv–cxxxvii.
15. *Interest and Effort in Education* was issued as an Arcturus Books paperback reprint in 1975 (Carbondale: Southern Illinois University Press).

was reprinted in *Characters and Events*, ed. Joseph Ratner (New York: Henry Holt and Co., 1929), 2: 790–97, which is cited as the first appearance of corrections that would have been made here editorially. When the essay was reprinted in Dewey's collective volume, PC: *Philosophy and Civilization* (New York: Minton, Balch and Co., 1931), the text was apparently based on the original journal publication; the *Characters and Events* corrections do not appear in that printing. Dewey's substantive revisions of the first publication for the PC edition are listed here in the "List of 1931 Variants" in the textual apparatus.

"Some Dangers in the Present Movement for Industrial Education" first appeared in January 1913 in AT: *American Teacher* 2 (1913): 2–4, with the title "An Undemocratic Proposal." The following month, it was printed in CLB: *Child Labor Bulletin* 1 (1913): 69–74, with an added one and one-half page introduction, the title "Some Dangers in the Present Movement for Industrial Education," and minor revisions in substantives and accidentals. This version also appeared as *Pamphlet 190* of the National Child Labor Committee (New York: The Committee, 1913), a reimpression from the original plates. In March, the article was reprinted "from the *American Teacher* for January," in S: *Survey* 29 (1913): 870–71 as Part II of "Industrial Education and Democracy." Part I, Dewey's reply to H. E. Miles's earlier statement on industrial education, appears on page 104 of this volume. Finally, in May the article was reprinted once more, with its original title, in VE: *Vocational Education* 2 (1913): 374–77, with several changes in both substantives and accidentals, including the addition of two new internal headings. The first appearance of this article in AT serves as copy-text for the present edition.

The chronological order of publication of the four texts falsely suggests a straight linear transmission, but collation reveals that CLB was revised and expanded independently, with both S and VE deriving from AT. To tailor the article, which deals with industrial education, for readers interested in child labor, Dewey wrote a new introductory section and revised the original first sentence for CLB.

As the editor of *Survey* indicated, the S text is based on

AT, although three substantives and five accidentals were altered by the S editor, who also added three internal headings to the text. The meager evidence suggests that VE also derives from AT or, which seems less likely, from S: in four instances of accidental variance from AT, S and VE agree (99.32, 100.30, lowercase 'State'; 100.30, lowercase 'City'; 102.12, 'curiculum' corrected). In eight other cases of accidental variance, VE differs from both S and AT (100.3, comma inserted after 'industrial education'; 100.23, comma after 'industrial'; 101.18, comma after 'noteworthy'; 101.16, 102.17–18, relative placement of punctuation changed; 101.31, 101.33–34, quotations set as extracts and italics removed; 103.10, 's' changed to 'z' in 'unadvertised'). VE also introduces several indifferent substantive changes that could well have been made by an editor, particularly an editor for a journal such as *Vocational Education*, as for instance the addition of 'and a separate Board' (99.35), altering 'vocation' to 'vocational' (101.12–13) and the insertion of headings. Dewey himself would have made this minor kind of revision only in conjunction with other more meaningful changes. In addition, it is unlikely that Dewey would address himself to a few substantive alterations in an article that had already appeared four times (including the pamphlet reprinting of CLB). The substantive variants in VE have therefore been considered to have no authority. Substantive and accidental variants in both S and VE appear, however, in the Emendations List, which thus serves also as a historical collation.

LIST OF SYMBOLS

Page-line number at left is from present edition; all lines of print except running heads are counted.

Reading before bracket is from present edition.

Square bracket signals end of reading from present edition, followed by the symbol identifying the first appearance of reading.

W means Works—the present edition—and is used for emendations made here for the first time.

The abbreviation [*om.*] means the reading before the bracket was omitted in the editions and impressions identified after the abbreviation; [*not present*] means the reading before the bracket was added to earlier material.

The abbreviation [*rom.*] means roman type and is used to signal the omission of italics.

For emendations restricted to punctuation, the curved dash ~ means the same word(s) as before the bracket, and the inferior caret ‸ indicates the absence of a punctuation mark.

EMENDATIONS LIST

All emendations in both substantives and accidentals introduced into the copy-texts are recorded in the list that follows, with the exception of certain regularizations described and listed in this introductory explanation. The reading to the left of the square bracket is from the present edition. The bracket is followed by the abbreviation for the source of the emendation's first appearance and by abbreviations for subsequent editions and printings collated that had the same reading. After the source abbreviations comes a semicolon, followed by the copy-text reading. Substantive variants in all texts collated are also recorded here; the list thus serves as a historical collation as well as a record of emendations.

The copy-text for each item is identified at the beginning of the list of emendations in that item; for items that had a single previous printing, no abbreviation for the copy-text appears in the list itself.

The following formal changes have been made throughout:

1. Book and journal titles are in italic type; articles and sections of books are in quotation marks. Book titles have been supplied and expanded where necessary.

2. Superior numbers have been assigned consecutively throughout an item to Dewey's footnotes; the asterisk is used only for editorial footnotes.

3. Single quotation marks have been changed to double when not inside quoted material; opening or closing quotation marks have been supplied where necessary, and recorded.

The following spellings have been editorially regularized to the known Dewey usage appearing before the brackets:

all-embracing] all embracing 232.28
although] altho 86.11, 89.22
anti-theological] antitheological 226.30–31
behavior] behaviour 35.15
centre (all forms)] center 10.20, 18n.25, 28.25, 86.18, 110.19, 205.6, 238.21, 268.16, 278.3, 279.26, 291.27, 294.22, 325.37, 340.1, 341.8, 354.11, 372.35
clue (all forms)] clew 23n.28, 25.40, 183.6, 193.14, 227.24, 243.13, 244.4, 280.30, 321.6
coadaptation] co-adaptation 236.10
common-sense (adj.)] common sense 3.4, 5.4, 358.18–19, 358.39–359.1
cooperation] co-operation 92.19–20, 98.25
cooperate (all forms)] coöperate 185.18, 233.34, 236.8, 247.39, 281.36, 298.37, 303.38, 316.35–36, 317.36
coordinate (all forms)] coördinate 235.24, 235.38, 261.36, 316.16, 316.39, 343.11, 375.16–17
didn't] did n't 164n.3
doesn't] does n't 164.12, 178.12
enclosed] inclosed 143.18
endorse] indorse 85.5–6, 88.40, 89.7
engrained] ingrained 285.25
evil-doing] evil doing 229.13
fibre] fiber 154.31
grown up] grown-up 374.22
half-century] half century 59.27
intraorganic] intra-organic 27.4, 319.19–20
laissez-faire (adj.)] *laissez faire* 58.7
life-blood] life blood 133.8
life-struggle] life struggle 36.17, 41.16
Middle Ages] middle ages 272.34
naïvely] naively 147.5
old-time (adj.)] old time 100.21
outdoor] out-door 55.16
outgoing] out-going 162.35
overstimulation] over-stimulation 154.39
pedagogues] pedagogs 87.5
preestablished] preëstablished 293.18
preexisting] preëxisting 76.23
program] programme 143.17
psycho-physical] psychophysical 136.4
ready-made] readymade 167.35, 168.27, 182.31
reenforce (all forms)] reënforce 216.25, 251.10, 257.1, 258.13, 301.10
role] rôle 22n.2, 136.33, 193.31, 201.11, 221.11(2), 235.21, 248.10, 256.9, 287.9, 299.11, 317.39, 329.4, 338.32
self-enclosed] self-inclosed 272.23, 354.16, 363.24–25
theatre] theater 42.3

thorough (all forms)] thoro 109.5, 132.7
thoroughgoing] thorogoing 86.2–3, 86.8–9, 92.10
though] tho 31.7, 35.18, 40.18, 89.8
through] thru 132.3, 132.22
wage-earners] wage earners 85.16
well-being] well being 104.30, 136.29
well-being] wellbeing 95.7
well-defined] well defined 32.30
well-known] well known 318.15
zoology] zoölogy 313.8, 336.17

"Perception and Organic Action"

Copy-text for "Perception and Organic Action" is its first publication in *Journal of Philosophy, Psychology and Scientific Methods* 9 (1912): 645–68. Variants between the copy-text and the later appearance of the article in PC: *Philosophy and Civilization* (New York: Minton, Balch and Co., 1931) are in the "List of 1931 Variants in 'Perception and Organic Action.'" PC is noted as the first appearance of three emendations that would have been made editorially for the present edition.

8.32 constructed] PC; connected
11.6–7 instantaneous" (p. 26); "an] W; instantaneous‸;[9] ‸an
12.38 upon] W; from
12n.1 233] W; 232
12n.2 images] W; objects
16.26 in so far] W; in so
17.19–20 body upon things] W; body
17.20 itself"] W; ~‸
23n.21 and] PC; and and
24n.1 74] W; 84
27.32 multitude] PC; mutitude

"What Are States of Mind?"

Copy-text for "What Are States of Mind?" is the previously unpublished typescript in the Philosophical Club Papers, Special Collections, Columbia University.

31.1 ARE] W; are
31.13 Club] W; club
32.6 object‸] W; ~,
33.9 in a] W; in

34.9 emotional] W; emotion
34.9 condition] W; conditon
35.29–30 indirectly,] W; ~‸
36.8 deeper-seated] W; ~‸~
36.9 environment.] W; ~,
36.27 nor] W; or
37.7 transcendence,"] W; ~",
37.7 "transsubjective reference,"] W; ‸transubjective reference",
37.10 organism‸] W; ~,
37n.8 pretty firm opinions] W; pretty opinion
38.16 biological nor] W; biological or
39.16 the behavior of physical] W; the of physical
39.38 objective] W; ejective
40.15 therefore] W; therefor
40.16 it were] W; twere
40.19 learn] W; leanr
40.29 because] W; bacause
40.32 destiny),] W; ~,)
42.17 Descartes] W; DesCartes
42.24 things.] W; ~?
43.3 But] W; By

"The Problem of Values"

Copy-text is the only previous impression of this article in the *Journal of Philosophy, Psychology and Scientific Methods* 10 (1913): 268–69. No editorial emendations have been made.

"Psychological Doctrine and Philosophical Teaching"

Copy-text is the only previous impression of this article in the *Journal of Philosophy, Psychology and Scientific Methods* 11 (1914): 505–11.

50.23 science‸] W; ~,
52.16 side)‸] W; ~),
53.26 movement‸] W; ~,
55.13 turning] W; truning

"Nature and Reason in Law"

The first printing, in *International Journal of Ethics* 25 (1914): 25–32, has served as copy-text. CE: *Characters and*

Events, ed. Joseph Ratner (New York: Henry Holt and Co., 1929), pp. 790–97, is noted as the first appearance of three changes that would have been made editorially.

57.7 In view] CE; In the view
57.27 causal] CE; casual
58.4 collectivistic] CE; collective
59.17 cases‸] W; ~,
59.27 half-century] W; ~‸~
60.4 ‸cannot] W; "~
60.5 "means] W; ‸~
60.30 meant‸] W; ~,
61.24 practice‸] W; ~,
62n.1 1911] W; 1912

"A Reply to Professor Royce's Critique of Instrumentalism"

Copy-text is the only previous appearance of this article, in *Philosophical Review* 21 (1912): 69–81.

64.6 perhaps,] W; ~‸
64.32 instrumentalism] W; instrumentalisn
65.20 dialectician] W; dialectian
71.14 *propria*] W; *propia*
75.23–24 confirming.] W; ~,

"In Response to Professor McGilvary"

Copy-text is the only previous appearance of this article, in the *Journal of Philosophy, Psychology and Scientific Methods* 9 (1912): 544–48.

79.8 predicament‸] W; ~,
80.1 to indefinitely] W; indefinitely to
80.3 has] W; had
83.9–10 happening‸ are,] W; ~, ~‸

"Should Michigan Have Vocational Education under 'Unit' or 'Dual' Control?"

Copy-text is the only previous appearance of this article, in *Bulletin 18* of the National Society for the Promotion of

Industrial Education (Peoria, Ill.: The Society, 1913), pp. 27–34.

90.32 lines),] W; ~)‸
91.18 dealt] W; dwelt
92.17 working out] W; working

"Some Dangers in the Present Movement for Industrial Education"

Copy-text is the first printing in AT: *American Teacher* 2 (1913): 2–4, with the title "An Undemocratic Proposal." Emendations have been adopted from CLB, the revised, expanded second printing in *Child Labor Bulletin* 1 (1913): 69–74. A third printing, based on AT, appeared in S: *Survey* 29 (1913): 870–71, as Part II of "Industrial Education and Democracy." The fourth printing was in VE: *Vocational Education* 2 (1913): 374–77. S and VE are noted as the first appearance of five changes that would have been made editorially.

Both substantive and accidental variants in VE and S, at those points where VE and S do not agree with the AT copy-text, are also listed here rather than in a separate historical collation.

98.1–99.16 SOME . . . placing bureaus.] CLB; [*not present*] AT, S, VE
99.17 *Industrial . . . Dangers*‸] W; INDUSTRIAL EDUCATION DANGERS.] CLB; AN UNDEMOCRATIC PROPOSAL AT, VE; INDUSTRIAL EDUCATION AND DEMOCRACY . . . / II *Two Movements on the Inside* S
99.18 The . . . is] CLB; No question at present under discussion in education AT, S, VE
99.18 fraught] CLB; so fraught AT, S, VE
99.19 democracy.] CLB; democracy as the question of industrial education. AT, S, VE
99.27 rather than] AT, CLB, VE; than to S
99.29 to the interests] AT, CLB, VE; in the interests S
99.32 State] AT, CLB; state S, VE
99.35 State Commission of Vocational Education] AT, CLB, VE; state commission of vocational education S
99.35–36 wherever] AT, CLB, S; and a separate Board wherever VE
100.3 industrial education‸] AT, S; ~, CLB, VE

100.23 industrial‸] AT, CLB, S; ~, VE
100.30 City] AT, CLB; city S, VE
100.30 State] AT, CLB; state S, VE
100.34–35 efficiency. [¶] These] AT, CLB; efficiency. / *Its Arresting Effect* [¶] These S; efficiency. / EVILS OF SEPARATE CONTROL WORK BOTH WAYS. [¶] These VE
101.8 although] S; altho AT, CLB, VE
101.9 five] AT, CLB, VE; 5 S
101.9 cent‸] S, VE; ~. AT, CLB
101.10–11 taxation. [¶] Thirdly] AT, CLB, VE; taxation. / *A European Example* [¶] Third S
101.12–13 vocational] VE; vocation AT, CLB, S
101.15–16 "Vocational . . . Europe."] AT, CLB; ‸~.‸ S; "~". VE
101.18 noteworthy‸] AT, CLB, S; ~, VE
101.20 Although] S; Altho AT, CLB, VE
101.31–32 *work . . . general*] AT, CLB, S; [*rom.*] VE
101.33–34 *its . . . bearings*] AT, CLB, S; [*rom.*] VE
101.35–36 society.‸ [¶] Whatever] W; society." [¶] Whatever AT, CLB, VE; society." / *Industrial "Classes" the Consequence* [¶] Whatever S
101.38 laborers] CLB; laborers for them AT, S, VE
101.38 quotations state] AT, CLB, S; quotation states VE
101.40–102.1 education,] AT, CLB, VE; ~‸ S
102.9 of intentions] AT, CLB, S; intentions VE
102.12 curriculum] CLB, S, VE; curiculum AT
102.17–18 general."] AT, CLB, S; ~". VE
102.23 would simply aim] AT, CLB, S; would be confined to aiming VE
102.24 lines. Those] AT, CLB, S; lines. / UNITY OF PUBLIC SCHOOL SYSTEM ESSENTIAL. [¶] Those VE
102.29 schools‸] AT, S, VE; ~, CLB
102.29 taxation‸] AT, S, VE; ~, CLB
103.2 that may] AT, CLB, S; may VE
103.4–5 actually . . . already] AT, CLB, S; already being done VE
103.10 though] CLB, S; tho AT, VE
103.10 unadvertised] AT, CLB, S; unadvertized VE

"Industrial Education and Democracy"

Copy-text is the only previous publication of this article, in *Survey* 29 (1913): 870.

104.25 intimates,] W; ~‸
104.28 Miles's] W; Miles

"Cut-and-Try School Methods"

Copy-text is the only previous impression of this article, in *Survey* 30 (1913): 691–92.

106.17 it on] W; it
107.24 more] W; mere
107.31,32 children,] W; ~‸
108.7 principle] W; principal
108.12 shown)‸] W; ~),

"Professional Spirit among Teachers"

Copy-text is the only previous publication of this article, in *American Teacher* 2 (1913): 114–16.

111.36 transmitting] W; transmiting
111.38 serious:] W; ~;
112.36 is you‸] W; ~,

Review of Schiller's Formal Logic: A Scientific and Social Problem

Copy-text is the only previous publication of this review, in *Independent* 73 (1912): 203–5.

132.2 predicables,] W; ~;
132.16 meaninglessness] W; meaningless

Review of Hall's Founders of Modern Psychology

Copy-text is the only previous publication of this article, in the *New York Times Book Review*, 25 August 1912, pp. 457–58.

137.33 sense),] W; ~,)
138.17 wrote,] W; ~‸
138.30 esthetic),] W; ~,)
138.37 psychic] W; physic
139.2 parallel] W; parrallel
139.24 probably,] W; ~‸
139.34 phenomena‸] W; ~,
139.34 general,] W; ~‸
139.36 led to] W; led
139.37 Jung] W; Yung
139.37–38 psycho-analysis] W; psycho-analysists

140.25 use] W; us
140.33 *Fach*] W; [*rom.*]

Review of James's Essays in Radical Empiricism

Copy-text is the only previous publication of this article, in the *New York Times Book Review*, 9 June 1912, p. 357.

142.13 was] W; were
143.5–6 demonstrations;] W; ~,

Interest and Effort in Education

The copyright deposit copy of *Interest and Effort in Education* (Boston: Houghton Mifflin Co., 1913) has served as copy-text for the present edition.

153.21 Practically,] W; ~‸
155.23 interest‸] W; ~,
156.23 he is] W; that he is
163.3 take] W; takes
170.5 excitement‸] W; ~,
171.17 ball,] W; ~‸
183.2 way,] W; ~.
184.1 excitement,] W; ~‸
188.2 illustrates] W; illustrate
194.33 realization‸] W; ~,
195.25 excitements‸] W; ~,

"Introduction to Bergson Bibliography"

Copy-text is the only previous publication, in Isadore Gilbert Mudge's *A Contribution to a Bibliography of Henri Bergson.*

201.12–13 associations] W; asssociations
201.15 super-scientific‸] W; ~,

"Introduction to Directory of the Trades and Occupations"

Copy-text is the only previous publication, in *Directory of the Trades and Occupations Taught at the Day and Evening Schools in Greater New York* (New York, 1913), 2–3.

205.21 sixteen$_\wedge$] W; ~,
206.13 education, keep] W; education$_\wedge$ keeps

Contributions to A Cyclopedia of Education, *Volumes 3, 4, and 5*

Copy-text for Dewey's articles in these three volumes of *A Cyclopedia of Education*, ed. Paul Monroe (New York: Macmillan Co., 1912–13) is the first printing of each volume.

212.3 acts:] W; ~;
212.24 hedonism,] W; ~;
213.4 1892] W; 1896
216.28 beliefs)$_\wedge$] W; ~),
216.31 exploitation$_\wedge$] W; ~,
219.8 principles or] W; principles of
220.16 phenomena,] W; ~;
223.36 psychical] W; psyc ical
225.38 scholasticism,] W; ~$_\wedge$
227.6 contents,] W; ~;
227.20 conception:] W; ~;
227.37 this$_\wedge$] W; ~,
228.16 Oxford] W; London
228.20 *gesammten*] W; *gesamten*
228.21 Tübingen] W; Leipzig
228.34 1864] W; 1896
229.39 is,] W; ~$_\wedge$
232.7–8 occupation,] W; ~$_\wedge$
232.35 nature;] W; ~,
235.34 feat,] W; ~$_\wedge$
235.37 only the] W; the only
237.12 *in*] W; *of*
237.13 1897] W; 1895
237.15 McDougall] W; MacDougall
237.15 London] W; New York
237.18 E. C.] W; E. H.
241.31–32 *System of Logic*] W; Principles of Logic
243.18 Educationally, this means$_\wedge$] W; ~$_\wedge$ ~,
244.25 system.] W; ~$_\wedge$
245.21 *A system* . . . 1900.)] W; *Principles of Logic.*
245.22 1909] W; 1910
248.32 Hall] W; Hally
248.34 *Text-Book*] W; *Textbook*
248.35 1911] W; 1910
254.13 upon$_\wedge$] W; ~,
254.27 way$_\wedge$] W; ~,
259.28 matter, of content,] W; ~$_\wedge$ ~$_\wedge$

260.24 discursive] W; discussive

261.31 besides] W; beside

262.10 unity‸] W; ~,

263.5 valid, conclusion‸] W; ~‸ ~,

264.1 subject‸matter] W; ~-~

264.6 the] W; in the

268.7 late,] W; ~‸

268.19 knowledge‸] W; ~,

270.8 obedience,] W; ~‸

272.25–26 imperfection;] W; ~,

272.27 divine,] W; ~‸

283.11 illogical—and the logical] W; illogical—

284.33 Subject-Matter] W; ~‸~

284.34 XXXI] W; XXX

284.35 I. E.] W; I. F.

284.35 1909] W; 1910

289.29 philosophers‸] W; ~,

291.1 *Education*‸] W; ~,

291.2 London] W; New York

294.36 1901] W; 1904

294.37 *Ethic*] W; *Ethics*

295.11–12 humanists'] W; ~‸

295.30 law] W; laws

298.28 values,] W; ~;

298.34 the general] W; general

304.15 minds] W; mind

312.3 *Text-Book*] W; *Textbook*

312.4 1911] W; 1903

312.9 1903] W; 1906

312.10 *Genetic*] W; *The Genetic*

312.13 1903] W; 1894

312.29 NEO-PLATONISM] W; NEOPLATONISM

318.26 1880] W; 1883

319.25 in order] W; order

323.34 *Children*:] W; ~.

323.37 Christian] W; Chr.

323.39 1884] W; 1864

323.40 Groos] W; Gross

324.8 McDougall] W; MacDougall

324.13 1896] W; 1895–96

324.15 *A Physiological*] W; *a physiological*

324.34; 326.19 Auguste] W; August

326.23 1893] W; 1902

326.26,33; 327.5 Peirce] W; Pierce

326.27 1878] W; 1879

326.27 *Science*] W; *Scientific*

329.25 *pragmatiste*. Vol. I, *Le*] W; *pragmatiste, le*

329.32 "Does . . . Character?" In] W; [*not present*]

329.35 van] W; von
329.35 *Philosophy*] W; *Philosophy of*
329.36 *Critically . . . Present-Day*] W; *critically considered in relation to present-day*
330.4 *Philosophical*] W; *Philosophic*
330.6 *droits*] W; *Droits*
330.6 *respectifs*] W; *respectif*
330.7 *l'aristocratie*] W; *l'Aristocratie*
330.7 *démocratie*] W; *Democratie*
330.17 aspect‸] W; ~,
332.29 eighteenth-century] W; ~‸~
332.34 poverty,] W; ~‸
338.13 terminology] W; teminology
340.8 become] W; becomes
347.19 1909] W; 1910
350.4 energy),] W; ~,)
352.20 assimilate,] W; ~‸
353.10 important] W; inportant
353.30 deism:] W; ~.
360.1 1906] W; 1907
360.3 F. C. S.] W; F. C. M.
360.36 doer,] W; ~‸
362.13 Oxford] W; Cambridge
362.17 *Concerning*] W; *on the*
362.39 another] W; an other
363.40 that‸ which,] W; ~, ~‸
364.18 knowledge,] W; ~‸

Report of "Reasoning in Early Childhood"

367.16 *Psychology*‸] W; Psychology,
370.21 which it] W; which
371.36 do the] W; the

Lectures to Federation for Child Study

378.21 believed in] W; believed
381.18 education‸"] W; ~.'
381.27 impressions] W; imprescions
385.32 Dewey to] W; D. to

Lectures on "Psychology of Social Behavior"

396.24 occurring] W; occuring
399.18 readjustable] W; readjustible
400.29 in] W; is
408.24 cent‸] W; ~.

LIST OF 1931 VARIANTS IN "PERCEPTION AND ORGANIC ACTION"

In the list that follows appear all variants between the copy-text printing of "Perception and Organic Action," in *Journal of Philosophy, Psychology and Scientific Methods* 9 (1912): 645–68, and its revision for reprinting in *Philosophy and Civilization* (New York: Minton, Balch and Co., 1931), pp. 202–32. Both substantive and accidental variants are listed except for those formal matters normally regularized silently in the present edition: consecutive numbering of footnotes, book titles in italic type, "page" or "pages" abbreviated. The reading before the bracket is from the copy-text and will not coincide with the present edition in readings that have been emended; the 1931 variants follow the brackets.

3.1 PERCEPTION AND ORGANIC ACTION] *Perception and Organic Action*
3.5 knowledge‸] ~,
3.19 action‸] ~,
4.13; 6.10 that] which
4.14–15 which has not been] not
4.18 It . . . supposing] Bergson supposes
4.20 have been] can be
4.26 follow‸] ~,
4.26–27 considerations,] ~‸
4.37 a knowledge] knowledge
5.21 it also holds] also holding
5.29 "reality," . . . knowledge] "reality." Then knowledge
5.40 in its] since
5.40 theoretic character] theoretic
6.23(2),24–25 practise] practice
6.27 around] round
6.35–36 of the growth of an] of
8.8,16 so] as
8.32 connected] constructed
9.10–11 inconsistency, but] inconsistency. It
9.13–20 One . . . perception.] [*om.*]
9.28 its presence] presence of the object

9.31–32 we . . . Since] note that since

10.16–17 perceived] then perceived

12.31 *i.e.*] [*rom.*]

14.30 abandonment] "suppression"

15.12–13 real actions] actual doing

15.35 instantaneous, that] instantaneous, one that

15.36 that qualifies] one that qualifies

16.26 in so] so far

16.37 action$_\wedge$] ~,

16.38 sort$_\wedge$] ~,

18n.2 panpsychic] pan-psychic

19.39–40 it . . . *constituting*] it operates to *constitute*

21.9 here] then

22.23 a choice] making a choice

23n.21 and and] and

23n.23 is as perceived] as perceived is

23n.30,34 preestablished] pre-established

23n.33 uniquely] unique

24.1 focusing] focus

27.22 coordinating] co-ordinating

27.32 mutitude] multitude

27n.2 655] 217

28.19 If] If it is

28.20 this] there

28.20 in a] a

28.20–21 in an] an

28.22–23 handling,] ~$_\wedge$

28.28 coordinated] co-ordinated

28n.4 of] in

30.15 revision.] revision. With *this* revision, follows also that of "intuition" severed from practical knowledge.

LIST OF 1931 VARIANTS IN "NATURE AND REASON IN LAW"

All variants between the copy-text impression in *International Journal of Ethics* 25 (1914): 25–32 and the impression in *Philosophy and Civilization* (New York: Minton, Balch and Co., 1931), pp. 166–72, appear in the list that follows. Readings to the left of the bracket are from the copy-text; *Philosophy and Civilization* readings follow the bracket.

56.27 obstructed] obstruct
56.27 furthered] further
57.33,37 meant] means
58.10 and then to] with the intent of
59.3 the influence] a direct influence
60.4 court] Court
60.23–24 courts, in] courts have done in
61.17 wilful] willful
61.26 of the idea of nature] of "nature"
61.40–63.11 My point . . . intelligence.] [*om.*]

LINE-END HYPHENATION

I. *Copy-text list.*

The following are the editorially established forms of possible compounds which were hyphenated at the ends of lines in the copy-text:

4.26	overboard
13.13	subject-matter
18n.3	panpsychic
28.14	sensori-motor
33.24	so-called
35.12	non-living
60.22–23	ready-made
65.24	presuppositions
90.22	part-time
91.17	prevocational
132.5	semi-logical
137.13	commonplace
138.39–40	psycho-physics
144.33	non-dogmatic
146.26	thoroughgoing
147.33	well-known
161.19[2]	cross-eyedness
163.33	thoroughgoing
166.21	food-power
178.37	*mis*educative
179.7	twofold
181.38	subject-matter
182.30	subject-matter
183.10–11	thoroughgoing
184.20–21	offspring
185.33	sense-training
186.24	day-dreaming
187.38	sensori-motor
217.25	sidetrack
225.20	sense-perception
232.9	quasi-mystic
240.3	widespread
249.38	store-house
254.5	whole-heartedly
255.4–5	non-intellectual
262.23	interdependence
286.12	spread-outness
286.18	non-acquired
287.16	deep-lying
290.26	Neo-humanism
298.37	long-continued
304.15	by-product
308.4	ready-made
308.15	homespun
310.12	forethought
324.29	coexistence
334.34	sense-perception
336.26	Everyday
340.18	self-hood
340.27	self-hood
341.16	Self-hood
349.21	Neo-realism
376.2	open-mindedness

II. Critical-text list.

In transcriptions from the present edition, no line-end hyphens in ambiguously broken possible compounds are to be retained except the following:

9.15 subject-matter
16.8 subject-matter
29.30 subject-matter
30.12 subject-matter
37.26 so-called
40.18 half-hearted
48.38 subject-matter
60.22 ready-made
82.1 non-natural
98.16 non-educational
109.16 every-day
138.39 psycho-physics
139.20 psycho-therapists
139.37 psycho-analysis
220.22 cross-examine
222.21 to-day
223.14 so-called
226.30 anti-theological
236.25 so-called
255.4 non-intellectual
261.22 Neo-Platonism
268.19 second-handed
275.27 so-called
325.2 non-human
338.20 ready-made
342.35 self-hood
358.18 common-sense
358.39 common-sense
378.13 pre-eminently
386.1 pre-vocational

CORRECTION OF QUOTATIONS

Dewey represented source material in varying ways, from memorial paraphrase to verbatim copy, sometimes citing his source fully, in others mentioning only authors' names, and in still others, omitting documentation altogether.

To prepare the critical text, all material inside quotation marks, except that obviously being emphasized or restated, has been searched out and the documentation has been verified and emended when necessary. Steps regularly used to emend documentation are described in "Textual Principles and Procedures" (*Middle Works* 1:358), but Dewey's substantive variations from the original in his quotations have been considered important enough to warrant a special list.

All quotations have been retained within the texts as they were first published, except for corrections required by special circumstances and noted in the Emendations List. Substantive changes that restore original readings in cases of possible compositorial or typographical errors are similarly noted as "W" emendations. The variable form of quotation suggests that Dewey, like many scholars of the period, was unconcerned about precision in matters of form, but many of the changes in cited materials may have arisen in the printing process. For example, comparing Dewey's quotations with the originals reveals that some journals house-styled the quoted materials as well as Dewey's own. In the present edition, therefore, the spelling and capitalization of the source have been reproduced, except in concept words where Dewey changed the form of the source.

The source of Dewey's quotations from Kant appears in the Checklist of References, but no correction of the quotations is included here because Dewey translated from the original German. For a fuller discussion of Dewey's translation methods, see *The Early Works of John Dewey*, 1:lxi–lxiv, xc.

Dewey's most frequent alteration in quoted material was changing or omitting punctuation. No citation of the Dewey material or of the original appears here if the changes were only of this kind. He also often failed to use ellipses or to separate quotations to show that material had been left out. In the case of Dewey's failure to use ellipses, omitted short phrases appear in this list; if, however, a line or more has been left out, an ellipsis in brackets calls attention to the omission. When a substantive difference between Dewey's material and its source has been caused by the context in which the quotation appears, that difference is not recorded.

Italics in source material have been treated as accidentals. When Dewey omitted those italics, the omission is not noted, though Dewey's added italics are listed. If changed or omitted accidentals have substantive implications, as in the capitalization or failure to capitalize concept words, the quotation is noted.

The form used in this section is designed to assist the reader in determining whether Dewey had the book open before him or was relying on his memory. Notations in this section follow the formula: page-line numbers from the present text, followed by the text condensed to first and last words or such as make for sufficient clarity, followed by a bracket. Next comes the necessary correction, whether of one word or a longer passage, as required. Finally, in parentheses, the author's surname and shortened source-title from the Checklist of Dewey's References are followed by a comma and the page-line reference to the source.

8.36 it] that it (Bergson, *Matter and Memory*, 306.6)
9.36 all its] its (Bergson, *Matter and Memory*, 30.31)
11.2 can retain] retain (Bergson, *Matter and Memory*, 304.24)
11.17 things] regard to things (Bergson, *Matter and Memory*, 21.18)
12.11 the way] its way (Bergson, *Matter and Memory*, 29.10)
12.28 is] is to say (Bergson, *Matter and Memory*, 30.14)
12.29 *action*] influence (Bergson, *Matter and Memory*, 30.15)

14.19 are . . . indetermination] are, within the universe, just 'centres of indetermination,' (Bergson, *Matter and Memory*, 28.23–24)

17.23 *actually . . . organs*] [*rom.*] (Bergson, *Matter and Memory*, 233.17–18)

21.3 consists] lies (Bergson, *Matter and Memory*, 31.6)

21n.17–18 decreases] diminishes (Bergson, *Matter and Memory*, 6.16–17)

22.26 of *ensuring*] is merely to ensure (Bergson, *Matter and Memory*, 84.11)

23n.3 living] these (Bergson, *Matter and Memory*, 69.19)

26.11 *so to*] [*rom.*] (Bergson, *Matter and Memory*, 19.16)

59.36 on . . . implies] on its part implies (U.S. Reports 107.454.7–8)

60.3 men] officers (U.S. Reports 107.460.33)

66.19 biological] their biological (Royce, *William James*, 194.8)

67.15 objective] objective constitution of a certain (Royce, *William James*, 221.18)

67.16 is true, then,] is, then, true (Royce, *William James*, 221.20)

67.32 no man] no one man (Royce, *William James*, 220.22)

69.9–11 *are . . . world*] [*rom.*] (Royce, *William James*, 193.18–19)

74.6 needs] intelligent needs (Royce, *William James*, 224.18)

80n.4 How] Now (McGilvary, "Present Philosophical Tendencies," 466.34)

101.31–32 *work . . . general*] [*rom.*] (Cooley, *Vocational Education*, 99.36–37)

101.33–34 *its scientific . . . social*] [*rom.*] (Cooley, *Vocational Education*, 100.1–2)

101.34 *bearings*, will] bearings—who comprehends the inner connection that must exist in the work of all members of society—will (Cooley, *Vocational Education*, 100.2–4)

131.14 logic] Logic (Schiller, *Formal Logic*, 409.31)

133.39 ‸logic‸] 'Logic' (Schiller, *Formal Logic*, xi.3)

133.39 science can] Science could (Schiller, *Formal Logic*, xi.3)

134.1 science] Science (Schiller, *Formal Logic*, xi.5)

134.3[1] science] Science (Schiller, *Formal Logic*, xi.7)

134.3[2] science] Science (Schiller, *Formal Logic*, xi.8)

140.3 supremely] felt supremely (Hall, *Psychology*, 303.18)

143.33 makes] make (James, *Radical Empiricism*, 277.3)

143.37 philosophy seems] philosophy, as it actually exists,

reminds many of us of that clergyman. It seems (James, *Radical Empiricism*, 277.20–22)

143.39 Kosmos] unconscious Kosmos (James, *Radical Empiricism*, 277.24–278.1)

144.39 fact except] fact, it says, except (James, *Radical Empiricism*, 160.5)

145.2 philosophy] reality (James, *Radical Empiricism*, 160.9)

145.9 their] the (James, *Radical Empiricism*, 243.8)

145.28 we find] The statement of fact is that (James, *Radical Empiricism*, x.13)

145.28 things are] *things, conjunctive as well as disjunctive, are* (James, *Radical Empiricism*, x.14–15)

145.40 experience] *our experience* (James, *Radical Empiricism*, 193.13)

146.2 self-sustaining] *self-containing* (James, *Radical Empiricism*, 193.16)

146.3 nothing else] *nothing* (James, *Radical Empiricism*, 193.17)

CHECKLIST OF DEWEY'S REFERENCES

Titles and authors' names in Dewey references have been corrected and expanded to conform accurately and consistently to the original works; all corrections appear in the Emendations List.

This section gives full publication information for each work cited by Dewey. When Dewey gave page numbers for a reference, the edition he used was identified exactly by locating the citation. Similarly, the books in Dewey's personal library have been used to verify his use of a particular edition. For other references, the edition listed here is the one from among the various editions possibly available to him that was his most likely source by reason of place or date of publication, or on the evidence from correspondence and other materials, and its general accessibility during the period.

Albee, Ernest. *A History of English Utilitarianism*. London: Swan Sonnenschein and Co., 1902.

Alexander, Samuel. *Moral Order and Progress: An Analysis of Ethical Conceptions*. The English and Foreign Philosophical Library. London: Trübner and Co., 1889.

Angell, James Rowland. *Psychology: An Introductory Study of the Structure and Function of Human Consciousness*. 3d ed. New York: Henry Holt and Co., 1906.

Appleton, Lilla Estelle. *A Comparative Study of the Play Activities of Adult Savages and Civilized Children: An Investigation of the Scientific Basis of Education*. Chicago: University of Chicago Press, 1910.

Bagley, William Chandler. *The Educative Process*. New York: Macmillan Co., 1908.

Bain, Alexander. *The Emotions and the Will*. 3d ed. London: Longmans, Green, and Co., 1875.

Baldwin, James Mark, ed. *Dictionary of Philosophy and Psychology*. 3 vols. in 4. New York: Macmillan Co., 1901–5.

———. *Mental Development in the Child and the Race*. New York: Macmillan Co., 1895.

———. *Social and Ethical Interpretations in Mental Development: A Study in Social Psychology*. New York: Macmillan Co., 1897.

Bawden, Henry Heath. *The Principles of Pragmatism: A Philosophical Interpretation of Experience*. Boston: Houghton Mifflin Co., 1910.

Bentham, Jeremy. *An Introduction to the Principles of Morals and Legislation*. Oxford: Clarendon Press, 1879.

Bergson, Henri. *Matter and Memory*. Translated by Nancy Margaret Paul and W. Scott Palmer. New York: Macmillan Co., 1911.

Berkeley, George. *Works*. Edited by A. C. Fraser. 4 vols. Oxford: Clarendon Press, 1901.

Berthelot, René. *Le Pragmatisme chez Nietzsche et chez Poincaré*. Un Romantisme utilitaire. Étude sur le mouvement pragmatiste, vol. 1. Paris: F. Alcan, 1911.

Bosanquet, Bernard. *The Education of the Young in the Republic of Plato*. Translated by Bernard Bosanquet. Cambridge: University Press, 1901.

Bradley, Francis Herbert. *Appearance and Reality: A Metaphysical Essay*. Library of Philosophy. 2d ed., rev. London: Swan Sonnenschein and Co., 1897.

Bryant, Sophie. *Educational Ends; or, The Ideal of Personal Development*. London: Longmans, Green, Reader and Dyer, 1887.

Butler, Nicholas Murray. *The Meaning of Education, and Other Essays and Addresses*. New York: Macmillan Co., 1905.

Caird, Edward. *The Critical Philosophy of Immanuel Kant*. 2 vols. Glasgow: James Maclehose and Sons, 1889.

———. *The Social Philosophy and Religion of Comte*. 2d ed. Glasgow: James Maclehose and Sons, 1893.

Carus, Paul. *Truth on Trial: An Exposition of the Nature of Truth, Preceded by a Critique of Pragmatism and an Appreciation of Its Leader*. Chicago: Open Court Publishing Co., 1911.

Chamberlain, Alexander Francis. *The Child: A Study in the Evolution of Man*. The Contemporary Science Series, vol. 39. Edited by H. Ellis. London: W. Scott, 1900.

Colozza, Giovanni Antonio. *Psychologie und Pädagogik des Kinderspiels*. Translated by Christian Ufer. Internationale Bibliothek für Pädagogik und deren Hilfswissenschaften, vol. 2. Altenburg: O. Bonde, 1900.

Colvin, Stephen Sheldon. *The Learning Process*. New York: Macmillan Co., 1911.

Cooley, Charles Horton. *Human Nature and the Social Order*. New York: Charles Scribner's Sons, 1910.

Dewey, John. *The Child and the Curriculum*. University of Chicago Contributions to Education, no. 5. Chicago: University of Chicago Press, 1902. [*The Middle Works of John Dewey, 1899–1924*, edited by Jo Ann Boydston, 2:271–91. Carbondale: Southern Illinois University Press, 1976.]

———. *Educational Essays.* Edited by Joseph John Findlay. London: Blackie & Son, 1910.

———. *How We Think.* Boston: D. C. Heath and Co., 1910. [*Middle Works* 6:177–356.]

———. *The Influence of Darwin on Philosophy and Other Essays in Contemporary Thought.* New York: Henry Holt and Co., 1910.

———. *Moral Principles in Education.* Riverside Educational Monographs, edited by Henry Suzzallo. Boston: Houghton Mifflin Co., 1909. [*Middle Works* 4:265–91.]

———. *My Pedagogic Creed.* New York: E. L. Kellogg & Co., 1897. [*The Early Works of John Dewey, 1882–1898*, edited by Jo Ann Boydston, 5:84–95. Carbondale: Southern Illinois University Press, 1972.]

———. *The School and the Child: Being Selections from the Educational Essays of John Dewey.* Edited by Joseph John Findlay. The Library of Pedagogics. London: Blackie & Son, 1907.

———. *The School and Society.* Chicago: University of Chicago Press, 1900. London: P. S. King & Son, 1900. [*Middle Works* 1:1–109.]

———. "The Reflex Arc Concept in Psychology." *Psychological Review* 3 (1896): 357–70. [*Early Works* 5:96–109.]

———. "Science as Subject-Matter and as Method." *Science*, n.s. 31 (1910):121–27. [*Middle Works* 6:69–79.]

———, and Tufts, James H. *Ethics.* New York: Henry Holt and Co., 1908. Reprinted, 1909. [*Middle Works* 5:1–540.]

———, et al. *Essays, Philosophical and Psychological, in Honor of William James.* New York: Longmans, Green, and Co., 1908.

———, et al. *Studies in Logical Theory.* University of Chicago Decennial Publications, vol. 11. Second Series. Chicago: University of Chicago Press, 1903. [Dewey's contributions, *Middle Works* 2:293–375.]

Eastman, Max. *The Enjoyment of Poetry.* New York: Charles Scribner's Sons, 1913.

Ennis v. *The Maharajah.* 40 Federal Reporter 784 (S.D.N.Y. 1889).

Farrar, Frederic William, ed. *Essays on Liberal Education.* London: Macmillan and Co., 1867.

Fichte, Johann Gottlieb. *The Destination of Man.* Translated by Mrs. Percy Sinnett. London: Chapman Bros., 1846.

———. *Grundlage der gesammten Wissenschaftslehre und Grundriss des Eigenthümlichen der Wissenschaftslehre in Rück-*

sicht auf das theoretische Vermögen. New unaltered ed. Tübingen: Cotta, 1802.

Findlay, Joseph John. *Principles of Class Teaching.* Macmillan's Manuals for Teachers, edited by O. Browning and S. S. F. Fletcher. London: Macmillan and Co., 1902.

Fiske, John. *The Meaning of Infancy.* Riverside Educational Monographs, edited by H. Suzzallo. Boston: Houghton Mifflin Co., 1909.

Fite, Warner. *Individualism: Four Lectures on the Significance of Consciousness for Social Relations.* New York: Longmans, Green, and Co., 1911.

Fouillée, Alfred Jules Émile. *Le mouvement idéaliste et la réaction contre la science positive.* 2d ed. Paris: F. Alcan, 1896.

Francke, Kuno. *A History of German Literature as Determined by Social Forces.* New York: Henry Holt and Co., 1905.

Froebel, Friedrich Wilhelm August. *The Education of Man.* Translated by W. H. Hailmann. International Education Series, edited by W. T. Harris, vol. 5. New York: D. Appleton and Co., 1912.

Georgens, Jan Daniel. *Das Spiel und die Spiele der Jugend.* Leipzig: O. Spamer, 1884.

Goethe, Johann Wolfgang von. *Goethe's Popular Works.* 10 vols. Cambridge ed. Edited by Frederic H. Hedge and Leopold Noa. Boston: Estes and Lauriat, 1883.

Goodsell, Willystine. *The Conflict of Naturalism and Humanism.* New York: N.Y.C. Teachers College, Columbia University, 1910.

Green, Thomas Hill. *Prolegomena to Ethics.* 4th ed. Edited by A. C. Bradley. Oxford: Clarendon Press, 1889.

Groos, Karl. *The Play of Animals.* Translated by Elizabeth L. Baldwin. New York: D. Appleton and Co., 1898.

———. *The Play of Man.* Translated by Elizabeth L. Baldwin. New York: D. Appleton and Co., 1901.

Halévy, Élie. *La jeunesse de Bentham.* La Formation du radicalisme philosophique, vol. 1. Bibliothèque de philosophie contemporaine. Paris: F. Alcan, 1901.

Hall, Granville Stanley. *Adolescence: Its Psychology and Its Relations to Physiology, Anthropology, Sociology, Sex, Crime, Religion and Education.* 2 vols. New York: D. Appleton and Co., 1908.

———. *Aspects of Child Life and Education.* Edited by Theodore L. Smith. Boston: Ginn and Co., 1907.

———. *Youth: Its Education, Regimen, and Hygiene.* New York: D. Appleton and Co., 1906.

Harris, William Torrey. *Psychologic Foundations of Education: An Attempt to Show the Genesis of the Higher Faculties of the Mind.* International Education Series, vol. 37. New York: D. Appleton and Co., 1908.

Hegel, Georg Wilhelm Friedrich. *Phänomenologie des Geistes.* 2d ed. Leipzig: Felix Meiner, 1911.

Helmholtz, Hermann Ludwig Ferdinand von. *On the Sensations of Tone as a Physiological Basis for the Theory of Music.* 4th ed., rev. Translated by Alexander J. Ellis. New York: Longmans, Green, and Co., 1912.

———. *Optique physiologique.* Translated by Émile Javal and N. Th. Klein. Paris: V. Masson and Son, 1867.

Henderson, Ernest Norton. *A Text-Book in the Principles of Education.* New York: Macmillan Co., 1911.

Herbert, Thomas Martin. *The Realistic Assumptions of Modern Science Examined.* Edited by James M. Hodgson. London: Macmillan and Co., 1879.

Höffding, Harald. *A History of Modern Philosophy: A Sketch of the History of Philosophy from the Close of the Renaissance to Our Own Day.* Translated by B. Ethel Meyer. 2 vols. London: Macmillan and Co., 1908.

Horne, Herman Harrell. *Idealism in Education; or, First Principles in the Making of Men and Women.* New York: Macmillan Co., 1910.

———. *The Philosophy of Education: Being the Foundations of Education in the Related Natural and Mental Sciences.* New York: Macmillan Co., 1905.

Huizinga, Arnold van Couthen Piccardt. *The American Philosophy Pragmatism Critically Considered in Relation to Present-Day Theology.* Boston: Sherman, French, and Co., 1911.

Hume, David. *The Philosophical Works.* Edited by Thomas Hill Green and Thomas Hodge Grose. 4 vols. London: Longmans, Green, and Co., 1874–75.

Jacoby, Gunther. *Der Pragmatismus. Neue Bahnen in der Wissenschaftslehre des Auslands.* Eine Würdigung von Gunther Jacoby. Leipzig: Dürr, 1909.

James, William. *Essays in Radical Empiricism.* New York: Longmans, Green, and Co., 1912.

———. *The Meaning of Truth.* New York: Longmans, Green, and Co., 1909.

———. *A Pluralistic Universe: Hibbert Lectures at Manchester College on the Present Situation in Philosophy.* New York: Longmans, Green, and Co., 1909.

———. *Pragmatism: A New Name for Some Old Ways of Thinking.* New York: Longmans, Green, and Co., 1907. [Reissued, 1909.]

———. *The Principles of Psychology.* 2 vols. New York: Henry Holt and Co., 1890. [Reissued, 1899.]

———. *The Varieties of Religious Experience: A Study in Hu-*

man Nature. 16th impression. New York: Longmans, Green, and Co., 1910.

———. *The Will to Believe, and Other Essays in Popular Philosophy*. New York: Longmans, Green, and Co., 1897.

Joachim, Harold Henry. *The Nature of Truth: An Essay*. Oxford: Clarendon Press, 1906.

Johnson, George Ellsworth. *Education by Plays and Games*. Boston: Ginn and Co., 1907.

Kant, Immanuel. *Kritik der reinen Vernunft*. 2d ed. Riga: J. F. Hartknoch, 1787.

Kirkpatrick, Edwin Asbury. *Fundamentals of Child Study: A Discussion of Instincts and Other Factors in Human Development*. New York: Macmillan Co., 1903.

Ladd, George Trumbull. *A Theory of Reality: An Essay in Metaphysical System Upon the Basis of Human Cognitive Experience*. New York: Charles Scribner's Sons, 1899.

Leibniz, Gottfried Wilhelm. *Die Théodicée*. Edited by J. H. von Kirchman. Philosophische Bibliothek, vol. 79. Leipzig: E. Koschny, 1879.

Locke, John. *An Essay concerning Human Understanding*. 2 vols. Oxford: Clarendon Press, 1894.

Lotze, Rudolph Hermann. *Logik*. System der Philosophie, vol. 1. Leipzig: S. Hirzel, 1880.

———. *Medicinische Psychologie; oder, Physiologie der Seele*. Leipzig: Weidmann, 1852.

McDougall, William. *An Introduction to Social Psychology*. London: Methuen and Co., 1908. [Reissued, 1910.]

McGilvary, E. B., W. B. Pitkin, H. A. Overstreet, and E. G. Spaulding. "The Problem of Values." *Journal of Philosophy, Psychology and Scientific Methods* 10 (1913): 168.

Mackenzie, John Stuart. *A Manual of Ethics*. 4th ed. London: University Tutorial Press, 1900.

MacVannell, John Angus. *Outline of a Course in the Philosophy of Education*. New York: Macmillan Co., 1912.

Mill, John Stuart. *A System of Logic, Ratiocinative and Inductive*. 8th ed. New York: Harper and Bros., 1900.

———. *Utilitarianism*. London: Parker, Son, and Bourn, 1863.

Miller, Irving Elgar. *The Psychology of Thinking*. New York: Macmillan Co., 1909.

Moore, Addison Webster. *Pragmatism and Its Critics*. Chicago: University of Chicago Press, 1910.

Muirhead, John Henry. *The Elements of Ethics*. University Extension Manuals. New York: Charles Scribner's Sons, 1892.

Nettleship, Richard Lewis. "The Theory of Education in the *Republic* of Plato." In *Hellenica: A Collection of Essays on Greek Poetry, Philosophy, History and Religion*, edited by Evelyn Abbott, pp. 67–180. London: Rivingtons, 1880.

Ormond, Alexander Thomas. *Foundations of Knowledge, in Three Parts*. London: Macmillan and Co., 1900.

O'Shea, Michael Vincent. *Education as Adjustment: Educational Theory Viewed in the Light of Contemporary Thought*. New York: Longmans, Green, and Co., 1903.

Partridge, George Everett. *Genetic Philosophy of Education: An Epitome of the Published Educational Writings of President G. Stanley Hall*. New York: Sturgis and Walton Co., 1912.

Pater, Walter Horatio. *Marius the Epicurean: His Sensations and Ideas*. New York: Macmillan Co., 1900.

Paulsen, Friedrich. *German Education Past and Present*. Translated by Theodor Lorenz. London: T. Fisher Unwin, 1908.

Peirce, Charles Sanders. "How to Make Our Ideas Clear." *Popular Science Monthly* 12 (1878): 286–302.

Plato. *The Dialogues of Plato*. Translated by Benjamin Jowett. 4 vols. Boston: Jefferson Press, 1871. [*Gorgias*, 3:1–119; *Republic*, 2:1–452; *Laws*, 4:1–480.]

Pollock, Frederick. *The Expansion of the Common Law*. London: Stevens and Sons, 1904.

Pound, Roscoe. "The End of Law as Developed in Legal Rules and Doctrines." *Harvard Law Review* 27 (1914): 195–234.

Rickaby, Joseph John, S. J. *Moral Philosophy; or, Ethics and Natural Law*. English Manuals of Catholic Philosophy. New York: Benziger Brothers, 1888.

Rosenkranz, Johann Karl Friedrich. *The Philosophy of Education*. Translated by Anna C. Brackett. 2d ed., rev. International Education Series, vol. 1, edited by W. T. Harris. New York: D. Appleton and Co., 1903.

Royce, Josiah. *Nature, Man, and the Moral Order*. The World and the Individual, second series. New York: Macmillan Co., 1901.

———. *The Spirit of Modern Philosophy: An Essay in the Form of Lectures*. Boston: Houghton Mifflin Co., 1892.

———."The Imitative Functions, and Their Place in Human Nature." *Century Magazine* 48 (1894): 137–45.

———. "Preliminary Report on Imitation." *Psychological Review* 2 (1895): 217–35.

———. "Some Observations on the Anomalies of Self-Consciousness." I. *Psychological Review* 2 (1895): 433–57; II. ibid., pp. 574–84.

Ruediger, William Carl. *The Principles of Education*. Boston: Houghton Mifflin Co., 1910.

Russell, Bertrand. *Philosophical Essays*. London: Longmans, Green, and Co., 1910.

Sandys, Sir John Edwin. *The Eighteenth Century in Germany and the Nineteenth Century in Europe and the United States of America*. A History of Classical Scholarship, vol. 3. Cambridge: University Press, 1908.

Schiller, Ferdinand Canning Scott. *Formal Logic: A Scientific and Social Problem*. New York: Macmillan Co., 1912.

———. *Humanism: Philosophical Essays*. London: Macmillan and Co., 1903.

———. *Studies in Humanism*. London: Macmillan and Co., 1907.

Schinz, Albert. *Anti-pragmatisme: Examen des droits respectifs de l'aristocratie intellectuelle et de la démocratie sociale*. Bibliothèque de philosophie contemporaine. Paris: F. Alcan, 1909.

Schopenhauer, Arthur. *Arthur Schopenhauer's Sammtliche Werke*. 2d ed. Edited by Julius Frauenstadt. 6 vols. Leipzig: F. A. Brockhaus, 1891.

Sidgwick, Henry. *Outlines of the History of Ethics, for English Readers*. 3d ed. London: Macmillan and Co., 1892.

———. *The Methods of Ethics*. 4th ed. London: Macmillan and Co., 1890. [6th ed., 1901.]

Sigwart, Christoph von. *Logic*. 2d ed., rev. and enl. 2 vols. Translated by Helen Dendy. Library of Philosophy, 4th series, edited by John Henry Muirhead. London: Swan Sonnenschein and Co., 1895.

Sinclair, Samuel Bower. *The Possibility of a Science of Education*. Chicago: University of Chicago Press, 1903.

Spencer, Herbert. *The Principles of Ethics*. A System of Synthetic Philosophy, vols. 9, 10. London: Williams and Norgate, 1892–93.

———. *The Principles of Psychology*. 2 vols. in 3. New York: D. Appleton and Co., 1896.

Spinoza, Benedictus de. *Ethic*. 4th ed., rev. Translated by William Hale White. Rev. by Amelia Hutchison Stirling. New York: H. Froude, 1910.

Spranger, Eduard. *Wilhelm von Humboldt und die Reform des Bildungswesens*. Berlin: Reuther Reichard, 1910.

Stephen, Leslie. *The English Utilitarians*. 3 vols. London: Cuckworth and Co., 1900.

Strachan, John. *What Is Play? Its Bearing upon Education and Training. A Physiological Inquiry*. Edinburgh: D. Douglas, 1877.

Taine, Hippolyte Adolphe. *L'Idéalisme anglais. Etude sur Carlyle*. Bibliothèque de philosophie contemporaine. Paris: G. Baillière, 1864.

Tarde, Gabriel de. *Les lois de l'imitation; étude sociologique*. Paris: F. Alcan, 1890.

———. *The Laws of Imitation*. Translated by Elsie Clews Parsons. New York: Henry Holt and Co., 1903.

Tufts, James H., and Dewey, John. *Ethics*. New York: Henry Holt and Co., 1908. Reprinted, 1909. [*Middle Works* 5:1–540.]

United States Reports. *Wabash Railway* v. *McDaniels.* 107 (1882): 454–63.

Venn, John. *The Principles of Empirical or Inductive Logic.* London: Macmillan and Co., 1889.

Vincent, George Edgar. *The Social Mind and Education.* New York: Macmillan Co., 1897.

Watson, John. *Christianity and Idealism: The Christian Ideal of Life in Its Relations to the Greek and Jewish Ideals and to Modern Philosophy.* New ed. London: Macmillan and Co., 1897.

———. *Hedonistic Theories from Aristippus to Spencer.* Glasgow: James Maclehose and Sons, 1895.

Wundt, Wilhelm Max. *Principles of Physiological Psychology.* 5th German ed. Translated by Edward Bradford Titchener. New York: Macmillan Co., 1910.

INDEX